## About This Book

### Why is this topic important?

More and more offshore training and outsourcing are done globally, making the ability to provide training to global audiences more important and lucrative. Too many foreign and international companies have rolled out a curriculum designed for a U.S. audience and have then watched it fail. Additionally, more and more programs are being presented in new countries and to a variety of audiences while companies try to expand their cultures and their businesses across borders. In general, speakers and trainers know what is acceptable and expected and how to address audiences within the United States. This book helps broaden the opportunities for presenters by serving as a quick reference of important information on global audiences.

### What can you achieve with this book?

This book is designed to help trainers, teachers, and presenters prepare to train successfully in a new country on any of a variety of topics. This companion resource is not a comprehensive reference on any specific country, but instead focuses on the key elements that will have to be adjusted to be country-specific. Trainers should use it before traveling to plan and design the training and to learn what they can about an audience. The book will also serve as a resource during training, helping the trainer avoid unintentionally alienating the audience, providing tips and resources for further development. It is written to help people be successful the first time. Trainers and presenters working with translators, interpreters, and localization for the first time will also learn techniques to make the process more efficient.

### How is the book organized?

This book is divided into three major sections. The first provides general information on training in foreign countries without getting into the specifics of any country. Tips are given on translation, program design, and presentation, and general insights are given for training international audiences. Specific recommendations and resources for each stage of the process are provided. The second major section of the book is divided into regions, including Africa/Middle East, Asia, Australia, Europe, and The Americas. Within each region, the specific requirements of countries that are likely to request training are addressed. Each chapter includes information on requests that are likely, getting there, program design and delivery, logistics, technical requirements, accommodations, moving around, the people, preparation, and the presentation. The third major section provides a conclusion, and appendices with additional examples, tips for dealing with the unexpected, mentoring global employees, using technology, and helpful resources.

This will be an adventure!

# About Pfeiffer

Pfeiffer serves the professional development and hands-on resource needs of training and human resource practitioners and gives them products to do their jobs better. We deliver proven ideas and solutions from experts in HR development and HR management, and we offer effective and customizable tools to improve workplace performance. From novice to seasoned professional, Pfeiffer is the source you can trust to make yourself and your organization more successful.

**Essential Knowledge** Pfeiffer produces insightful, practical, and comprehensive materials on topics that matter the most to training and HR professionals. Our Essential Knowledge resources translate the expertise of seasoned professionals into practical, how-to guidance on critical workplace issues and problems. These resources are supported by case studies, worksheets, and job aids and are frequently supplemented with CD-ROMs, websites, and other means of making the content easier to read, understand, and use.

**Essential Tools** Pfeiffer's Essential Tools resources save time and expense by offering proven, ready-to-use materials—including exercises, activities, games, instruments, and assessments—for use during a training or team-learning event. These resources are frequently offered in looseleaf or CD-ROM format to facilitate copying and customization of the material.

Pfeiffer also recognizes the remarkable power of new technologies in expanding the reach and effectiveness of training. While e-hype has often created whizbang solutions in search of a problem, we are dedicated to bringing convenience and enhancements to proven training solutions. All our e-tools comply with rigorous functionality standards. The most appropriate technology wrapped around essential content yields the perfect solution for today's on-the-go trainers and human resource professionals.

**Pfeiffer**
www.pfeiffer.com

*Essential resources for training and HR professionals*

# The Essential Guide to Training Global Audiences

## YOUR PLANNING RESOURCE OF USEFUL TIPS AND TECHNIQUES

## LuAnn Irwin and Renie McClay

**Pfeiffer**

A Wiley Imprint
www.pfeiffer.com

Published by Pfeiffer

An Imprint of Wiley

989 Market Street, San Francisco, CA 94103-1741

www.pfeiffer.com

For additional copies/bulk purchases of this book in the U.S. please contact 800-274-4434.

Pfeiffer books and products are available through most bookstores. To contact Pfeiffer directly call our Customer Care Department within the U.S. at 800-274-4434, outside the U.S. at 317-572-3985, fax 317-572-4002, or visit www.pfeiffer.com.

Pfeiffer also publishes its books in a variety of electronic formats. Some content that appears in print may not be available in electronic books.

McClay, Renie.
    The essential guide to training global audiences : your planning resource of useful tips and techniques / Renie McClay and LuAnn Irwin.
        p.   cm.
    Includes bibliographical references and index.
    ISBN 978-0-7879-9661-1 (pbk.)
        1. International business enterprises—Employees—Training of.    I. Irwin, LuAnn, 1949-    II. Title.
    HF5549.5.T7M36937    2008
    658.3'124—dc22

                                                                                2008010926

Acquiring Editor: Matthew Davis
Marketing Manager: Brian Grimm
Director of Development: Kathleen Dolan Davies
Developmental Editor: Susan Rachmeler

Production Editor: Michael Kay
Editor: Rebecca Taff
Editorial Assistant: Lindsay Morton
Manufacturing Supervisor: Becky Morgan

Printed in the United States of America

Printing    10 9 8 7 6 5 4 3 2 1

# CONTENTS

*To Lee, Michael, and Alicia, who have always made travel and life full of joy and excitement!*

*And to Nick, whose insights and cultural sensitivity will serve him well whatever path he chooses.*

# ACKNOWLEDGMENTS

## TO OUR VALUED CONTRIBUTORS

We are so very grateful to all those who have contributed information for this book. Some people gave us a lot of time and information and insights; others gave us quick ideas or comments. Some reviewed existing chapters and checked for accuracy. Many resources and contributors are listed at the end of the book, but it is impossible to list or thank every person who made a contribution.

We treasure your input and truly appreciate your willingness to share your knowledge and experiences with all of us.

Thank you!!

# Introduction

Thomas Friedman provides very convincing detail in his book, *The World Is Flat* (2006), that shows us how important it is to quickly and carefully learn how to effectively communicate with people from all over the world. Friedman writes that Americans need to set an example, collaborate, and nurture imagination in intercultural settings. When we receive requests to train, teach, and present to others across the globe, it gives us a chance to share our knowledge and experience, and to learn from others. What a powerful responsibility and opportunity that is!

This book is designed to provide information and ideas for anyone who trains, teaches, or presents to people from a culture other than his or her own (or who just wants to!). It can be used by people who are in a variety of professions and have expertise that needs to be shared by traveling to another country, presenting to a multicultural audience in their own country, or conducting a session through virtual or electronic means such as computer, phone, or other technical devices. The subjects of training that we give as examples cover a broad range of topics, from computer systems, aircraft maintenance, and management training to organization development (OD) interventions, sales, and coaching. The examples come from large and small organizations, including multinational corporations as well as non-profit, government, academic, and independent consultants. Topics are both non-technical and technical to provide the largest range of ideas possible.

The purpose is to enable the reader to design and deliver an excellent learning experience to an unfamiliar audience by providing techniques and tips gained by practicing experts from all over the world.

When we tried to find such a book, we were surprised that most of the available resources focused on doing business in a foreign country, negotiating, or traveling for fun. We wanted more information that addressed the need to teach or present to people from other cultures. So we decided to create a useful guide by asking experts who do this often and well to share their knowledge.

The book is designed to be used as a resource. We would not imagine this to be read cover-to-cover by most readers. Rather, we would expect people to look up the new place where they will be training or presenting, and gain some insights.

The initial chapters of this book cover basic insights, design, translation, and presentation information.

Parts of the book are divided by regions of the world. Some of these regions may have training that includes participants from neighboring countries; for example, representatives of several European countries may be together in one session. This does not mean that they feel like neighbors or are from overly similar cultures, but rather that they are closer in travel, time zone, and often in language, so it is more convenient and cost-effective for companies or organizations to have participants together in a program that represents a variety of languages, cultures, and views.

We have also divided the information by country because you may have a group of learners who are from a particular location or may be training in a particular city. Although it is a mistake for any of us to assume that participants are the same, just because they are all from the same country.

The chapters on each country include information about preparation, program design, accommodations, communications, travel, presentation, evaluation, and reinforcement of learning for many of the typical countries that trainers, teachers, and presenters are asked to visit or present in. We also include details we have learned and experiences we have had along the way that can save you time, frustration, and money if you read them before you travel to the countries.

You can go to any of the chapters to explore information specific to a location that interests you. Some common elements are appropriate across countries as well. If you are teaching or presenting (either in person or electronically) to a mixed audience from many countries, you can look up information about each of the countries that is represented. This can help you to prepare for some of the differences you may encounter.

We want to sincerely thank all the contributors to this work. A number of contributors wrote for this book. We made the decision to maintain the contributing author's "voice," so if different chapters read as though they were written by different authors, there's a good reason for that. Our interviews with the contributors were enlightening and fun. Our intent was to capture their experiences and insights to share with you.

At times we received conflicting information from different contributors about a region. That makes sense, because everyone's experience is different, so we tried not to make generalizations based on one person's experiences. Often, instead of providing conflicting information, we identify what you need to find out in order to be successful in a given country and, when we can, we give the resources to find that information. It would be nice to be able to give you the "ten steps to success" in any given country, but the reality is that different parts of a country differ—and audiences will differ as well. For example, an audience in the north of India will be very different from one in the south of India. An audience in China in their twenties and thirties will be different from an audience in their fifties and sixties. So where we didn't provide the answers, we hope we gave you the right questions.

While each continent provided its own excitement and challenges, Africa in particular turned out to be quite a journey. An entire book could be written about Africa. With fifty-three independent countries and things changing daily, we decided to use a different format for this region. We wrote one chapter on South Africa (it is very unique and where a lot of business training is happening), Egypt (which may also be considered as a Middle Eastern example) and then a general chapter on the rest of the continent. We also identify what you should find out and some places to look for that information.

## HOW THIS BOOK IS ORGANIZED

Part One includes general information for training or presenting to international audiences. The following chapters are included:

- Chapter One: Insights and Suggestions for Training and Presenting to International Audiences
- Chapter Two: Designing the Program for International Audiences
- Chapter Three: Translation for International Audiences
- Chapter Four: Presentation Techniques for International Audiences

Parts Two through six cover specific regions of the world. They include the following divisions:

- Part Two: The Continent of Africa
- Part Three: Asia

- Part Four: Australia
- Part Five: Europe
- Part Six: The Americas

Each chapter within the parts includes information regarding communication, cultural sensitivities, learning styles, preparation tips, and examples for a particular country. Please be aware that any price estimates provided are subject to change.

Part Seven, the Conclusion, includes a chapter on human resource development trends currently and five appendices relevant to trainers dealing with the global environment.

## ??? THE REQUEST

In the Request section of each chapter, we outline typical requests for training (software, technical training, English, call centers) and give examples of some requesting organizations. If there are specific details that should be clarified before accepting a training opportunity, we list those for you as well.

## • • • GETTING THERE

Once you've agreed to travel internationally to do training, the idea of actually getting there becomes important. Information on passport requirements, visas, airports, cities to travel into, time zones, and any holidays that can affect travel or training are included.

## PROGRAM DESIGN

Program design means using a needs assessment to ensure that you are meeting the needs of the participants and the requestor, as you would with any training program. In this book, we won't teach you how to perform the needs analysis, but we will tell you about language, translation requirements, and key characteristics of the country's learners that may affect your program design.

## LOGISTICS

The Logistics sections cover some of the details that might otherwise go unnoticed in your planning. Information in this section includes how to be sure your training materials are delivered on time and in one piece, currency issues, information about exchanging money, and tips on importing any technology you may need.

## PROGRAM DELIVERY

In this section of the chapters, you will find information about some of the design choices you'll have to make about the actual delivery of your material. Specifics include types of training that will work well in a given culture (Will a lecture work well, or will participants want to be active?) as well as classroom issues such as introductions, group work etiquette, taking breaks for religious or cultural reasons, etc.

## TECHNICAL REQUIREMENTS

More and more training is dependent on technology for successful delivery. In this section we'll cover some of the most common issues, such as electricity rates and plugs, common equipment, Internet availability, and cell phone coverage.

## ACCOMMODATIONS

Your accommodations serve as your home away from home while training, so it's important to find accommodations that suit your needs. Information on hotels in specific cities, staying safe, food, and water is available in this section of each chapter.

## GETTING AROUND

Transportation is an important element of your planning and execution of your program delivery. It also can relieve stress when you know how and when you will be arriving, to ensure there is enough time to set up your program and focus your attention on your learners. In the "Getting Around" section, we make recommendations on modes of transportation in different areas and ways to stay safe.

## THE PEOPLE

There is too much to learn about the people of any country for us to cover it in the short space of a chapter. Instead, we cover some of the basic elements that you should consider: background, primary language, likely attitude about the topic of the program, level of expertise in the topic before entering the program, cultural sensitivities, background on the country and major cities, as well as gender or hospitality expectations.

## PREPARATION

In addition to reviewing and practicing your presentation, it is important that you prepare yourself physically and emotionally to be at your very best. This means getting enough sleep before you leave, keeping well hydrated, arriving with time to rest and set up, and so forth. In the preparation section, we tell you what expectations different countries have about what an instructor or teacher should be like, as well as provide some common phrases for each culture that may help you navigate basic social situations.

## THE PRESENTATION

Many classroom tips can help to ensure smooth delivery of your presentation. Topics in this section include likely locations for training, speaking and visual aid suggestions, and recommendations for how much student participation to attempt to create.

## LEARNING FROM THE EXPERTS

Trainers and presenters typically not only like to share information and expertise, but are also skilled at explaining so others can quickly understand. Their willingness to help others improve their knowledge and capability is rewarded by their satisfaction in seeing someone else grow and develop.

We are thankful that we worked with such a talented and giving group of experts, and we can never repay what they have done to fill this book with ideas. We can only attempt to repay them by sharing their information with our readers.

The world has become "smaller." We can now interact with people we might never have met in the past, and we can share knowledge and insights. This has created opportunities to work more closely together to solve important problems and achieve success in many ways.

We hope you enjoy reading this book as much as we have enjoyed creating it for you. This is such fun work, and we want to share our energy and excitement as we explore these areas together. Enjoy the sights, sounds, flavors, and people with us as we journey on!

# PART ONE

# General Information for Training or Presenting to International Audiences

# Insights and Suggestions for Training, Teaching, and Presenting to International Audiences

**S**peaking to groups around the world will spice up your life!

There are choices to be made when you receive a request from a client to train, teach, or present to an audience that has different culture, language, and experience from your own. How should you prepare?

This book is designed to help you to plan and complete your assignment with confidence and comfort. We cover various techniques and tips, as well as provide examples and suggestions.

Let's start with an example:

All your senses are piqued. From the moment you step off of the plane or get on the phone with an international audience, you know this experience is going to be very different.

You have just traveled to China to demonstrate some new technology products.

You arrived at the airport expecting your pre-arranged ride, but there is no one there to pick you up. Somehow you reach your destination.

Now you are looking at a room full of people and can tell from their blank faces and silence that they do not understand what you have just asked them to do. It is the opening of Day 1 and you still have two full days of a program to teach. You were told "they understand English, but don't speak it so well." It seems that this was a bit of an overstatement.

You have shipped the technology products in advance, and have found out that they have been delayed getting through customs. You won't have them this week. Because you shipped the student materials with the products, you don't have those either.

The adapter you brought for your computer power supply does not fit the socket.

You have split the participants into small groups and given them an assignment. No one is speaking; they are just looking at each other.

The dinner you had last night is not agreeing with you and you are not sure how you are going to make it through the day.

There is a thirteen-hour time difference between where you are and home. You slept little on the plane. It is 11:00 P.M. your time, but you can't sleep now. This is going to be a long day.

You ask questions to test for understanding and get no response.

Your translated slides looked fine on your computer in the office. Now they look like weird, unrecognizable characters with lots of rectangles.

These are just a few examples of dilemmas you can face when you have been asked to train in a foreign country or present to an international audience. The more you do this, the more you can potentially learn lessons the hard way.

What do you do next? And what do you do next time?

This scenario required you to travel to another country and present in person. Other examples will cover virtual training to an international audience from a separate location.

There are lots of things to do to help avoid troubles and inconveniences when training, teaching, or presenting internationally. We address some in this chapter and more specifics in later chapters.

One of the first things you can do when you are working with a new country is to look through the books at your local bookstore for the country or countries you will visit or teach in. You can order Frommer's travel guides for the appropriate locations at www.frommers.com. Also, buy a small dictionary of terms and phrases for the primary language spoken in the locations where you will visit or present. Practice some of the phrases that you think you will need. You can start with how you will greet the class (will it be "Hello" or "Good morning"?). Read everything you can about the country and its culture. Check the weather for about a week before leaving, to determine what to pack.

Being prepared for the unexpected is perhaps the best advice we can give you. No matter how much you prepare, there will be surprises. So open your mind and spirit to an adventure! You will most likely experience frustration, embarrassment, strangeness, and confusion, but it is all part of the adventure. Be open to a variety of experiences, and be willing to vary your technique and plans. As long as you are well prepared and flexible, it will be the experience of a lifetime. You may never cease to be surprised when traveling, working abroad, or training an international audience, as there is so much to learn from people of different countries!

Even though you are supposed to be the teacher or "expert," you can learn at least as much as your student/audience does. And speaking of being a teacher, it carries a very special and venerated honor in many countries.

## THE BASICS

To prepare for an international training assignment, obtain agreement with your country management contacts or hosts regarding your learning objectives to ensure that their expectations will be met. This should include what each learner will be able to know and do by the end of your session. List actions that can be easily observed for your program objectives, such as describe, explain, perform, or demonstrate (see more about this in Chapter Two).

### Questions to Ask

- Timing (dates, start times, end times) (Don't assume an 8:00 A.M. start time.)
- Location (city, hotel, meeting room)
- Participants (number of people, positions, managers)
- Expenses (costs, who will pay for what)
- Materials collateral (who will make copies, deadlines for final versions)
- Translation (if so, who will do it and associated deadlines)

One person should be the final decision-maker, but you may have to communicate with several stakeholders to make sure that everyone knows the final arrangements. We provide many more ideas from a variety of experts throughout this book.

## TRAVEL

Making arrangements for and confirming flights and accommodations are important details, and the proper arrangements ensure you are well rested and prepared for conducting your important training/education sessions. Try arriving early to adjust to the new time zone and culture. There are many choices of where to stay. Safety and proximity to the training may be key. An alternative may be to stay in a bed and breakfast/pension (guest house) environment. This allows you to stay with a family, dine and live as a guest in their home, learn about the culture, and make good friends. Karen Brown's guides provide good recommendations (www.karenbrown.com).

### Tips for Travel Documents

- Always maintain a current passport with at least six months left before expiration; some countries won't allow entrance with less than that. It is best to update when it is not needed, rather than to wait until the last minute when so many details require attention. You will also need a visa to enter certain countries. It is simpler if you have an up-to-date passport to start that process.

- Sign your passport in ink.

- Fill in emergency information in case the passport is lost. Use pencil for your home contact and in-country contact information so it can be changed as needed.

- Bring a photocopy of the passport with you, stored in a different location than your passport, just in case of loss or theft.

- Leave a copy of your passport, itinerary, and in-country contacts at home with a friend or family member—again, just in case.

- Check early to see whether a visa is required to visit the country you are traveling to.

- Before leaving home, buy an under-your-clothes money pouch in a light color. You can keep your passport and most of your money there (it will not be visible, even if you are wearing a light colored shirt). Keep a smaller amount of money in a pocket or purse for easy access and to avoid exposing your major cash and documents.

- We recommend keeping your passport with you in your under-the-clothes money pouch or placing it in the hotel safe. There are times when a hotel will ask for your passport to check in, but they should return it to you within a short period of time. Check your locale to see whether it is safer to carry the passport with you or not.

- In some countries, larger bills have a better exchange rate than smaller bills. For those locations (India and parts of Africa, for instance), take $100 bills or travelers checks instead of $20 bills. Exchange your money into small bills of the country currency because you will need them to pay for transportation and water. In some countries they cannot make change for you from large bills.

- ATM (automated teller machine) use will give a varied exchange rate. We actually walked miles checking different banks in Bangalore, India, trying to find one that accepted a bank card. At the sixth bank, we were finally able to get cash.

## HEALTH

Make sure you are as healthy and rested as possible before you leave home for your trip, and leave enough time to overcome jet lag when you arrive.

### Tips for Overcoming Jetlag

- Allow an extra day so you will not have to work on the first day and can adjust to a new time zone and surroundings, as needed.
- Work hard to stay hydrated. Avoid diuretics while traveling (caffeine and alcohol). They get in the way of staying hydrated and will increase jet lag symptoms.
- Whenever possible, sleep on the plane.
- Start to adjust your sleep schedule to the new time zone, if possible, before you leave.
- Exposure to sunlight helps with overcoming jetlag.
- Avoid naps at the new destination and get on the new sleep schedule as soon as possible. (This may seem impossible, as that nap feels so good! If you need a nap, limit it to twenty minutes so it doesn't interfere with your night's sleep.)
- Some people try melatonin (this works best in darkness, so you may need an eye mask), an herbal sleep remedy, or a sleep aid to assist those first couple of nights adjusting to a new time zone.
- Some exercise (walking, for example) can help release tension and bring on sleep.

Check with your physician and the Center for Disease Control (www.cdc.gov) before you leave for any needed inoculations or medications to make your stay safe and healthy. Read and follow the advice in the travel book that you purchase to prepare yourself for an enjoyable trip. Check the news for recent significant events that may be distracting people's attention when attending your program, so you can be aware of what is going on.

## SHOWING RESPECT

Typically, the oldest or most senior person, such as a manager, is introduced first in a training session, but you must be sensitive to the possibility that someone may be insulted if you guess wrong about hierarchy. Ask your host for the recommended protocol for introductions and seating arrangements, for example, by position, by alphabet, or by location in the room (first person on the left and so on). Tent cards and name tags with markers should be at each person's place. The presence of management may cause stress for some participants, who may not be comfortable participating in the same session with their managers. In other groups, you may need a manager present to bring up the tough questions or topics that others may be uncomfortable bringing up. Check with your sponsor to see whether you should have a separate session for management.

Always be on your very best professional behavior. Remember that you are a guest in their country and your most polite behavior will be appreciated. We tend to be used to very casual behavior in the United States, which is often too casual for those in other countries. We find that it is helpful to remember all of our best manners and avoid showing anger or frustration. Practice patience, because it is very easy to be misunderstood. Errors in interpretation are common. Remember to honor traditions of other cultures and try to speak the language for at least a few key words. These efforts are greatly appreciated by those you meet and those who are watching you as a representative of your country.

## PREPARING AND PRESENTING YOUR TRAINING MATERIALS

Now let's talk about the preparation of training materials. Language and visuals are critically important when you are presenting to an international audience. The audience members do not have the same frame of reference as you do, often do not understand jokes you may tell, and could easily be offended and confused by your casual way of presenting material (jargon and terms). Use words for your presentation that can be quickly looked up in an English dictionary. Use key words and concepts on each page, instead of long sentences, so that translations can be done (many languages take more letters per word and more words per concept than ours). Test out pictures, graphics, and language with someone you know who has a background in the culture you will be visiting. For example, when preparing materials for one presentation, we were surprised to find out that a picture of a child holding a stuffed bunny was a shock to a person from China, where they would not consider holding such an animal as a pet or toy.

Case studies can work well, but they must be carefully crafted to be clear and provide sufficient context. It is critical that you have a reliable contact in the country you will visit so you can check your content and ensure a maximum learning environment. You should ask whether all people who will be in the session can read English and whether the host can help you to translate the materials ahead of time, or if that is something you need to do. Does the host require and provide interpreters? Are the translations simultaneous, or do you need to double your training time for them to translate each sentence after you say it? Will they reproduce the materials, or do you need to ship materials ahead of time? Shipping may take much longer than you would imagine and videos/CDs may not be allowed to go through their mail system (depending on the country's shipping protocols).

Bring an international electrical appliance converter and adaptor plugs. If you are planning on using videos, the NTSC format from North America may not work in the equipment. PAL is the preferred format in much of Europe, and SECAM is standard for France and French-based countries. Videos must be converted into the appropriate format before you leave, so be sure to ask your host what format is required. CDs or DVDs should not pose a problem, as long as your computer and projector electrical hookups are international. It is better to be prepared for any possible complications. It is also important to have contingency plans (such as handouts and presentation notes) in case technology fails. Be prepared to change to "Plan B" without your students knowing about your technical difficulties. Your job is to help them to learn, without wasting their time when problems occur.

## TIPS FOR DEVELOPING A CULTURALLY INCLUSIVE VIDEO, BY MARCIE AUSTEN, DIRECTOR, HUMAN RESOURCES, FROM SHURE, INC.

We included a short video presentation as part of our "Values in Action" global training initiative in an effort to bridge the past and present of Shure's corporate culture and demonstrate how the company's core values have remained constant since 1925, when Mr. Shure founded the organization.

We wanted the video to be inclusive of the many global cultures of Shure for all of our associates around the world. In order to make that happen, we

*(continued)*

conducted focus groups in each of our international regions: Europe, Asia, and Latin America. The participants actually helped us choose the music and photos. In addition to interviews with Shure associates, the video included interviews with some of our customers, with subtitles when necessary.

Ultimately, the video and the training were very well received, and we feel this has helped us to establish a successful foundation for our next training initiative.

If you are going to use global SMEs to help develop content or materials, allow for plenty of time and involve them early in the process. It sounds intuitive, but if you haven't been through this before, you will be surprised at how long it will take. You can't walk down the hall to talk to someone, and you often can only catch the person by phone during very narrow time windows.

You may typically be seen as a VIP (very important person) with expertise, so participants in your program may be reluctant to ask questions and betray lack of knowledge, or they might hesitate because of lack of language skills or because their culture does not approve of asking questions of someone in a position of authority. Offline conversations are critical to finding out whether people are understanding the content. That means you often get no breaks!

If the participants in your program are from different countries, they should be grouped with persons from their own county, not mixed together (unless they are used to being mixed). This provides participants with a support system and helps with translations, as well as eliminating conflicts. Some countries have been conquered and humiliated by others in the past, so there may be hard feelings that cannot be changed in a training session. Even students from the same country may come from drastically different backgrounds and levels of protocol, so be very sensitive to this. You may be able to tell by observing body language, such as confusion, forced smiles, or frowns of worry, to see whether your trainees are uncomfortable. If so, you can pay special attention to alleviating their discomfort (without embarrassing them or calling attention to it). Not all body language translates well, however. Participants may be watching you and smiling and nodding their heads because they hear you or are polite, not because they understand the concepts you are discussing. Because each culture has its own body language, it is helpful to partner with a participant who would be willing to provide feedback to you regarding your presentation and its effectiveness. Whenever you can, let people sit and interact with the people they choose. This gives them an opportunity to discuss issues among themselves and speak to you as a group if they wish.

## FEELING GOOD

While in another country, take care to eat fully cooked foods. Don't eat those tempting fruits with the skins on or salads with raw vegetables in countries where the water they've been washed with may make you sick. In Ghana we were told it is safest to stick to fruit with skins that you peel yourself (with your own clean hands/knives). We craved and lived on pineapples, mangoes, and bananas that we peeled each night. Street vendor foods look and smell delicious, but may cause you to have stomach problems because you are not used to the bacteria in other countries. Drink and use bottled water (even for brushing your teeth), making sure that the bottle has not been opened (in some countries they re-use the water bottles by filling them with tap water and selling them). A little caution helps to ensure that you will feel your best throughout your trip.

Most training sessions are arranged in major cities, so use the same security techniques that you might in any large city. Ask your hotel or host to set up transportation so you will be with a reputable company. Ask your hotel or host how much it should cost to your destination so you have an idea how much money to have ready. Ask your driver how much the trip to your destination will cost before you get into the vehicle. If it seems like too much, try another vehicle or company. In some countries, tourists are charged more (commonly referred to as a "skin tax"). Always be aware of your surroundings and get out of them if you don't feel comfortable. Trust your instincts. Keep to the streets that are busy with people and go to restaurants where there are many patrons (this usually means the food is good). Watch and observe how others behave and try to "fit in." For example, your clothes should be conservative and respectful; this means no tank tops or shorts. If you must wear a sleeveless top, it is a good idea to cover it with a sleeved shirt or jacket. Suits with below the knee length skirts are usually appropriate for women. In some countries, it is wise for a woman to have a scarf or shawl, in case she needs or wants to cover her head out of respect and/or comfort from the heat. We do not recommend that you "go native" and dress as the people who live in the culture do, because it is often easy for them to tell that you are a foreigner who is trying to look like a native.

## VIRTUAL PRESENTATION

For virtual presentation via conference phone and computer, it is even more important that you clearly communicate everything ahead of time, such as computer specifications required by the participants. It is extremely useful to have the capability of a "hands-free" conference phone. Design your program to a minimum requirement of student capability to ensure success, because it is harder to coach individuals having difficulty if you are on a group conference call. Engage a conference support company (for example, WebEx) to ensure smooth technology usage. Practice ahead of time to remove any obvious roadblocks and gain experience in using the tools smoothly.

Develop a comfort level with a contact in the country you are working with. The person can ask tough questions during your program or help with clarification when possible when you're on the conference call. Engage this person in advance and share your expectations. Explain the role you would like him or her to play. If appropriate, explain the role the person is playing to others who are in on the call.

If the number of people is not too large, have each person or group spokesperson *briefly* introduce him- or herself (with name, organization, and location) at the beginning of the session. Provide online chat opportunities on an ongoing basis after the session and a web location for documents, resources, and continued learning/sharing opportunities.

These are just a few ideas for you to consider. We will cover this topic more in the next chapter.

## GAINING WISDOM

There is much history and wisdom in other lands. Many countries have thousands of years of history; some may have been united for only a short time, or not at all. Their music, art, dance, tastes, and animal species are rich and varied. If you have time to explore, take it! Their stories and perspectives are very different from what most of us have experienced. Expect the unexpected, such as all vehicles stopping for the sacred cow that has just laid down in the middle of the road in India or the elephant's leg that is brushing your arm and sharing the same road that your open air vehicle is using. Your meals and accommodations may be quite different from anything you have ever experienced. Treasure the variety and try not to show frustration, which can be easily misinterpreted. This is their world—you are a guest in their country. Many citizens of other countries have experienced poor behavior from foreigners, either in person or in the media. If they are deeply religious people, they may have seen very disrespectful behaviors from some visitors and may be sensitive to these actions and angry or disappointed to witness them. They are also curious about any country where citizens have a great deal of freedom and often see the extremes of this freedom in the media and movies. We heard a presentation recently where someone was coming to the United States for the first time from the Middle East. The presenter's friend had told him to be very careful; it is very dangerous in the U.S., and everyone carries a gun. Some countries know the U.S. by movies they see. Just remember: When you visit some places, they may be watching and making decisions based on your actions and their expectations.

We remember two men following us through the square in Beijing, China, because they wanted to practice their English. Even in English-speaking countries, the speakers' accents are often difficult for us to understand. Words that we think we know may mean something completely different to the speaker. Misunderstanding is easy. Clarification and writing things down is helpful, as is pointing to the word in the language dictionary so people can see it in both languages.

These are just a few thoughts to consider as you begin your journey.

Traveling is a wonderful and fascinating experience, one you may never forget.

Enjoy it and relish the opportunity to learn from every minute of it!

## MANAGING GLOBAL LEARNING PROJECTS

### TIPS FROM CAROLE WALD, ACCOUNT MANAGER, CORPORATE EDUCATION, LAKE FOREST GRADUATE SCHOOL OF MANAGEMENT

- Having a structured project management method is vital.
- Time differences require having guidelines and communication ground rules. (If you don't, you could receive "emergency" calls at 11:00 P.M. or 2:00 A.M.)
- Set up an electronic collaboration website (Wiki) for the project. Keep project plans, documents, and a "to do" list current.
- Bring attention to action items. If someone is not fulfilling his or her job, document it in writing weekly and verbally. Follow-up and attention to details carry different urgencies in different places. Be attentive to derailing tasks.
- Set rules of engagement up front. Clearly state rules in terms of "your role" and "my role."
- Schedule weekly status calls. You may need to adjust the time; for example, 7:00 A.M. or 7:00 P.M. is very common for contact with India.

*(continued)*

- Have a well-written agreement outlining assumptions about what your sponsor will do and pay for and what you will take care of and pay for. Define the cancellation policy clearly.

- Early on, add the country's holidays to the project calendar. Get those from the client.

- Build relationships with the main leader or sponsor. Meet in person if possible. If you cannot meet face-to-face, share photos or video conference to build a relationship. Think about ways to build the relationship and how you will be working together.

- Buy a cell phone that works where you are going and Internet connectivity arranged for the trainers who are visiting. Trainers need an easy way to communicate. Make these arrangements in advance.

Here are some tips for working with an internal training staff or manager in a different country:

- Get to know each other, and use formal communication practices. Continually ask for questions and feedback.

- Talk through misunderstandings. Show patience.

- Expectations of management may differ from country to country. Some places will expect direction from management, others will expect participation. Set clear roles and communication guidelines.

- When English is their second language, people may be hesitant to speak up and offer ideas. Those in Asian countries may not ask questions because of concern for showing respect. It will take probing and work to get feedback under those circumstances.

- When looking for feedback, send the request in writing in advance and let people respond in writing. Feedback can be consolidated so that no one feels exposed.

- Silence should not be interpreted as agreement or understanding. People will not want to embarrass themselves and may be cautious.

- Team members should learn expectations and preferences of the leader and of others on the team.

Additional details will need to be spelled out with costing a project when foreign work and travel are concerned. Discuss things like these:

- Will flights be coach class or business class?

- Who pays shipping costs (these may be significant and even overnight shipping may take five days)?

- Who will pay for the cost of copying materials? Getting materials there may be troublesome, but if the client is responsible, you won't have control over the quality or even know whether your materials will be in the classroom when you arrive. Companies' business centers will vary in reliability.

- Clearly define travel expenses. A five-star hotel may be appropriate because of safety concerns.

- Make sure of pre-arranged airport transportation where appropriate.

When choosing the right trainer for international work, look for:

- Flexibility

- Adventurousness

- Intercultural sensitivity

- Ability to develop quick rapport

- Knowledge of content and ability to contextualize content

- Knowledge of what training methods work best in a situation

- Ability to pick up on adjustments that need to be made

- Awareness of when things are not working

An additional consideration for global learning projects is how to pay contract facilitators. After research with several companies that pay contractors and conversations with contract facilitators, here are some considerations:

- Some companies pay a day rate for two travel days (one going, one returning), in addition to the training days at the destination. Others pay a half-day rate for the two travel days. (Might be a difference when the travel day is six hours versus when the travel time is twenty-three hours!)

- One company gives trainers a choice. They can have an upgraded flight to first or business class or they can be paid for the travel time. The idea is that, if you fly in the big seats, you can show up rested. If you fly in the cheap seats, you lose more time on both sides of the trip.

- Facilitators definitely receive an increase in their day rate for training internationally. The increases start at 20 percent, it was common to receive a 50 percent increase, and it goes up to a 75 percent increase in the typical day rate. (If they receive a 75 percent increase in their day rate, that covers the travel costs. One independent facilitator said that her clients have an easier time paying the increased day rate, rather than the travel rate.)

- Everyone seems to agree. Use a good hotel, arrange for reliable transportation, have an in-country contact who is attentive to helping with arrangements or problem solving. And most people fly at least business class.

For anyone who has done this, there is no argument. The facilitators are working harder and are earning their compensation.

## OVERALL RECOMMENDATIONS

*Watch, listen, ask, and try*. Discuss topics that unite people for example: food, weather, or lodging. Politely change the topic if asked about hot issues such as politics and religion, or change the direction of the conversation back to them and ask what they would like to share with you about their perspective.

Don't expect perfection and work hard to take things in stride. Have contingency plans, develop relationships and rely on local contacts to give advice and help you through. Everyone is learning here!

Here are some helpful tips.

### TIPS FROM SUSAN ONAITIS, PRESIDENT OF GLOBAL LEARNING LINK

Having traveled four continents and trained people in over seventy-five countries, I'd like to pass along a few tips to trainers who might be doing the same thing. Some of the tips may seem like "no brainers." However, when your brain is jet-lagged you might forget them. Some have to do with pre-travel action items that will make your trip go a lot more smoothly. These tips are organized into what to do before, during, and after your training—a kind of checklist approach to help you get organized. You may even have a few of your own to add!

**Before**

1. Plan your trip with an extra day or two on the front end. You may think you can power through jet lag, but your body has a way of undermining the best intentions. Allow yourself time to get on the clock of the country you are visiting.

2. Fly a major airline, preferably one with many flights to your destination. That way if there is a problem, you have options.

3. Lots of people believe in melatonin as a natural way to adjust your body to your destination's clock. Many have successfully used the three-day jet-lag diet recommended in *Overcoming Jet Lag* by Dr. Charles Ehret.

4. Check to make sure your passport is valid and will be for your whole trip.

5. Determine what shots or medications you might need prior to traveling. Schedule them enough in advance of your travel that you are not suffering any side-effects while on the trip.

6. Take only enough of the local currency to buy a meal and a cab ride from the airport. It is almost always less costly to exchange money in the country you are visiting than at home. Many hotels exchange currency and don't charge the outrageous fees you find at the airports. Banks in the destination country often have the best exchange rates.

7. Pack light. You never know where and how far you might end up having to carry your luggage. Leave the steamer trunks at home.

8. Remember to pack all medications you need in their original bottles or plan to carry a copy of the prescription.

9. Check that your destination location has copy facilities. Then you can send your materials ahead and not worry about having to carry them. Remember that overseas packages might get waylaid for some reason in customs, so allow plenty of time for materials to arrive.

*(continued)*

10. Always carry a master copy of all your materials.

11. Check out the power and voltage situation to bring adapters so your equipment works "over there."

12. Learn something about the culture you will be working in so you don't do something offensive in your attire, greeting, dining, or training. A wonderful resource is the book *Kiss, Bow, or Shake Hands: The Bestselling Guide to Doing Business in More than 60 Countries* (2006) by Terri Morrison and Wayne Conaway.

13. Design your training program with the culture and language differences in mind. Not all cultures love interaction in the classroom. Don't assume that what works at home also works abroad. Create an environment that is safe for participants, but that also accomplishes your objectives.

14. Designing the training so that you divide the class into small groups to work gives participants a chance to help each other, clear up any confusion, or ask questions in their own language. Very often the most confident English speaker in the group will ask a question that has the whole group confused.

15. As you design the program, keep in mind that if you are using an interpreter during your program it will take about one-third to one-half again as much time for the translation, and factor that into the timing of your program.

16. Use a local interpreter in the destination, if possible. He/she will know the local references, jargon, and colloquialisms.

17. Try to arrange a meeting with the interpreter prior to the training so you can get to know how he/she works best.

18. Have the materials translated by someone in the destination and keep all materials in both English and the local language. That way, if there is a question about the materials, you will know where participants are looking and to what they are referring.

19. Before you leave, plan your ground transportation upon arrival. It's one less thing you have to worry about when you get off the airplane tired and possibly disoriented.

20. Once you arrive at your destination, try to check out the training room a day before to see whether you have everything you need.

21. Do a dry run with your equipment and your interpreter (if possible) to make certain everything works as you expect.

22. Check a day or two in advance of your training to be sure your materials have arrived and you can get your hands on them. If they haven't arrived, you still have time to make copies.

### During

1. If you are teaching in English and not using an interpreter, remember to slow down your speech. Articulate clearly. Eliminate slang expressions, jokes, and colloquialisms common at home that might confuse participants.

2. If you are using an interpreter, slow down your speech so he/she can get the full meaning. Remember, English may be the interpreter's second or third language. Pause regularly to be sure he/she has caught up with you.

3. Give frequent breaks—your interpreter needs them. Translating is intense work and can be very tiring. Make sure your interpreter can stay rested and fresh or he/she may miss important points in the training.

4. Check in with your participants frequently to allow them to ask questions. This is extremely important when the audience comes from a non-English-speaking country and English is their second or third language.

5. Listen carefully. Ask the interpreter for help if you don't understand what a participant is saying.

6. Enjoy yourself and have fun. Participants will relax if they see you are relaxed and confident. Let your warmth and personality come through.

7. Have participants complete a feedback form. Ask open-ended questions to gain insight into whether the training / program met their needs.

8. Give participants an easy way to contact you if they have questions following the program.

### After

1. Evaluate the training with the participants' managers. Review any areas of confusion that came out in the feedback forms.

*(continued)*

2. Assist managers with a follow-up plan for each participant based on what you observed in the classroom.

3. The rule of thumb on recovery from jet lag is about one day of recovery for every time zone you have crossed. So if you live in New York and have just returned from Singapore, you will probably need about thirteen days to recapture your body clock completely.

Reprinted with permission of Susan Onaitis.

# Designing the Program for International Audiences

In this chapter we will cover some of the elements of program design and general considerations along the way to help ensure success with international audiences. Even though the delivery of training may cross an ocean or continent, the design process doesn't need to be foreign. The same fundamental concepts hold true. We'll be following the outline of a typical design process: Analyze, Design, Develop, Implement, Evaluate (ADDIE), but won't give step-by-step instructions. Instead, we'll provide tips in each section based on our research and point out parts of the process that may require extra attention when designing for an international audience.

To help illustrate the process, we will follow a fictitious scenario in this chapter, and *you* can play a big part. Put yourself into the scenario and try to envision it playing out. Your role is one of an experienced designer who has been engaged to develop sales training on a new product line for an international company with an international audience. Sales representatives from a variety of countries will attend the event. All attendees speak English to one degree or another. You will need to learn a bit more about the project before giving your recommendation about the best approach to take. Are you ready to start?

## ANALYZE

Just like any other well-planned project, this international training program should be designed based on the results of a needs assessment or some other analysis to better understand the needs of the organization, the project, and the learners. This analysis helps the designer to focus on what the participants need to know and helps keep the design and delivery on track. Whether you conduct the needs assessment or it has already been done and you are reviewing the results, consider the following points:

- Review the request.
- Obtain information from the program sponsor.
- Leverage communication vehicles.
- Gather additional information.
- Communicate with potential participants.
- Do your homework.
- Present your proposal.

Let's look at each of these in more detail.

### Review the Request

Who is requesting this training? Be sure to consider the cultural impact of the requester, for example, what is the role or position of the requester in the organization? What is his or her background? Consider gender and stereotypes for a moment. Based on the culture served, are there any things we need to consider? If interviews or data gathering are required, will gender impact the results? Consider your gender and culture and try to imagine what the client may perceive about you. *Note:* Be sure to check out other chapters in this book for information about specific countries and regions.

### Obtain Information from the Program Sponsor

Clarity of scope and information to be covered, as well as a solid understanding of your audience, is even more important when dealing with international audiences. To enhance success, be politely persistent about hearing the vision of the program sponsor in his or her own words. Clarify the project background and how it impacts this program.

### Leverage Communication Vehicles

Consider which communication methods best meet your needs. Should you use in-person meetings, phone conversations, email, or some other means? Whenever possible, it is a best practice to meet in person, at least initially. Being face-to-face with the sponsor and/ or other team members gives you the ability to truly meet each person, observe body language, and see whether all parties are on the same page.

Phone conversations or conference calls are useful if you have already established rapport with the individual and are helpful for status meetings and updates. Although it is possible to conduct an interview or gather content via the phone, timing delays, poor quality connections, and the inability to read body language make this more challenging.

Electronic communication such as email can be used for quick updates and sending information back and forth. All too often the message and intent are misconstrued, even if the sender and recipient are communicating in the same native language. Imagine how tricky this can be when team members are from differing cultures and countries!

### Best Practice Tips (for Meetings)

- Be sure to organize your thoughts and questions in a logical flow to avoid confusion.
- Use short and simple questions.
- Speak clearly and slowly (particularly if meeting over the phone).
- Be very polite and respectful (typically refer to your contact formally by addressing him or her as Mr. or Ms. Client, until he or she tells you differently). Use "please," "thank you," and other polite words.
- Continually check for understanding by rephrasing and clarifying as you go along.
- Consider organizing your questions to follow a "who, what, when, where, why" flow. See the sample below.

### Who

- Who is the audience for this program?
- Would you describe a typical participant please? (Try to get at age range, gender, education level, language proficiency, successful past learning events, job experience level, and so on.)
- How many participants will attend?
- Are these participants required to attend? (Try to get at the motivation for the participants to attend. Is this mandatory, or are they attending because they want to?)

### What

- What is the need for the topic requested?
- Does the content exist in an electronic format (Word, Portable Document Format [PDF], or Excel)? If not, how can we gather the content?

- What do you imagine this program being like?
- What constitutes success? How do you define success?

**When**

- When is the program needed?
- How long do you expect the training to take (hours/days)?
- Will there be one session or several?

**Where**

- Which location(s) are best for delivering the program? (Think about audience size, technical considerations, time zones, and travel requirements.)

**Why**

- Why do the intended participants need this program?
- What are they not doing that they should be able to do?
- What do they need to learn to be able to do this?
- What do they already know about this topic? (This gets at related materials/courses.)

## Gather Additional Information

If you are not able to find all of the information or detail needed from the sponsor, ask for permission to contact others who have that information. Even if you feel you have all of the information you need at this stage (for analysis purposes), most likely you will need to gather information from another contact (or several) within the organization as the project progresses.

- Who can I work with to make sure the content of the program is correct? (Again, be aware of gender/cultural influences. What is the best mode of communication to take into account preferences and time zones: email, telephone, in-person meetings, video conferences?)
- Who can I work with to confirm details such as setup of the location, materials, and logistics?
- May I contact some of the participants to obtain more information?
- Who else should I speak with to be sure that this program is successful (other key stakeholders)?

## Communicate with Potential Participants

In addition to some of the questions asked above, here are some questions to get further clarification when you speak with potential participants or subject-matter experts (SMEs).

- What do you hope to learn by attending a program on this topic? What information and/or skills would you like to gain in this topic?

- What is your previous level of training on this topic (so we don't cover information that you already know)?

- Provide your initial thoughts on timing and location of this program, and then ask: "Can you think of any major problems with this approach?"

## Do Your Homework

Get your bearings by doing your homework and being prepared. If you haven't done so already, benchmark the current state of this topic. There are many ways to do this including:

- Research the newest information on this topic to get yourself up-to-speed.

- Find out what other excellent organizations are doing regarding this topic (in this country and internationally).

- Analyze the current state of this topic in the countries you are targeting for this program.

- Consider learning styles and possible cultural aspects of this topic. In our international company scenario, although it is one organization, each country may be operated as a separate business unit with policies and practices reflecting the culture or environment. For example, there may be some aspects of training that are country-specific, such as access to technology (due to transportation, infrastructure, or technical expertise in the region). Another cultural preference of global audiences may be established by the company. Case in point: A number of international organizations prefer in-person training for leadership and management topics because it helps develop relationships among peers/colleagues.

Len and Zeace Nadler tell us in their book *Designing Training Programs* (1994) that we can identify needs from various sources like performance reports, production or service problems, and changes in technology, customers, competition, or government requirements.

In the *Basics of Instructional Systems Development* (2002), Chuck Hodell reminds us that when you are teaching job tasks, you need to perform a task analysis by identifying the critical outputs, major tasks, knowledge and skills required. Once you have collected data to document job tasks in detail, you need to validate and obtain approval from the client.

## Present Your Proposal

After gathering more information about the project (in our scenario), you recommend a blended learning approach to best meet the needs of this audience. By using a variety of instructional methods, learners are more likely to absorb and retain the new information. Your immediate solution for this situation includes:

- Pre-reading materials to be reviewed prior to the training to give learners an overview of the new products
- A facilitated workshop to present the main content and provide practice with role-play situations
- Short podcasts to reinforce key points after the training session

Your proposal is met with overwhelming enthusiasm. You receive the approval to continue, and you are asked how soon you can deliver. It is time to move on to creating the program design.

To summarize the Analysis phase, this is where you get your bearings by reviewing the

- Program request
- Project goals
- Vision
- Content type
- Audience characteristics
- Industry trends
- Information about the organization

You figure out who the players are and begin communicating with project team members to start filling content gaps.

## DESIGN

By the end of the design phase you should obtain agreement from all key stakeholders approving the program objectives (what the participants will be able to do by the end of the program). You should also have reached an agreement regarding the approach and purpose of each component of the training.

Typical documents created during this phase of the project can be called by a variety of names and include:

- Design document
- High-level design
- Initial outline
- Detailed outline

Project timelines, budgets and cultural aspects of the client dictate which of these deliverables are completed for the project and how robust each may be. For our scenario, as you probably noticed at the end of the Analysis phase, time is of the essence. The client wants this training program as soon as possible, so you decide to create an initial outline that includes some design elements. You will then take this one step further in the detailed outline.

## Create an Initial Outline

The main purposes of this outline are to

- Document what you have heard in your initial and subsequent meetings with the project sponsor and SMEs (Subject Matter Experts)
- Give it a training/learning context (include effective learning principles such as interactivity)
- Obtain approval to continue to the next step of the project

A simple Word document containing the purpose and objectives of each training component is a good start.

---

### SCENARIO

To follow our scenario, here is a sample of what your initial outline may contain:

**I. Pre-Reading Materials**
Format/Timing: Materials will be sent electronically one week in advance of the workshop to each participant. Participants are required to read the materials before attending the workshop.

*(continued)*

---

Purpose: The materials will be ten to fifteen pages in length and will provide a general positioning and overview of the new products.

Objective: Provide a high-level overview of the new products.

Design Elements: A Word or PDF document will contain the text and graphics to provide an overview of the new products.

- Since no template exists, text will be provided in Arial font in 12-point type. The use of bold text and simple styles display a simple and clear structure of the information.
- Information will be formatted so that learners can review the information on the computer or it can be printed.

### II. New Product Workshop Components

Format/Timing: A one-day instructor-led workshop will be conducted (location to be determined).

Purpose: The purpose of the workshop is to provide the international sales team with more detailed information about the new products, give opportunities to interact with the products, and provide role-play scenarios to practice sales calls for the new products.

Objectives

- Describe the features of product X
- Describe the features of product Y
- Explain product positioning
- Conduct sales calls on new products

Design Elements

- PowerPoint slides will contain the majority of the workshop content.
- Existing PowerPoint slide templates will be used.
- Supplemental materials (for handouts) will be created as Word or PDF files and will use the same styles as the pre-reading materials.
- Participants will receive a copy of the PowerPoint slides with an area for note-taking.

- A written assessment will be taken at the end of the workshop to help gauge learning. Twenty questions will be developed in the format of multiple-choice, true/false, and fill-in-the-blank question types.

- A training evaluation form will be given to learners to provide feedback on the program.

### III. New Product Podcasts

Format/Timing: One week following the workshop, participants will be able to listen to two ten-minute podcasts. The first podcast will cover a review of the products. The second will highlight sales tips and techniques for the new products. These podcasts can be available for future review as well.

Purpose: The purpose of the podcasts is to reinforce key features and benefits of the product and review key sales techniques.

Objectives

- Review product features and benefits

- List sales tips and techniques

Design Elements

- Podcasts will use a professional narrator and be upbeat and energetic.

- For the first podcast, the narrator conducts a brief interview of the sales vice president who provides product highlights.

- For the second podcast, the narrator conducts a quick interview of two leading sales representatives, who provide sales tips and techniques.

Once you have submitted the initial outline, be sure to walk through any documents you've created to make sure all stakeholders have the same understanding regarding objectives and general approach to the training. Resolve any questions or issues. Include any revisions or changes on your next deliverable, the detailed outline.

## Develop a Detailed Outline

Once the initial outline has been approved, it is time to be more specific. A detailed outline can provide key learning points and possible techniques or activities to illustrate learning points or objectives. Here again, simple language and formatting are key. It may also be a good idea at this juncture to create a mocked-up sample of the materials for your sponsor to review. Show how you plan to use color, white space, a clear tone, and concise sentences to help reviewers see what your audience will experience.

The detailed outline incorporates the research and information you gathered, by helping to determine the best formats to use in developing the presentation. Here are a few words about common activities and how to use them.

### Using Case Studies

For certain learning objectives, a case study is a terrific learning experience. If participants need to discuss and explore a variety of concepts or a broad concept, case studies can be very effective. In small groups, a scenario can be given to participants to read. Discussion questions about the scenario provide the opportunity to analyze the situation and recommend solutions. An added benefit of this technique is that it also helps to build confidence and foster camaraderie among the participants.

Again, with global audiences, simplicity is the key. Describe the situation and allow the participants to discuss it in small groups using a common language. It does not matter whether one group is speaking Italian and another group is discussing the case in French. A common language such as English can be designated for the large group debriefing of the case. Be sure that the case study "works" for the audience you are targeting. You can do this ahead of time by asking a representative of the audience to tell you whether the case study is clear and appropriate for their culture. Ask the reviewer to provide suggestions to make the case even better. Make sure the case study is short, relevant (both culturally and conceptually), and easy to understand.

### Developing Role Plays

A role play can be used when participants need to learn how to respond to a new or different situation. If sales representatives need to conduct sales calls with their customers, role plays can provide practice. Participants can obtain feedback and learn from seeing how others do it.

Provide an observation checklist that covers critical points to be reviewed for a more successful role play. Give time guidelines to the "sales representatives" and have them conduct the practice role play. Ask observers to provide constructive feedback regarding the "sales representatives'" questions and responses to the "customers." Then allow discussion of the entire practice among the group members, to identify key points to remember.

Many people are not comfortable with role plays, so have an alternative approach prepared, such as asking someone who would be willing to practice ahead of time and perform a demonstration.

### Adding Activities

The use of games, question-and-answer techniques, brainstorming sessions, and other activities can work just as well with global audiences *if* you review them through the eyes of the participant. When using activities for global audiences, ask yourself these questions:

- Are the instructions clear?
- Do the visuals convey the desired meaning?
- Could the actions or activities be considered offensive or go against cultural norms?

## SCENARIO

To follow our scenario, here is a sample of what your detailed outline may contain for the new product workshop deliverable. Note that the objectives have to be further refined from the initial outline, and each has one or more techniques defined.

| Learning Objective | Technique(s) |
|---|---|
| Describe the features and benefits of product X | Review of pre-reading materials in group question-and-answer format |
| | Lecture and slides provide more detailed product information |
| Describe the features and benefits of product Y | Review of pre-reading materials in group question-and-answer format |
| | Lecture and slides provide more detailed product information |

*(continued)*

| Learning Objective | Technique(s) |
|---|---|
| Explain product positioning | Small group activity (groups review several customer scenarios and match the best product with the customer needs). |
| | Debrief activity as a large group |
| | Lecture and slides provide more detailed positioning information and examples |
| | Group activity to create a job aid with product features, benefits, and positioning |
| Conduct sales calls about new products | Small group activity to role play sales calls; one person plays customer, one plays sales person, one is observer. Each person has at least one chance to play each role. |

**Best Practice Tips**

- Use action-oriented words when developing learning objectives so others will easily understand what they need to do as a result of the learning. These words also provide observable clues that can be used to provide feedback on performance, to aid in students' learning and practice.

- Be sure to include a variety of techniques to address different learning styles and preferences.

- When designing activities, provide a verbal overview or demonstration to the group. Make sure instructions and rules are simple and clear.

Once the detailed design has been reviewed, revised, and agreed on by key stakeholders, you are ready to begin development of your program content. As you may have guessed, in our scenario, your detailed design has been approved and the project continues. The client is so pleased with your work that he is insisting that you facilitate the workshop.

To summarize the Design phase, this is where:

- The general structure of the program begins to take shape.
- The objectives and design are refined.
- Consideration has been given to learning styles, preferences and cultural implications.
- Deliverables are beginning to form in your mind.

## DEVELOP

Development involves putting what you want to convey into what the participants will see and use, such as PowerPoint slides, handout materials, and job aids. Factors to continue to consider during this phase are learning styles and preferences, cultural implications for the audience(s) being served by the training program, and effective ways to convey information. Typically, the Development phase includes several rounds of review and edits. Each iteration of this process will help more clearly hone the content for the audience.

Although the people in many countries speak English, the deliverables need to be targeted to the learners' command of the English language and cultural influences, as well as accommodating different learning styles and preferences.

### Considering Learning Styles and Preferences

Most learners seem to have a dominant learning style, such as auditory, visual, or kinesthetic and tactile. In addition, each learner has his or her own approach to learning. Some attack learning with great enthusiasm, and others avoid anything that sounds like it involves new learning. Consciously or unconsciously, each learner brings previous memories into new learning situations. It is important to recognize that a participant in a session may be reacting to something from the past, not necessarily to the current situation.

Learners also have preferences for learning. Some need to have the big picture and then the pieces presented right in the beginning of a program or else they are distracted until they can understand major concepts. Others would like to hear every detail right now and have a hard time waiting while a presenter is covering the big picture. Sometimes these preferences are a result of cultural influences – sometimes these are individual preferences.

It is crucial to keep these considerations of style, approach, and preference in mind as you begin developing the program materials. Deliverables should be broad enough and have enough variety to appeal to all learners.

One other consideration of learner style is the facilitator style and activity type that would be most effective for several categories of learners: Dependent, Collaborative, and Independent.

Susan Russell (2005) cites Barbara Schneider-Fuhrmann and Paul Jacobs, who indicate that people with a "Dependent" learner style respond best to a trainer who uses structure such as lecture and demonstration.

Participants who have more of a "Collaborative" learning style respond best to interaction, experimentation and practice.

Participants with an "Independent" learning style respond well to an instructor who provides resources, opportunities for negotiating, and requests for feedback.

According to the Myers-Briggs Type Indicator, Isabel Briggs Myers, *Introduction to Type* (1998) tells us that people around the world may fall into type categories that respond best to certain design techniques. For example:

- An Extrovert may enjoy discussion and role-play activities.

- An Introvert will typically not like role plays but will respond better to individual exercises, reading or listening to the instructor lecture.

- There are some people who look for the data, facts, and detail of your topic and others who look for the whole picture and how pieces fit together.

- There are those who like structure, order, and sticking to the time frames. They look for the presenter to provide closure on one topic before going on to the next and look for summaries and conclusions.

- There are also people who learn best by doing hands-on activities.

This awareness of the variety of preferences, in any group of people, encourages us to include different learning options in our programs, to meet the needs of as many learners as possible. We, of course, still need to keep in mind the cultural preferences of our audience.

David Kolb, in *Training and Learning Styles* (2005) identifies learning styles that can be classified into:

- Those who prefer one right answer, are strong on solving technical problems, and are decisive (Convergers)

- Those who are imaginative, sensitive to meanings, values, and feelings, keep an open mind, gather information, and envision implications of situations and choices (Divergers)

- People who are able to create abstract models, organize information, analyze, and experiment (Assimilators)
- Learners who take risks, adapt to circumstances, take action, get involved, and are often viewed as impatient (Accommodators).

Knowing something about these styles can help us design our program so that people with any of these styles can have their interests piqued, and each can experience some success. For example, we need to include all of these in our design, if possible:

- Examples
- Practice
- Opportunities for reflection and observation
- Presentation of concepts and information.

### Best Practice Tips for Text

- Use short words that are common or can be looked up in any dictionary.
- If the content will be translated into multiple languages, use short dictionary words that can be easily translated.
- Use common fonts, particularly if the content will be translated.
- Spell out all words of any acronyms used.
- Avoid jargon, but if you must use it, explain it in context.
- For written materials, be generous with the amount of white space you use. Give your text some "breathing" room on the page and a place for the eyes to rest.
- Consider whether the text will be viewed on a computer screen, printed out, or be part of an overhead slide presentation and make adjustments to font size, spacing, and use of white space.

### Best Practice Tips for Graphics

- Be very selective about any pictures or clip art that is used. What works in one country may be offensive or confusing in another.
- Use simple images that convey universal concepts even better than words. Check with someone from that culture to ensure that the images convey what you want people to learn.
- Avoid using gestures or hand signs as part of graphics.

**Tips for Audiovisuals**

- Carefully consider cultural aspects of any visuals chosen.

- Try to put yourself in the learners' shoes. Consider the timing and pacing of any audio or video content. Add time to let the words or content "soak in."

- Keep movement on the minimal side, so as not to distract from the learning message.

## SCENARIO

To continue with our scenario of the blended approach to the new product training, you have come up with development standards and styles for creating your deliverables. Here's what you have come up with.

**Pre-Reading Materials**

- Clear, concise text in a simple and readable font

- Bold headings used to introduce concepts

- Lots of white space to let the eyes rest on the page (generous margins and blank lines separating distinct thoughts and paragraphs)

- Pictures of the products to accompany descriptive text

- Information about the product in simple and clear terminology; acronyms are spelled out; no jargon is used

- The text and graphics laid out in a manner that prints well

- Color used sparingly so as not to distract the learner and for ease of printing

**New Product Workshop Materials**

- Created primarily as PowerPoint slides (An idea to help learners focus on the content is to incorporate a graphic of the product on the slides. It could be used in the title of the slide or as a watermark image in the background of the slide.)

- Simple slide text, clean and similar to the style used for the pre-reading materials

- Facilitation notes (Notes section of each slide)

- A slide introducing the activities and separate handouts for the activities to be developed following the same general style for the pre-reading materials
- Participant materials with a copy of each slide and an area to be used for writing the learner's own personal comments/notes on each slide (This is where it is important to know about the language and culture of your participants because you may need to leave space on each slide for translations.)

**Podcasts**
- No longer than fifteen minutes in length (due to file size implications as well as learner attention spans)
- The same "narrator" is used for all podcasts. This narrator has a Midwestern U.S. accent (which has been determined to be the simplest to decode) and is asked to speak more slowly for this audience than he would for his local audience.
- The narrator gives a brief introduction to remind the learner of the topic and then introduces the person to be interviewed.
- The format is a radio-show-style interview of a question posed by the narrator followed by the response of the featured guest.

Using these styles as guides, you create the PowerPoint slides, handout materials, pre-reading materials, and the speaker notes for the podcasts. You send drafts to your program sponsor and subject-matter experts and other team members for their review and feedback. At last the materials are just right for the audience. Now, the task that remains is to deliver the training.

The Development phase leverages the decisions that had been made in the Design phase by creating the deliverables agreed on. Generally style guides that make the materials acceptable for the learners are developed first, then scripting and course development begin.

## IMPLEMENT/PROGRAM DELIVERY

When presenting the final materials to the client or presenting your program in person, you will need to consider language, translations, customs, protocols, and visibility. If at all possible with diverse audiences, plan for a pilot test or a dry run with a sample audience.

This helps to fine-tune any last-minute details or clarify any things that could be lost in translation.

Try to give yourself plenty of lead time. This applies to sending materials via postal service, a delivery service, or the company's intranet or delivering the materials in person. Things always seem to go wrong when there is no margin for errors.

To continue with our scenario, you have completed the pre-reading materials. The PDF file has been sent electronically to your program sponsor. He has drafted a cover email to accompany the materials when they are sent electronically to participants. All has gone well so far. You are preparing to travel to a foreign location to facilitate the workshop. There are many factors to keep in mind when delivering the program. The following is not an exhaustive list, but it contains key tips as you prepare for the trip and to conduct the program.

### Best Practice Tips for Getting There

- Carry a complete set of materials with you in case you arrive and nothing else has made it.

- Be prepared to be surprised. It would be very unique if you arrived and everything went smoothly because there are so many new variables that could affect your plans.

- Wear professional clothing that is acceptable for the culture by being aware of the color and cut of your garments. This holds true for traveling as well as facilitating the program.

- Allow extra time on each leg of the trip for delays or unexpected events.

### Best Practice Tips for Reviewing the Room

- If you can go to the room ahead of time (or even look at a digital photograph of the room before you arrive), look at the projection surface to make sure it allows participants to easily see any visuals.

- Make sure that all equipment works.

- Position yourself and materials so you can be easily seen and access your materials without having to move too far away from the front of the room.

- Ensure that seating is roomy enough but also positioned so that participants can see and hear each other for discussion and asking questions.

### Best Practice Tips for Conducting the Program

- Use an appropriate mode of address for participants such as Mr. or Ms. or first name, based on what is acceptable and respectful.

- Do not take it personally if learners do not respond as you would like. Remember that there are many factors (such as culture, learning style, and preferences) that could be affecting their experience.

- Watch for signs that indicate it may be necessary to vary the technique used to help learners comprehend the content. Looks of confusion, boredom, embarrassment, or panic may indicate that the message is not getting through.

- Determine whether the group feels comfortable asking questions or asking for help. In some cultures, asking questions or pushing back is considered disrespectful. Come up with various ways to give permission to ask questions. Small group activities may provide a more comfortable setting for asking questions.

- If any managers are present, leverage them to add their thoughts, articulate the concerns for the group, and start discussions.

- If you have one, let your interpreter know you are looking for particular information. If the audience is struggling, you need to know this to be able to address it, and your interpreter may be able to help.

- Be prepared to shift gears if necessary. Perhaps the big picture overview is needed, maybe a quick drawing on the whiteboard will help, or maybe a break is needed.

- Make sure there is extra time in the agenda in case you need to provide more examples, practice time, or discussion time.

- Choose simple language and watch participants to ensure that they understand what is being said. If they look confused, explain again more clearly, in different words. Speak slowly enough to enunciate each word, making sure that you clearly speak the beginning and ending of each word. (We tend to drop our voices when we are using our native language.) We may speak too fast and not enunciate enough of the words for people to understand, if they are not familiar with the language we are using.

- Don't ask people to work through lunch and break times. In some cultures this can be a major mistake of disrespect.

- Be aware that typical feedback techniques may not work well. Plan to walk around during activities or exercises to read body language and answer questions. Seek out participants, the interpreter, customer staff, or managers present to see how well they think the learning transfer is going. Be prepared to make modifications as needed.

If the program is held in your location, but attended by multi-national participants, much of what we just covered regarding the design of the program still applies. It may be easier for you to deliver on your own home "turf," but the participants will be struggling with a new location as well as customs they are not as familiar with, so it may be an additional challenge for them. Above all, be patient, polite, and understanding.

## EVALUATE

Using what you have been told by your sponsor/requestor of the program, design the evaluation to check if people have learned what the objectives have said they will learn.

Evaluation can include a paper-and-pencil quiz, case study, role play, game, practice exercise, or a variety of other possible ways to determine whether people are comfortable with the material provided. This should be checked with your project team to ensure that it is appropriate for the culture of the participants. For example, tests may create very high-pressure situations and should not be used unless necessary or required by the sponsor of the program.

In our scenario, the sponsor has decided that the learners will not be given an evaluation (Level 2) test. Instead you have developed an instrument to gather feedback about the workshop (the style, pacing of information, reaction to activities, suggestions for improvement, and a list of the three most important things each participant learned, that is, Level 1 program feedback). Be sure to review this information and gather any learning for next time before passing the completed evaluations along to the project team.

In the case that you may need to design a paper-and-pencil test to evaluate what the students have learned, Alice Waagen gives us some advice in C. Hodell's *Basics of Instructional Systems Development* (2002), telling us to create a draft of sample questions, using objective questions such as multiple-choice and true or false, and presenting only one correct answer.

- We should write questions for easy comprehension, that reveal how well the participants understand the material.

- We should also use a random arrangement of answers, vary the level of difficulty, try not to signal the correct answer, and provide thorough but consistent directions.

Introduce the test in a non-threatening way and explain how the test takers will get their results (for example, privately) to show them how much they have learned. Tell them that you will be available to clarify any of the answers after the test, if they wish further discussion.

## FOLLOW-UP/REINFORCEMENT

After the program is complete, participants could be given worksheets, additional sessions, or further activities to reinforce the learning. People tend to remember the information and skills better if they use them immediately after the program and the material is reviewed at intervals such as three or six months after program completion. Follow-up can be provided by email reminders, hints, and newsletters or by forming learning groups who can meet and discuss the application of skills learned. In our scenario, the two podcasts will serve as reinforcement.

The program can be more effective if you have involved managers and supervisors before, during, and after the training. Interview the managers and supervisors about their needs when you are developing the program. Then have the managers introduce the program to tell the participants how important it is. After the training, the managers and supervisors can provide ongoing reinforcement of the learning by sending follow-up letters that you have created and by ongoing recognition of the program completion.

You can also ask supervisors to observe and reward good performance, and collect performance data to show the return on investment (ROI) through:

- Increased productivity

- Increased savings

- Better quality

- Fewer errors, grievances, and problems.

Your follow-up plan for each country may be different. Think about who the right people and methods are to best follow up and reinforce.

## VIRTUAL PRESENTATIONS

Although we have not spent much time in this chapter discussing virtual presentations such as webcasts and conference calls, many of the elements discussed earlier still apply. In a later chapter we provide specific details about conducting webcasts. Here are some other considerations:

- Be aware of the locations of participants. How many participants are joining in? What time zones and languages are represented?

- Find out what kind of equipment the participants have. What minimum specifications are required for effective reception? What computer configurations do most participants have?

- Think of ways to keep learners' attention without having eye contact. Use things like making presentations visually interesting, using more voice inflections, and leveraging the tools of the presentation mechanism such as polls, voting, and online question submission.

- Set aside time for question-and-answer periods. If possible, provide an email question submission option as well as one on the phone.

- Send the presentation ahead of time to all participants.

- Set up an electronic location for participants to access the presentation on a file server or a website.

- Create detailed directions for participants to sign in, access the information, and download it, if necessary.

- Have all participants (or participant groups) introduce themselves (with their locations) if the numbers are not too large.

- Ask participants to identify themselves before speaking so that others know who is asking the question or making a comment.

- Stick to your agenda. By doing so you will respect everyone's time.

- Allow time for breaks.

- Include activities to keep participants involved.

- Run a test ahead of time to make sure that your computer, phone, and webcasting system work effectively with participants from different locations.

- Keep looking and listening for body language and voice changes to notice confusion or frustration.

- If you happen to have an interpreter, ask him or her to check for understanding.

- Ask for questions and clarifications from the participants throughout the session.

- Provide opportunities for the participants to discuss concepts with others to deepen understanding and comprehension.

- Leave time to go into depth in areas that have to be clarified.

- Be available during breaks and after the program for individual and small group discussion, as needed.

In this chapter we covered some of the elements of program design and general considerations along to the way to help ensure success with international audiences. More information about specific cultures can be found in subsequent chapters.

## PRACTICE EXERCISE

Here's a quick practice exercise for you to identify language that may be confusing to international audiences. The list below are some examples of words or phrases from this chapter that you may not have noticed as you read along, but that may easily be misinterpreted by students from another country.

- play a big part
- get a better handle on
- on track
- are on the same page
- tricky
- get your bearings by doing
- up to speed
- case in point
- move on to
- figure out
- filling content gaps
- in essence of time
- getting through
- come up with

These phrases and words, even when looked up in the dictionary, may not be clear. See whether you can revise them to be less confusing.

Here are some potential answers:

play a big part → help

get a better handle on → determine

on track → organized

are on the same page → understood

tricky → difficult

get your bearings by doing → delete it and revise to: Do your homework and be prepared

up to speed → prepared

case in point → delete it

move on to → delete and revise to: Create

figure out → identify

filling content gaps → obtain additional information

in essence of time → to save time

getting through → clear

come up with → identify

These phrases are common only to the people who have lived in a particular culture. Every language has such terms, which is why it is important to have the materials localized (translated for the location of the program participants) and interpreted by a local resident. With practice, we can become more aware of causes of potential misunderstandings and try to prevent them by revising the wording that we use.

We hope that you enjoyed this exercise and continue to look for areas of potential confusion and misunderstanding in your own designs, so that you can be ready to enhance the learning of the participants in your programs.

## References

Hodell, C. (2002). *Basics of instructional systems development* (ISD). Alexandria, VA: ASTD Press.

Myers, I.B. (1998). *Introduction to type.* Mountain View, California: Consulting Psychology Press.

Nadler, L., & Nadler , Z. (1994). *Designing training programs* (2nd ed.). Houston, TX: Gulf.

Russell, S. (2005). Training and learning styles. *Info-Line 8804.* Alexandria, VA: ASTD Press.

Swedberg, Louann M . Writer and instructional designer

# Translation for International Audiences

**A**s experts in organizations present and train globally, they will often need to have materials and presentations translated and interpreted. In this chapter you will find tips for translating documents and presentations, working with classroom interpreters, and choosing resources to help with these processes.

When training people from different cultures, it is important to be a learner BEFORE being a teacher—there is so much to learn from other cultures. When possible, try not to present your ideas as a replacement for their ideas. True teaching is creating new ideas within the learners' experience and making it work. Understanding learning preferences of your audience may help you in helping them connect with the content you are presenting. Are they visual? Do they need interaction? Do they prefer hands-on? or Do they prefer lecture? For example, many people can read a second language better than they can understand that language as spoken, so projecting PowerPoint slides or having well-annotated handouts may provide an advantage—the audience can both see and hear what you say, leading to better understanding.

## TRANSLATING DOCUMENTS AND PRESENTATIONS

If presentations must be translated, much expense can be saved if they are designed with translation in mind. This means creating simplified wording as well as simpler graphics for translation later. We provide some tips for creating materials and presentations that will be easily translatable below. You will find that we mention this topic throughout the book. Our purpose here is simply to provide some general guidelines. Information specific to various countries is within the country chapters.

### Use Caution with

- Cultural or geographic references.
- Sports analogies that do not apply across cultures. Soccer references will be familiar in many cultures, but baseball in far fewer. (For example, avoid phrases like: "We need to hit it out of the park.")
- Jargon, slang, and cliches. These are often not translatable. At best they are unclear, and at worst they are confusing. (For example, avoid: "It's like looking for a needle in a hay stack." If you have to explain a hay stack, it isn't going to make your point.)
- Gender, geographical, or historical references.
- Acronyms and abbreviations.
- Homophones (same or similar sound, different meaning such as hear and here).
- References to the human body, animals, sex, alcohol, politics, or religion.

### Tips for Making It Easier Later

- Stick to six lines per slide, not full sentences. Chinese uses 50 percent less space, Spanish can take 50 percent more. Less slide reformatting will be required if the slides are designed with the end in mind.
- When writing documentation or content, use short and simple sentences. A more formal tone rather than a casual tone will work for all cultures.
- Use simple formats for slides, handouts, or documentation to make it easier to allow for expansion.
- Special fonts may make it difficult to translate. Also, video and audio clips will add more translation costs.
- Use the same term for things referred to repeatedly. A translating firm will likely create a glossary of unusual/industry terms, particularly if more than one project will be translated.
- Static graphics and pictures really help. They can help solidify and clarify. Use caution to make them appropriate for the audience. Keep graphics in separate files, rather than imbedding them.

- Only translate a final work product. Changes and edits after translation will cost additional time and money.

- Include translators in the project discussions. They can help you give them files in the most efficient manner. Make sure they know your audience.

- Check software and versions. Some Windows versions are more language friendly (particularly Chinese translations). You may spend a lot of money on a translated version and end up projecting boxes. Take printed materials with you, just in case you need them.

- Add time to training. Plan on at least a third more time for interpreting.

- Spanish isn't just Spanish. Are you presenting in Spain or Argentina? The same goes for other languages, including English.

- Target a specific reading level for written material.

- Include an editing review of in-country experts in the design and translation cycle.

## USING A CLASSROOM INTERPRETER EFFECTIVELY

When someone translates live for you, he or she is called an interpreter. An interpreter can be a valuable resource. Plan to get to know him or her personally. Don't meet at 9:30 for a 10:00 presentation. Share details about the audience. Let the interpreter become comfortable with your accent and manner of speaking. If the person is going to interpret training for you, plan time to run through the materials first. Remember that the interpreter will actually be doing the training and helping participants make connections. If the material is complex, allow time to actually train him or her on the content.

An experienced interpreter told us about a time he was asked to translate complex information at a very large conference with very short notice. "When I took the podium with the speaker, the speaker began to talk in very BIG words with complex, philosophical ideas. I understood the words, but wasn't completely prepared to translate them. Spontaneously, I managed to put some words together and translated as best I could. However, I knew it was not completely accurate and the speaker had no idea what was being translated. The speaker left the conference happy because of a warm response from the audience. What he did not know was that I was preaching words of my own. Still today, I feel embarrassed every time I think about it. I wish I had known what was coming and could have been prepared."

**Tips for Working with a Classroom Interpreter**

- Plan for extra classroom time for interpretation, at least one third more.

- Establish rapport with the interpreter. Let the person get to know you. You want him or her to feel comfortable so he or she is not just interpreting your words, but understands you. This will make the interpreter more effective and will help him or her feel comfortable pushing back or asking for clarification when the need arises.

- Set expectations of how to relate to each other and with the group.

- Communicate details about the audience (include any sensitivities you are aware of).

- Set a rhythm with the interpreter, speaking in manageable amounts of information.

- Develop signals or signs with the interpreter when you need to slow down or take a drink of water.

- Make the interpreter feel comfortable asking for more information or clarification when needed. Better to be clear than to translate something incorrectly.

- Use simple sentences and communicate one idea at a time.

- Learn cultural protocols in order to engage with the audience (learn a few words of greeting, key words or concepts in the local language, and culturally sensitive manners and postures)

- Use stories. Don't just talk about the idea but "show and tell" by sharing real-life stories.

- Plan for more frequent breaks.

- There is no way of knowing whether your ideas are being delivered correctly. Ask for feedback after each session.

- Communicate key concepts and the flow in advance so the interpreter has a mind map of where you are going

- Be gender sensitive. There may be an advantage to using a female interpreter with a female speaker and a male interpreter with a male speaker.

Many of these tips are not just useful when training globally. The issues are the same any time you are speaking to a culturally diverse group anywhere. Many of our normal terms will not be effective.

The American Translators Association (http://atanet.org/) can help you find resources.

Another issue to be sensitive to is whether the group will speak up and ask questions or bring up difficulties. In some cultures, asking questions or pushing back is considered disrespectful. Figure out a way to give permission and get the questions you need to hear; let your interpreter know you want feedback from the audience and welcome their questions. If the audience is struggling, you have to know it to be able to address it; your interpreter may be able to help. You may be able to find out the information you are looking from smaller groups. Management may also be able to help with this issue. They can articulate any concerns for the group and start a discussion. Whatever method works for you, plan for extra time to implement it.

## TRANSLATION RESOURCES/LOCALIZATION

We have used the term "translation" in this chapter, but the larger term is "localization." What is the difference? I asked Welocalize, and here is what they said:

Translation is the actual process of translating the text elements of a training course, workbook, online course, software application, documentation, or other materials. This is the work a native speaker would perform on the actual text strings and sentences in your training material.

Localization includes translation, but also the process of customizing the structure, visuals, display, and the formatting of the material. This includes changes to page layout for printed materials to accommodate different page sizes used in other countries. It includes the cultural preference for time, date, calendar, monetary format, number format, and display. Time in most non-U.S. countries is a 24-hour format instead of the AM/PM format used in United States. Another example is day, month, and year preference in Europe (DD/MM/YYYY) instead of month, day, and year (MM/DD/YYYY) used in the United States. In Germany, the common format for numbers is 23 444,09 instead of 23,444.09, as in the United States. Localization often includes adjustments to software application components like buttons, graphics, and other visual elements for online courseware and applications. Translated text for most European languages is as much as 200% longer than English. So, the visual elements used to enhance the text often have to be adjusted or re-sized to accommodate the longer translation.

Localization can also include modification to the structure and the learning design of a course to accommodate different learning contexts and/or performance contexts of learners around the world. For instructor-led training, this can include changes to adopt more leader-directed activities and fewer learner-directed activities. In many Asian cultures, it is not as common for learners to lead activities as it is in United States. Often social interactions and norms may interfere with learning design. Gender can often be an impediment in group activities the designer did not anticipate. These are different by each market and learning context, so they should be carefully evaluated during the design. Other accommodations may have to be made for online learning. Widely available Internet access at home or even work is not the norm for many countries. Internet access and low bandwidth connections can dictate online design and format. Localization will bring out these issues and assist in the solution.

Thanks to Welocalize, for that clarification. My view is that localization is translation on steroids, making sure the original intent has been accomplished. For instance, translating just words may not get your point across. "Country ham" may turn into "ham in country." In the United States, "breaking into small groups" may be similar to "working in teams." In other places, those terms may have a very different context. There are often choices of what word to use when translating. Localization ensures your original intent is intact after the translation. The edit cycle should be used to ensure this, which is why in-country reviewers are so important to the translation or localization process.

How do you choose a translator/localization firm? If you need a workshop or small amount of materials translated into one language, you can probably go to a local language translator with good success. (Try American Translators Association at www.atanet.org or the resources section of *MultiLingual* magazine at www.multilingual.com.) If it is a large translation project or you are translating into three or more languages, we recommend talking to a company like Transware, Welocalize, The Big Word, Merrill Brink, Lionbridge, or SDL International. These companies offer services for larger projects such as project management and managing work flow; the technical skills to make the PowerPoint and workbooks look professional, and a quality assurance process to help ensure success. You may find *The Guide to Translation and Localization* to be a helpful resource. At the time of this writing, it is available free electronically from the Lingo Systems website: www.lingosys.com.

I set up and managed a localization process, having hundreds of documents translated into two languages. As are many who approach these types of projects, I was naïve about the complexity of this task. I initially used a local person because she was referred by someone else in my company. She was an independent who used local translators on a contractual basis. My project very soon outgrew her. As our volume increased, she found it difficult to keep up. Our Brazilian in-country reviewer very gently asked me if I could find someone else to translate. He noticed the translator's depth wasn't that great with the language. I looked for a firm that could manage more quantities and who had a better quality assurance cycle.

But just because we were working with a larger company didn't mean we didn't have trouble. We had firewall challenges transferring files to our in-country reviewers. Our Chinese audience had difficulties viewing the completed files, depending on which version of Windows they had. Completing the in-country reviews were challenging for our people. Our internal people had to do it because we needed some depth of industry and product knowledge. However, we were adding this responsibility to an already demanding job. Finding the time to do this work was frequently difficult. I sent little appreciation gifts as they completed milestones (often chocolate or company logo items they couldn't easily access). I learned that you may need to get on a plane and schedule a meeting (or bring the local subject-matter expert to you) in order to complete projects on a timely basis. So many things are competing for mind share. Instead of using the person originally assigned to review my program, I frequently ended up with an administrative assistant who reviewed it. There are two possible downsides to this. You will always wonder whether you are getting the best quality review with the right depth of subject knowledge. You can also lose control of your documents, which can lead to version control issues.

We asked Transware what the key internal challenges for localizing training curriculum are. Their response:

1. Definition of scope and span of the localization program
2. Target market
3. Identification, arrangement, and selection of the source data
4. Definition and agreement on information technology (IT) platform
5. Identifying budgets and stakeholders
6. Setting program timing and deliverables
7. Defining measurements to see if the training objectives were met

> The challenges faced by clients who wish to localize can be very daunting. Many have varying experience in the field of localization and require advice and consultancy on how best to proceed. Localization frequently occurs once the development cycle is complete. Localization schedules are frequently pressured and deadlines are very tight—localization under these circumstances can be very demanding.

This is also a fragmented industry. There are thousands of independents, there are local language specialists, there are companies who localize websites, e-learning, and documents for languages across the globe. With all of these options, how should people choose the right vendor? Again, we asked Transware.

> The process by which an organization goes about selecting a localization program service provider can be as daunting as the execution of the program itself. But there are critical questions and discussions that should be included in the selection process to secure the success of your localization program by a localization services provider.

### Basic Questions

1. Which languages does the service work with?
2. Does the vendor use in-country translators?

3. What content types can be submitted for translation? (ASCII, comma delimited files, Word documents, JPEGs, TIFFs, MP3s, PPT, WAV files, PDFs)

4. What experti.se do you have in web, audio/video, and DTP?

**Process Questions**

5. Which translation management (TM) system do you support and use?

6. Can the localization services connect to a content management system (CMS) (documentum, stellent, percussion) or learning management system (LMS)?

7. How are reporting and progress/status presented during the program?

**High-Level Questions**

8. Which translation and localization standards do you use?

9. What is your quality assurance process, and do you have a process improvement approach in place?

It is helpful to send a sample document when asking for a quote so that the quote will be more accurate.

We provide some names of vendors and resources below. We hope that you now know some good questions to ask and can find some people to ask. We wish you success as you have documents translated and presentations interpreted for your audiences!

**Resources**

Transware: www.transware.com

Welocalize: www.welocalize.com

**Helpful Websites and References**

The American Translators Association: http://atanet.org/

*The Guide to Translation and Localization:* www.lingosys.com

*MultiLingual* magazine: www.multilingual.com

# Presentation Techniques for International Audiences

## PREPARING TO PRESENT

As with any presentation that you make, there are steps you can take to make your presentation effective and memorable. Here are some tips for preparing to present a program to your international audience:

- Know your audience.
- Know yourself.
- Practice your presentation.
- Check materials.
- Contact your interpreter.
- Communicate with your hosts.

Let's look at each of these in a little more detail:

### Know Your Audience

- Who are the people who will be attending?
- What can we learn about them, that is, jobs, education, interests?
- Where do they come from, that is, city, country, status, socio-economic background, family?
- What is going on in their country right now regarding politics, holidays, transportation, and work issues, economy, leaders, and the weather?
- How do they feel about coming to your program? Have they been selected to come, forced to come, or offered the opportunity?

- What do they already know about your topic?
- What do they need and want to know about your topic?
- What does their management want them to be able to do as a result of their participation in your program?

### Know Yourself

- Are you the type of person who prefers to have everything planned and scheduled?
- What are your strengths that can be applied to this situation?
- If your Myers-Briggs type preference usually relies on "judging" (likes to have things decided, come to closure), can you expand your style to include more "perceiving" (flexible, open to change) based on what your participants are saying and doing?
- How do you feel about presenting to these people?
- What is your current energy level? Is there something you can do to recharge your own personal battery?
- How familiar/comfortable are you with this presentation? Will some extra review and practice help you to confidently present this material?
- What is your preferred presentation style, and can you vary it? If you like to facilitate instead of lecture, will the people of this culture respond well to a facilitation style or are they more comfortable with lecture?
- Who do you know you can rely on for assistance, if needed?

### Practice Your Presentation

- Can you take time to practice your entire presentation?
- Can you practice with someone who will give you feedback?
- What are your contingencies/backup plans that you can smoothly switch to, if something is not working with this audience?
- What are the key points that must be covered and objectives that must be achieved for your program to be considered successful?
- Does your timing include enough room for translation, clarification, and extra breaks?

### Check Materials

- Do you have hard copies and additional electronic storage device copies of your program that you can carry with you, in case materials that have been previously sent are not where you need them?

- How will materials be distributed to the participants?
- Do you have extra copies of materials, in case additional people drop in unexpectedly?

### Contact Your Interpreter

- Schedule a meeting to discuss the program and audience.
- Is your interpreter already familiar with the audience, so he or she can give you some insight into what techniques or gestures might be most effective and what should be avoided?
- Is your interpreter familiar with your topic and any terms that may be used in your presentation?
- Can you share the presentation with your interpreter ahead of time, so he or she will know the major sections and flow of the presentation?
- Have you obtained the correct spelling and pronunciation of the interpreter's name, so you can introduce the person?

### Communicate with Your Hosts

- What are your hosts' expectations of you and for the class?
- What will your hosts be able to provide for you as far as equipment, supplies, room setup, transportation, accommodation, food and beverage for breaks and lunch, technical support for equipment, and temperature control for the room where you will be presenting?
- Who will be paying for equipment rental, food, and transportation?

### Prepare to Be Surprised

- How do you typically react to surprises?
- Can you modify plans, as needed?
- Do you have names and phone numbers of people who can help you to answer questions or change plans quickly?
- Can you organize everything ahead of time, so you don't look rushed or unprepared?
- Do you know your presentation well enough that you can spend all your time focusing on the needs of the participants and the relationship you want to build with them?

**What Are the Keys to Success?**

- Focus on what your audience wants to know about your topic.

- Tune in to each person's reaction and interest in your presentation.

- Enjoy the challenge of persuading those who think they don't need to be in attendance that they can gain something from the investment of their time in this program.

- Help participants to feel confident and proud of what they know about this topic.

- Listen carefully to understand questions and comments, even if someone's accent is difficult to understand and make sure you thank everyone for their participation.

- Make reference to your agenda periodically, so participants always know where you are in your program. Summarize each topic and explain what you will be covering next.

- Make sure there are sufficient breaks and movement to keep people engaged and attentive.

- Ensure that your visuals are tasteful for the cultures that may be represented by participants in your program. Have someone review the program ahead of time and provide feedback to you, to assure there are no potential insults, mistakes, or confusion.

- Enjoy meeting and interacting with each participant.

- Have name signs for each participant and use their names when you ask or respond to a question or comment.

- Provide something that each participant will treasure and take away from your program. This can be something small and tangible or a piece of wisdom and joy that they can remember.

In their book *Intercultural Interactions: A Practical Guide,* Cushner and Brislin (1996) have noted the possibility of emotional reactions from people who are adjusting to work in cultures other than their own, such as anxiety and disconfirmed expectations (surprises), in addition to a need for belonging, tolerance for ambiguity, and willingness to confront ones own prejudices.

In addition to time, language, and personal space differences, misunderstandings can occur among cultures in areas such as roles, status, values, the importance of the group or individual, and one's approach to work.

These misunderstandings and misinterpretations arise because of the way we are each socialized in our own culture. Because of these differences, we may be tempted to categorize, differentiate, make people feel like they are in or out of a certain group, see different learning styles, and attribute behavior to others incorrectly, based on our own past experience. Being aware of and sensitive to these differences will help you to react quickly if you need to clarify a concept or action while presenting to people in another culture.

Cushner and Brislin have created scenarios for cross-cultural training that can be used to help trainers to practice being open to alternate interpretations. They call this the "cultural assimilator." Review and discussion of various scenarios such as theirs can sensitize trainers, teachers, and presenters to the variety of possible interpretations that might occur in cross-cultural communication.

It is important for each of us to not assume that we know what is going on in cross-cultural communications, but to test our assumptions and be open to other possible interpretations of people's behavior and language. It is also useful to not enter cross-cultural situations with the high expectations of success that you have been used to experiencing. Then you can be pleasantly surprised when everything goes as planned.

In preparing to present to an audience from any culture that is different from your own, it is helpful to consider any differences and be aware that these differences may influence people's behavior and their interpretation of your behavior. Harry Triandis explores this topic in *Essentials of Studying Cultures* (Landis & Brislin, 1983) and explains that in order to prepare for intercultural interaction, it is important for us to study the culture's norms, attitudes, and expectations.

Triandis identifies cultural elements that influence the way that people respond to communication and interactions such as education, beliefs, technology, decision-making style, and conflict-resolution patterns,

## INITIATING THE PRESENTATION

Here are some suggestions for the beginning of your presentation or program:

### Create a Bond Through Introductions

- Identify something that many participants have in common and state it in your introduction, for example, "We have all come together here in this location today to learn about. . . . "

- Introduce yourself, any interpreters, and any management or administrative staff who may be in the room, and graciously thank the appropriate people for inviting you there.

- Ask participants to introduce themselves and write their names on the name cards provided, so they can get to know each other better.

### Establish Common Goals for the Program

- People may be participating in this program for a variety of reasons. Your introduction can allow them to align with others who are there for the same reasons and validate whatever those reasons may be. For example, some people are participating because they have been told to do so or are required to attend to achieve some certificate of completion. Let participants know that these are legitimate reasons to participate and that they are welcome to share in and contribute to the learning, even if they are simply fulfilling a requirement. Say something like: "Even if you are here only to gain a completion mark on your record, we hope you will join us in the engaging discussion and experiences that are planned for the day."

- There are probably others who may really want to learn new skills and are worried about not gaining the information quickly enough. You can explain that one of the goals of this program is to build on whatever knowledge the participants enter the program with and that they will continue to increase their skill throughout the program.

- Some individuals may think that they should be teaching this program instead of you. A ground rule that could be established might be that those with experience and skill in this topic are invited to share their knowledge with others throughout the discussions.

### Make People Feel Welcome

- A quick exercise that requires participants to find answers to some easy questions that are related to the topic being presented can make them feel united.

- A team-building activity where participants work in small groups to discuss a question that is related to the topic and combine their ideas to come up with a summary to briefly present back to the large group can be helpful. Say something like: "What do you want to know about this topic?" or "Why is this topic important to you?"

### Create an Environment

- Help them feel connected in pursuing common goals.

- Invite people to stop you to ask questions or clarification any time throughout the program (this will enable you to slow down enough for those who are not familiar with the language to catch up).

- Explain that we all learn at different paces and that, by the end of the program, everyone will be able to achieve the objectives, so not to worry about asking you to slow down or speed up the presentation of certain elements of the program. (This kind of feedback gives the learners a sense of control and helps you to stay on track at a pace that is optimum for their learning.)

- Listen intently to those participants who may have heavy accents and make sure that all students are listening when each person is speaking. (This avoids a common occurrence of people tuning out and having side conversations when it is difficult to understand someone.) If you don't understand what someone has just said, and have already asked the person to repeat it, ask if others in the room would like to comment on the point. (Often someone else in the room has understood what was just said.)

- Avoid laughing at someone's mispronunciation or misinterpretation of something. Respectfully clarify the point that you were trying to get across. Make it your mistake instead of theirs, and they will feel supported to continue in their learning process.

### Build in Successes

- Start with activities that participants will be successful at completing and keep course sections short enough so the topics will successfully build on previous knowledge and skill.

- Ask questions that are not too difficult to answer, so people feel that they are making progress in their learning.

### Provide Quick References

- Explain how the participants can quickly access information, saying something like: "In the back of your notebook you will find a glossary of terms and a quick reference guide; the tabbed sections in your notebook include these topics. . . ."

- Hand out job aids so participants will have practice using them during the program.

### Clearly Outline the Day

- Refer participants to the objectives to be achieved and read through each of them.

- Ask whether there are additional objectives that should be considered. You may need to defer additional objectives to another session or complete them after the program, but at least you know what the participants are expecting.

- Show the agenda for the program and explain when and how long breaks will be scheduled, lunch times, etc.

- Explain administrative details such as location of rest rooms or telephones.

### Start with a Powerful Beginning

- Engaging participants in a "Wow!" experience right in the beginning of the program gets their attention on the topic to be learned. This can be done by showing captivating photographs and images of the success that can be gained by completing your program.

- Creating an experience during which participants realize how much they do not already know about the topic can provide a powerful beginning. For example: have participants answer some simple questions that actually have surprising answers.

Geert Hofstede's UNESCO article on his research, reprinted in *Intercultural Communication: A Global Reader* (Jandt, 2004), provides some thought-provoking considerations regarding five dimensions when communicating with people of other cultures: power distance, individualism, masculinity, uncertainty avoidance, and long-term orientation.

- In high power distance countries, people expect and accept inequality among people: (Mexico, Arab countries, India, West Africa). Low power distance countries are Greece, Thailand, East Africa, and Colombia.

- Individualism is the degree to which people of a country have learned to act as individuals rather than as members of cohesive groups (Individualism: United States, Australia, Great Britain, Canada. Collectivism: Colombia, Indonesia, Thailand, West and East Africa).

- Masculinity is the degree to which "masculine" values such as assertiveness and competition prevail over "feminine" values such as warm personal relationships, service, and solidarity (Masculine: Japan, Austria, Italy, Switzerland, Mexico. Feminine: Brazil, Canada, India, Argentina).

- Uncertainty avoidance is the degree to which people in a country prefer structured over unstructured situations, from extremely rigid to extremely flexible (High: Greece, Japan, France. Low: Denmark, Great Britain, and India).

- Long-term orientation is perseverance and respect for tradition versus short-term orientation and materialism. (Long-Term: China, Japan, Brazil, and India. Short-Term: Canada, Great Britain, United States, Australia).

What we can do in light of this information:

- If there is a large perceived power distance between you as a presenter or teacher and your students, they may be less likely to ask you the questions that they want to ask you. So you can write some typical questions and answers and provide them in a handout, thus shortening the time allotted for questions and answers during your program.

- If there is a strong sense of cohesiveness among members of a culture, you can provide opportunities to discuss topics in small groups, in addition to offering opportunities to answer questions individually.

- A strong "masculine" culture may respond well to competitive learning games. A strong "feminine" culture may respond better to group events that provide time to get to know each other.

- Uncertainty avoidance cultures will be more successful if the program is highly structured. Provide some flexibility during small group conversations and breaks, that can satisfy the needs of participants who look for these opportunities.

- Long-term orientation cultures will expect to know the effects over time of learning the information that is being presented, whereas, the short-term orientated culture requires that you explain immediate payback for the time and money invested in the program.

If participants can see by your objectives and agenda that you have provided elements that accommodate all of these differences into your program or presentation, it will help to satisfy the needs of most of your participants.

## THROUGHOUT THE PROGRAM

Nancy Adler provides good advice in her book, *International Dimensions of Organizational Behavior* (2002), especially in the chapter on "Communicating Across Cultures." Adler reminds us to:

- Use appropriate pictures and graphs to reinforce concepts.
- Provide summaries.
- Give extra time for a person to respond to a question.
- Remember that mispronunciation does not mean lack of intelligence.
- Assume difference, not similarity.
- Make the assumption that your learners do not understand.

Build periodic question-and-answer periods into the program so that even people from cultures that are less likely to ask questions can be encouraged to participate. Even if the majority of participants are from such a culture, have learners discuss their questions in small groups and then ask them to submit the questions in writing or through a spokesperson.

In Robert Kohls and Herbert Brussow's *Training Know-How for Cross Cultural and Diversity Trainers* (1995), the authors share their opinion of methodologies that they have found to work well. Lectures are considered most effective and role plays are considered least effective.

Robert Kohls and Michael Paige also provide trainer competencies or personal attributes for effectiveness, which include patience, empathy, openness, flexibility, tolerance of ambiguity, humility, and a sense of humor.

## BEST PRACTICES FOR GLOBAL WEBCASTS

Renie McClay shares some great tips for successful webcasting:

- Have an in-country contact as a resource when possible. Establish a relationship to ask questions, make inquiries, and follow cultural protocols.

- Check what time it is as you start. Don't say "good morning" if it is evening for them.

- Establish a personal connection. Show them a photo of you or use a web-cam.

- Practice names in advance. Run through them with your local contact if necessary. It makes a large personal connection, and even if you make mistakes, it shows you are trying.

- Plan interaction: polls, yes-and-no questions, pace, speed up or slow down indicators.

- Talk slowly so they can get used to your accent. Encourage them to talk slowly, and don't be afraid to ask them to repeat or send in a chat (easier to read sometimes than hear).

- Set yourself up to stand during the presentation if you can, just as you would in front of a classroom. This helps with energy.

- Have a co-facilitator if possible. If you don't have a co-facilitator, have someone else sign on as a speaker, just to be safe. If the leader loses connectivity or the computer freezes, someone else can advance slides and the conversation can still move ahead. Develop a genuine rapport with your co-facilitator. Sound natural together. Think of it as two radio personalities working with each other. You want an easy back-and-forth style. Conduct a practice session.

- If possible, the leader should sign on with two computers, one as a leader and one as a participant. He or she can see what the audience is seeing, and it may be helpful in troubleshooting.

- Be prepared to handle connection issues. People will have trouble. Either have some notes of basics to help troubleshoot, or have someone online who can help. The first time people are signing on, have them log on in advance of the call or show up fifteen minutes early. Make sure that you have signed on early as well.

- Language issues abound. If people respond via chat (in writing), it may be easier to understand. If working with ESL (English as a second language) participants, chat may be easier. Even English-speaking countries may use terms differently, and dialects can be difficult to understand.

- Create presenter and participant folders.

- Label polls and files so they are easily accessible.

- Close out of all windows you won't be using for the webcast.

- Adjust attendee privileges.

### Pre-Meeting

- Create polls in advance.

- Save all polls and handouts in the Notes section of PowerPoint files, in preparation for easy use.

- Test recording and any playback you will be using.

- Sign on early in case of connectivity issues. Load all presentations and polls at least forty minutes ahead of time (in case of trouble, there is time to respond). After everything is ready, you can get a drink of water and/or visit the washroom. Be available fifteen minutes in advance to help people in case they need it.

- Test video on several target audience computers. It will likely be slow and may not work well if shared from the desktop. Imbed video into PowerPoint (WebEx can show you how) and it will be more likely to work.

### The Day of Training

- Enable privileges for participants.

- Load polls and presentations.

- Open any documents or applications you want to use.

### During the Session

- Create an engagement activity every ten minutes, something to connect participants to their computers or the content or each other.

- Build in real-world examples.

- Save chat, notes, or poll results if helpful for future reference.

- End with: "What did you find the most helpful [actionable]?"

- Plan for audience connection up-front. If it is a series of calls, use something different for each call. Some examples: a poll asking "What is it like outside where you are [sunny, dark, cloudy, raining]?" Have them write the last movie they saw on a whiteboard. Ask them to send in a chat regarding what city they are calling from. It helps to engage participants early and helps to remind them how to use the tools. (Don't forget to assign privileges so they can participate.)

- If longer than two hours' worth of content, consider chunking the material and making it a series of calls. If that isn't possible, give them breaks with something they need to do (WebEx has breakout rooms). Then tell them what time to come back and share. Plan interactivity every ten minutes, a break every hour.

- Greet each individual as he or she comes on when audiences are fewer than twenty. For larger audiences, have a welcome poll that people can fill out as they join and say welcome to the group.

## EVALUATION AND INTERCULTURAL COMMUNICATION

Evaluation is a sensitive topic in any culture. Many people do not like to be evaluated, and some do not like to evaluate others. This is an important topic to discuss with your host and sponsor for the program you are presenting.

- Is evaluation required?

- What kind of evaluation would you prefer?

- What are the participants' expectations and experiences regarding different types of evaluation?

- Will you review evaluation instruments and provide feedback on their usefulness?

   We will look at two major aspects of evaluation:

- *Program evaluation* provides feedback on the success of the program and is often a short survey that each participant is asked to complete to explain what he or she liked or disliked about the program, including the instructor, materials. and facilities. This type of evaluation is often called Level 1.

- *Student evaluation* is used to verify that the students learned what they were supposed to learn. This can consist of a variety of techniques, including paper-and-pencil tests, observations, checklists, and performance evaluations. This type of evaluation is called Level 2 when done as part of the course or Level 3 when done after the program, to see whether students are able to apply what they have learned when they return to work.

The program evaluation may not provide valuable information if it is administered in a culture that respects authority and puts a high value on "saving face." The student evaluation can be a source of anxiety and stress that may impact the students' ability to learn and participate throughout the program.

In *An Introduction to Intercultural Communication: Identities in a Global Community*, Fred Jandt (2004) explains culture's influence on perception, barriers, and dimensions. These explanations can provide valuable insight to us as we present programs to people from cultures other than our own.

Jandt explains that culture strongly influences our perceptions of everything. Each of us has a cultural identity, reflected in the words we use and our symbols, rituals, values, heroes, and myths. Factors such as race, social class, ethnicity, superstitions, and rules influence how we see situations. Religion, history, education, economy, and climate also influence how we perceive the world. In high-context cultures such as China, Japan, Korea, and Greece, most of the information is already shared among people, so less has to be spoken or written. In low-context cultures such as Switzerland, Germany, the United States, and Denmark, verbal messages tend to be elaborate and highly specified, detailed, and redundant. High value is placed on verbal abilities, logic, and reasoning.

Jandt highlights significant barriers to effective intercultural communication that should be considered such as anxiety, assuming similarity instead of difference, stereotypes, language, and non-verbal misinterpretations.

Here is some information to keep in mind as we consider ways to evaluate a program:

- Since anxiety is a barrier to effective intercultural communication, we reduce the effects when we make the evaluation non-threatening, for example, not using the word "test" for student evaluation.

- If our culture is more used to test-taking, we should not assume that all cultures see tests as necessary or helpful.

- Avoid using stereotypes and prejudice in administering evaluations, that is, thinking that some nationalities will have better results than others.

- Take care to control non-verbal communication and verbal language when explaining what the evaluation is and how the information will be used. Say something like: "This is anonymous feedback regarding the program that we will use to improve the course. The results of your student evaluation information will be provided back to you and not be shared with your supervisor."

Evaluation should focus on improvement and development. The supportive environment that is created by the presenter can enable the participants to focus on their learning and not be distracted by the evaluation planned to occur when the program ends.

## FOLLOW-UP/REINFORCEMENT OF LEARNING

Tell the participants what follow-up and reinforcement of what they have learned are available to them, such as a list of resources for further study, ongoing emails, or newsletters and opportunities for a community of practice to discuss application of the learning. These methods can help people to remember and use what they have learned.

For international programs, it is most helpful if an in-country representative can be in charge of ongoing communication, follow-up, and reinforcement of the learning. This provides an opportunity for someone who really knows the culture to help with continued application of the learning. Materials and activities can be provided to the local representative for review and recommendations prior to the program to increase the program's effectiveness.

### References

Adler, N. (2002). Communicating across cultures. In N. Adler, *International dimensions of organizational behavior.* Cincinnati, OH: South-Western.

Cushner, K., & Brislin, R.W. (1996). *Intercultural interactions: A practical guide.* Thousand Oaks, CA: Sage.

Hofstede, G. (2004). Business cultures. *UNESCO courier, 1994.* In F. Jandt (Ed.), *Intercultural communication: A global reader.* Thousand Oaks, CA: Sage.

Jandt, F. (2004). *An introduction to intercultural communication: Identities in a global community.* Thousand Oaks, CA: Sage.

Kohls, R., & Brussow, H. (1995). *Training know-how for cross-cultural and diversity trainers.* Duncanville, TX: Adult Learning Systems.

Triandis, H. (1983). *Essentials of studying cultures.* In D. Landis & R.W. Brislin (Eds.), *Handbook of intercultural training.* Elmsford, NY: Pergamon Press.

**PART TWO**

# Africa

# The Continent of Africa

The continent of Africa, including its island groups, is comprised of fifty-three independent countries. Its population, estimated at over 900 million, is made up of countless tribes and ethnic groups, each with its own history, language, beliefs, culture, and traditions. It is therefore easy to see how inappropriate it is to generalize about Africa. Instead of attempting to dissect the changing training environment of each country, we will attempt to provide a comprehensive list of research topics and basic information that can be applied to your particular requirement in Africa. You will need to do some of your own digging into specifics, but clearly the time will be well spent when you are able to incorporate the appropriate customization to your training or presentation based on your research, guided by this overview. We have attempted to slice and dice the information into bits that can be stitched together to create a picture of the particular country you will work in as well as the people you will be trying to reach. Before we move into the typical format we are using with other countries, a general discussion about historical and regional influences seems appropriate. Then we move into the structure used in other chapters and provide the questions to be answered to prepare yourself for each step in your process.

## Background

In general, the continent has two relevant periods of history that influence the customs, politics, and people of each nation in ways important to trainers—their specific Colonial history and the history since their independence. As a time reference, Colonialism peaked from 1900 to 1960. A struggle between the two histories exists in everything from religion to who gets their Nescafe first at break time. In general, countries previously colonized have maintained a language and some traditions from their occupiers. Many such traditions are based on established hierarchies. Ask questions about how this plays out for your audience and the people you will meet and work with on your project. Below is a list of most countries and which country/countries colonized them:

- Britain: Botswana, Cameroon*, Egypt, and Eritrea (just before their independence), Gambia, Ghana, Kenya, Libya[+], Malawi, Mauritius, Nigeria, South Africa, Sudan (also occupied by Egypt), Swaziland, Zambia, and Zimbabwe.

- France: Algeria, Benin, Cameroon*, Central African Republic, Chad, Djibouti, Gabon, Guinea, Libya[+], Mali, Morocco, Senegal, and Tunisia.

- Portugal: Angola, Guinea-Bissau, Mozambique, Cape Verde, and Sao Tome e Principe.

- Belgium: Burundi and Rwanda (also occupied by Germany), and Republic of the Congo (also occupied by France).

- Germany: Burundi and Rwanda (also occupied by Belgium), and Namibia[^].

- Spain: Equatorial Guinea and Western Sahara (currently held without UN approval by Morocco).

- United States: Liberia.

Absent from this list is Africa's oldest independent country, which, except for a four-year occupation by Mussolini's Italy at the end of the 1930s, has never been colonized. Ethiopia inspired the rest of Africa in its path to independence.

## Regions

Each region of the continent has been influenced by different factors as well. Here is a snapshot of those considerations and the countries they affect:

- North Africa: heavily influenced by ancient European civilizations such as Rome as well as the more recent expansion of Islam. Northern Africa countries include Algeria, Egypt, Libya, Morocco, Tunisia, and Western Sahara.

*The British southern sector joined Cameroon in 1961, while the northern sector joined Nigeria.
[+]Portions of Libya were held by Britain and France before its independence was ultimately achieved from Italy.
[^]Namibia's independence was ultimately achieved from South Africa.

- East Africa: exhibits the strong influences of Arab traders and European colonization. East Africa consists of Burundi, Djibouti, Eritrea, Ethiopia, Kenya, Rwanda, and Sudan.

- Central Africa: was relatively free of European influence until the end of the 19th century when France and Belgium developed colonies. Central Africa is made up of Cameroon, Central African Republic, Chad, Equatorial Guinea, Gabon, and Republic of the Congo.

- West Africa: known for the rich natural resources and the slave trade, the spread of Islam and the aggressive competition between France and Britain to exploit the region has left a powerful legacy. West Africa countries include Benin, Gambia, Ghana, Guinea, Guinea-Bissau, Liberia, Mali, Nigeria, and Senegal.

- Southern Africa: overshadowed by the era of Apartheid, this region has a rich and well-documented history. Southern Africa countries are Angola, Botswana, Malawi, Mauritius, Mozambique, Namibia, South Africa, Swaziland, Zambia, and Zimbabwe.

## ??? THE REQUEST

There are an infinite number of types of requests that could be made of you as a trainer, each one with its own unique set of expectations and objectives. As with any other project, data gathering about the assignment is critical. Find out everything you can during your initial talks with your customer. Important questions include:

- What do they see as the objectives of the training?
- Who will be your audience?
- Are they educated professionals or laborers?
- Where will you be conducting the program?
- What resources will you have at your disposal?

All the typical questions are necessary. Once this information is gathered, you can begin to craft your program using additional research about the country and even the city you will be visiting.

## • • • GETTING THERE

All trips from the United States to Africa are long. The time differences are significant regardless of country. Build several extra days into your schedule, not only to acclimate to the time (and possibly the climate), but to get to know your surroundings. The cultural differences between Western society and African cultures are significant. You will be much more relaxed if you are not on stage your first day in a new country. Discuss travel suggestions with your in-country contact before booking your flight. Visa and passport requirements vary from country to country. Start your research with the Department of State at www.travel.state.gov. From there, you may want to visit the individual embassy or consulates of the nations you plan to visit. Not all have resources, but many do. Verify their individual requirements; even if you have traveled recently, they change frequently.

Check with the Center for Disease Control and Prevention for required vaccines you will need. There are U.S. health centers specifically for international travelers. They will do an assessment on your history and make recommendations for what vaccines you will need. (Likely, your physician can recommend a source.) For example, if visiting Ghana you will likely need yellow fever, hepatitis A, hepatitis B, typhoid, meningococcal, rabies, and maybe polio vaccines. Malaria may be a consideration, depending on where you are traveling. Wearing long sleeves, long pants, using bug spray, and sleeping in a mosquito net will likely be needed for protection. Spray your room before retiring.

If you are a natural treatment type of person, ask a health food store about using something like the herb goldenseal or echinacea in your diet to strengthen your immune system before traveling and while you are there. Bring things like decongestants, charcoal tablets or diarrheal remedies, pain relievers, and maybe melatonin to help sleep. Don't forget a hat and sunscreen.

AIDS is a large concern in Africa. It is wiping out entire villages. Some travelers bring their own syringes, in case one is needed.

When you pack, consider the location and condition of the training facilities. Will you have air conditioning? What type of weather will you expect? Local fashion may vary, but conservative business dress is a safe bet if you can't determine a specific type of apparel. Men who bring coat and ties may remove them if they find them unnecessary. Longer skirts for women are better than shorter skirts or even pants in most places. To be safe, women should avoid showing thighs, which means no shorts or shorter skirts. In Muslim countries, women should wear blouses that cover at least their upper arms.

## PROGRAM DESIGN

The first suggestion for program design is a general one of flexibility. Even with the best due diligence, you may still find yourself making last-minute changes to your presentation. With so many factors to consider, it is likely you will need to make some adjustments. We recommend going with a plan and then being totally willing to adjust to make it work. We all know that being absolutely comfortable with your subject makes this possible. If you do not have control of the material, you will not be able to make necessary, unexpected modifications.

With that said, you can minimize the number and magnitude of your changes by thoroughly researching the country's background and incorporating your findings into your training.

## Audience

As with any training, the more you know about the audience members and the individual participants, the better. If you are able to work with an in-country contact who can lend this insight, you can build the materials, exercises, and agenda customized to specific audiences. Education as we know it rarely exists in many parts of Africa. Growing up, your participants may have gone to school for four weeks and then been pulled out, or their school may have been closed. They likely didn't have their own textbooks; they shared with three or four other children. Quite possibly, there may have been one textbook for the entire class. Homework was likely not part of the curriculum, since paper and pencils in some areas were only available in the wealthiest of homes. Students attending in large cities have had different experiences as well; many families are transient because of jobs and children attend many different schools. Schools vary greatly in quality. Even those who attend college have a variety of university experiences. Be sure you verify, even if you are told the audience is college-educated.

Here are some questions to start with:

- What is the highest achieved level of education of the participants?
- What type of educational experiences have they had in the past?
- Have they participated in shared learning where they are accustomed to working in groups to facilitate learning?
- Do they follow any specific European learning style?
- How well do they show retention of information/knowledge transfer?
- In what ways can you validate knowledge transfer/retention?
- Can you establish a baseline level of current knowledge of the subject?

We anticipate that the answers to these questions will point you in the direction of highly participative learning style preferences. In that case, incorporate brainstorming and discussion activities in small groups. Try to avoid exercises where it is easy for a few people to dominate the discussions; encourage all participants to say something. Let the groups elect leaders, which must be changed periodically. These methods move away from the reliance on written materials, slide decks, and PowerPoint presentations. These lecture-style methods are difficult for those who are not used to them. If your audience has little such experience, build your materials around experiential learning. Consider singing, dancing, and other unconventional classroom practices (by Western standards), which could be not only acceptable, but preferable in many nations. You may not know this until you arrive, or even after a few hours with your group. Again, flexibility is key to your success. If you can determine, mid-course, a new method of reaching your participants, use it.

Don't rely on questions to verify and validate knowledge transfer. Use hands-on exercises whereby participants can demonstrate their learning (or lack of learning) for your validation and correction, if need be.

## Language

Since there are so many spoken languages in Africa, determine your audience's ability to understand English or any other languages you speak to avoid using an interpreter or translator. It seems like a simple question, but it may not be. Simply asking what the official language of a country may not give you a true picture of your audience's ability to understand written materials or your spoken lecture. The agenda and timing for your topics will hinge on these factors. Build in more time if you use an interpreter, but you will still want ample time for questions and clarifications if they do understand English (or any other language you speak fluently).

Here are some ways to get to the critical information about language:

- What is the native language of each participant?
- What is the official language of the country?
- Will I need an interpreter or translator?
- Should I translate my written materials?
- How much interaction can I expect from my audience? How comfortable will they be speaking English in class?

These questions can be asked of your in-country contact. If you do not have an in-country contact, you will likely have a client who can find out. If nothing else, see whether you can get in touch with a participant. The following is a list of "safe bets" as far as language goes. They are the "official languages" of these countries, but don't assume that your audience will learn with accommodations for these alone. Ask your in-country contact to verify.

- Portuguese: Angola, Cape Verde, Guinea-Bissau, Mozambique, and Sao Tome e Principe.
- French: Benin, Burkina Faso, Burundi, Cameroon, Central African Republic, Chad, Comoros, Democratic Republic of the Congo, Ivory Coast, Djibouti, Gabon, Guinea, Madagascar, Mali, Mauritius, Niger, Rwanda, Senegal, Seychelles, and Togo.
- English: Cameroon
- Arabic: Chad, Comoros

Don't forget to include a local view. If you can incorporate the names of local towns, cities, buildings, and landmarks into your presentation, then do so. It is impressive and respectful in any country.

## Religion

Religious influences and beliefs can affect training classes in many ways. Not only will they dictate days off (for holy days) or times of prayer, but other important customs and rituals that you may be expected to participate in and respect. You may open your sessions in prayer or conduct training during certain hours. The three most influential religions (although others are practiced, so be sure to ask) are Islam, Christianity, and African Traditional Religion. Each has its own set of customs to be aware of; for example, Muslims do not accept food or money with their left hands.

## Politics and Social Norms

Politics and the political climate affect the mindset of participants as well as logistics for your travels to Africa. Political unrest is common in many regions for various reasons. This current event information is important for your safety and for your use during times of casual conversation with participants. Remember that speech isn't always free in other parts of the world; do not criticize the government, even if your in-country hosts do. At best, it will be looked upon poorly and at worst; you could get yourself into trouble with the local police or government. Extreme patriarchy and extreme matriarchy co-exist in this land. Be careful not to voice your more Western opinions about such hierarchies. Our freedoms are not necessarily appreciated by people in other parts of the world, and our ideals are not always shared. Of course, South Africa's history of Apartheid is the most notorious of social practices and is still an influential time in certain countries' histories. If you are traveling to South Africa, we have outlined some of the risks and opportunities that Apartheid provides, but your own research on how this practice affected your participants is warranted if you are going to work there.

In all of these areas, the more you know, the better off you will be. Many countries have websites filled with information for the foreign traveler. (Consulate sites, American Chamber of Commerce sites for the individual countries, Wikipedia, and more resources are listed at the end of this chapter.) Take advantage of them. Also, the Harvard Business School and Wharton School of Business publish online newsletters with portions focused on information and case studies from Africa. CNN network has an extensive foreign correspondents' area on their website with current events information. All are great sources for design and preparation.

 **LOGISTICS**

Shipping to Africa is expensive and its reliability varies from country to country. There are inconsistencies within countries as well. There is a high risk of pilfering or confiscation. If you attempt to ship your materials, it would be wise to send printed materials separate from give-aways or other reward trinkets in case they "disappear." If it is feasible, have materials printed in-country. This will allow you to be flexible and make changes to your content after meeting with your client and/or audience members. You may decide to pack other training items with you on your flight. It may be well worth the extra expense of having heavy luggage, just to ensure your items arrive with you and don't get caught up in shipping.

Don't be surprised at agonizing bureaucracy. Many African nations have a much slower-paced way of doing business, which includes quite a bit of red tape. That can include places like the post office for picking up materials.

There is no standard of currency amongst the countries, so currency and its issues should be researched on a country-by-country basis. Find out the safe places to complete your exchanges and what local customs call for in the way of tips and other gratuities. Other questions to consider asking:

- Are credit cards readily accepted?
- Are there ATM (automated teller) machines available? If so, will my card work?
- Should I expect exchange charges?
- Is it safe to exchange money only in certain locations?
- Should I carry cash with me? How much? For what purposes?

## RENIE McCLAY'S EXPERIENCE IN GHANA

I remember being in Ghana and picking up a box of training materials at the local post office. We didn't have the required notice to pick up the box. The man at the post office was not the least bit helpful at getting us the box. He ranted and said we couldn't get it without the slip of paper. My peer was upset with him, and they had a fight. The post office was not an easy place to get to and we did not want to come back another time to try and solve this. I took the man aside and told him what we were trying to do. I explained that someone had lost the slip of paper, that we were volunteers at a new school being built, and we were to conduct the training the next day at a new school and needed the supplies in the box. I told him he was obviously in charge, and asked if there was anything at all he could do to help us. This conversation was very quiet and excluded my peer who had been angry. He went into the back and in fifteen minutes brought us the box. Red tape is everywhere. It will not always end like this, but this was a happy ending.

## PROGRAM DELIVERY

Assuming you have asked the right questions and structured your program to fit the background and the needs of your participants, delivery may be the easiest part of the process. Find out from your in-country contact about cultural concerns or other customs you should be aware of. Some include:

- Male/female status issues.

- Age gaps between participants and how they are important to interaction.

- If you are working with groups that include many members of the same family, ask about social norms with respect to these relationships, in particular parent/child, father/daughter-in-law, and mother/son-in-law.

- Timeliness: are people generally on time or not? How can you appropriately set expectations?

If you have men and women come in a classroom, let them seat themselves; you may see women wanting to sit on one side, so let them do it. Be sensitive to people's beliefs and traditions; all traditional values must be taken seriously.

Let the in-country contact guide you about how to open the session. It may be appropriate to start with a prayer. Communicate your hope to participate, but not lead such an interaction. It may also be appropriate to show humility and gratitude before beginning, thanking the participants for the opportunity to work with them. These customs vary greatly from place to place.

## TECHNICAL REQUIREMENTS

You will not find access to technology in the way you are accustomed. Many meetings are conducted without technology as we know it. Ask about the following:

- Will there be electricity in the classroom? What is the voltage?
- What other resources will be available? Chalk board? Overhead projector? Other?
- Should you rely strictly on handouts?
- Will your cell phone work?
- Can you rent local cell phones for emergency or communication use?
- Will your adaptors work with their plugs and voltage?
- Will there be Internet availability?

In many very urban settings, there are blackouts and brownouts (regions dropping to lower voltage). Always have a backup if you plan to rely on your laptop or other electrical device. Even devices we take for granted work intermittently. In some countries, phones work sporadically, often with both parties loudly saying, "Hello?" for literally minutes waiting for a connection.

Again, many meetings are held without technology. To play it safe, plan on using handouts.

## ACCOMMODATIONS

Accommodations in Africa vary as widely as the people. Some large, urban areas will have hotel names you are used to hearing. In more remote locations, you will not recognize a single name in the list of options. Your first concern should be safety; the less important second concern is for comfort. The best way to ensure your personal safety is to research hotels and other options using three sources: your in-country contact, the local police and or embassy/consulate for the country, and the Internet (if applicable). Your in-country contact can get you started by identifying the location of your training and possible suitable accommodations. Take this information to the local police authorities or to the country's U.S. Embassy or consulate to discuss the safety of specific neighborhoods and properties. Finally, if the hotel has a website, look online at pictures to determine your comfort level with the accommodations. Using all three of these sources, you have a much better chance of finding a place to stay that is safe and comfortable.

## GETTING AROUND

Again, safety is the biggest issue when traveling inside African countries. It is most advisable to have your in-country contact or group escort you as much as possible. You will want to ask about how to go from the airport to your hotel or training facility. It is best to arrange a ride or have someone pick you up. If you are accustomed to driving in other countries, research the laws concerning the type of drivers licenses required for renting a vehicle and driving yourself. If you do decide to rent a car, be sure you know where to go and the exact way to get there. As with any city, there are less desirable places to drive through—particularly for a foreigner. Large city driving can be very frenetic. It is safe to say that if you can rely on locals to do the driving, you probably should. If there are storms, people may not show up for training, meetings, or appointments. With hard storms, unpaved streets can become rivers. Cars stall out because of the height of the water running down the streets. Sometimes meetings are put off until the storm stops. That can be minutes or hours. It will be unpredictable. During one training in a school in Ghana, there was a big parents' night planned with lots of interaction. The trainers were warned that if there was a rainstorm, no one would come. They wouldn't call and cancel; it was just assumed they would not show up.

## THE PEOPLE

In general, the people of Africa have been described as warm, colorful, vibrant, and extroverted. But, as with any generalization, it is difficult to truly capture the essence of any group of people in a few words, and Africans are so diverse that you should not expect to find any one type of person. Refer to the country's history (both Colonial and Independence) to glean some insights. The educational background of the people of this continent varies greatly. Economic differences are vast, and racism in the form of Apartheid greatly influenced portions of this land.

If you can delve into the pop culture of the country, you can gain clues to the people. What is the music or popular artist of the day? What is being shown at the local theatres? Are there dance productions? Art exhibits? Live music? Are they influenced by Western society? Eastern culture? European influences? You may be able to incorporate music in your teaching if you find it is a large part of their culture. This may also indicate that written materials will not have the impact you expect.

Several contributors have told us that creativity is likely not a strong skill for this audience. It is not taught or emphasized in many places or in many circles. A much more practical, tactical approach is typical.

## !!! PREPARATION

In addition to those topics already discussed, we should consider a few more. At this point you will have already decided whether you will use a translator or interpreter. If so, preparation time should be dedicated to developing a rapport with this person. Be sure to connect not only on the content of your session, but on a personal level. This individual can be another valuable resource to you when needing direction or advice about a cultural situation in class or working out a logistical issue. This is another reason to travel to your destination well before the training event, since this work is best done face-to-face.

Once in-country, ask questions of the locals about the specifics of everyday customs, such as manners for eating, making introductions, and other social situations. Ask for a tour of your training environment to verify the resources you expected. Is there a chalkboard, projector, or flip chart, as you were promised? What modifications must you make based on the actual situation once you are there? Conduct a run-through of a portion of your materials. Become comfortable with your surroundings if they are much different than you are used to. Remember our mantra of flexibility, and try to roll with whatever comes your way. A good trainer will learn from these types of experiences to become better at preparing for the unexpected.

## THE PRESENTATION

Go for broke! If you have worked your way through the research, design, logistics, and execution to this point, you couldn't be any more ready. We recommend more hands-on approaches than strictly lecture. Small group discussions will help solidify the content, but you may have to work to keep them on topic. They also will be freer to express their opinions in a small group than a large group. Also, incentives for learning and retention may be helpful. Review quizzes may be very popular. You will likely find your group to be animated and fun. We recommend you let them get to know you. Use humor at your own expense and have fun.

We asked Tom Archibald, Peace Corp volunteer, what advice he would give to someone who has not done this before. His experience was with west central Africa (Gabon), but there may be similarities to other regions as well:

- Be patient.

- During non-formal times, use humor and sarcasm; they like comedy.

- Before speaking at any meeting, thank everyone for either coming or inviting you. Start with the most powerful person. You can thank the president even if he's not there. Get all the titles right.

Remember the privilege and the honor you have traveling to one of the most diverse locales on the planet. You have navigated your way to a unique experience, customized by you for the exact audience you wish to reach. Good luck and good teaching!

**Helpful websites and references include:**

- de Bruyn, Pippa. (2006). *Frommer's: South Africa*. Hoboken, NJ: John Wiley & Sons.

- Devine, Elizabeth, & Branganti, Nancy L. (1995). *The Travelers' Guide to African Customs and Manners: How to Converse, Dine, Tip, Drive, Bargain, Dress, Make Friends, and Conduct Business While in Sub-Saharan Africa*. New York: St. Martin's Griffin, 1995.

- Foster, Dean. (2002). *Global Etiquette Guide to Africa and the Middle East*. Hoboken, NJ: John Wiley & Sons.

- Harvard Business School Publishing (HBSP) Newsletters, Online website, and articles, http://www.hbsp.harvard.edu

- www.cdc.gov: Center for Disease Control and Prevention

- www.cnn.com: CNN foreign/world news and current events

- www.state.gov/p/af/- Bureau of African Affairs

- www.travel.state.gov- U.S. Department of State

- Yale, Richmond, & Gestrin, Phyllis. (1998). *Into Africa: Intercultural Insights*. Yarmouth, ME: Intercultural Press.

The following list shows consulate and embassy information and websites for many African countries. It was compiled by Amy Pletcher, independent writer and consultant.

| Region | Country | Capital | Embassy | Consulate Information |
|---|---|---|---|---|
| Eastern Africa | Burundi | Bujumbura | http://bujumbura.usembassy.gov/ | http://travel.state.gov/travel/cis_pa_tw/cis/cis_1078.html |
| | Comoros | Moroni | | http://travel.state.gov/travel/cis_pa_tw/cis/cis_1091.html |
| | Djibouti | Djibouti | http://djibouti.usembassy.gov/ | http://travel.state.gov/travel/cis_pa_tw/cis/cis_1101.html |
| | Eritea | Asmara | http://eritrea.usembassy.gov/ | http://travel.state.gov/travel/cis_pa_tw/cis/cis_1111.html |
| | Ethiopia | Addis Ababa | http://addisababa.usembassy.gov/ | http://travel.state.gov/travel/cis_pa_tw/cis/cis_1113.html |
| | Kenya | Nairobi | http://nairobi.usembassy.gov/ | http://travel.state.gov/travel/cis_pa_tw/cis/cis_1151.html |
| | Madagascar | Antananarivo | http://www.usmission.mg/ | http://travel.state.gov/travel/cis_pa_tw/cis/cis_957.html |
| | Malawi | Lilongwe | http://lilongwe.usembassy.gov/ | http://travel.state.gov/travel/cis_pa_tw/cis/cis_959.html |
| | Mauritius | Port Louis | http://mauritius.usembassy.gov/ | http://travel.state.gov/travel/cis_pa_tw/cis/cis_967.html |
| | Mozambique | Maputo | http://maputo.usembassy.gov/ | http://travel.state.gov/travel/cis_pa_tw/cis/cis_976.html |
| | Rwanda | Kigali | http://kigali.usembassy.gov/ | http://travel.state.gov/travel/cis_pa_tw/cis/cis_1007.html |
| | Seychelles | Victoria | http://seychelles.usvpp.gov/ | http://travel.state.gov/travel/cis_pa_tw/cis/cis_1015.html |
| | Somalia | Mogadishu | http://somalia.usvpp.gov/ | http://travel.state.gov/travel/cis_pa_tw/cis/cis_1016.html |

| | Country | Capital | | |
|---|---|---|---|---|
| | Tanzania | Dodoma | http://mbabane.usembassy.gov/ | http://travel.state.gov/travel/cis_pa_tw/cis/cis_1038.html |
| | Uganda | Kampala | http://kampala.usembassy.gov/ | http://travel.state.gov/travel/cis_pa_tw/cis/cis_1051.html |
| | Zambia | Lusaka | http://zambia.usembassy.gov/ | http://travel.state.gov/travel/cis_pa_tw/cis/cis_1062.html |
| | Zimbabwe | Harare | http://harare.usembassy.gov/ | http://travel.state.gov/travel/cis_pa_tw/cis/cis_1063.html |
| Middle Africa | Angola | Luanda | http://luanda.usembassy.gov/ | http://travel.state.gov/travel/cis_pa_tw/cis/cis_1096.html |
| | Cameroon | Yaoundé | http://yaounde.usembassy.gov/ | http://travel.state.gov/travel/cis_pa_tw/cis/cis_1081.html |
| | Central African Republic | Bangui | | http://travel.state.gov/travel/cis_pa_tw/cis/cis_1085.html |
| | Chad | N'Djamena | http://praia.usembassy.gov/ | http://travel.state.gov/travel/cis_pa_tw/cis/cis_1086.html |
| | Congo | Brazzaville | | http://travel.state.gov/travel/cis_pa_tw/cis/cis_1092.html |
| | Democratic Republic of Congo | Kinshasa | http://kinshasa.usembassy.gov/ | http://travel.state.gov/travel/cis_pa_tw/cis/cis_1104.html |
| | Equitorial Guinea | Malabo | http://malabo.usembassy.gov/ | http://travel.state.gov/travel/cis_pa_tw/cis/cis_1110.html |
| | Gabon | Libreville | http://libreville.usembassy.gov/ | http://travel.state.gov/travel/cis_pa_tw/cis/cis_1120.html |
| | Sao Tome and Principe | São Tomé | | http://travel.state.gov/travel/cis_pa_tw/cis/cis_1010.html |

(continued)

| Region | Country | Capital | Embassy | Consulate Information |
| --- | --- | --- | --- | --- |
| Northern Africa | Algeria | Algiers | http://algiers.usembassy.gov/ | http://travel.state.gov/travel/cis_pa_tw/cis/cis_1087.html |
| | Egypt | Cairo | http://cairo.usembassy.gov/ | http://travel.state.gov/travel/cis_pa_tw/cis/cis_1108.html |
| | Libya | Tripoli | http://libya.usembassy.gov | http://travel.state.gov/travel/cis_pa_tw/cis/cis_951.html |
| | Morocco | Rabat | http://usembassy.ma/ http://casablanca.usconsulate.gov | http://travel.state.gov/travel/cis_pa_tw/cis/cis_975.html |
| | Sudan | Khartoum | http://khartoum.usembassy.gov/ | http://travel.state.gov/travel/cis_pa_tw/cis/cis_1029.html |
| | Tunisia | Tunis | http://tunis.usembassy.gov/ | http://travel.state.gov/travel/cis_pa_tw/cis/cis_1045.html |
| Southern Africa | Botswana | Gaborone | http://botswana.usembassy.gov/ | http://travel.state.gov/travel/cis_pa_tw/cis/cis_1071.html |
| | Lesotho | Maseru | http://maseru.usembassy.gov/ | http://travel.state.gov/travel/cis_pa_tw/cis/cis_949.html |
| | Namibia | Windhoek | http://windhoek.usembassy.gov/ | http://travel.state.gov/travel/cis_pa_tw/cis/cis_977.html |
| | South Africa | Bloemfontein, Cape Town, Pretoria | http://pretoria.usembassy.gov/ | http://travel.state.gov/travel/cis_pa_tw/cis/cis_1008.html |
| | Swaziland | Mbabane | http://mbabane.usembassy.gov/ | http://travel.state.gov/travel/cis_pa_tw/cis/cis_1031.html |

| Region | Country | Capital | Embassy | Travel Information |
|---|---|---|---|---|
| Western Africa | Benin | Porto-Novo | http://cotonou.usembassy.gov/ | http://travel.state.gov/travel/cis_pa_tw/cis/cis_1066.html |
| | Burkina Faso | Ouagadougou | http://ouagadougou.usembassy.gov/ | http://travel.state.gov/travel/cis_pa_tw/cis/cis_1075.html |
| | Cape Verde | Praia | http://praia.usembassy.gov/ | http://travel.state.gov/travel/cis_pa_tw/cis/cis_1083.html |
| | Cote d'Ivoire | Abidjan, Yamoussoukro | http://abidjan.usembassy.gov/ | http://travel.state.gov/travel/cis_pa_tw/cis/cis_1094.html |
| | Gambia | Banjul | http://www.usembassybanjul.gm/ | http://travel.state.gov/travel/cis_pa_tw/cis/cis_1121.html |
| | Ghana | Accra | http://accra.usembassy.gov/ | http://travel.state.gov/travel/cis_pa_tw/cis/cis_1124.html |
| | Guinea | Conakry | http://conakry.usembassy.gov/ | http://travel.state.gov/travel/cis_pa_tw/cis/cis_1132.html |
| | Liberia | Monrovia | http://monrovia.usembassy.gov/ | http://travel.state.gov/travel/cis_pa_tw/cis/cis_950.html |
| | Mali | Bamako | http://mali.usembassy.gov/ | http://travel.state.gov/travel/cis_pa_tw/cis/cis_962.html |
| | Mauritania | Nouakchott | http://mauritania.usembassy.gov/ | http://travel.state.gov/travel/cis_pa_tw/cis/cis_966.html |
| | Niger | Niamey | http://niamey.usembassy.gov/ | http://travel.state.gov/travel/cis_pa_tw/cis/cis_986.html |
| | Nigeria | Abuja | http://abuja.usembassy.gov/ | http://travel.state.gov/travel/cis_pa_tw/cis/cis_987.html |
| | Senegal | Dakar | http://dakar.usembassy.gov/ | http://travel.state.gov/travel/cis_pa_tw/cis/cis_1013.html |
| | Sierra Leone | Freetown | http://freetown.usembassy.gov/ | http://travel.state.gov/travel/cis_pa_tw/cis/cis_1016.html |
| | Togo | Lomé | http://lome.usembassy.gov/ | http://travel.state.gov/travel/cis_pa_tw/cis/cis_1041.html |

# Egypt (Middle East)

**E**xotic and chaotic are two words that come to mind when traveling in Egypt. Egypt is an African country that is also considered a Middle Eastern country. The sights, sounds, tastes, and smells are very different from what many of us are used to. Egypt is such an ancient land that you may feel as if you have been transported into an action movie. Upon our arrival, we had arranged for someone to take us through the airport maze of paperwork and take us to our hotel. That was such a good idea. We were provided with an armed guard, a translator, and a driver. That may seem a little too much, but it is also a very good idea. You need to feel safe and understood when things are confusing. Then you can enjoy the richness of the culture and the people of Egypt.

This section will provide information regarding what to expect and tips for success when training, teaching, or presenting to an Egyptian audience.

## ??? THE REQUEST

The request for a program, presentation, or course may come through a company, university, or government agency. Ensure that all of the arrangements have been made and approved before leaving for Egypt. Clarify the commitments, timing, and outcomes required in writing. This should include specific deliverables, who will help to customize materials, and who is printing materials.

# • • • GETTING THERE

Make sure you have a valid passport. Check visa requirements because they change on short notice. According to www.traveldocs.com/eg/vr.htm. for a business visa to Egypt you will need:

Your valid, signed passport (passport must have at least six months' validity remaining)

One application form, fully completed and signed

Completed cover page (print from browser)

One recent passport-type photograph

Copy of airline tickets or itinerary

A business letter of responsibility is required, to be typewritten on your company letterhead and addressed to:

Embassy of Egypt, Visa Section, Washington, D.C.

The letter should explain the following:

- Purpose of the trip

- Name and address of company to be visited, and that financial responsibility and return transportation are guaranteed.

Arriving in Cairo, Egypt, is an explosion of excitement and confusion for most of us. Have someone (your driver) who can bring you through the maze of requirements and paperwork that allow you to leave the airport meet you at the Cairo International Airport (CAI). You can arrange this when you make your hotel reservation.

If you need to take one, taxis are available at any time and are operated on a flat-fee basis. Official Cairo taxis are predominantly black and white. Agree on the fee before getting into the car. Expect to pay a small airport exit fee as well. Have small change available or they may take the rest as the "tip."

Limousine services are offered by nineteen different companies.

The Airport Bus Service (both air-conditioned and non-air-conditioned) operates from Terminal 1. There are several bus stops, including downtown Cairo.

The native name of Egypt is Misr.

Cairo is also known as Al Qâhirah.

Cairo is the capital of Egypt.

The standard time zone is GMT/UTC (Greenwich Mean Time/Universal time, Coordinated) plus two hours

This is also known as EET or Eastern European Time.

Daylight Savings Time (DST) (EEST–Eastern European Summer Time) starts around the end of April and returns in September.

Egypt has two seasons: mild winter from November through April and hot summer May through October. In Cairo the lows in winter can go into the 50s (F), highs in the 60s. In the summer it will typically be in the 90s with lows in the 70s. Although it rarely rains, it can get humid in the summer and windy in the spring.

Check the weather before you leave home to decide what to pack at www.timeanddate.com/worldclock

National holidays that may affect your travel and program scheduling include:

- January: Christmas (7th)
- April: Sinai Liberation Day (25th)
- May: Labour Day (1st)
- July: Revolution Day (23rd)
- October: Armed Forces Day (6th)

Since Islam is the state religion, the Islamic holidays are observed by all Egyptians:

- Sham El Nessim (Spring Festival): The Monday following Orthodox Easter
- Islamic New Year: The New Year based on the lunar Islamic calendar
- The Prophet Mohammed's birthday
- Ramadan Feast: Religious holiday for three days
- Sacrifice Feast: Religious holiday for four days

Other holidays that may be observed:

- January: New Year's Day (1st)
- March: Mother's Day (21st)
- June: Evacuation Day (18th)
- August: Flooding of the Nile (15th)
- October: Egyptian Naval Day (21st)
- October: Suez Day/Popular Resistance Day (24th)
- December: Victory Day (23rd)

## PROGRAM DESIGN

Your materials should be in Arabic as well as English. An interpreter should be used, to ensure that people have the opportunity to hear the presentation in their native language. Egypt has a strong Muslim influence, but the true natives are the Nubians, who speak their own language. It is not likely that you will meet many Nubians, because they live south along the Nile and are not often in the cities of Cairo or Alexandria.

## LOGISTICS

The most likely location for your presentation will be a hotel. Work with the hotel staff to make arrangements for necessary equipment and room setup. Bring your program on an electronic storage device. Send materials way ahead of time (at least one month). Bring a hard copy of materials to be used, if needed, to make copies before the program. Bring your own computer to assure your program will display correctly.

Egyptian paper money comes in denominations of 25 Piastres (quarter pound note), 50 Piastres, 1, 5 10, 20, 50, and 100 Pound Notes. Egyptian Pound (EGP; symbol E£) = 100 piastres. Coins are rarely used. Exchange of foreign currency is through official banks or money exchange offices/official bureaux de change and most hotels. Banks often have better exchange rates than bureaux de change or hotels.

American Express, MasterCard, and Visa are accepted in some locations, but paper money is more widely accepted.

## PROGRAM DELIVERY

Because there is often an interesting (tense) relationship between the West and the East, it would be best to have an Egyptian who is respected and recognized by the audience introduce and co-teach the program. This provides greater credibility and respect to the culture. Co-teaching is not an easy task. You will need to communicate with and work with this person ahead of time to ensure that you are partners in the program. Arrive early and schedule time to prepare with the person before the program is to begin. The co-presenter does not need to know all of the aspects of each topic. He or she can leave that to you. He or she can introduce sections, interpret, answer questions, and reinforce and support the learning process. If the person is seen as an integral part of the learning, it will enhance the learners' experience and your credibility. Co-presenters can also provide post-program support to increase the effectiveness of application of skills learned. Lecture, carefully chosen PowerPoint slides, and small group discussion would be appropriate. The slides and handouts should include no pictures because most images are not allowed in the Muslim culture. Only put words on the slides, with enough room to have them translated into Arabic.

Expect the women and men to choose to sit separately.

## TECHNICAL REQUIREMENTS

Technical requirements should be discussed with the host and hotel and agreed on prior to the program presentation.

Electricity in Egypt is 220 volts, alternating at 50 cycles per second. If you travel to Egypt with a device that does not accept 220 volts at 50 hertz, you will need a voltage converter.

There are three main types of voltage converter. Resistor-network converters will usually be advertised as supporting something like 50 to 1600 watts. They are lightweight and support high-wattage electrical appliances like hair dryers and irons. However, they can only be used for short periods of time and are not ideal for digital devices.

Transformers will have a much lower maximum watt rating, usually 50 or 100. Transformers can often be used continuously and provide better electricity for low wattage appliances like battery chargers, radios, laptop computers, cameras, MP3 players, and camcorders. However, they are heavy because they contain large iron rods and lots of copper wire.

Some companies sell combination converters that include both a resistor network and a transformer in the same package. This kind of converter will usually come with a switch that switches between the two modes. If you absolutely need both types of converter, then this is the type to buy.

Outlets in Egypt generally accept one type of plug: two round pins.

If your appliances plug has a different shape, you may need a plug adapter.

Depending on how much you plan to travel in the future, it may be worthwhile to purchase a combination voltage converter and plug adapter.

These are available through http://treehouse.ofb.net/go/en/voltage/Egypt.

Check to see whether the Internet is available in the location of your presentation, if you need it for your program.

You can rent a cell phone and purchase a SIM card if you will be staying for a long enough period of time. A SIM card or subscriber identity module is a portable memory chip used in some phones.

## ACCOMMODATIONS

Make sure you are staying in a five-star hotel. You will probably go through metal detectors and see armed guards. This is for your safety. They are there to ensure that nothing happens to you. It is for your peace of mind. You get used to it.

You can work with the hotel staff to prepare your presentation site, if it is in the hotel.

The hotel bar will not serve liquor. You will be able to rent a large water pipe and smoke flavored tobacco as you sit and have conversations. It is very relaxing once you get used to it.

Drink bottled water to ensure good health during your stay. Most Egyptians start their morning with a light breakfast of beans (or bean cakes), eggs, and/or pickles, cheeses, and jams. Most people eat their large, starchy lunch around 1400 to 1700 (2 P.M. to 5 P.M.) and follow it with a siesta. They may take a British-style tea at 1700 or 1800 and eat a light supper (often leftovers from lunch) late in the evening. The food is very tasty. It is appropriate for some foods to be eaten with your right hand. Do not use your left hand to eat (it is considered unsanitary). Ask your servers how a particular dish should be eaten if you are in doubt. They will be happy to tell you more about the dish and how best to eat it.

## GETTING AROUND

Everything is tightly controlled by the government. Things like traffic that are not tightly controlled are in chaos, according to the experience of most Westerners. When you are crossing the street, walking is truly a challenge. Six lanes of traffic move at breakneck speed, and there are no designated crosswalks. The traffic is supposed to avoid hitting pedestrians, and it is amazing to watch people dart between vehicles to cross to the other side. Be careful!

Taxis are readily available. Ask your hotel to call a taxi for you and write your destination in Arabic as well as your hotel name and address for your return. Most hotels have cards with the hotel information at their front desks.

Wear sun screen and a hat to protect yourself from the intensity of the sun. Carry and drink bottled water to replenish your fluids.

## THE PEOPLE

The Nile is the lifeblood of the city and the country. Everything centers on it. Water is precious and is revered by all.

City residents are more progressive than villagers and thus move at hectic paces to get where they are going. There is also a calm demeanor of some people who move in accordance with their own pace to go about their business. They are curious but wary of foreigners. Foreigners provide a good source of income for them, but they do not want to be unduly influenced by Westerners. Some people may love you on sight, and others may hate you on sight. It is easy to find out which is which by the way they look at you or avoid you.

Young people in the city are often very assertive, self-confident, and curious. Most people will assume that you are rich, so they will try to sell you things.

Egypt's industry includes the textile industry, mining and the production of cement, iron and steel, chemicals, fertilizers, rubber products, refined sugar, tobacco, canned foods, cottonseed oil, small metal products, shoes, and furniture. Agriculture and fishing are also important elements of the economy.

Historically, Egypt has had to fight Persians and be under the rule of the Romans, Greeks, Turks, Arabs, the French, and the British. Pharaohs ruled and built famous pyramids as their tombs. The massive monuments still provide a huge draw for tourists.

The majority of people in Cairo follow the Muslim religion. The call to prayer dominates daily life five times a day and can be heard via loudspeakers for the mosque minarets or towers. Women often cover their heads, faces, and bodies. Women should not be photographed. Government buildings cannot be photographed. Always ask first if you would like to take a picture. Expect that people will ask you to pay for the photo.

Historically, the religion of Ancient Egypt has been a polytheistic (many gods) religion with one short period of monotheism (one god). Their religion hosted about seven hundred different gods and goddesses. In addition, it was not uncommon for deities to be combined to form a new deity.

One of the more famous aspects of the Egyptian religious beliefs was their idea of the afterlife. They believed the physical body had to be preserved to allow a place for the spirit to dwell in the afterlife. Because of this, mummification was performed to preserve the body. In addition, large pyramids were constructed as tombs for the pharaohs.

## !!! PREPARATION

If you travel to any other locations, hire a guide through your hotel and have the guide arrange transport. This will ensure that you will have an interpreter and protector. In some cases, you may be provided with an armed guard and driver. Do not be alarmed; this is to ensure that you have a good trip. The government wants to know who you are, where you are going, and what time you will leave each location. Security is tight. This is serious business and nothing to take lightly. Always dress conservatively and professionally. People may pester you to make purchases, but you should just smile and politely say "No, thank you." If invited into a mosque by your guide, women must cover their heads and quietly ask any questions you may have.

It may be unbelievably hot. Make sure you wear cool clothing, but nothing sleeveless or clothing that would be considered too bold (showing skin). This is a very conservative culture. Always have a hat, lots of water available, and something to cover your skin to protect it from the sun.

It is extremely important that you represent your own country well. People draw conclusions about an entire country from meeting just one person. You will constantly be watched because people are curious about a country that provides such freedom to its citizens. When you find yourself being watched, just smile, nod, and go about your business.

## THE PRESENTATION

You will be successful if you show respect for the Egyptian culture, awe for their monuments, appreciation for their food, and confidence in your area of expertise.

There will be discussion and participation in activities that are clear and straightforward. Physical activity is not recommended because of their reluctance to touch each other.

Breaks must be provided for the participants to pray at appropriate times. This is a requirement of the culture. They may not use them as such, but will certainly appreciate your respect for their culture.

Images should be restricted and avoided. Use word slides to make sure that you will not offend anyone. With preparation and caution, Egypt should be a great learning experience. We hope it is a great teaching experience as well!

**Here are some useful websites and resources:**

- http://historylink101.net/egypt_1/religion.htm
- http://lexicorient.com/e.o/egypt_2.htm
- http://touregypt.net
- http://travelguides.lastminute.com

- http://treehouse.ofb.net/go/en/voltage/Egypt
- www.timeanddate.com/worldclock/timezone.html
- www.traveldocs.com/eg/vr.htm
- www.wisegeek.com/what-is-a-sim-card.htm
- www.wordtravels.com/Cities/Egypt/Cairo/Climate

# South Africa

As we have discussed, Africa is a large continent with a great variety of backgrounds, history, and cultures. We have chosen South Africa to write about individually because it is a totally unique country in many aspects, and because a great deal of training is going on there.

South Africa has about forty-eight million people and has at least eleven different languages. The government is a democracy, and there are currently nine different provinces. This country has vast differences in the distribution of wealth. Both severe poverty and amazing riches exist. Here is what to expect when training, teaching, or presenting to international audiences from South Africa.

## ??? THE REQUEST

Since the days of Apartheid, two important pieces of legislation have been passed in an effort to bridge the economic gap between the races of South Africa. The Equity Act and its companion legislation, the Skills Development Act, require employers to submit annual plans and progress reports on worker training programs. Many American companies have historically led the charge, complying with and adhering to affirmative-action laws. As a means to this end, many South Africans have been and continue to be re-skilled and trained to gain employment and to rise through the ranks. Companies are careful not to hire unqualified people as "tokenism" (hiring a person as a quota-filler not based on skills), which can undermine individual confidence and causes devastation to companies and individuals who are chosen strictly based on their race. This social climate and need for development makes South Africa a rich environment for training.

Agriculture is a main source of income for the country, and education in the area of land management and use of natural resources is a major focus.

## • • • GETTING THERE

Whether flying into the legislative capital of Cape Town or the largest city of Johannesburg, expect to dedicate a full day to travel. There are very few direct flights from the United States to South Africa; almost all flights will make an intermediate stop. There are nine different capital cities. If you can, plan the majority of your flight during the night and arrive during daylight hours. If you have the luxury of building time into your schedule to recuperate from jet lag, do it. The local time is GMT +2, which is six to nine hours ahead of U.S. time zones.

If your stay is for fewer than ninety days, a visa is not required. However, the U.S. State Department warns that passports of all travelers to South Africa must be valid for at least six months and contain at least two blank/unstamped visa pages each time entry is sought. These pages are in addition to the endorsement/amendment pages at the back of the passport. Without these additional blank pages, entry into South Africa may be refused. In addition to this refusal, you could be fined, returned to your point of origin at your expense, and/or detained for up to several days until extra visa pages are obtained. As with other travel abroad, it is important to keep a photocopy of your passport in a location separate from the passport. The U.S. State Department also recommends checking the latest requirements before traveling. This information may be obtained from the Embassy of South Africa at 3051 Massachusetts Avenue, NW, Washington, D.C. 20008 or by phone at (202) 232-4400. There are also South African consulates in Chicago, Los Angeles, and New York. The Embassy of South Africa's website is www.saembassy.org, and it has the most current visa information. It is advisable to register your trip with the U.S. State Department online at https://travelregistration.state.gov as a "short-term traveler." The U.S. Embassy website is http://usembassy.state.gov/pretoria/.

The climate in South Africa is moderate, similar to Southern California. Because it is below the equator, its seasons are the opposite of those in North America. The peak summer months are December and January. Cape Town and the southernmost part of the Western Cape have a Mediterranean-type climate, with warm to hot summers. Winter brings gentle rain showers around Cape Town and the West Coast. No specific formalities stand out in terms of what to wear or what to bring. Layers are always a good choice, especially in the warmer, sunnier months to stay cool.

The Johannesburg and Cape Town international airports have had baggage pilferage problems. Secure your luggage with Transportation Security Administration (TSA) approved locks, use an airport plastic wrapping service, and avoid putting personal valuables in checked luggage. Make an inventory of items in your checked baggage in case a theft does occur.

## PROGRAM DESIGN

Country-specific design considerations are few, but those few could possibly be quite complex. Language challenges are a possibility. South Africa has eleven official languages: Afrikaans, English, Ndebele, Northern Sotho, Southern Sotho, Swati, Tsonga, Tswana, Venda, Xhosa, and Zulu. Incidentally, each language has its own official name for South Africa. English is said to be widely spoken; however, if your work takes you into more remote or less urban classrooms, you may be contending with the compounded problem of multiple languages. In this case, interpreters are difficult to use unless you can narrow down the multiple native languages to a common one or two, hoping one of them is English. You can have people divided up into table groups by common language. Then as you speak, it can be simultaneously interpreted for each table. Making the content more hands-on and experiential and less lecture will help greatly.

When using interpreters, one-third more time should be built into the program design phase to account for translation issues. An in-country contact is critical to successful translation and for identifying capable interpreters. Participants appreciate team teaching, so consider partnering with a local subject-matter expert to present your content.

South Africans are accustomed to mid-morning tea. This includes a meal-like break and prayers. Afternoon breaks are also similar to a meal break, and both will cut into your classroom time by at least thirty minutes.

When building examples or anecdotes, you can try sports (cricket, soccer, rugby, boxing, and for younger audiences skateboarding) or music. Do not assume that examples from other countries in Africa will make sense here. Countries can be very distinct in their background, educational systems, politics, and interests.

## LOGISTICS

If you can avoid shipping materials, you will escape several potential headaches. Shipping is slow and unpredictable. Boxes and even manila envelopes are subject to high taxes and are often pilfered. If you typically use give-aways or other trinkets to encourage participation, consider bringing them with you in your luggage or shipping them separately from training materials. The extra cost of baggage outweighs the risk of not having them at all. Bring training materials with you or have them produced in-country. There is no chain of printer/copier stores, so be sure your in-country contact knows how to have things produced and how long it will take.

Wikipedia shows a list of public holidays as well as a list of historical holidays. The list of public holidays is:

- New Year's Day, January 1
- Human Rights Day, March 21
- Easter varies, the Friday before is Good Friday and the Monday after is Family Day
- Freedom Day, April 27
- Workers' Day, May 1
- Youth Day, June 16
- National Women's Day, August 9
- Heritage Day, September 24
- Day of Reconciliation, December 16
- Christmas Day, December 25
- Day of Goodwill, December 26

The currency is the South African Rand (R), which is divided into 100 cents (c). Notes issued are R200, R100, R50, R20, and R10. Coins are R5, R2, R1, 50c, 20c, 10c, 5c, 2c, and 1c. It is not advisable to obtain Rand money before entering the country, since it must be declared on entry and is restricted to R500. Major credit cards are widely accepted, with some restrictions in small towns and rural areas. When using your credit card, don't allow the card to leave your sight for processing, as there is an increasing amount of credit card fraud in South Africa. Automated teller machines (ATMs) are situated outside most banks. Do not accept "assistance" from anyone or agree to assist others with ATM transactions. Use ATMs only during bank business hours and in well-populated locations. Gasoline must be purchased with cash.

Additionally, South Africans are not in as much of a hurry as Westerners typically are. When asking directions or inquiring about anything, introduce yourself first and start a casual conversation. You will receive a more positive response. You can tip waiters and taxi drivers 10 percent of the bill, unless a service charge has been added. In general, 2 Rand (about 50 U.S. cents) per bag is recommended for porters.

## PROGRAM DELIVERY

Dress conservatively for your presentation. Women should consider wearing long skirts and men dress slacks, even in casual environments. Because of their laid-back nature in regard to time, don't be surprised if your class wanders in just at or after your scheduled start time. Have some tricks up your sleeve to keep them coming back on time after breaks. (One bite of candy goes a remarkable long way, or try giving out tickets that will be used later for a drawing for a prize of some kind.)

If you don't have language issues and are working without an interpreter, you will find participation will be much like it is with your audiences here at home. Adult learning principles hold true here, hands-on training is better received than straight lecture. Humor is welcomed, but don't overdo it. Keep your examples and illustrations localized with pictures and company names they will recognize. Even when speaking to an audience that understands English, watch for puzzled expressions that indicate clarification is needed. Participants will be forthcoming with their questions, but you should be perceptive enough to know to ask. Use good teaching technique and ask for questions before moving on to the next subject.

A small item of note, most South Africans relay the time in military fashion. They are culturally late to arrive, but expect things will begin on time. They have a relative sense of time when they use terms like "now" or "just now." These terms are more like our "soon" and "sometime today."

## TECHNICAL REQUIREMENTS

If your laptop doesn't already have a built-in converter, you will need to purchase one. It will be needed as well as a transformer (240V) and an adapter for local power outlets. Adapters are inexpensive once in South Africa, but transformers are difficult to find. Even with an adapter, we had a contributor whose computer was fried there. It is a risk. Take files on a portable USB drive as a backup. Power systems are generally 220/230 volts AC, 50 cycles, except in Pretoria, where the currency is 250 volts AC. Three-pronged plugs are universal, so take an adaptor. Most hotel rooms have 110 volt outlets for electric shavers and small appliances.

You will have to check around for Internet availability and cell phone coverage. This will vary based on where you are traveling.

## ACCOMMODATIONS

South Africa's major urban areas offer budget and luxury, world-class hotels, guest and country houses, bed-and-breakfast establishments, and resorts. Your budget is the determining factor here. Our recommendation would be to stay at a larger, luxury hotel with their amenities and security. If this is not within your budget, you can contact local police officials for help with choosing a safe neighborhood and hotel. Don't book a stay without at least seeing pictures of the establishment. South Africa is in many respects a developed country, but much of its population lives in poverty. Expect to see armed police on street corners in some cities. Tap water is safe to drink throughout South Africa. You can swim safely at beaches along the entire coastline. You shouldn't swim in rivers or lakes in the eastern and northern regions, as the bilharzia parasite (otherwise known as snail fever or swimmers itch) may be in the water. This can lead to infections with serious effects. Warning signs are usually posted. The Eastern Cape is bilharzia-free.

No vaccinations are required of visitors coming from the United States or Canada. You should take anti-malaria tablets before visiting the game reserves and parks of the Northern, Mpumalanga, and KwaZulu-Natal provinces. You can take tablets twenty-four hours before entering a malaria-affected area and then on a weekly basis for five to six weeks. They are available without prescription at South African drugstores. Consult a doctor or pharmacist for advice on best drugs or combinations.

 **GETTING AROUND**

If you are comfortable driving on the left side of the road (keep this in mind when you are a pedestrian in the city too!), your valid driver's license is accepted in South Africa, provided it bears your photo and signature and is printed in English. Wearing seatbelts is required and some highways and roads require tolls, so carry small currency or coins if you intend to drive. If you are like me, you will rely on the efficient taxi system in the cities. Public transport is not as well developed as in U.S. cities, so don't expect to catch a bus or train to your destinations. When riding a car/taxi, leave your valuables in the trunk out of sight. Take advantage of your hotel's safe for your passport, cameras, and other expensive items. Keep your wits about you when moving through the city; avoid any large gathering, particularly protests and demonstrations, since the possibility of violence is real. The South African Police are easily recognized by their blue uniforms and white and blue patrol vehicles. It wouldn't be a bad idea to pick up a rental mobile phone, available from kiosks at the major airports. Your U.S. mobile phone may not work in South Africa, but a rented one could, at the very least, ease your fears. The nationwide emergency number for the police is 10111, and the nationwide number for ambulance service is 10177. Just dial these digits without any country code or other prefixes. Another option is to dial 107 from a land line for an emergency or to dial 112 from a cell phone.

## THE PEOPLE

South Africa has one of the most complex and diverse populations in the world. As mentioned previously, there is a large gap between the economic status of the wealthy and the poor. This is a historically important topic in this part of the world. Class has been based on skin color: Black, Brown, or White. Various cultures living there include local tribes, English descendents because of British rule for many years, slaves and indentured servants who were brought in from different African countries, India, Malaysia, Indonesia, and other locations. However, one can find several grass-roots efforts to improve South Africa's image and any racial stereotypes. The land of Nelson Mandela is eager to renew itself in the eyes of tourists and travelers. One such effort is being made by two specific organizations that strive to increase security, tourism, and a sense of community: eblockwatch and Travelbuddy. The groups are amassing an army of native volunteers to be an OnStar equivalent in South Africa. The services are relatively new and we are unable to validate their effectiveness or reliability, but they are recommended to travelers by the South African Embassy. What a wonderfully spirited effort to bring peace of mind to the traveler and thereby bring more people into this amazing, beautiful, and diverse country.

## PREPARATION

Your preparation will include the typical exercise of getting to know your audience, but it will also have a healthy dose of getting to know your surroundings. Once again, the issue of safety should be on your mind. If you are in Los Angeles, Chicago, or New York, visit the South African Consulate. Ask questions about the areas you will be traveling in, gather brochures to help you choose your accommodations, and inquire about current political conditions. Be sure you confirm your itinerary details and you have an in-country contact who is personally responsible to help you find your way to all events during your trip. If you have enlisted the help of an interpreter, be sure to schedule an advance meeting with him or her to go over your material and answer any questions.

A well-thought-out trip with some local assistance can provide you with a safe and enjoyable trip to this exotic land. Remember to bring a camera, since any time of year is beautiful in South Africa. Keep your head about you, but enjoy all this rich land has to offer!

Some common greetings generally understood are "howzit," meaning "How is it?"; "hallo" meaning "hello"; and "dankie," which means "thanks."

## PRESENTATION

Your audience will likely speak Africaans or English. Many Africaans-speaking people also have some knowledge of English, because of the English rule for so many years. You will need to check on this. If you need an in-class interpreter, allow the usual one-third extra time. If not, still allow extra time and plan on speaking slowly to account for the accent issues. Steve Gawrys, a sergeant from a U.S. police department, conducted several forms of safety training for audiences in several cities in South Africa. His experience was that the U.S. speaker is considered THE authority, and people were very attentive to everything he said and totally saw him as the expert. Also, the audience was not shy and asked many questions.

Steve recommends these "to dos":

- Ask your in-country contact about sensitivities regarding race, gender, or leadership issues in your training groups.
- Arrive in the classroom early so you can be ready for whatever happens.
- Use adult learning principles and everything should work.
- Hands-on methods work better than lecture.
- Stay flexible. For example, you may want a "U," but you may need to take what you get.

Talk about flexible; Steve was hired to design and conduct training with NO local subject-matter expert (SME). He used the Internet to research the region and the topic. Then he found some old acquaintances from college to give him a local perspective. He went with a plan and was totally ready to adapt.

South Africa is a place where you can create real relationships. One contributor said he hung out around a bonfire at the beach with participants until 4:00 A.M. talking about the session topic and making friends. To this day, friends from South Africa visit him each Christmas as a result of his training trip there. This is a visit from which you will learn as much as you teach.

### Helpful websites and references include:

- Frommer's: South Africa by Pippa de Bruyn
- https://travelregistration.state.gov
- http://usembassy.state.gov/pretoria/
- www.saembassy.org (most current visa information)

**PART THREE**

# Asia

# China

**A**s with any new country you travel to, it is always a good idea to gather as much information as you can about your host country and its current events before you start planning your training, most certainly before you board the plane. This is especially true in Asia. Eastern countries pose significant cultural challenges. Be sure to have an understanding of any tensions that currently exist between your two countries, for example, for Taiwan, the trade deficit, the Yuan tied to the dollar, lack of copyright laws, etc. Not only must cultural difference be understood but also differences in business practices, laws, and government policies.

Obvious, yet important, China is still a communist country. You must understand that many businesses are government-owned or are joint ventures whereby foreign firms invest with Chinese partners, which may be the communist government. It would serve the traveler well to read not only books about doing business in China but novels about life in China pre- and post-Mao and about Communism. As you travel, do so in a spirit of humility with a genuine desire to learn. The Chinese are learning more English, but it is still nice to be able to speak a few words of Chinese when you arrive.

Here is some helpful information and what to expect for training, teaching, or presenting to international audiences from China.

## ??? THE REQUEST

Common requests for training come in two flavors. The first is required training from Headquarters or Corporate U.S. Affiliates within Chinese organizations who often find that certain topics are important to communicate in-country. The typical stigma about being from company headquarters may apply here, but most likely you will experience a warm welcome and open acceptance of how things are run in the United States. They want and need to hear what is being offered. Adhering to company business practices, standards, and knowledge of how to get things done internally are paramount to getting a division up and running in a country that is twelve to fourteen hours ahead of North America and will likely be working without as much infrastructure. Thus, job descriptions are more fluid and people are going to be wearing many different hats throughout the organization. They will be eager to have help.

A second, larger request classification is from Chinese corporations and universities proactively seeking out the knowledge and wisdom of North American authorities on various topics, possibly business practices, global trends, communication skills, project management, problem solving, and other train-the-trainer topics. In all of these situations, build in extra time for curious questions about you and your culture that may or may not be related to the topic at hand.

### • • • GETTING THERE

Most large corporations and universities are located in one of the three largest cities in China. Shanghai is in the east. Things move very quickly in Shanghai and because of that it has been compared to New York City. Beijing, in the north, has been compared to Washington, D.C., because of a very political environment. A major city in the south is Guangzhou. Southern China has a Hong Kong influence and is likened to the Wild West, where millions of people are moving in and out for jobs. Flights are long to get to any of these locations, close to twenty hours if you are traveling from the East Coast of North America, so proper hydration and good travel planning are necessary to reduce jetlag. The time zone is UTC +8. The U.S. State Department has individual websites with updated travel information at http://travel.state.gov/, which is very helpful. The U.S. State Department website also posts updates about the avian flu. Also check for any health concerns at the Center for Disease Control website at www.cdc.gov.

There are seven major Chinese dialects and many sub-dialects. Mandarin, the predominant dialect, is spoken by over 70 percent of the population. You will want to work with a local contact who knows your audience to determine whether a translator is necessary, and if so which dialect he or she should speak.

A valid passport and visa are required to enter China and must be obtained from Chinese embassies and consulates before traveling to China. Visa applications should be made at least a month prior to departure for China. Passports must be valid for at least six months for a single or double-entry visa and at least nine months for a multiple-entry visa. Visas are granted only for the points of entry indicated in the passport. All documents necessary for further travel and sufficient funds to cover intended period of stay are required. Care should be taken when reading dates on visas for China, as they are written in year/month/day format. (This information came from http://beijing.usembassy.gov/living_traveling_in_china.html.)

Research should be done to make sure you are not planning training for major holidays or festivals. There are three major holidays for the entire country. National Day (October 1), Chinese New Year (January to February), and Labour Day (May 1). There are many regional holidays and festivals, too many to list here. For some holidays, people are off work or school for a week or more. This is a good thing to research for the particular region you are visiting.

## PROGRAM DESIGN

If your program has not yet been designed, call some of the participants to find out how well they speak English, if at all. If their English is at all suspect, create materials and build in time to have them translated, even if you are not planning to have an interpreter in the session with you. Surprisingly, some organizations have lumped all their Asia Pacific regional locals together, including Australia, which is problematic for the Australians with regard to language and culture. Be sensitive to all of your audiences.

With this culture in a business setting, management support is necessary. Their participation is optimal, but if that isn't possible, be sure that management starts the session with a short speech reinforcing the importance of the topic. If you have a client or contact in-country who is assisting with content, schedule a dry run of the materials. What something looks like on paper and what will work in China may be two different things. The pre-delivery conversation could be the most valuable piece of the design. Make sure you tell the audience why they are being trained, as they may see it as a punishment. If they know why it is important, and that it has management support, you will more likely be successful. Here are other valuable considerations:

- Use simple English (not as easy to do as it sounds). Leave big words out.

- Do not use popular colloquialisms or phrases such as "step up to the plate," "maiden voyage," or "hit the ball out of the park." They will translate these literally and be confused. You'll lose the audience during your presentation.

- Use humor carefully, but if you choose to tell a joke, explain it thoroughly. Some people recommend avoiding jokes altogether because it can be risky.

- If doing case studies in English, allow for more time to read them in English. Do them in Chinese if possible.

- Be clear about objectives and what you are trying to accomplish. Have ways to determine whether learning happened.

- Be aware of reporting structure dynamics. It will give you insight as to who will be "tuned in" or "tuned out" during the training session.

- Embarrassment or pressure in front of their peers is very stressful for the Chinese. So allow for a good amount of time for them to prepare for presentations or exercises where they have to present.

- Be cautious about choosing and rewarding with prizes or gifts. They don't carry large bags, notebooks, or portfolios. Standard paper is a different size. Get ideas from the Chinese regarding what gifts or prizes would be most appropriate.

- Cut the number of lectures per day to half of what you would build in for English-speaking participants. It takes a lot of energy and focus to translate words. Build in more activities where they can speak Chinese instead.

- If you are working with a classroom interpreter, explain to that person that it is okay to let you know when he or she doesn't understand.

- Reviews or feedback may be difficult to obtain due to lack of participation. You may want a "coach" to do this in Chinese at the beginning or end of the day. You may receive better feedback that way.

- Written feedback will get a larger response if you pass the forms out early in the day.

An instructor in a Chinese classroom will be respected going in. In many environments, frequently American audiences, an instructor needs to earn the respect of the group. That is not the way it is in China. The instructor is seen as knowledgeable, and participants will have great expectations of wisdom. Companies should send their best and brightest person to train or present. The person facilitating should also be the subject-matter expert on the topic. Just facilitating a discussion in the room is not for them; the facilitator needs to add value to the topic. Training itself is often not seen as particularly helpful or vital in China. It needs to be positioned as solving problems or helping business in some way. As a true expert, they will want access to you before and after training to continue to receive coaching and have questions answered. (Consultants may want to build extra time into contracts for this purpose.) To really make training come alive for them, make it personal. Show how this knowledge will help THEM be promoted or earn more money. While adults will be very team focused, young people see the need to distinguish themselves from their peers, to be noticed.

Bill Wiggenhorn, principle of Main-Captiva and the founder and past president of Motorola University, suggests including as much local material as possible. Make examples, cases, vignettes, and role plays relevant to the people being trained. What if you don't have this and don't know how to get it? Look at Chinese newsletters for seeds of ideas, interview local managers (Skype provides free computer-to-computer conversations and very inexpensive phone calls). Contact local cultural clubs (for example, the Chinese American club). Check out websites, read speeches from CEOs from China-based companies. Watch CNN Asia CEO interviews. Harvard, Macenzie, and Wharton all have newsletters full of information. The Internet and Amazon.com have resources, also. All of these sources will give insights into how people think, which will add relevance to training. Think of the end user: How will the student use this method? How will it help him or her learn?

 ## LOGISTICS

Complications with customs are very common when sending materials to China. Send printed materials separate from any electronics or demo equipment. Printed materials seem to not be a problem in passing through customs, but electronics may be a different issue. Our best advice is to ship early and keep in touch with contacts in China about shipping standards. If you have the opportunity, think about shipping to Hong Kong or Singapore and then into China. It is often easier than shipping directly from the United States. Always bring electronic versions and a hard copy of your materials with you and know where you can do some last-minute copying if necessary. If you are coordinating logistics with an in-country contact, a weekly conference call is necessary to ensure details are being handled properly. That in-country contact should become the designated owner of the project plan to follow up on tasks with other task owners if you don't get a response or they miss calls.

The currency used in China is the Renminbi Yuan (RMB or ¥). The Yuan is divided into 10 Jiao or 100 fens. Notes come in denominations of ¥100, 50, 20, 10, 5, 2, and 1. Exchange your leftover Yuan before returning home because it can be exchanged only within China's borders. Traveler's checks, preferably in U.S. dollars, and foreign cash can be exchanged in cities at the Bank of China. The larger hotels and the special "Friendship Stores" designed for foreigners will accept most Western currencies for purchases. Major credit cards are accepted in the main cities at various establishments, but outside the major cities, acceptance is limited. ATMs are scarce outside the main cities. Travelers should have small bills (RMB 10, 20, and 50 notes) for travel by taxi. Reports of taxi drivers using counterfeit RMB 50 and 100 notes to make change for large bills are increasingly common. Be sure to get a receipt from the taxi driver. Gratuities are not permitted and are generally considered an insult.

## PROGRAM DELIVERY

They will expect lectures. They see interaction as a Western teaching method, although localized case studies will work well. You will need to be very engaging if you are going to get interaction from the group. Have it be problem solving in nature.

Online education is acceptable to the young, but not the older generation. The more mature workers don't see it as real education. Another challenge with it is finding a place to do it. Most homes are crowded with lots of people living there. People need a quiet place to do this work. Companies that provide online learning must provide a place, perhaps a wireless cafeteria, for people to get away and learn online. They are not resistant to using technology; they just need an environment in which to do it.

It is important to never embarrass anyone in the learning process. No one should be publicly wrong. Not just in a workshop, but before, during, and after. Be careful with tests and assessments; they must be presented very carefully. Position them as instruments to help become more successful. But then live up to that. Showing managers the participants' test scores, for example, is reporting and will be inconsistent with their view of using the results for development.

Let participants present and complete activities in Chinese. This is particularly important if they won't be using the skills taught while speaking English. It is particularly interesting to note that most Chinese colleges and universities don't require students to speak in front of the class, so this will be challenging for them. If you are not providing an interpreter, it will be important to have a "coach" or manager there during these activities to debrief in Chinese.

If you hire Asian vendors for translations and/or you are working with third-party instructors delivering your materials, make sure the instructor speaks proficiently in the languages you request. This is not always obvious until you get there and meet the instructors. Specifically, be sure the English instructor speaks English well if you have participants who will select this as their preferred language. It is best to order books in Chinese (Mandarin) for them to read prior to or after the training session. Plan on cell phone interruptions, even if you request that they turn them off. It is a culture difference with regard to cell phone etiquette. To avoid some interruptions, allow for longer cell phone breaks if you have the time.

Some companies may think there is an advantage to sending a presenter with an Asian background, and there may be an advantage if the person knows the local culture and some of the language. If the person doesn't have language AND local culture knowledge, this strategy may backfire.

Smoking is allowed in the break areas and at the dinner table. If the majority of the group is Chinese, they will likely not drink very much at dinner and want to go back to the hotel no later than 8:30 or 9:00 P.M. For those who will be spending leisure time with their audience, karaoke that is guided by an emcee is actually a lot of fun for groups and not as embarrassing as it would be at home (not as much drinking occurs, and little to no alcohol is required to get people to sing).

If you are expecting things to go smoothly, be ready to be disappointed. Have an attitude of adventure and go with the flow.

## TECHNICAL REQUIREMENTS

Electrical current is 220 volts, 50Hz. Plug types vary, but the two narrow-pin type is most common. Adapters are generally required. CD/DVD and VCR or PAL video media formats may vary slightly, so it is important to send media ahead to be tested by local contacts or don't count on their use. You may choose to use your own laptop/hardware with adaptors. LCD projectors are compatible. Most business professionals have cell phones and can be reached easily by phone while in the country.

Internet accessibility will vary based on where you are.

## ACCOMMODATIONS

In the major cities, you will find many comfortable, albeit expensive, hotels to choose from. Most have enough Western familiarity. Because of the political situation, security personnel may at times place foreign visitors under surveillance. Hotel rooms, telephones, and fax machines may be monitored, and personal possessions in hotel rooms may be searched. Taking photographs of anything that could be perceived as being of military or security interest may result in problems with authorities. Keep your passport with you in a secure location at all times; pick-pocketing is the most common form of crime. Make photocopies of your passport and Chinese visas, keep these in a separate, secure location, and register with the nearest U.S. embassy or consulate general, according to http://beijing.usembassy.gov/living_traveling_in_china.html. It is best to stay in the company of locals or a group, rather than to explore alone.

In the event of an emergency, no matter where you are in China, dial:

- 110 for local police
- 114 for operator
- 119 for fire department
- 120 for medical emergencies
- 122 for traffic emergencies

Use bottled water only, and check the seal to make sure it is a new bottle, rather than a refilled bottle.

## GETTING AROUND

Taxis will be your most likely form of transportation around the city. It will be more difficult to get a taxi during rush hour and very difficult to get one when it is raining. It is best to write down your location and show the driver if you cannot pronounce it. Major cities have subway systems, and they are known for being clean and safe. Some cities also have pedicabs (human powered, similar to bicycles) as alternatives to taxis.

## THE PEOPLE

Most people in business are under the age of forty. Real economic change did not take place until after Mao's death in 1976. Older people have no office experience, since that type of business did not really exist until the reform. Young people are eager to change jobs to move up, and they will change jobs for a very small amount of pay increase. Training has questionable value for some. Businesses worry that if people are better trained, then they will leave to go work for a foreign company. Young people, however, expect to be trained. The social network once provided by the socialistic/communistic government no longer exists. Retirement does not provide the security it once did. People are wonderful and friendly. They like and are curious about Americans. They are eager to acquire Western training. Trainers have been asked to place their pictures on the certificate of completion so people could see that they had been trained by a Westerner. They are eager to learn anything there is to know about your culture. Asians have been raised not to humiliate the teacher. They will not challenge you because they don't want to embarrass you out of respect. That means that you may not know whether they understand your content. Smiling and nodding is polite, not an indication of understanding and comprehension.

Some contributors have told us that young people entering the workplace can tend to have an entitlement mentality. They are often only children whose parents and most likely grandparents are all working. Young people will need to be taught a work ethic, where for their parents it came naturally.

You will find a range of literacy, comprehension, ability to apply knowledge, and motivation. Education is very good for the elite, but for the rest of the population it will vary. Education is often theoretical in nature. You will find many women in business, including in high-level positions.

People will ask about your family, where you are from, what your income is (you can gently answer, "Enough to live on"). Some questions may be personal and may feel inappropriate. Ask them where they are from and where their parents are from. It is important. Show interest in them as people, outside of business. A "Type A" personality, wanting to get in and get a deal done in twenty minutes, won't be very successful here. Running in, giving a presentation, and heading on to the next customer will not be viewed positively.

The Chinese nod or bow when greeting each other. Shaking hands is common also, but wait for them to extend their hands first. Using Mr., Mrs., Miss, or Madam is polite when addressing people.

## ▌▌▌ PREPARATION
For China it would be worthwhile to take an intercultural class. It is a relationship-based country and learning nuances will be helpful in building those relationships. It is respectful to learn some Chinese phrases before you go. It shows you care about their culture. Read *The World Is Flat*, by Thomas L. Friedman (2006) for some additional insights.

---

### GRETCHEN LINZING, MANAGER, TRAINING AND COMMUNICATIONS, UNITED HEALTH GROUP

A sense of adventure is an attitude that I think helped me as I headed over the North Pole. It didn't make the fact that all of my training materials I had sent over weeks in advance were stuck in customs (and eventually sent back to the United States) such a bad experience. I also noticed that, prior to coming to China; it was very difficult to find books on training in China. There were loads of books on business practices and negotiating, but not much on training. I'm happy to share my experiences and hope it will be of help to others.

Research the history of the cities you will be visiting. Know current events and cities in the area. Know enough that you can talk to people and ask for more information. You want people to know that you cared enough to find out. Have some bilingual slides and greetings prepared.

A couple of Mandarin words that may come in handy are hello ("Nǐ hǎo") and good-bye ("Bai-bai") (pronounced byebye).

## THE PRESENTATION

Icebreakers really help to make Chinese participants feel more relaxed; work with your in-country contact to determine the most appropriate one to use. You should be almost painfully aware of the language barrier and remember to ask open-ended questions and wait for a longer period of time for answers. Get comfortable with silence. Even with ample opportunity, don't be surprised if you do not receive many answers. If it seems participants are holding back, you can bring in their authority figures. The audience will answer questions posed by their managers. It is important to give deference to status, however. In America we tend to treat everyone in the room the same. In China it is important to show respect to the senior managers.

Jon Anderson, partner, Lake Point Partners, has lived and worked in China for years. He says participants will smile and nod and thank you for the great performance. You still won't know whether they understand the content. He suggests building relationships in order to get past that. Ask questions over dinner about what makes sense. Get information about what is working so you can tweak the remaining content or revisit topics that need clarification.

It is important for everyone's sake to take frequent breaks, whether you work with an interpreter or not. Everyone must work harder to understand and communicate in an unfamiliar language. If participants like to socialize after class, this can become

---

### A BRIEF STORY FROM ONE OF OUR CONTRIBUTORS

During one of my first lectures we had no breaks and a participant fell asleep and fell completely off his chair and hit the hard floor with a thump. I thought I had killed him. It gave new meaning to the term, "Death by lecture."

particularly tiring with everyone straining to understand each other with the "Chinglish" spoken. Even with an interpreter, expect to work effectively for only about five hours a day before everyone is exhausted from listening and speaking. If you don't have any translations, be sure to print the materials written in English since people can read more English than they can speak.

With that said, don't shy away from using exercises. They work well but require clear instructions. Many Chinese have never worked for companies that have provided formal training. Some participants won't know how to respond or act. You or the managers will need to prepare them in advance, if possible.

**Tips for Success**

- Start your presentation with a humble introduction. Chinese like their presenters educated but humble, so even after you share your credentials, be humble and suggest that you are "honored by this opportunity" to teach.

- Warm up your audience. Start your training formally and then gradually increase the interactions you want from them.

- Try the food. Be polite even if you don't like it. Learn to use chopsticks. One person reported fumbling with their chopsticks during a business lunch and the host removed them from the table. All the Chinese colleagues were forced to use forks. This was not a comfortable situation.

- Chinese do not talk about sad events in public conversations. Do not bring up a death or tragedy, for example.

- If you work with an interpreter, the person may know English but not the nuances of the language, so your message may not be exactly what you think it is.

- The Chinese have a great sense of humor. One Chinese colleague had a contributor drinking beer out of a bowl and saying it was the local custom. They will laugh in class if you laugh. Saving face is still important to them, so don't make fun of anyone. But you can make fun of yourself.

- Business cards are passed and received with two hands and lingered on.

Take these lessons and a healthy sense of adventure with you as you head over the North Pole. Contributor Bill Wiggenhorn, suggests you take two suitcases with you. One is filled with the knowledge you bring with you. The other goes over empty and returns full of the knowledge you learn and bring back with you. We wish you well on this journey, and don't forget one of the most popular Chinese characters used in Chinese New Year celebrations, the Fu.

---

*Fu—Blessing, Good Fortune,*
*Good Luck*

---

**Helpful websites and references include:**

- http://beijing.usembassy.gov/living_traveling_in_china.html

- http://travel.state.gov/

- www.cdc.gov

- Bill Wiggenhorn, principle of Main-Captiva. LLC, founder and former president of Motorola University

- Gretchen Linzing, Manager–Training and Communications, United Health Group

- Jon Anderson, partner, Lake Point Partners, www.lakepointepartners.com

- Friedman, T. L. (2006). *The World Is Flat.* New York: Farrar, Straus and Giroux.

# Hong Kong

**H**ong Kong began as a trading port in the 19th century as a colony of the United Kingdom, but its sovereignty was transferred to China in 1997 under the condition that the region operates with autonomy in its legal system, police force, currency, and immigration policies until at least 2047, and it has since become a major financial and business center.

Here is what to expect when training, teaching, and presenting to international audiences from Hong Kong.

## ??? THE REQUEST

The request for a program is likely to come from a major corporation on the northern side of Hong Kong Island, but can cover any number of sales, business, financial, or other topics.

## • • • GETTING THERE

Getting to Hong Kong is relatively uncomplicated. Because Hong Kong retains control over its own immigration policies, most Western visitors do not need a visa as long as they are not continuing on to mainland China. Passports are still required, and if you do need to continue on to mainland China, there are kiosks in the Hong Kong International Airport that issue visas and take photos.

Flying into Hong Kong is easy, and the airport at Chek Lap Kok (an island on the western side of Hong Kong) serves as a hub for several major Southeast Asian airlines such as Cathay Pacific, Dragon Air, Air Hong Kong, Oasis Hong Kong, and others. Do take the time change into consideration though, as Hong Kong is at GMT +8.

Embassy information is available at http://hongkong.usconsulate.gov/.

Once you've landed in Hong Kong and collected your baggage, there are several options for transportation into the major areas. The Airport Express is a train that takes about twenty minutes, and from the terminal shuttle buses are provided to the major hotels in Kowloon and Central. You should also check into combination passes that combine Airport Express fare with local transportation options (the Octopus). There are also buses (airbuses) and taxis that are slower and can vary greatly in price. Be careful though, as there are often taxis and vans operating illegally as taxis. These drivers and vehicles are not licensed, so in case of accidents, your insurance won't cover you.

Hong Kong has extremes of weather in both directions. In the summer months the climate can be downright subtropical, but in January and February there can be cold fronts. Tropical cyclones can occur anytime between May and November, causing rain, landslides, and flooding, which can all interfere with both training and travel.

There are also several holidays that may interfere with your travel and program scheduling:

- New Year's Day (January 1)
- Chinese (Lunar) New Year (in January, depends on the lunar calendar)
- Ching Ming Festival (April 5)
- Labour Day (May 1)
- Tuen Ng Festival (Dragon Boat Festival, usually in June)
- Hong Kong Special Administrative Region Establishment Day (July 1)
- Mid-Autumn Festival (around September)
- National Day of the People's Republic of China (October 1)
- Chung Yeung Festival (usually October)
- Winter Solstice or Christmas Day (December)

 ## PROGRAM DESIGN

Cantonese, a Chinese language, is spoken by 95 percent of people in Hong Kong. The amount of English spoken and understood can be somewhat limited in non-tourist areas, even though Hong Kong was a British colony until the end of the 1990s. However, most people in service industries and business communities speak English fluently, although you can help by sticking to simple sentence structures. You will also want to confirm the level of English spoken by your participants.

Standard lecturing will be the most familiar way of learning for your participants, but you can also mix it up with some interaction. The students will not feel comfortable presenting to the group on a subject they are not an expert in, so small group discussions will likely work best. Remember that many of your participants will be Chinese in heritage. For more information on training in China, see that chapter in this book.

 ## LOGISTICS

Getting your materials to Hong Kong is relatively easy and can be done using standard shipping companies such as UPS. Be sure to verify country-specific weight limits and standards and get all of your documentation in order, but there should be no difficulties in getting material delivered. However, as always, it is better to send your materials early to your in-country contact to ensure delivery and to take copies with you in case of last-minute problems.

The currency in Hong Kong is the Hong Kong dollar (HK), which fluctuates in rates between about 7.75 and 7.85 HK per U.S. dollar. Hong Kong dollars are issued by three different banks (all of which can exchange money) and come in banknotes:

- $10, green or purple (paper or plastic)
- $20, dark blue or light blue (old or new)
- $50, purple or green (old or new)
- $100, red
- $500, brown
- $1,000, gold (may not always be accepted due to counterfeiting concerns)

Coins include:

- $10, in bronze/silver, circular
- $5, in silver, circular, thicker
- $2, in silver, wavy-circular
- $1, in silver, circular, thinner
- 50c, in bronze, circular, larger

- 20c, in bronze, wavy-circular
- 10c, in bronze, circular, smaller

The Octopus card, originally introduced as a transit payment mechanism, can now be used all over the city as well.

##  PROGRAM DELIVERY

The expectations in terms of social roles are similar in Hong Kong to those in China. The expectation will be for lectures and minimal interaction, but localized case studies can be effective.

When being introduced to people and when teaching, respect is very important. You should always greet the most senior person in a meeting first and by his or her full title. While you are not expected to bow and will likely shake hands instead, be prepared for a less firm handshake. In terms of teaching, no one should ever be publicly told that he or she is wrong before, during, or after training. Instead, position yourself as a facilitator to help people become more effective by sharing your expertise, rather than as someone evaluating them and their knowledge.

Hong Kong business usually runs from 9 A.M. to 5 P.M. Monday through Friday, so try to keep your training within those standard business hours. Gift exchanges are also part of doing business in Hong Kong and are a part of establishing relationships. Gifts should be presented with both hands (so should business cards) and should be reciprocated. For more information, check out the chapter on China.

##  TECHNICAL REQUIREMENTS

Electricity in Hong Kong is run on 220V, so you can use the same adapters that you would for traveling to the UK (United Kingdom).

Internet access is plentiful in Hong Kong, with the region having one of the highest concentrations of broadband access anywhere. Most homes and businesses are connected to the Internet, so it is reasonable to assume that most hotels are as well. Wi-Fi is also beginning to become popular in public locations like airports and libraries.

##  ACCOMMODATIONS

Accommodations in Hong Kong can vary greatly from luxurious five-star hotels on Hong Kong Island to youth hostels and cheaper hotels in Kowloon. The best recommendation is to find somewhere close to your training site and to check with your in-country contact for recommendations. The government does maintain an online list of licensed hotels and guesthouses that can be found at www.hadla.gov.hk/english/.

Hong Kong is known for its cuisine, which integrates regional Chinese cuisine with other Asian and Western restaurants. Hong Kong is known for its dim sum, but there are many types of food that are worth trying. Be adventurous!

Do keep in mind that tipping is not a standard tradition in Hong Kong, and in some restaurants it can be seen as patronizing not to take your change or to leave a tip.

Hong Kong in general is one of the safest cities in terms of crime and personal safety, but you should still always be aware of your surroundings and use common sense. Don't give shopkeepers money until you've seen the object you're trying to buy, as you may find that they have suddenly run out. Hold bags and purses in front of you in crowded areas, and keep an eye on wallets and other valuables.

## GETTING AROUND

Hong Kong has myriad transportation options, including subways (MTR and KCR), trains, buses, a tram, light rail, and, of course, taxis. If you aren't staying at the same place where you are conducting your training, consider getting an Octopus card, which is valid on all public transportation (except a few minibuses and taxis). The Octopus card is a contact-free smart card that you don't have to take out of your wallet to use and that offers lower rates than paying cash directly for each ride. In addition to using the Octopus card in mass transit, you can use it in most convenience stores, vending machines, parking machines, and even some restaurant chains. You can add money at machines in most transportation stations, as well as at any merchants that accept the Octopus cards.

If for some reason you do decide not to take advantage of the transit system and you rent a car, remember that they drive on the left in Hong Kong!

## THE PEOPLE

Hong Kong is sometimes characterized as a place with multiple personalities due to its history as a British colony, its status as a refuge from the Communist Party of China during the Chinese Civil War, and as the only point of contact between China and the Western World before finally becoming mostly autonomous. Due to the mix of influences, Hong Kong is highly industrialized and is a center for finance and business.

About 95 percent of Hong Kong's population is of Chinese descent, with the rest being a mix of Indians, Pakistanis, Nepalese, Vietnamese, Filipinos, Indonesians, Europeans, Americans, Australians, Canadians, and Japanese. This mix can provide quite the variety in any meeting, so come prepared to learn!

Hong Kong is divided into four primary areas:

- Hong Kong Island is the site of the original British colony. The main business night-life, and government areas are still in this area. Your training is likely to occur in the densely populated northern part of the island, where business is centered, rather than the more leisurely southern part of the island.

- The New Territories (a name that is strangely outdated, as the islands where leased by the British in 1898) are a mix of cities and rural areas, but none of the cities is likely to be large enough to require trainers.

- Kowloon is the peninsula sticking out toward Hong Kong Island and the primary population center.

- The Outlying Islands are the 234 other islands incorporated as part of Hong Kong, with the largest being a residential island called Lantau.

## ‼️ PREPARATION

In addition to maintaining your professionalism and being prepared to experience new things, you can show some respect for your participants and contacts by learning a few phrases in Cantonese that may he helpful:

| | |
|---|---|
| Thank you | "dòjeh" |
| Hello | "néih hóu" |
| Welcome | "fòonying" |

Additional information can be found at www.amcham.org.hk/ or www.ethnologue.com.

If you need translation or an in-class interpreter, it will be interesting. There will likely be different languages represented. Check with your in-country contact, but at the very least plan on speaking slowly and distinctly and using simple sentences, at least in the beginning.

## PRESENTATION

Many of the same cultural standards of China hold true in Hong Kong as well, in terms of interacting with participants, so read that chapter for more in-depth information, but we'll cover some of the basics here.

Presenters are expected to be calm, patient, and modest. Showing impatience, anger, or seeming to brag can cause you to lose face and the respect of your participants. As we've said before, Hong Kong can have a significant diversity of cultures, so apologizing at the beginning of training for anything you may say that is inadvertently offensive may help smooth the training process.

Asian cultures in general will try to show as much respect for you as possible and so will rarely disagree or question anything you say, even when they don't understand. Make sure to ask clarifying questions to ensure comprehension, instead of just relying on affirmations. On the flip side of that, you should also avoid saying "No" outright to anyone. If someone has answered a question incorrectly, ask for other viewpoints, or ask how the person came up with that answer. Always maintain respect for the participants.

You will also want to take training slowly and include lots of breaks as, even if English is spoken, it can be hard for listeners and for you to communicate clearly. You will be tired at the end of the day and so will your participants!

Hong Kong is a vibrant area and conducting training in the city can be very exciting. Just remember this research and read up on Chinese customs and you should have a wonderful time!

**Helpful websites and references include:**

- http://hongkong.usconsulate.gov/
- www.hadla.gov.hk/english/
- www.hkta.org/login.html
- www.kwintessential.co.uk/etiquette/doing-business-hongkong.html
- www.wikipedia.com
- Amy Pletcher, independent writer and consultant, www.amypletcher.com

# India

**T**he best description for India is "large." Large geographically, large differences in people and culture, large differences in financial wealth and education. It is a largely English-speaking country because of previous British rule. The job market is large and continues to attract companies from around the world because of an attractive workforce and wages, among other things.

Here is information and what to expect when training, teaching, or presenting to international audiences from India.

## ??? THE REQUEST

American training is popular in India. Call center training is a very common request, as described in a great book, *The World Is Flat* by Thomas L Freidman (2006). And with all the outsourcing being done to India, American culture training is also very popular; companies want to know how to work successfully with Americans. Colleges and universities are receptive to American business speakers, in case you can work that in while you are there. Most people find Indians very receptive to American training.

## • • • GETTING THERE

The flight is long and you are likely to arrive at night, so you will be tired and confused by all of the noise and activity. Depending on where you are flying from in the United States and your connections, it could be twenty-three hours from the time you leave your home airport until you land in an Indian airport. The cities that training would likely occur in are Mumbai (formerly Bombay), Delhi, Kolkata (formerly Calcutta), Chennai (formerly Madras), Bangalore, and Hyderabad. And more. The time in India is UTC +5 ½, which is "on the other side of the clock."

Try to have someone meet you at the airport and take you to your hotel. A pre-arranged ride is important because there are taxi-related crimes that can happen to the unaware traveler. You can ask your hotel when making the reservation whether they can send a car to bring you from the airport to the hotel, and how much it will cost. If you do not have an arranged ride, go to the pre-paid taxi stand at the airport. Many people speak English so, theoretically, you will be able to understand and communicate with them. Just ask them to talk slowly because you will be adjusting to the accent. And you will likely need to do the same for them. You may have difficulty distinguishing between a "V" and a "W" sound. Asking people to repeat what they said is not considered rude.

You will need a valid passport and visa. Information can be found at www.indianembassy.org. Do not do what I did here. Check to see whether the embassy is open if you are going in person. I drove to the train station, took the train into Chicago, and took a cab to the embassy to get my visa for the trip. When I arrived, I found out it was closed for an Islam holiday that I had never heard of. Call before you make the trip.

Make sure you know when holidays are occurring, especially those that may affect your travel or training. The public holidays are Independence Day, Republic Day, and Gandhi Jayanti. There are also Hindu, Islam, and Christian holidays that some areas celebrate. The list of all these holidays is long, with some on the lunar calendar, which changes yearly, so we will not try and list them here.

The most favorable times to visit India are October through March. If you are able to travel then, you should miss the extreme heat and monsoon season.

 ## PROGRAM DESIGN

Hindi is the primary language, and English is commonly used for business and politics. Even though many people speak English, there may be language barriers. Their English is British English and people will likely have a heavy accent, so you should provide lots of handouts and written materials, because reading will help to convey the message. Take care if you are using only U.S.-based case studies. It is best if you can use an Indian or Asian case study or, at the very least, have someone who knows the culture review for relevance.

There are many more languages other than Hindi. Ethnologue.com lists twenty-two official languages at the writing of this book and says the total for India is 428. One contributor reports that the number of dialects is over 1,600.

Ronnie Sarkar (Senior Vice President, Digital Solutions, R.R. Donnelley), Indian-born with many years of offshoring experience, recommends a combination of training and certification to really get solid learning and skills. He does job skills training with a tiered approach. He recommends first doing a train-the-trainer, where Indian subject-matter experts (SMEs) come to the United States and learn fundamentals. Those SMEs then go back and train more participants. Participants are given some time to try skills out and practice. This helps them get the fundamentals. Then American trainers go to India and conduct Phase 2. This provides more advanced information/skills and includes skill practice. Phase 3 is certification. People must actually demonstrate the skills. Participants know in advance they will be given two chances to successfully demonstrate the skills necessary to do their jobs. They work very hard to complete this, take it seriously, and under these circumstances will ask the questions they need to be successful. Sarkar says this helps to make sure the participants have the theory as well as the practical application.

Education, diplomas, and certifications are very important to these audiences. Advanced education is respected. This means they will be willing participants and hungry for additional information, and they will respect a presenter's credentials. These credentials will mean more if they will give a company an edge over their competitor in the global market, and a company will be more likely to invest in training in that case.

Be cautious of subjectivity when you design the course. Many Indians deal best with black and white. Concepts and material become much less clear when there is a need to problem solve and troubleshoot because more than one answer might be correct. Make training and processes as precise as you can, and then give guidelines to handle the less precise stuff!

---

### TIPS FOR SUCCESS FROM KATHY LECK, EXECUTIVE VP CORPORATE EDUCATION, LAKE FOREST GRADUATE SCHOOL OF MANAGEMENT

- Make sure the class knows what the expectations are and review often.
- Obtain feedback regularly on what is being understood and adjust the course if needed.
- Manage the atmosphere of the class. Don't let questions take you off-track.
- Deliver on your promises in class. Teach them what you have promised to teach them.
- Help them make the leap from "knowing" to "being able to demonstrate" the concepts.

## LOGISTICS

Arrange for reliable airport transportation and have some Indian rupees with you when you arrive. You can exchange them in airports and banks. Avoid mailing materials if possible. Email is a better option for sending materials. Shipped materials can get lost or stolen. I shipped a box to Bangalore and several items and envelopes were missing from the box; it arrived wide open. FedEx and other companies are available in India. Offices can be bureaucratic and it can take a while to get things done. Be ready to be patient.

Take backups of everything in hard copy and on a memory stick.

Always have extra passport photos with you. You may be asked for one to use the Internet, or for other reasons.

## PROGRAM DELIVERY

Design the program to include fun, activities, and even role plays. Demonstrations, culturally appropriate case studies, and working in small groups work well. They love games, music, movies, and cricket. Those topics all work well for illustrations or examples. It is good to start with something fun and end with something fun. One contributor says to put something that is not important at the beginning, because people will not necessarily arrive on time. Indians, like many Asians, tend to be event-oriented and not necessarily time-oriented.

Relationships are highly valued. You should plan to include extra time for interaction. And use the interaction to gauge whether people are understanding the content or not. You will likely find this audience has an appetite for knowledge.

Jo Paulson, consultant/coach with HR Anexi Pvt Ltd., recommends that you let people sit where they want in the classroom. Women will probably sit together and men will probably sit together. Males and females tend to mix less in most settings. Let them choose so that they will be comfortable. Be attentive as to whether mixed-gender activities will work.

Watch for head signals in India. We are familiar with left to right meaning no and up and down meaning yes. A side-to-side head motion means "maybe" or "okay."

Cell phone interruptions are very common. Group activities will keep them engaged. Use adult learning principles and never embarrass anyone publicly.

## TECHNICAL REQUIREMENTS

Power supply is 220V/50Hz. Carry a universal adaptor. Be very cautious about computer viruses and careful about using other people's files or discs on your computer. Expect electricity outages; they happen regularly and are sometimes short and sometimes not (major corporate facilities will likely have backup power). PowerPoint presentations are common, but always have a backup presentation method ready. Virtual learning is fairly common, especially in Bangalore, Bombay (Mumbai), and Chennai.

Cell phones are very common and Internet access is generally available, although affected by power outages.

## ACCOMMODATIONS

There is a broad range of hotels. Get advice locally as to where to stay. Training will likely be scheduled at hotels or on company sites. Your in-country contact can recommend accommodations that will be suitable. In fact, ask the in-country contact to handle that for you. If you are making your own reservations, going with five-star hotels will help to ensure safety. Making hotel reservations in advance is recommended. I took a side trip to Mysore and tried to get a hotel room when I arrived. I tried three hotels in the region I wanted to be in. None had vacancies. The last one had a sister hotel that they directed me to. I went directly there, toured a room, and as I approached the front desk someone off the street was asking for the room. I reserved it just in time. Whew! What a relief.

Don't drink the water or anything that has been touched by water (if you can see that it is still wet). Always check the bottle seal to make sure the water bottle has not been opened and refilled with tap water. Only eat cooked foods, not raw. Never eat or touch food with your left hand. It is the hand people clean themselves with and is considered unclean. Wash your hands before and after meals. Don't be surprised if you see cockroaches.

## GETTING AROUND

In the cities you will see huge mansions and nice neighborhoods, right next to slums and people living in shanties. Ask for advice if you are going to take a walk.

Cabs are common transportation methods. (I am pretty committed to not drive in India.) It is possible for a cab driver to refuse to pick up a Caucasian. Some people will reserve a driver and car for hours or a day. They will be available for you at any time. It is fairly reasonable and very convenient and reliable. From the airport, hire a pre-paid taxi to take you to your destination (the booth is outside of the airport and open twenty-four hours a day). Check to be sure your fare includes luggage; you may be charged extra for that when you reach the destination. Honking is very common. It is a signal that "I am here" and not a sign that they are mad at you.

Travelers are advised not to give money to beggars (unless they are performing for you and you want to). You can give money to the church or temple to distribute to those in need instead of giving it directly to the beggars. Direct giving only encourages them to do this begging more aggressively. When you give to one person, you will likely have many more approach you. Some beggars carry a child with them and ask you to give something so the child can eat. Some beggars actually borrow children for this purpose to get sympathy contributions. Women should ignore the stares of men on the streets and should wear skirts below knee length. Any bags that you carry should zip closed. Hold carried items close to you to avoid pickpockets. Put valuables in an under-clothing pouch.

 ## THE PEOPLE

There are over a billion people in India. Castes are prevalent. There are four basic castes and many sub-castes. These statuses are born into and are indicators of social standing, and often educational opportunity. In the upper castes, women often have the opportunity for education. That is not always true in the lower castes. Gender differences will often come up in business settings. This is why participants should sit where they are comfortable. Talk to your in-country contact regarding any additional sensitivity.

Eighty-eight percent of the country is Hindu. Islam is common in some parts of India. Christianity is present, but only about 2 percent. Again, ask your in-country contact whether there is anything you should know about this topic and the groups you will be training. Avoiding any references to religion is a good start.

The country had British rule for many years, which is why English is so very common. Independence for that part of the country was achieved in 1947, when the territory became India, Pakistan, and Bangladesh. The history and culture are so rich that we can't possibly give you everything here. It will help to do some extra research.

People are fairly open. They will ask a lot of questions initially. They are knowledge, information, and evidence hungry. They are proud of their education.

Do not make any assumptions if men are holding hands; it is very common. Men and women holding hands in some conservative parts of the country is not encouraged.

One contributor tells us that sometimes you will hear "It's not possible," but that's not always true. Be prepared for outrageous rules and don't always believe they are true (for example, if someone says a building is locked, check it). If they say "no" it could mean "I don't understand." Ask open-ended questions and not "yes or no" questions. You may witness larger swings in emotions, both outrage and joy, than you would see in the West.

Use caution when asking for directions. People will want to help you, and you may hear "I think it is this way," but they may not be sure and may inadvertently send you in the wrong direction. You may find standing in line to be different. People will often all go to the front of the line and crowd, rather than waiting patiently in a straight Western line.

## !!! PREPARATION

Practice speaking slowly and deliberately. The main language of India is Hindi, although, depending on where you go, there might be a different language or dialect spoken. (In Hindi, "namaste" can be either hello or goodbye.)

Women should make sure they always cover their shoulders and never wear shorts. Suits are good. Long pants and long skirts are fine. Men are fine with dress pants and a shirt and should check with their in-country contact on whether they should take a sport coat or suit.

Bring toilet paper with you. And rest up for your flight!

## THE PRESENTATION

Most people in corporate settings understand English, so translation is generally not needed. Building in interaction will be helpful in the learning, but lectures are accepted as well. People will take pride in learning and understanding. Pre-work and homework will likely be helpful and taken seriously.

John Chandra, technical project lead from India, suggests you "know your subject matter really, really well." He says your Indian audience is likely to be very well educated and will not be shy about pointing out mistakes to the trainer.

There may be a large mix of talent and academic background in your audience. Plan to train for the lowest common denominator in the classroom. Be very direct and detailed and help them to figure it out. Don't rely on standard methods of measuring whether or not the participants have learned. The Indians are polite and will smile and shake their heads. You may interpret this to mean they understand. But they may not. Ask application questions to see whether they understand and can apply what they are learning.

Aldrin Bogi, leader from Youth with a Mission, tells us Indians are motivated when the environment in the classroom is competitive. He has had success starting each session with review questions from the previous sessions. He calls it a "Mad Minute" and asks five quick questions and rewards the people who are right. It is a great energizer and it also gets people back from breaks on time.

### Tips for Success

- Be approachable and open.

- Stay humble. Don't assume your methods are better.

- Use plenty of handouts and written materials.

- Plan to let the audience talk and participate.

- Plan for how to see application of learning. Understanding it and being able to do it are two different things.

- Allow for gender differences in a classroom setting. Women may not mix comfortably with men.

- A female trainer should stay humble and show respect, particularly to men who are older than she is.

## A TRUE EXPERIENCE FROM RENIE MCCLAY

I swear this happened. I was speaking with a peer to a group of professors at Mt. Carmel College in Bangalore. As my peer was speaking, I noticed some chipmunks/ground squirrels running in and out of the air conditioner unit in the back of the room. There were four or five of them. My peer didn't notice as she was speaking to the group. As I was speaking, they began to run to the front of the room, toward the stage. She started squealing (won't she be happy to read this), and they veered to the audience. The teachers lifted up their feet, the chipmunks ran underneath their chairs and to an open door. The teachers made no noise, just sat waiting for us to continue. I said, "You don't really see this much in Chicago." They said, "It happens all the time."

India is a relatively easy country to train in because the language barriers are reduced compared to other countries. Being sensitive to the culture will help to ensure success. The fact that they love and see the value of education helps keeps things exciting. Many trainers develop relationships here that last a long time.

**Helpful websites and references include:**

- Freidman, T.L (2006). *The World Is Flat*. New York: Farrar, Straus and Giroux.

- www.indianembassy.org

# Indonesia

The Republic of Indonesia is a Southeast Asian country made up of over 17,000 islands and 230 million people. There are over three hundred ethnic groups there, ranging from modern cities to isolated tribes. Locals speak many different languages. There is vast diversity here, from the people to the vegetation and the wildlife.

Here is what to expect when training, teaching or presenting to international audiences from Indonesia.

## ??? THE REQUEST

The request for a program could come from a company, university, or government agency.

Clarify the purpose of the presentation, the audience, dates, times, and locations. Communicate on an ongoing basis to have your hosts review the objectives and agenda for the program. They can give you feedback and suggestions for success.

## • • • GETTING THERE

The most common location for a program to be presented in Indonesia would be on the island of Java. Jakarta is the capital city and the traffic is frantic. If you are presenting at a hotel, it is best to stay right there and not have to deal with the traffic issues. It is often hot and hectic, with lots of traffic.

All foreign nationals need a visa to enter, go to www.passportsandvisas.com/visas/indonesia.asp. Avoid training during the month of Ramadan. This is a thirty-day Islamic holiday and it moves up eleven days each year, based on the new moon sighting. This makes it difficult to list here, although through the year 2010 it is in the months of

September and August. The Indonesian holiday calendar is a mix of Islam, Christian, and Hindu celebrations. There are too many to list here, but check before planning your trip.

Dates are written in the day/month/year format. Indonesia is made up of three time zones. Java and Bali are GMT +7. Also check for any health concerns at the Center for Disease Control website. You will likely need shots and anti-malarial meds.

There are reasons to leave your travel agenda with friends and to register with your country's consulate when you arrive. This is a tsunami/flooding/typhoon region as well as an active volcano region. And in the past U.S. and Australian travelers have been targets for violence. This is likely because of the past U.S. policy regarding East Timor. Although most agree this shouldn't be an issue today, it is best to take precautions. Let people know where you will be when traveling there and check for government travel advisories on the U.S. Department of State's website (www.travel.state.gov).

## PROGRAM DESIGN

Dr. Cisca Sugiro is a senior research scientist who has trained technicians on complex x-ray data acquisition. Cisca was born and raised in Jakarta, Indonesia. She suggests that training is best conducted in a hotel or restaurant (because Indonesians like to eat regularly).

The official language is Bahasa Indonesian. (There are many regional languages.) The translated words will be larger, so you should leave enough space on your slides to have the words expanded. Paper is A4 size, so expect the length of the pages to be longer when they are printed on paper for handouts.

A contributor tells us role plays will not work well because people are uncomfortable playing a role and will not like feedback unless it is all positive. Localized case studies and group discussion will likely work better. Compliments and praise are very well received, so we recommend you build on people's strengths. If you decide to have a competition such as a learning game, it should be designed as a team competition. Individual competition will not work well. For prizes, the winning team members will like pins or pens with the name of the company or event on it. Food is always appreciated as well, so treats from home (candy or cookies) will likely be a hit.

## LOGISTICS

The money is rupiah. We are told everything is cheap in Indonesia. ATMs, banks, and currency exchange places are available on Java, Bali, and Lambok for exchanging money. It is advised that you get your cash before you visit other islands. Also, be wary of credit card fraud.

## PROGRAM DELIVERY

An interpreter should be available to help with discussions and clarifications. Provide finger foods for regular snacking. Have tea bottles, tea boxes, and mineral water available for people to drink.

Participants are very sensitive. They don't want to say what they feel. They will often say "yes" when they mean "no." There are language subtleties that will give clues that this yes doesn't really mean yes. You will need to be tuned in for that. They would rather not say a direct no. (Look for "yes, but" or evading the question altogether.) Design for feedback to be gathered in small groups to allow for anonymity.

Indonesian participants will let trainers make mistakes rather than correcting them in public. They will want to let them "save face." They consider it an embarrassment to be corrected in public. They will be most appreciative of praise for a group accomplishment, rather than individually.

## TECHNICAL REQUIREMENTS

Converters and plugs will need to be used for 220 volt outlets. Some places will still use slide projectors, so you will need to bring your own computer and projector if you wish to use one.

If you use videos, have them subtitled in Indonesian. If you are going to use PowerPoint projectors, DVDs, CDs, or videos (PAL format), check for compatibility before you go. Internet usage and cell phone coverage will vary based on where you are located.

## ACCOMMODATIONS

Book a higher-end hotel for your stay; this is not a place to try to save money. Everything is quite cheap though, so that should not be much of a problem.

The food is hot and spicy. You can ask for your food to be less spicy or with no pepper in it. Never drink the tap water; always use bottled water (even for brushing your teeth).

To be safe, don't eat street food. Be selective with restaurants. We suggest that you ask your host for suggestions. Some restaurants will be set up so you will sit on the floor to eat.

It is hot and humid. There is lots of pollution and dust. Wash hands often. Wash fruits and vegetables with clear bottled water, even if you are removing the skin, because the dirt or water they have been previously washed in will contaminate the inside of the fruit or vegetable.

For breakfast, lunch, and dinner, rice is eaten with chicken, beef, vegetables, fish, or shrimp. Noodles are sometimes eaten. Bowls with spoons and plates with forks are used. No bread is used except as a snack or finger food. Never put your elbows on the table.

Second-story toilets are never built over the stove on the first floor. Toilets are typically ceramic holes on the floor. Public toilets are unisex, but the doors are built from the floor to the ceiling so you will have privacy. Bring your own toilet paper or tissue.

##  GETTING AROUND

The traffic is extreme. They don't seem to obey any traffic rules. However, they are very cautious, so there are not that many accidents. Take a Blue Bird taxi (at least at the time of this writing). They will be dependable and use a meter.

Getting to your location, you might take a three-wheeled bicycle seat ride to get you there fastest.

Jakarta is a harbor town. Shipping has always been central to the commerce of the islands. There is a heavy Dutch influence that is evident. This is a prosperous city. There are lots of western shopping and night club opportunities.

##  THE PEOPLE

Hospitality is outstanding. If you stay with a family, your host will give you his or her bed and sleep on the floor. You are a guest and will not be allowed to stay where there is no bed to offer you. Mosquito nets are very important because they always have mosquitoes. Insect repellent and closing of windows also helps. Cold water is available to wash with, not hot water. Water can be "cooked" for you to have heated water. The beds will likely be on a low raised platform. Sometimes you will have floor mattresses. Food is usually cooked on a gas stove. If you are invited to someone's home to stay, you can bring gifts for your host such as a scarf or serving platter for a woman and pen for a man. Christmas gift giving is not too common. The primary vacation occurs during Ramadan. Everything closes down.

Many families have several rooms for the maid and boarders. The maid will clean and cook for the family. Boarders are men from the outlying villages who work in the city. They pay to stay during the week so they can work and then return to their families in the village on the weekend. This provides income to families in the city and accommodations for the workers who need it.

The mixture of religions is unique. The country is over 80 percent Muslim, about 10 percent Christian, and also Hindu and Buddhism. All must be respected. It is best to not discuss religion, but recognize that it is integral to people's lives. Indonesian people are from many ethnic groups, including Chinese, Javanese, Sundanese, Madurese, Buginese, Batak, Kayak, Balinese, Minangkabau, and more. Many Indonesians go by only one name.

Indonesia is made up of at least 13,000 islands (published numbers show between 13,000 and 17,000). It contains both Australia and Asian wildlife and plants. Nature has blessed the island with dramatic volcano activity as well as great aquatic biodiversity. The country started early as a trading outpost.

Indonesian is the primary language, but often not people's primary language. Most people speak one of seven hundred local languages. Ask your in-country contact if translation is necessary.

### Do's and Don'ts

- Don't talk with your face too close to the other person's.
- Never put your feet on the table or desk.
- Always use your right hand, never the left, to shake hands or eat. The left hand is used for cleansing the body and is considered unclean.
- Always try to smile; never use a stern face. Politeness is very important in this culture.
- Have someone you know introduce you to someone you don't.
- Use a travel agency or guide to find places instead of stopping someone on the street to ask for directions.
- Don't look people in the eyes. It is considered rude.
- Do not criticize the government; journalists have been arrested or ordered to leave the country.
- Be on time for business events, but don't expect your audience to be prompt.
- Allow for pauses and time to think. A fifteen-second pause would not be unusual in a conversation.
- Do not kiss in public.
- Don't interrupt people who are talking. If you need to pass in between them, wait until one of them gives you permission by nodding, then hold your head down. You do not have to say "excuse me" if you have been given permission. Interruptions are considered very rude.

The Indonesians respect the elderly a lot. The older you are, the wiser you are. There is nothing wrong with aging. They are surprised by countries that use chemicals and surgeries to look young again.

## PREPARATION

Clothing must be businesslike. Wear solid colors, nothing flowery. Wear cotton, nothing too heavy, because it is hot and humid. This is a Muslim country, so women should dress conservatively. Always wear sleeves. Never wear anything sleeveless or use low-cut necklines. Never wear shorts. Pants and skirts are acceptable. If skirts are worn, they must be below the knee or ankle length. Dark, conservative colors will be preferred. Even when swimming, bathing suits are unacceptable. Bathing shorts are okay. Women should never wear dangling earrings. Only posts or ear knots are acceptable.

Eating is a non-stop ritual in Indonesia, so make sure that there is always food available for the participants and allow people to partake often of small breaks. The bottled tea is also important to provide to them.

Seating in the program should never mix levels. Executives should be at a separate table from employees if they are all in the same program.

English is common in business; you may or may not need a translator. A couple of Indonesian words that may be helpful include:

| hello | "halo" |
| more informal hello | "he" pronounced "hey" |
| thank you | "terima kasih" |
| goodbye | "dadah," pronounced "duh-duh." |

## THE PRESENTATION

Avoid boring presentations. They will enjoy clean jokes. Also avoid topics of human rights, religion, and politics. Do not make jokes or criticize customs. Talk about travel and food. Discussing your accomplishments will be considered bragging.

You will need to provide breaks for the Muslim participants to pray, so lunch should be one to one and a half hours long to allow time for eating and praying for those who choose to pray. Providing a separate room that is available for prayer will be appreciated and be considered respectful. Islamic participants will wear a head covering throughout the program. The program will often be scheduled to start at 7 A.M. and continue until 5 P.M. Their dinner time is typically around 6 or 7 P.M.

People enjoy making small amounts of money as prizes for performing well. You can use these as incentives to learn in a supportive, not strongly competitive, way.

If you have a test, it is okay, but the results must be kept private (only the individual should see his or her own results) and not be shared with anyone else.

Badminton and tennis are common sports, so you can use these in examples if you wish. Weather is not a good topic for conversations. The Indonesians have suffered many weather effects from tsunamis, earthquakes, floods, mud slides, and volcano eruptions.

Indonesia is a very multi-ethnic country, with strong traditions that need to be respected. This is a country in which your in-country contact will be valuable to provide you with feedback and advice. You may want to begin training sessions by apologizing for any mistakes you may make culturally and telling them your intention is to honor their culture. Enjoy this very different land!

**Helpful websites include:**

- www.passportsandvisas.com/visas/indonesia.asp
- www.travel.state.gov
- www.wikipedia.org

# Japan

*"Culture is more often a source of conflict than of synergy.
Cultural differences are a nuisance at best and often a disaster."*

*Dr. Geert Hofstede*

**D**r. Hofstede's words are more true for Westerners in Japan than in many other countries. His work includes a comprehensive study of how culture influences values in the workplace. He was able to identify a model with five primary dimensions of differentiating cultures: Power Distance, Individualism, Masculinity, Uncertainty Avoidance, and Long-Term Orientation. An interactive display of these dimensions can be accessed on his website (www.geert-hofstede.com), where you can view the differences on each dimension for your culture and that of the culture you are visiting. When you conduct the analysis for the United States and Japan, you see the significant differences between the two cultures, which gives you some insight into this interesting place to do business.

You will, at some point, embarrass yourself or others during your trip to this land. Your worries are well-founded, yet most infractions will be pardoned. Much of this chapter will be spent on the cultural challenges in Japan. If you can avoid a few simple cultural missteps, you can use the principles in the other chapters of the book to create your content and conduct a successful training session. All efforts made to familiarize yourself with customs and protocol will be appreciated, but there are many.

## ??? THE REQUEST

Once you know you will be traveling to Japan for training, start the process of making name cards or meishi (pronounced may-she). They are similar to our business cards and include your name, title, and other business contact information. They are two-sided, one side in English and the other in Japanese. There are many online companies that can assist you with layout and produce these cards. In Japan, the meishi is an extension of the person. They are treated with much respect and there is ceremony surrounding their exchange. Be sure you have enough produced for every person you will encounter during your trip. More about the exchange later.

Typical training requests could be anything related to business or teaching English.

## • • • GETTING THERE

A valid passport and visa are required for travel to Japan. We recommend registering your trip with the U.S. State Department online at https://travelregistration.state.gov as a "Short-Term Traveler." As with all other destinations for international travel, be sure to leave ample time for this process. If you have a choice in the matter, try to schedule your trip for early to mid-April or late October. The temperatures are milder and it is drier at these times. The climate varies greatly throughout the year across the country, so check weather averages for the dates you are scheduled to teach. Avoid packing in large suitcases, and choose several smaller bags instead. There isn't much space in storage compartments for large baggage. Do leave space for travel tissues. Public restrooms are often void of paper products, people are expected to bring their own. A handkerchief is a good idea for drying washed hands throughout the trip.

Tokyo is nine hours ahead of GMT, as are other cities you may be asked to work in such as Hiroshima, Kyoto, Nagasaki, Osaka, and Yokohama. Since the days are totally reversed, our sources recommend arriving at least two days in advance to give your body a chance to adjust to the new clock. The language spoken is Japanese, but some people in the larger cities know a little English.

Major holidays are scheduled nationally and the whole country is off work. This also means that trains, planes, and hotel rooms are booked and busy during these times. Try to avoid the following dates and their adjoining weekends:

- New Year's: December 27 to January 4
- Golden Week: April 29 to May 5
- OBon: August 15
- School breaks: end of March to beginning of April and from end of July through August There are other holidays, but some are on a lunar calendar.

## PROGRAM DESIGN

Like name cards, gifts are a unique exchange in this culture. They are often expected, but they need not be extravagant. It is important to plan for gift exchanges before you leave on your adventure. Ideas include some small items representing your home town: wine, whiskey, bourbon, fruit, or small items from high-end department stores. Name brands are very popular. Avoid gift sets of four items, the number 4 is considered unlucky since its pronunciation is similar to the word "death." Gifts should be wrapped neatly (no white paper), given with two hands (like name cards) at the end of your visit, and are not expected to be opened in front of you.

Additionally when planning your trip, you should know that conservative business attire is the norm. Casual or over-accessorizing (for women) is never appropriate in a business setting, so select clothes that are simple and conservative. Think about your shoes (and your socks for that matter!) because you will be removing them frequently. Slip-ons are your best choice. Women should chose a low heel to avoid being taller than men.

Give yourself ample time for building relationships if this is a new group you are working with. The social aspect of business is important, and much time can be consumed getting to know one another and not necessarily building your content. A good in-country contact will be critical to the success of your program for many reasons, so it is important to cultivate that relationship carefully and without haste. You will also want to add an additional one-third more time to your plan for working with interpreters and translators. Verify with your in-country contact that your audience will require translation, but if you aren't sure at the start, build it into your plan for a conservative estimate of the time it will take to complete the work. An experienced translator recommends giving material to the translator more than one day in advance so that he or she is able to review it.

For the Japanese, learning is typically a very passive experience. Teachers are seen as authorities on their subjects, and participants are in attendance to listen only. Because learning in Japan is rarely an interactive experience, you will want to think about your subject and how it can be appropriately communicated with little or no assistance from your audience. Although the Japanese do appreciate engaging and interactive training when it is done well, they will not facilitate the process without first establishing their level of comfort. Making in-roads into their social networks will enable you to break down those barriers; however, if your presentation is short, there may not be time to get there. Don't be alarmed if the feeling in the room seems like disinterest. Do not mistake this mood for disagreement either. That is not necessarily the case. The Japanese culture teaches people to avoid uncertainty, so lack of participation is simply a product of that aversion. You need to decide whether you are willing to break out of the typical role of teacher and go to the next level. Your efforts will not go unappreciated. Since they are not taught this way typically, they do appreciate it when they see it.

Regardless, know that you should not build a large chunk of time into your presentation for questions and answers. This will not happen as it does in other countries, even if you have laid the foundation for "interactive" discussions. Use your in-country contacts to anticipate questions and build the responses into your presentation instead of as a technique to engage the audience. If soliciting opinions—especially where frankness is important—consider using anonymous surveys/questionnaires rather than forum discussion or Q&A sessions. Build in time for smoke breaks.

Consider the audience and their relationships to each other. Do they all know each other? If not, they will be reluctant to participate and risk being wrong in a situation in which they are not established. Is there a wide range of experience levels in the crowd? If so, the less-experienced participants will defer their responses to the more experienced learners.

Because you can't always count on building in interactions, you must heavily rely on the presentation materials, making them as interesting and engaging as possible. If there was ever a time to avoid bullet points, this would be it. When planning interaction, consider the fact that Japanese people are not used to making presentations to other people. Do not expect them to present to the class. In colleges it is not common—younger people may adjust, but people over thirty will not be used to it. Group teach-backs or role plays in front of the class should be avoided. Small discussion groups may be a better bet.

The Japan External Trade Organization (JETRO) has created a document entitled *Communicating with Japanese in Business* that can be another good source of information for intercultural communication with Japanese.

## LOGISTICS

Planning and logistics can be a bit tricky.

The currency is the yen (JPY - ¥). Notes are in denominations of ¥10,000, 5,000, 2,000, and 1,000. Coins are in denominations of ¥500, 100, 50, 10, 5, and 1. All money must be exchanged at an authorized bank or currency exchange. Major credit cards are accepted in urban areas at stores, hotels, and restaurants; however, Japan has a strong cash culture. Credit cards may not be accepted in the country. It is always good to have some Japanese yen cash on hand. Few ATMs accept foreign credit or debit cards. Traveler's Cheques in Japanese yen or U.S. dollars are best to avoid additional exchange rate charges.

Allow lots of time for shipping materials, or bring them with you.

## PROGRAM DELIVERY

When you reach to Japan, you will need to meet with your in-country contact and possibly your interpreter. There may be others to visit before your training. This is the appropriate time to exchange meishi (name cards). Personal attention to this activity will serve you well. Most Japanese will greet you with a bow, but some may offer a hand for a handshake. If you are bowed to, try to imitate the bow back to the person. The bow's length and depth signify different things in the Japanese culture, but if you imitate exactly what was given to you, this is a safe rule. After exchanging bows, offer or accept the meishi with two hands. When offering your card, be sure the Japanese side is facing up. Take time to read and pronounce the name on the card before moving to the next (if your group is large). The senior-most people are introduced first. The cards themselves must be treated with respect, held in a case and never written on (except on your own), don't ever pass them out playing-card style or stuff them into a pocket or purse. Remember, they are an extension of the person and must be treated with great respect. If you are with a large group, it is appropriate to spread the cards on the table in front of you and refer to them during conversation. Once introductions are finished, the meeting begins. Long pauses or significant periods of silence are common, so don't let them throw you off. The Japanese use the time to think about what has been said and formulate their responses or questions.

Business is conducted punctually. You should plan to begin on time, stick to scheduled breaks, and end your session at the scheduled time. Your participants will expect it and they will adhere to it. However, after the session is over, social timeframes become more unstructured.

Because few Japanese speak fluent English (most have taken English in high school but not much beyond), it is recommended that you obtain the help of an interpreter.

As with any other country, it is important to plan time into your schedule to meet with and rehearse the presentation with the interpreter. The Japanese word order for speaking is exactly opposite from English. The earlier you can give material to the translator, the better quality your translation will be, particularly if the topic is unfamiliar to them. Whether you have engaged an interpreter or not, speak at a moderate rate and use correct grammatical English. If you try to "make it easier" and speak broken English, your listener will become confused and frustrated. Be sure to provide written copies of all materials and presentations. If you can have documents translated, be sure you are able to have all translations approved by an in-country representative. It is acceptable to repeat important points during a spoken presentation to ensure they were received and understood.

As with all other cultures that do not speak your native language, be sure you are not giving examples unfamiliar to them or using jargon, idioms, or colloquialisms that will not translate. Since your audience will not feel comfortable enough to ask questions, it is important to remove any common barriers to learning that you can before, during, and after the presentation. Common interests are sumo wrestling, martial arts (judo or karate), baseball, football, and soccer. Examples or anecdotes with these topics will likely be understood.

Once the session has concluded, you will likely be expected to socialize with some of your contacts. This too is the way of the Japanese and their social way of doing business. If you anticipate many such opportunities, a little research on restaurant etiquette is advised, in addition to the tips in the People section of this chapter.

Although this is often overstated, many Japanese do tend to avoid sticking out and disrupting harmony. Japanese tend to be very flexible with foreigners and customs. Be polite, warm, and friendly, but don't be overly casual or close, or your audience may consider you insincere. Treat all of these situations as great opportunities to expand your mind and your horizons, and I think you will be delighted at what you will learn while teaching.

Julie Jacques shares her experience as the manager of sales training in the audiovisual field. She was training in Japan in 1998:

> The training was geared toward product features and benefits selling for one of our newer printers. I worked with an interpreter and one of our company product managers. The group consisted of distributors for our products. One of the first things that struck me was that, in most cases, the Japanese internalize what they are learning by strictly listening, and many times their eyes

are closed while doing so. This was extremely disarming, as we are so accustomed to making eye contact with our learners (even though, unfortunately, they may sometimes appear to be sleeping!). The Japanese culture learns, in many cases, through a "brain dump." It was difficult for me to engage them by asking or answering questions, as they typically don't learn that way. I experienced resistance to our Western-style experiential training approach (although when training in Beijing, China, I found the trainees much more open to hands-on role play involvement). They understood the content, but went about it differently.

There were some other dynamics going on while I was in Japan as well. Being an American female was tough. There still existed some cultural and gender credibility issues. As a result, I had to defer some of their operational questions to the head of our Japanese subsidiary, a Japanese male. I insisted that he remain in the room throughout the training to help address questions and issues.

## TECHNICAL REQUIREMENTS

The electricity in Japan is 100 volts, and there are two cycles (50/60). In Northeast (including Tokyo) it is 50 cycles and in the Southwest (including Osaka, Kyoto, and Nagoya), it is 60 cycles. Bring your converter, although a contributor said he used his equipment from the United States with no difficulties. Japanese outlets are two-pronged; there are no three-pronged outlets. Remember, U.S. DVDs may not play in Japanese players (and vice-versa). Videotapes are fine—both use the NTSC standard. CDs and cassettes are fine, as well. If you're borrowing a computer for a presentation, be prepared to see menus, labels, and dialog boxes in Japanese. Internet access tends to be somewhat more limited than in the United States, so confirm that access will be available if you expect to need it (and check the speed of the connection, as well, if bandwidth is a concern). There is Internet access from major hotels and Internet cafes, but it can be pricy.

Your cell phone will very likely not work in Japan. Public phones are often around, you can rent a phone, or you can buy a prepaid phone very easily.

## ACCOMMODATIONS

When choosing where to stay, you can certainly find Western-style hotels, or you could be more adventuresome and select a Japanese-style hotel or ryokan. You will find few

Western brand-named hotels, but the large Japanese-named hotels will be costly. There are business hotels, often with cramped quarters but lesser price tags. If you choose to go with a ryokan, you will receive wooden clogs and kimonos. These inns are more expensive because of a government "accommodation tax," but may well be worth the extra cost just for the experience.

A little advice for the new traveler: Do research on Japanese toilets and their proper use. We will not go into the proper techniques here, but suffice it to say, they are not always self-explanatory and it will be quite unnerving to experience them without knowing what you are doing. There are many resources on the Internet for this information, so be sure to do a little research on your own. You may want to bring hand sanitizer or wipes with you.

You will find tap water acceptable, and food preparation standards are high.

## GETTING AROUND

Tokyo's subway and rail systems are efficient and comprehensive. Once you understand them, you can get anywhere in the city. They publish timetables in English for ease of use. Emergency numbers on all phones are 110 for police and 119 for fire or ambulance. On a public phone, press the red button and then the digits and no money is needed. Police kiosks (called Koban) have a metallic pentagon symbol on the front of the building and are open to assist you. The AMDA International Medical Information Center (http://homepage3.nifty.com/amdack/english/E-index.html) provides English-speaking personnel if calling during the work week. Also available is the Tokyo English Lifeline (www.telljp.com) or the Japan Helpline (www.jhelp.com/en/jhlp.html), where English-speaking counseling and referrals are provided. The U.S, Embassy is in Tokyo and in Osaka. The U.S. Embassy in Japan website is http://tokyo.usembassy.gov.

There are many major cities where training may take place. Tokyo is one, others are Osaka, Yokohama, Sapporo, Nagoya, Kobe, or Kyoto. There is great diversity in terrain in Japan, with much of it mountainous and uninhabitable. For this reason, the cities are very crowded.

Taxis are very available to take you from place to place, and they are considered very safe. Ask about the fare before you go, so you are not surprised. You may need cash to pay it.

## THE PEOPLE

Business in Japan is done through networks. Familiarity is important for successful interactions. People conduct themselves quite formally and cordially. The service in Japan is exceptional, each professional taking the customer service aspect of his or her job quite seriously. Drinking is part of business. Many people will go out for drinks, and if you are asked, you should go. If you do not drink alcohol, drink juice or a soft drink. Being that they are a very polite and quiet society, drinking is an icebreaker and a place to get to know a person. At lunch or dinner, don't proceed with eating or drinking until the host has invited you to begin. Never pour yourself a drink, but allow someone else to do it. Typically, the youngest will pour drinks for the elders. If you take your hosts out, take them to a Western restaurant and insist on paying. It is polite for them to decline, but it is appropriate for you to pay if you invite them out. Learn some key phrases surrounding going out for a meal:

- "itadakimasu" means before dinner
- "gochisou-sama-deshita" means after
- "Sumimasen" means excuse me
- "kekko desu" is to say you have had enough

Tipping is not expected and, when paying the bill, do not openly display money. They rarely say "no" directly, so use your keen observation to determine whether they really mean "yes" or not. If it is any consolation, even the Japanese have a difficult time distinguishing between the non-committal yes and a true answer of agreement.

Japanese will ask direct, and sometimes forward or even embarrassing questions, such as your age, how much money you make, or how you live. They are not trying to be rude, and you don't have to answer, but be gracious. Find out from your in-country contact about addressing people by name; typically the Japanese do not address each other by first name, as this is reserved for children and close friends only. A good rule to follow is to add "san" to the last name of the person you are addressing, so Mr. Yamaguchi becomes Yamaguchi-san.

Naturally, personalities and values vary from person to person, but one of our contributors found many Japanese to be friendly and polite, if somewhat distant, thoughtful, punctual, sometimes ethnocentric, and often trusting. Earnestness, diligence, and accountability were among the most important traits to exhibit.

## ‖‖ PREPARATION

Research the specific area you will be visiting. Have Japanese yen with you. We suggest you know the material cold, as you will be seen as an expert. This will not be a great culture for facilitating the knowledge within the group (unless that has been identified as your purpose). Be prepared to add some value.

A few words that may come in handy are

thank you      "Dōmo"

hello          "Konnichiwa"

goodbye        "sayōnara"

## THE PRESENTATION

First and foremost, whether translated or not, speak slowly, clearly, and in uncomplicated sentences. Listen carefully as well. Japanese study English in middle and high school, but many don't advance beyond this. Even for those who do, listening comprehension and pronunciation can continue to be challenging. In addition, avoid the perfect tenses.

---

### TIPS FROM CHRIS WATKINS, SENIOR INTERACTION DESIGNER

- Come with an itinerary and know people will be attentive to it.
- Use visuals to illustrate points where appropriate.
- Use simple sentence structure and avoid slang and idioms.
- Speak slowly and clearly.
- Try small group activities and discussions.
- Don't expect sarcasm or other language subtleties to be understood.
- Don't expect a lot of response to question-and-answer periods.
- Don't expect vocal expression of opinions, especially on controversial topics.
- Don't mistake head nodding as understanding; it means "I heard you."
- Don't put participants on the spot.

---

The Japanese spoken language is more ambiguous and vague than most languages, so often you will encounter presentations given in Japanese filled with slides containing lots of text. Content-laden slides decrease the chances that the spoken word will be misinterpreted. Don't use U.S. slide best practices when developing slides for Japan. Adding additional text may be helpful. It might make sense when using an interpreter to provide a whiteboard for the translator to write the key terms in kanji to avoid confusion. Japanese study English in middle school and high school, but many do not advance beyond this. Use simple language and allow for comprehension or pronunciation difficulties.

Keep the training visual and limit the amount of text on the slides so your audience is not reading, listening, and trying to keep up. Japanese culture is very visual. Their written language is pictorial. Their culture is rich. Anime and other graphic images abound. Show your understanding and appreciation of this culture and create slides and

## ANECDOTE FROM BRIAN DIETMEYER, FOUNDER OF THINK, INC!

This is a quick story that might be counter-intuitive. I was facilitating a negotiating skills session in Japan and was told two things that are musts. One, don't expect people to interact, it's just not culturally sound and, two, expect to go out at night . . . . and to be out late. The first morning of the workshop, I asked a question and everyone stared back at me, then stared at their tables. I stopped the workshop and told them I was aware that it was not in their culture to interact but that the workshop was built to be about 80 percent interactive, not didactic, and that we couldn't effectively help them learn unless there was dialogue. I then started with some safe audience participation, hand-raising, yes and no answers, etc., and by noon, we had a pretty healthy dialogue going on.

At the end of day one, I let them know that I couldn't go out with them that evening as I couldn't function on day two with jet lag AND a hangover and I wanted to do my best for them personally. They understood, and one man even went so far as to tell me over lunch the next day that getting home late is a sign of importance in Japan and, even if there is nothing happening after work, some people might intentionally come home late. He also thanked me for perhaps bringing another mindset to the table as I told him that in the United States, he who gets his work done and gets home earliest wins! In fact, she who works from her home has the best of all jobs!

handouts that support your material in a visual way. This is true of most learners, but especially true in Japan.

Don't point or use exaggerated facial expressions or hand gestures. They are not socially acceptable and can be seen as distracting. The "ok" symbol with your hand means "money" to the Japanese; use it only in appropriate context if at all. Know that head-nodding is not necessarily a sign of agreement or understanding—in many cases it simply means, "I heard you." It may be surprising to know that students who do not understand a topic are often more inclined to struggle silently then to speak up, even privately, after a class/session. Similarly, even participants with strong opinions on a topic will often keep them to themselves in a public forum.

Have fun!

**Some helpful sources include:**

- Japan External Trade Organization (JETRO)
- www.presentationzen.com
- www.venturejapan.com
- International Business Etiquette & Manners, web-based resource, www.cyborlink .com/

# Malaysia

**M**alaysia is a constitutional monarchy made of thirteen states in Southeast Asia. In these states are twenty-seven million multi-ethnic people. It is a country of two clearly distinguishable land masses divided by the South China Sea. Western Malaysia and its citizens are connected to Thailand on the northern border. Eastern Malaysia is divided into individual states with different citizenship and is connected to Indonesia. Major industries in Malaysia include agriculture (palm oil, rubber, tobacco, pineapple, pepper, cocoa), minerals (tin and petroleum), forestry, and manufacturing.

## ??? THE REQUEST

Training requests may come in for any business purpose, but training will likely occur in the more populated areas of Malaysia, such as the capital city Kuala Lampur (KL).

## • • • GETTING THERE

Kuala Lumpur at GMT +8 and has one major international airport (KLIA) that will likely be your destination when arriving in Malaysia. Other international airports that may be your destination include Kota Kinabalu International Airport, Penang International Airport, Kuching International Airport, Langkawi International Airport, and Senai International Airport. Putrajaya may also be a site for training as it is the administrative capital for the government.

A U.S. citizen does not need a visa to visit Malaysia; however you do need one if you are looking for employment. You will, of course, need a passport to travel there, and you should always have at least six months remaining on your passport before you travel. If you have questions, check the Malaysian embassy site at www.kln.gov.my/perwakilan/washington. There you will also find information on any vaccines such as diphtheria that you will need.

When making plans to travel and train in Malaysia, you should be aware of Malaysian holidays. Federal holidays include:

Malaysian Independence Day (August 31st)

Labour Day (September 1st)

Celebration of the king's birthday (first Saturday in June.)

Because Malaysia is such a multi-cultural and multi-religious country, Islamic, Hindu, and Christian holidays are celebrated in some areas, as well as Chinese holidays.

Be sure to check the weather as well, as Malaysia's climate is relatively tropical with storms and flooding common.

## PROGRAM DESIGN

The official language of Malaysia is Malay, but English is taught in schools and is commonly spoken in the cities. However, you should check with your in-country contact to verify the languages of your participants, as a variety of Chinese and indigenous dialects are also spoken. One contributor was able to train and present completely in English, but you may need to use translation.

In general, Malaysians are well-educated, with a variety of schooling options open to them, including state schools, specialized schools, and international schools. When it comes to your presentation, the audience is likely to be reserved but will not have a problem answering questions. We suggest checking with your in-country contact to verify which interactive methods work best. We have contributors who say any method can work, the purpose just needs to be explained. Also, be careful about putting people on the spot.

## LOGISTICS

When sending your training materials into the country, you have a couple of options. You can mail them in advance (well enough in advance that you can confirm their arrival and completeness before you leave home) or, perhaps simpler, you can email them to the client and have them make copies and order books.

Another logistical issue in Malaysia is exchanging your money for the local currency, the ringgit, which can be divided into 100 sen. Coins and bills are available and you should change your currency, as foreign currency is not commonly accepted.

According to one source, when you need to exchange money you should look for licensed money changers in shopping areas who may have better rates than either banks or airports. On the other hand, banks will be trained to handle international transactions should the need arise. ATMs are also available in cities but not in rural areas. Credit cards can be used in reputable establishments, but fraud can be a problem in less reputable areas.

## PROGRAM DELIVERY

Many Malaysians come from traditional backgrounds and are likely to treat you with respect. This manifests in a reticence to speak up in class, people indicating that they understand material that they do not, and relatively limited interaction in class. However, it does not have to be this way.

Case studies, role plays, and discussions will work in class, but may need some warming up. Beginning with easy questions to heighten confidence may help break the ice and get students involved in the materials.

Other factors you should remember include adding in time for prayers. You can ask your in-country contact for specifics, but plan on taking multiple breaks throughout the day.

Also, build some flexibility into your starting time for each day. In general, people are not on time. It is very common for people to be late for a meeting. Traffic congestion can definitely make it difficult to be prompt. Regardless, they do expect foreigners to be prompt.

Laughing is not always a sign of happiness. In Malaysia it can be used to cover up shame, bitterness, or disagreement. Laughing or smiling in a meeting may express anxiety and not happiness. Courtesy is also very important. Because of this, you will not hear an open "No" in the meeting. If someone says "Yes, but . . ." or "That would be difficult," he or she is probably saying no.

It is important not to lose your temper. It will affect people's ability to trust you or it could be an indication that you are not able to control yourself. Malaysians would rather do business with people they like. Even though creating a relationship takes time, it is very important for successful business. Good conversational topics are travel, tourism, and plans for the future. Avoid topics on religion, sex, gender roles, politics, or anything that criticizes the Malaysian culture.

## TECHNICAL REQUIREMENTS

Electricity in Malaysia runs at 240 volts, alternating at 50 cycles per second, so most presenters will need converters. Local training sites will likely have their own equipment but may or may not have converters for you, so either check with them beforehand or bring your own. Standard 220V converters may support this range so check. If you're using a DVD or video, verify that your formatting matches whatever machines they use for presentation as well.

Internet connectivity is fairly common throughout Malaysia and can be accessed in cities and most mid-sized towns. It is also common in hotels, restaurants, and cafes, so connecting should not be a problem.

## ACCOMMODATIONS

There is great diversity in terms of accommodation in the cities. Malaysians are building the largest skyscraper in the world, but there are cows on the street, across the street from the skyscrapers. We recommend staying at major hotels and having clients make arrangements for the hotel because they will know what is close to the training.

If you do decide to make your own reservations, avoid any hotels marked with "Rumah Tumpangan" instead of "hotel," as one source indicated that these are typically lower-rate hotels for foreign workers and not pleasant accommodations.

Standard safety precautions are needed in Malaysia. Individuals traveling alone should stay alert, valuables must be deposited in the hotel safe, and being wary of vendors is appropriate. In addition, public demonstrations of any kind are uncommon and so when they happen are treated harshly by the police and should be avoided. Drug trafficking is also treated with a mandatory death sentence in Malaysia. Be careful to watch all of your possessions and luggage when traveling in and out of the country.

Tap water is drinkable in some areas, but even the locals boil or filter most of it so to stay safe, just stick to bottled water. This also means avoiding any cold or iced drinks or cut fruit.

The food in Malaysia reflects the myriad of cultures that inhabit the region. The Indians and Malaysians use strong spices in their food, while the Chinese food is more subtle. Food is sold on the streets, but we don't recommend that you try it. Stick to the food that is served where you are staying or at places specifically recommended by your hosts.

## GETTING AROUND

For traveling around Malaysia at large, you can use trains, airplanes, buses, or the highway system (people drive on the left!). However, for travel within a given city, you will likely want to rely on your in-country contact's recommendations.

You can get around by taxi in the cities, but traffic jams are very common. This is especially so in rush hour. Taxis have also been known to charge very large fees to tourists, so it is advised to use a taxi that uses a meter. There are car rentals available but traffic laws are commonly treated as merely suggestions in Malaysia, so be careful if you decide to drive.

## THE PEOPLE/CULTURE

There are many things you need to know about the people. The population of Malaysia is mostly made up of three ethnic groups. They are Indian, Chinese, and Malay. Islam and Buddhism are practiced in this country.

Because Malaysia is located on a popular sea route, it has been a source of extensive international trading with India, China, and Europe. It was also very attractive to Britain (who colonized it) and Japan (who drove out the British in World War II). They continue to have a strong and wealthy Chinese population, although it is a minority.

## PREPARATION

Women should dress conservatively. Dress in blue or black suits, without much jewelry. Skirts should be below knees, or trousers are preferable. Covering your shoulders is also respectful of the local culture. Men in dress pants or a suit will be fine; check with the client to see which is appropriate for your event.

A few additional cultural issues to be aware of:

- When entering a home or place of worship, take off your shoes.
- Never eat or give a gift with your left hand.
- Don't touch a person's head.
- Avoid displays of affection (especially in same-sex relationships, which are taboo).
- Never point with your forefinger.

Some phrases in Malay that you might find helpful are:

| "hello" | hello |
| "selamat jalan" | good bye |
| "tolong" | please |
| "terima kasih" | thank you |

| "sama-sama" | you're welcome |
| "apa khabar?" | How are you? |
| "khabar baik" | I'm fine |
| "khabar terbaru?" | What's new? |

## THE PRESENTATION

One of our contributors, recommends saying at the beginning of any training, "Help me out. If I do or say anything considered wrong or offensive, please let me know so I can fix the problem." Participants feel more comfortable when they know you are trying to be sensitive to their needs and culture. Simply let people know that you care and are trying.

Be very kind and gentle in a classroom, very respectful of feelings. You can get interaction. Try asking questions, but don't put people on the spot. Do not ask a direct question of a specific person in class. Be ready to allow time for prayers.

When building in participation, give instructions carefully and do not call on people directly. If you are having difficulty getting answers within the larger group, try having some small group discussions. People will need to get comfortable, and a "safe" learning environment here will include not being asked to do something publicly without proper preparation and a chance to do it well. Role plays will work, but do them in triads, not in front of the group.

Your visit to Malaysia should be educational for you as well as your audience. Your audience will very likely be diverse in culture, background, language, and religion. Be sensitive to differences and flexible in your approach. Go with a plan and be ready to adjust if required. And enjoy yourself.

**Resources include the following:**

- Morrison, T., & Conaway, W.A., and Borden, G.A. (2006). *Kiss, Bow and Shake Hands: Asia.* Avon, MA: Adams Media.

- www.asiarecipe.com

- www.wikipedia.org

chapter
**FOURTEEN**

# Philippines

Around ninety million people are estimated to live in the two thousand islands that make up the Republic of the Philippines, with more than one in ten living in the capital of Manila. The country is incredibly varied, with influences from China, Spain, the United States, and Japan and the people living anywhere from jungles and isolated islands to large modern cities.

Here is some information and what to expect when training, teaching, or presenting to international audiences from the Philippines.

## ??? THE REQUEST

Manila is the primary population center and many training requests will come from there. Some likely training topics include sales training, strategic planning, selling skills, negotiation skills, handling distributors, category management (space management), promotions management, and handling key accounts. There may also be some soft-skill training requests such as writing effectively and face-to-face communication skills.

## • • • GETTING THERE

Before you go to the Philippines, be sure to check any applicable visa and passport requirements (www.travel.state.gov/travel), but your passport should have at least six months left before expiration. One of our local training resources recommended medical evacuation insurance in case of serious illness. To help prevent any serious illness, check with the Center for Disease Control (www.cdc.gov) for vaccines that are needed, most likely cholera, malaria, and typhus.

In terms of getting to the Philippines, flying into Manila is the easiest option, although the trip can be long, with the Philippines at GMT +8. There may be an airport tax to pay before leaving from an airport in the Philippines, so be prepared to pay that. Tipping is also customary, so be prepared if you take a cab from the airport. Manila is full of traffic and you should plan for all trips to take at least an hour. This is important to remember if you are training somewhere other than in your hotel.

Have prearranged transportation from the airport. Taxi crimes (robberies) can happen to both visitor and locals. It is best to arrange a ride from your hotel or a prearranged car. Your hotel will have information.

Other factors that may complicate your travel include weather and holidays. Be aware of national disaster seasons before you go, as monsoons, storms, mudslides, earthquakes, and volcanoes can all occur within the Philippines. September to May is the best time to travel if you want to avoid monsoons. Earthquakes and volcanoes are fairly unpredictable. Even in relatively calm seasons, the weather is hot so wear light (but business appropriate) clothing.

You may also want to avoid Catholic/Christian holidays like Easter and Christmas, as many Filipinos will celebrate by traveling to see family and friends making seats on transportation hard to get.

## PROGRAM DESIGN

When designing training for the Philippines, Tagalog and English are both common languages, although there are over 170 languages used, so be sure to check with your in-country contact to verify the appropriate language for your participants.

In terms of sequencing your program, always begin with objectives and state what the participants can expect to have gained at the end of the seminar; that will help Filipinos fix their attention on your program. From there, small units of instruction work with extra time at the end to connect all of the units will help Filipinos take things more seriously.

Music and sports like basketball, billiards, and soccer are all popular, which means that using those to illustrate a point and incorporating them throughout the program can be helpful.

## LOGISTICS

In general, logistics like materials and equipment needed should be pre-planned with hotel or conference site staff and reconfirmed the day before presentation. Specifically, verify the following:

- Projectors or video equipment
- Seating arrangement

- Easel boards
- Pens
- Paper
- Breakout rooms
- Microphone and speakers
- Any catering

It is advisable to bring your own materials and laptop unless you have a training partner or consultant in the Philippines. Training materials on paper or handouts may need to be prepared beforehand. If you don't have your own projector, you can usually rent one, but prior arrangements are necessary.

The currency in the Philippines is the Philippine Peso.

## PROGRAM DELIVERY

Seminars usually start at 8 A.M. and end at 5 P.M., but Filipinos like to eat regularly so make sure to factor in coffee breaks at 10 A.M. and 3 P.M., and a full hour at noon for lunch.

In general, Filipinos like to talk, so starting with an icebreaker and employing small group discussions or debates is preferable to lecture, which may or may not make sense. You also may not know when something doesn't make sense, as the participants are likely to be passive—their education growing up is primarily by rote. You may want to incorporate questions about the training and the content to draw learners out and ensure participation by everyone. At the end, you may also want to have a presentation or quiz just to verify understanding, but make sure the rules and expectations are clear and consider having a small prize for the winner or winning group.

Relationships are very important in the Philippines, so be polite and make connections. It's important to treat participants with respect as well. For example, it is appropriate to call participants Miss, Mrs., or Mr. with their surname to show respect. Titles are important, so know people's titles. Treat leaders with reverence and preference.

## TECHNICAL REQUIREMENTS

Bring an adapter for 220 volts electricity. Cell phones and texting are very common. You will need to ask in advance for equipment for training rooms, and it is recommended that you bring your own laptop.

You will find Internet access in Starbucks, coffee shops, hotels, and shopping malls. Many Starbucks and coffee shops will have Wi-Fi; some may charge a small fee.

You can exchange your dollars into pesos in banks, exchange centers in malls, airports, and hotels.

## ACCOMMODATIONS

Usually, trainers will want to stay in the hotel where training will be conducted to promote safety and to save themselves some travel time. The good hotels are Makati Shangrila, Manila Peninsula, Mandarin, New World Hotel, and Edsa Shangrila (Ortigas area).

English is spoken regularly in hotels and restaurants. There is usually continental food available as well. Go with bottled water.

## GETTING AROUND

Airport taxis and hotel taxis have a supervised queue, and that is the best place to find reputable transportation. Some independents may neglect maintenance of vehicles, and there are instances of taxi crimes, particularly for tourists. We are told that even some locals have family pick them up rather than taking unknown transportation. If you are going to take a ferry, look it over before you get on. If it seems overloaded, it's best to wait or find an alternative.

Remember that traffic can be intense in the Philippines, so you should walk defensively as pedestrians are expected to yield to vehicles regardless of the right of way. Expect cars to honk.

If you do get lost, English is spoken by many people, so finding someone to help you should not be too difficult.

## THE PEOPLE

History and culture are very important in the Philippines. Because of some very early trading, the Chinese are major players there in business today. Spain ruled the country for over three hundred years, and there are many Latino influences in the language and customs even today. The United States have also been influential in the Philippines, helping to build infrastructure and schools and increasing the prevalence of English in the country. In 1946 the Philippines became independent, although they have had many internal political conflicts between different groups. All of these cultures continue to have influence within the Philippines.

The people are friendly and hospitable. While getting to know you, they will ask about your personal life and family. This is a good way to get to know people, because it is very important to them. They may ask you very personal questions about marriage or having children or how much you spent on something. Other people's opinions will have an effect on their decisions, so if one person is outspoken against an idea, it may impact others as well.

Networking is very important here. Knowing someone (even though it may be a distant relationship) is helpful in making contacts and connecting with people. Family is very important. Family elders are very important and stay involved with their grandchildren. Many grandparents live with and baby-sit for grandchildren while parents are working. Great sacrifices are made for the family, and the family unit is very strong.

Maintaining decorum in public is important; avoid angry displays and public rowdiness.

Men will shake hands. Women should offer their hands first to a man; the man will likely not initiate the contact.

## ‖‖‖ PREPARATION

Get some sleep because Filipinos definitely expect some energy from the trainer. Get the venue ready if possible the day before training. If you have a local person assisting you, coordinate with him or her before the training.

Maintain professionalism. Plan on dressing conservatively at least until you get there and have a read on the group. Dress for heat. Men wearing dress pants and light short-sleeved shirts will be acceptable; women wearing long sleeves and a skirt or suit or pant-suit will generally work.

You should also be on time (early to avoid traffic). The participants will arrive relatively on time.

A few words to know include:

| hello | "helo" |
| how are you | "kumustá" |
| thanks | "salamat" |

### THE PRESENTATION

Jojo Barraquias, Jr., UFC Philippines, Inc., a training professional with extensive experience and knowledge of the Philippines, gives the following tips for presentations and classroom training in the Philippines:

- Dress to impress. Business attire is customary.

- Prepare some stories with humor. People like to laugh out loud.

- Get some local information on the latest craze in entertainment (movies/local actors/actresses) to achieve some kind of cultural assimilation.

- Encourage participation early on. Encourage people to speak. Otherwise, they will be quiet the whole day.

- People need to be motivated, so try praising them when they contribute, even if the contribution is minor.

- Define house rules about issues like breaks, lunch, restroom breaks, cell phones (they like to text and entertain calls a lot), and smoking. The common reasons why some people are late to come back after breaks are phone calls and smoking breaks.

- Be sensitive to the energy level of the class. Games and other participatory activities can be used to increase energy levels.

- Explaining the house rules and/or salient training points helps, but they should be written out as well to ensure comprehension.

We think you will find your Filipino audience to be very social and fun. This will be a good place to network, socialize, and enjoy humor. Be sure to reinforce key concepts for retention. Stay cool and enjoy the trip!

**Some helpful websites and references include:**

- www.cdc.gov

- www.travel.state.gov/travel

- Jojo Barraquias, Jr., UFC Philippines, Inc., jbarraquias@yahoo.com

# South Korea

South Korea is the third-largest economy in Asia and the eleventh largest economy in the world, according to Wikipedia. Close to half of the forty-nine million people who live in South Korea live in or close to Seoul. Known for both technology and scientific advances, it is a country that values education and training. Here is information to help if you are asked to conduct training, teach or present to an international audience from South Korea.

**??? THE REQUEST**

Major industries are steel, cars, shipbuilding, semiconductors, and electronics (Samsung, LG, Hyundai KIA Automotive Group), so training in those industries is a common request. Teaching English is a very popular request in the education system as well as in business. Many Americans go over for extended periods to teach English, particularly Americans of Korean descent. For general information about Korea and the business and cultural landscape, check out the Korean Chamber of Commerce at http://amchamkorea.org/.

**• • • GETTING THERE**

There are eight international airports in Korea, but with so much of the population centered in and around Seoul, Incheon International Airport is your most likely destination. Before flying, you should verify your passport and apply for a visa. From the United States you can purchase a tourist visa for less than thirty days or a business visa for ninety days. Full passport and visa requirements are available at www.koreaembassyusa.org/.

The rainy season is June through September and typhoons can happen during that time. Once you've landed in Korea (GMT + 9) at Incheon, there are several airport limousine services that take you to major areas in Seoul, such as Hapjeong Station, Shinchon Station, City Hall, and Kangnam. You should take "legitimate"-looking taxis, and not just a car that will take you. The overall crime rate for the country is low, but burglaries and taxi crimes do happen. There are other public transportation options, including rail, bus, and subways. Signs are usually in English, but the system can be complicated.

As you're scheduling your trip and training, you may want to avoid mid-July to mid-August because this is a big vacation time for Korean workers and students. Early October and Christmas are also busy travel times. The two main holidays celebrated are Seollal (Korean New Year) and Chuseok or (Korea's Thanksgiving). The dates are by the lunar calendar, so they vary each year.

## PROGRAM DESIGN

Although Korean is the national language, many Koreans can read and write English well, but they will not always be able to speak and hear it effectively. English skills are valued in the workplace. The higher a person is in an organization, the more likely he or she is to speak and understand English well. For the same reasons, most Koreans are eager to learn more English, so if you do not speak Korean and your participants are not fluent in English, translators are often easy to find.

In the experience of some of our sources, Korean university students tend to be very accustomed to purely lecture and are not used to being active participants in the classroom. In a business setting, people might not be as open to expressing their opinions or asking questions in front of everyone else. Rather than take that as a sign of disinterest or failure on the presenter's part, it is more a sign of the reserved nature of Koreans. This is not to say that a really creative and active presentation should be avoided. Koreans might love something that breaks the norm, but it will take some work to get them to participate with you. It helps to understand the learning culture and design your program accordingly. To help make connections with your participants, when you need examples or analogies, you can use tae kwon do, judo, baseball, basketball, archery, golf, tennis, or ice hockey, as all are favorite pastimes.

## LOGISTICS

As in shipping materials to any foreign country, you should make sure to send things to your training destination in enough time to confirm their arrival before you leave so that you can bring additional materials with you as necessary. You can use any standard shipping company, and most will be able to help you negotiate sending materials overseas. There is also a Korean express courier company called Hanjin Express with offices in many major cities (New York, Philadelphia, San Francisco, and Atlanta) that is good for shipping materials in and out of Korea. (www.hanjin.com/en/company/officenetwork.jsp).

It is recommended that you allow for the normal one-third extra time in case an in-class interpreter is needed.

South Korea's currency is the won, and money can be exchanged at most banks and hotels, although most will also take traveler's checks. Currency can also be exchanged at the Incheon Airport. Some merchants may be willing to accept U.S. dollars, but the exchange rate will usually be worse. You can also get cash advances on non-Korean credit cards in most subway stations and banks, but exchanging your money will give you a better rate.

## PROGRAM DELIVERY

In a professional setting, most people will arrive on time. However, do not be surprised if there are a few stragglers. Timing may be more relaxed for social events.

The Korean culture has great respect for and deference to leaders and elders. Be very conscious not to disagree or make wrong a person with a high status in a classroom setting. Ask the person one-on-one if he or she wants to participate in a role play, for example. It is important for Koreans to "save face," just as for many other Asian countries. Never say outright that someone is "wrong." Be careful of "win" or "lose" games. If there are quizzes, do not share scores of individuals. Make gaining knowledge the reward, rather than rewarding an individual or team for "winning."

Cathy Hwang, educator, says the traditional education includes lecture, discussion, and listening. She thinks planning different interactive methods like role plays and case studies can work, but expect people to be a bit shy and reserved at first. If you have established rapport and a safe environment with them, it can work. Try it and explain the reason and benefit of the interaction. Chungme Bogi, (leader with Youth with a Mission and born in Korea), tells us that a younger or innovative crowd will participate in interaction and will enjoy humor.

You will find it particularly helpful to develop a relationship with the leaders who are involved with the training. Personal relationships are very important. Getting to know people and asking about their families will help solidify a relationship. Korean people are generally used to sitting and listening during meetings or training sessions so, while interaction can be introduced; it should be done with preparation and commitment as you may encounter resistance at first.

## TECHNICAL REQUIREMENTS

South Korea's electricity runs on 220V, so you'll need the adapters with two round plugs. Internet and cell phone accessibility is not a problem, particularly in cities, with wireless becoming more and more common in addition to standard connections. NTSC video format should work, but DVDs will likely not play on Western computers.

## ACCOMMODATIONS

Both hotels and motels are available in Korea; you should check with your in-country contact for recommendations at a nice, English-speaking hotel. Even in some of the nicer hotels, you should drink bottled water and use it exclusively, even to brush your teeth.

In terms of food, you will probably either really enjoy it or really dislike the very strong (and spicy!) flavors. You should be adventurous (pretty good vegetarian options), but be aware of anything that may be in a position to spoil, either because of the heat outside or because it is being sold in the street. Doing training with food poisoning isn't anyone's idea of fun.

Wherever you are, you should always keep safety in mind because if you look like a foreigner, you will already have the attention of many locals. That said, South Korea is generally a safe place with the same safety issues as most Western countries. In any major cities there can be dangers of pickpockets and anyone walking or traveling alone, especially at night, should use caution. In addition, be careful when crossing the streets. In the United States, cars must yield to pedestrians, but in Korea, the rules are not the same. Even if it is your right of way, make sure that you watch when you cross because cars/taxis/buses will tend to zip by you.

## GETTING AROUND

Public transportation is very good in South Korea. All taxis have a phone line whereby they can connect you with a translator if the taxi driver does not understand. All the signs are written in both Korean and English, so if you know where you need to go, you can write down the name and will most likely be able to find it with help. The bus is a little bit more difficult because the bus stop locations are all written in Korean, and they are written up and down instead of left to right. The subway system is labeled in English and Korean. It is pretty easy to access.

Navigating by yourself can be difficult, as only a few streets are named (making driving next to impossible)! Koreans never use street names, so don't bother learning them. Instead they use buildings and landmarks, like Kyobo Tower, Samsung Hospital, and History Museum. They also refer to subway station stops (Kangnam station exit 6, Shinchon station exit 5) or department stores. Try to find out ahead of time what is around the area where you are going. Also, if you are looking for a house, they are not ordered numerically because different buildings go up at different times and are torn down. It's best to have your friend come out and look for you when you reach a general area.

## THE PEOPLE

Korea is a country with an extremely long history, dating back to its foundation at least five thousand years ago. Since then, there have been various dynasties and occupations, but the current designation of South Korea as a Republic came fairly recently, in 1945. Koreans are descended primarily from the Mongolian race, but various occupations have intermingled both Chinese and Japanese cultures into Korea. In more recent times, there has been an upswing in Mexicans and Filipinos emigrating and working in Korea. There are also a variety of religions practiced in Korea, including Buddhism, Confucianism, Christianity, and increasing amounts of Islam.

Koreans are extremely relationship-oriented people. If you have friends there, Koreans are extremely hospitable and generous. Or if you are a guest at a hotel, usually the customer service is really excellent. Personal space differs from that in the United States. People will walk very close to one another, almost shoulder to shoulder.

Age is everything in Korea. It is how the social system functions and how people are often defined. People always ask about age so they know how to properly address and relate to the other. Older people receive initial respect and priority automatically. Giving and receiving respect is huge. Often you'll see middle-aged women on subways who push their way in and sit down first because they feel they have priority. Also, people still give up their seats for the elderly, although that is becoming rarer.

Social status is also important. Do not be surprised if people ask you personal questions such as how much money you make or how much your house costs. Koreans are very status conscious and they will likely ask questions to give clues about that. Being humble is very important, so letting people know your status and not bragging will be important.

Gender has also been a key issue in Korean society, but women are beginning to have more of a voice. More women are in the work force and are running for political office. In general though, our contributors suggest that South Korea is more of a male-dominated society.

## PREPARATION

Susan Sul, president of Morningware, Inc., recommends dressing in formal business attire for business dealings. Most Korean business people, young and old, wear a tie and suit every day at work. If you do presentations to businesspeople, you may want to wear a tie and suit to show the same level of professionalism and respect as your participants. Skirts, dresses, or suits for women are appropriate, but choose something that will work for sitting on the floor, in case you end up in that situation.

Researching your audience is important. Koreans treat each other differently depending on whether they are peers, senior, or younger. Knowing the demographics of the group is helpful. Asking an in-country contact what you need to know about those dynamics also helps. Greeting the most senior person in the room first is likely to be important. Ask questions in advance so you can be prepared for that.

Nicholas Lee, Factor and Lake, LTD, recommends keeping up with current affairs for your trip. His experience is that people are very keen on what is going on, not only in Korea but also in the world. Particularly professionals are very knowledgeable and enjoy discussing world events. They also are likely to have strong opinions. Be careful how you handle those situations if you disagree.

Common phrases that would be good to know include:

| | |
|---|---|
| "Ahn Young Ha Say Yo" | The formal way to say Hello, said with a head nod |
| "Gam Sah Hahp Knee Dah" | Thank you |

## THE PRESENTATION

Korean people are generally used to sitting and listening during meetings or training sessions. They don't generally get up to role play or do active learning activities. So if you are dealing with an older, more conventional, or more formal crowd, you can expect relatively little feedback and almost no questions to be asked during the session. You have to work especially hard to convince this type of group of the benefits of group work. People also may not ask questions during your presentation, so you should give some informal Q&A time during breaks for people to clarify their understanding. As in other Asian cultures, be careful calling out individuals or telling anyone that he or she is incorrect, as this can be seen as rude and disrespectful.

"Generally speaking, the audiences are used to one-way communication. Interaction is little, if any, and relegated to the end of the presentation. The interaction may be generally limited to Q&A. People may not be willing to share their stories/opinions/experiences. However, I have found that it takes time and familiarity to have interaction. Once the audience knows you and is comfortable with you, then they may be open to interaction. If one can draw them into interaction, they would be amazed by the knowledge and experience there is among the audience. I have also found that among the younger generation there is a bit more quest for interaction. Although it has been my experience to note a higher level of alertness when I begin to engage interaction (when I ask questions and wait for answers), I have found younger people respond more eagerly and enthusiastically. Younger people could ask good and difficult questions given the opportunity."

If you can set interaction up as "I am going to ask you to be active during the time that we are together," then the people are more willing to get up and do things (although they may be shy and unwilling at first). Elizabeth Seon, an American who went to Korea to teach English, says she had success convincing the group to be interactive. Enthusiasm and an animated persona did the trick for her. A lot of the times, it is about selling the concept, so if you are not fully convinced and confident that this is great, then they will obviously not reciprocate.

In meetings or training, be grounded in content and prepared with answers. Try to anticipate what questions will be asked and what additional information will be requested. Be prepared to give it at the event. This gains great credibility. If you need to find answers and get back to people, then be sure you follow up right away. They notice and appreciate it.

Korea can be a powerful place to present or conduct training, because of their keen interest and appreciation for education and credentials. Know your stuff, add value, show respect and deference to leaders and your elders. Enjoy the Korean barbequed beef (they bring a small charcoal grill to your table to cook it) and beware of the kimchi!

**Some helpful websites and references include:**

- http://amchamkorea.org/
- www.hanjin.com/en/company/officenetwork.jsp
- www.koreaembassyusa.org/
- www.wikipedia.org

# Thailand

**A**s the world seems to grow smaller, the borders between countries seem to grow closer. Yet there are cultural differences that cannot be ignored when conducting business outside of the United States. It does not matter whether the business is conducted in a division of the U.S. company abroad or whether it is a separate company. Success relies in part on following local custom and culture. In our business of training and development, we, too, need to be aware and sensitive to cultural differences to be successful.

If you have the opportunity to conduct training in Thailand (once known as Siam), here are some facts you will want to know about this nation of over sixty-five million people if you are training, teaching, or presenting to a Thai audience.

## ??? THE REQUEST

While Thai is the national language, English is frequently spoken in business circles, leading to training requests in all sorts of industries within Thailand. Most requests will come from large cities such as the capitol (Bangkok), but the subject matter can vary greatly. Some of the major cities in Thailand, by region are:

- North: ChiangMai
- South: Songkla
- Central: Ayutthaya (ancient capital of Siam) and Chonburi
- North Eastern: Nakhon Ratchasima and Khon Kaen
- Central: Bangkok

## • • • GETTING THERE

Thailand standard time is seven hours ahead of Greenwich Mean Time; Daylight Savings Time is not observed, so traveling from the United States means that you will experience a significant time difference. Build time into your trip for adjusting to the difference so that on training days you will be fresh and alert.

You will need a visa to travel to Thailand. For information on acquiring a visa, see http://passportdocs.com/visa.

You should also verify travel information from the Department of State website (www.travel.state.gov). There are currently no required vaccinations, unless you are coming from an infected area. Check for the latest medical information with the Center for Disease Control (www.cdc.gov) as soon as you know of your plans to travel.

Allow sufficient time for obtaining passports and visas. Keep your passport current by at least six months as some countries may require six months on the passport before they let you into the country. Here are some additional U.S. departments you may want to contact in advance of your travel (and their phone numbers):

| | |
|---|---|
| Getting Through Customs | 610.353.9894 |
| Department of State Citizens' Emergency Center | 202.647.5225 |
| Bureau of Consular Affairs Fax Services | 202.647.3000 |
| Bureau of Consular Affairs Electronic Bulletin Board | 202.647.9225 |
| Visa Information | 202.663.1225 |

In general, Thailand's climate is tropical with high humidity. Most places in Thailand are hot most of the year. If you have a choice, opt to conduct your training between November and February when temperatures are more bearable.

You should avoid scheduling training on or around public holidays, (holidays marked with an asterisk * are observed on the Full Moon Day):

- January 1: New Year's Day
- February: Maha Puja Day*
- April 6: Chakri Memorial Day
- April 12–14: Songkhran Festival Day (Thai New Year)
- May 1: National Labor Day
- May 5: Coronation Day

- May 7: Ploughing Ceremony
- May: Visakha Bucha Day* (Buddhist holiday)
- July: Khao Pansa* (Buddhist lent day)
- August 12: H.M. The Queen's birthday
- October 23: Chulalongkorn day
- December 5: H.M. The King's birthday
- December 10: Constitution Day
- December 31: New Year's Eve

In addition to the above, the residents of Chinese heritage celebrate Chinese New Year for one to three days on dates that generally fall in late January or early February.

 **PROGRAM DESIGN**

When you receive a training request, designate an in-country contact. Working with an in-country contact should help with the initial planning and development of your training program.

When you deliver training in Thailand, or for that matter in any country, you want to ensure that you avoid American English jargon, colloquialisms, and idioms. Using examples is always a good reinforcement of learning concepts, but be sure to use examples meaningful to Thailand. Soccer is wildly popular and kite flying is a popular pastime. Thai boxing is popular as well. You may be able to get additional ideas from your in-country contact!

The Thais live in a concrete and pragmatic society. They are present-centered. People take precedence over the rule or law. Thais educated in Europe or the United States may be more objective thinkers than those whose view is limited to local influences. Don't design a role play for use in Thailand because the Thai people do not understand acting or how to play a role.

If you are using an interpreter for your presentation, account for this when building the course. Thai is a very expressive language. Whereas presenting in other languages, the rule of thumb is to allow an extra one-third time for in-class interpretation, you may want to allow up to 50 percent more time for Thai. John Hwang, an experienced speaker who uses interpreters often, suggests you practice beforehand. Because Thai is very expressive and takes some time to translate completely, it is difficult to keep your rhythm and keep your train of thought. He suggests some words will not translate well and may need to be looked up in advance. Allow time for this for best results. If you have materials translated, allow sufficient time for this, as well as time for your interpreter to review them.

## LOGISTICS

The baht is the currency in circulation. They are issued in denominations of B1000 (gray), B500 (purple), B100 (red), B50 (blue), B20 (green), and B10 (brown). There are 10, 5, and 1 baht coin and 50 and 25 satang. There are 100 satangs in a baht.

Most major credit cards are accepted. Most foreign currencies and traveler's checks are easily changed at banks, hotels, or money exchangers in the cities. General banking hours are 9:30 A.M. to 3:30 P.M., Monday through Friday.

Tipping is not expected, although it is becoming more common. Most hotels and restaurants include a 10 percent service charge in the bill. Taxi drivers do not require a tip.

## PROGRAM DELIVERY

Punctuality is important in Thailand! Stick with your published training schedule. If you are going to be late, you should get this message relayed as soon as possible.

Most business is conducted in person, not over the telephone. Admittedly, this is difficult to do from abroad. Business cards are commonly exchanged at a first meeting. From the first meeting, Thais call each other by their first names, preceded by the title "Khun," which is our American equivalent of "Mr." or "Ms." Thais greet each other with the traditional "Wai." To do a "Wai," hold your hands in prayer position with a bowed head. The lower the head is bowed, the greater the respect shown. Although you may be greeted with a "Wai," handshakes are the typical greeting for Westerners.

If you are presented with a gift, do not open it immediately, unless invited to do so. Books and documents are treated with respect, so be careful not to place them on the floor.

If you plan case studies, make sure you describe the reason why and invite their participation. Do not ask them to present or speak publicly, unless you have "earned it." This would mean you are comfortable they can be successful and the learning environment is safe for them.

## TECHNICAL REQUIREMENTS

The electric system is 220 volt AC (50 cycles). Many plugs and sockets are in use. Bring a plug-adapter kit for your appliances. The video system is PAL. If traveling with any

American equipment, come prepared with a converter. Cell service and Internet availability will vary, based on the area you are staying in. You can rent a phone with a SIM card.

## ACCOMMODATIONS

Thai accommodations have the reputation for being clean, efficient, and friendly. Your in-country contact may have suggestions for hotels that are close to where the training will take place. This comes naturally to the Thais, because these are an integral part of their culture. Service and hospitality are excellent.

Bottled water is the norm. Although it is reported that tap water meets and even exceeds standards for drinking water, it is still recommended that you stick with bottled water when the tap water comes through the city water system. It is generally safe to brush your teeth with the tap water.

The water in cafes and restaurants is generally safe. Restaurant water may come from small, individual bottles served to you or a glass from a large bottle stored in the back of the restaurant. If the water has a pale color, chances are the water has been boiled. Another risk associated with drinking water is the glass it's poured into! Is it clean?

Speaking of water, hot water showers are not prevalent throughout all of Thailand. You'll be okay if you stay in a modern condo or upper-class hotel or some other places.

Eating is a pleasurable experience in Thailand. Good food can be found in all kinds of eateries from food stalls to floating restaurants on boats to high-end restaurants in hotels. An encouraging sign of a good restaurant is that it's busy! When you place your order, preface your order with the word "kaw" (pronounced like awe) and then your order, for example, "kaw Coke."

Unlike in the United States, if you are in a restaurant in Thailand, it is considered poor practice to divide the bill. So if you pick it up, plan on paying for it in its entirety!

## GETTING AROUND

Will you need transportation from the Thailand airport to your local Thai destination? The choices are similar to those in the United States. You can take a shuttle, a limo, a taxi, or a van. If you have large pieces of luggage, you should book a van instead of a car. Of course, it depends on which airport you fly into. Various transfer services are available.

If you take a taxi, beware of "unofficial" taxi services. Many visitors have literally been "taken for a ride" (robbed) by people claiming to be taxi drivers. A real taxi has a red and white taxi-meter on the roof. Airport taxis are white with green plates. If the taxi does not have a meter, be sure to agree on the fare before starting. If the taxi is metered, be sure that driver turns it on! You want to make sure that you have change because most taxi drivers do not! When driving on an expressway, it is the passenger's responsibility to pay any tolls.

## THE PEOPLE

As a visitor to Thailand, you should learn a little about the culture. The Thai people hold their monarchy in high regard, both earlier rulers and the present Royal Family. As a foreigner, you should never make disparaging comments about the Royal Family or its symbols.

Most Thais practice Buddhism. Showing respect for monks, temples, and Buddha images will be important to maintaining good relationships. Females must avoid any physical contact with monks.

In Thai society, it is important to avoid situations involving conflict. Criticism and anger should be avoided. If someone laughs for no apparent reason, it may be because he or she is embarrassed. Even in times of frustration or serious differences, it is important to remain calm. You will want to keep this in mind when you think about examples to use in your materials and when you facilitate discussion in the classroom.

It is taboo to touch another person's head. The head is viewed as "the seat of the soul." Feet are also taboo. Whether you are presenting in the classroom or in a meeting, do not let the soles of your feet point toward anyone (and especially toward an image of Buddha). Feet should be made as inconspicuous as possible. (Remove your shoes upon entering most homes and all temples.)

## PREPARATION

Thai behavior is formal. Impressions are important. The Thai people speak softly, smile easily, and act politely. They display consideration for the comfort and dignity of others. You will want to emulate this behavior when you develop your training content and when you deliver your course.

When in Thailand, dress for success! Although the temperatures are warm, both men and women should dress in business attire. For men, this means wearing a suit and tie or slacks and jacket, with a shirt and tie. For women, this means wearing a suit or dress. Women should avoid wearing black, as black is reserved for funerals.

Thai is not an easy language, but the local people will respect you for trying. Like other languages, some words have different masculine and feminine versions. Some examples you may need include these:

| Hello | "Sawat dii Khrap" (m) and "Sawat dii kha" (f) |
|---|---|
| What are you doing? or How are you? | "Bai nai?" |
| Thank you | "Khawp khun khrap" (m) "Khawp khnu kha" (f) |
| Very delicious | "Aroy maak" |
| Foreigner | "farang" |

## THE PRESENTATION

You will find that Thais are open to information on most issues. They are nonassertive and are very conscious of other people's feelings. Thais are also very conscious of others' positions in the social hierarchy. Since decision-making revolves around a hierarchical nature of society, the Thais obey decisions made by their superiors. Given this outlook, you would probably find that your participants do not ask many questions and that they respect your authority. This means you will need to find a safe way to obtain the kind of feedback you want in order to know they understand the content. Try discussions in small groups. Make a couple of relationships in the room with people who will tell you what you need to know. Ask at breaks very specific questions one-on-one. Have small group discussions on application and ask. what they will do with this information. How will they implement it on the job? These will give you clues as to how the materials are being received.

Finally, make this an enjoyable experience! Be receptive to a new culture. Be patient with yourself as well as with others. Surprise your hosts and learn a few words of Thai. Most of all, remember that learning is a mutual experience that brings our borders closer together!

**Helpful websites and references include:**

- Axtell, R.E. (1998). Gestures: *The DO's and TABOOs of Body Language Around the World.* Hoboken, NJ: John Wiley & Sons.
- Doing Business in Thailand. www.infoexport.gc.ca/ie-en/DisplayDocument.jsp?did=1547
- Morrison, T., Conaway, W.A., & Borden, G.A. (2006). *Kiss, Bow, or Shake Hands.* Avon, MA: Bob Adams, Inc.
- http://passportdocs.com/visa
- www.cdc.gov Center for Disease Control
- www.travel.state.gov

# Uzbekistan

**U**zbekistan is a republic in Central Asia, part of the former Soviet Union. Landlocked Uzbekistan is bordered by Turkmenistan, Kazakhstan, Tajikistan, Kyrgyzstan, and Afghanistan. Uzbekistan is divided into twelve provinces.

Here is what to expect and tips for success when training, teaching or presenting in Uzbekistan.

## ??? THE REQUEST

Requests for a program might come from a company, organization, or government agency. For our example, we will discuss training for Boeing.

When you receive a request, ask your host what the purpose and objectives of the program should be. Send drafted objectives and a detailed outline for their review. Make sure you have clear written agreements regarding length of the program, dates, times, and location.

Work with the hotel and/or office secretary to confirm administrative details.

## • • • GETTING THERE

You will probably be flying in to Tashkent, Uzbekistan, the capital. Ask your hotel when you make your reservation whether they will be sending a car to pick you up at the airport, and if so, how much it will cost. If not, you can take a taxi to travel to your hotel.

Of course, you will need a valid passport to enter the country. Check the current visa requirements for entry and stay in the country at www.traveldocs.com/uz/vr.htm. Currently, here are the steps to obtain a business visa:

- Submit your U.S. passport (must have at least six months remaining).
- One Visa Application Form must be completed ONLINE, then printed and signed.
- One passport-type photograph.
- Completed Cover Page (print from browser).
- Your host company or organization in Uzbekistan must also contact the Consular Department of the Uzbek Ministry of Foreign Affairs to have an invitation approved and sent to the Embassy of the Republic of Uzbekistan in Washington, D.C. (and a copy sent to the traveler if possible) on your behalf. The visa is not issued until the approval is received by the embassy.

Flights to Tashkent from New York take about twenty hours, depending on your airline and location of your interim stop (Moscow, London, etc.).

Baggage reclaim and customs formalities can take as long as two hours. Make sure to retain the customs declaration form you will be given as you pass through customs. You will need it when you leave the country and may find it difficult to leave without the form.

A short and inexpensive ($2 to $3) taxi journey is the easiest way to get to the city center. When you exit the international terminal, a large number of men will be crowded at the (sole) exit door offering "taxi" services. Most of these are not "official" taxis. These unofficial "taxi" drivers will attempt to charge whatever they believe the market will bear. For those without Russian or Uzbek language skills, it is best to arrange to have someone meet you at the airport. $2 to $3 fares are usually only obtainable by those who understand the system and speak at least some Russian or Uzbek. Taxi drivers will rarely accept small bills (dollars, euros, or pounds), and cannot be counted on to give change (in any currency).

Allow plenty of time when leaving the country via Tashkent airport. Check-in, customs, and passport control can be very time-consuming, especially if there are large numbers of passengers. Make sure to have the customs form you were given when you entered the country.

Uzbekistan/Tashkent time zone: UTC/GMT +5 hours

Holidays that may affect your program scheduling include:

- January: New Year's Day (1st)
- March: International Women's Day (8th), Navruz (Persian New Year) (21st)

- May: Labor Day (1st), Day of Memory and Remembrance (9th)

- September: Independence Day (1st)

- December: Constitution Day (8th)

There are also Muslim holidays that are timed with phases of the moon in March, October, and December.

## PROGRAM DESIGN

You will need to design your program so that it can be translated into Uzbek.

Design a clear structure and agenda for the training and make sure each section of the program is easily referenced back to the agenda. This ensures that participants can check and see where you are in the program at any time. Some lecture is okay, but try to design some of the program to be interactive with small group discussion plus question-and-answer (Q&A) periods.

## LOGISTICS

Request the necessary equipment to be set up and tested in the room before your arrival. If they cannot provide the equipment, bring your computer, projector, converter, plugs, and extension cord. Send your program to your hosts ahead of time as a backup precaution. Check with your hosts to determine whether they will photocopy materials for the program or to see whether they would prefer that you ship the materials directly to them ahead of time. Arrange for an interpreter by asking your host for a recommendation.

The local currency is SOM, SUM, or UZS. Exchange offices should be used, since the black market is illegal and rates are poor. U.S. dollars, euros, British pounds, or Japanese yen are the only currencies that can be readily exchanged, but notes must be in perfect condition with no marks or damage. Local ATMs (known as Bankomats) do not work with foreign cards. Dollars are available inside banks using international credit cards with commission of about 4 percent. The dollars can then be changed for local currency with another commission charge. Newer shops and hotels accept credit cards.

- Currency: coins: 1, 5, 10, 25, 50 som

- Bank note denominations: 1, 3, 5, 10, 25, 50, 100, 200, 500, 1,000 som

- British Embassy, Tel. +998(71)1207852

- Embassy of the United States, Tel. +998(71)1205450

The average summer temperature in Tashkent tends to be 35 degrees C, while the average winter temperature is around 10 degrees C. Uzbekistan does not receive much precipitation and includes desert, long, hot summers, mild winters, plus semi-arid grassland in the east.

Other major cities in Uzbekistan include: Bukhara and Samarqand.

## PROGRAM DELIVERY

The most likely locations for program delivery would be at the office or at a hotel. Speak slowly using simple terms and concepts that can be easily translated and interpreted.

Ron Webb, Customer Service Representative for Boeing in China, Kuwait, Italy, and Uzbekistan, has worked for Boeing for thirty-four years in many different engineering, sales, and customer service organizations. For the last thirteen years he has been a customer service representative, providing assistance and training for operators of Boeing Airplanes in many different countries. He has a B.S. degree in electrical engineering and an MBA. He is currently working in Boeing Field Service at Tashkent, Uzbekistan.

The subjects Ron presents are usually technical, problem solving, and training for procedures the airline requires to maintain Boeing airplanes as on-the-job training (OJT) for airline personnel.

Rons says: "Relationships with management and the people are developed over time as you interact with them. Simply try to observe, listen, respond, and adapt to the communication style that you feel each person prefers."

For Ron, because he is the expert, no presentation planning is involved. What he presents depends on the situation as it develops.

## TECHNICAL REQUIREMENTS

Be sure to bring 220/240 voltage converters, plugs, and back-up systems to use if needed. Plugs need to have two round pins or three rectangular prongs. Bring your program on an electronic storage device, send it to your host ahead of time, hand-carry hard copies of translated and English versions of handouts. Bring videotapes reproduced in PAL format and subtitled in Uzbek. Do not plan on everything working. Have contingency backup plans for any technical requirement.

For Ron, a laptop computer with the appropriate software installed and access to the Internet with acceptable line speed has become absolutely necessary in the last few years. In remote locations like Uzbekistan, finding dependable and stable Internet access, with an adequate acceptable line speed for your presentation, continues to be one of the biggest problems.

## ACCOMMODATIONS

Ron Webb (Boeing) suggests that your hotel accommodations should be limited to Western hotel chains.

The Radisson is more expensive than the local hotels, but may provide more of the typical accommodations (such as room, food, and Internet access) that Western travelers expect.

He advises that you make reservations at an accommodation that advertises their ability to speak English, so your stay will be comfortable. Plugs and converters will be required or you will burn up any electrical items that are not able to be switched to 220/240 volts.

Uzbek national dishes are similar to other Central Asian countries. The national dish is Plov (also called Osh, "Pulau" in Hindi), a mixture of rice, mild spices, carrots, mutton, meat, and sometimes other ingredients. Try Shashlik, which is- meat (usually mutton, beef, or chicken) and chunks of fat roasted kebab style over charcoal. Samsa ("Samosa" in Hindi) are similar to South American empanadas, meat (beef or mutton) and onion encased in pastry and baked in wood-fired, clay ovens shaped like upside-down beehives called tandories. The local bread, round and flat, is also baked in tandories. It is called Non (or in Russian, "lepioshki," "Naan" in Hindi) and is usually delicious. Tea, coffee, alcoholic, and non-alcoholic drinks are readily available.

There are hundreds of small cafes in Tashkent offering these and other local dishes at very inexpensive prices. A meal of salad, bread, tea, soup, and shashlik is usually around $2 to $3. Sanitation standards leave a lot to be desired in many of these cafes. Especially on warm days, look to see whether the meat is kept refrigerated before it is cooked. Often, it is not.

Typical big city crime may occur, such as theft or robbery. Refrain from political activities or confrontations of any kind. Usual safety precautions should be taken, as when traveling in any large city.

## GETTING AROUND

The city has a good, inexpensive public transport system. The metro/underground system is typical of the old Soviet style with large and impressive stations and is actually quite modern. There are also trams and modern buses. Tickets on the metro are small blue coin size tokens and cost about 250 SUM for any single journey. Photographs are not permitted in the metro stations. Police will usually be present on all platforms.

Obtain maps in the airport, train station, or hotel. Practice your questions ahead of time, so you can be understood. Point to the location on the map and ask for help. Don't be surprised if there are not a lot of people who speak English.

## THE PEOPLE

The people are serious and dedicated. Careful communication is critical. You need to establish trust with the people by doing what you say you will do. Show interest in the people and their country by doing your research and homework before you arrive. Find out what the events of the day are, when the holidays occur, what people are talking about, and what the weather is like, so that you can be prepared.

The people of Uzbekistan face economic challenges, unemployment, underemployment, and corruption.

The primary export is cotton. Gold, natural gas, coal, copper, oil, silver, and uranium are all produced in Uzbekistan.

Favorite sports include football (soccer), boxing, wrestling, and horseback riding.

In past centuries, Tashkent has been called Chach, Shash, and Binkent at various times. Each of the names is a part of the city's history. Tashkent has always been an important international transport junction. Unfortunately, only a small part of its architectural past is preserved, due to demolition of historical and religious buildings after the revolution of 1917 and a massive earthquake in 1966. Some old buildings are in the old town, west of the downtown. Narrow winding alleys seem to be in sharp contrast to the more modern Tashkent. Many of the Islamic sites in Tashkent, such as Khast-Imam, are not open to non-Muslims, and visitors should always ask permission before entering them.

Uzbekistan is called a country of sun and hospitality. They welcome tourists.

In Uzbekistan, there are several programs that help enable the active integration of women into the labor market. These programs include training and loans for women entrepreneurs.

## PREPARATION

Call the hotel or secretary to check to see whether everything is ready. Ask about any equipment that you will need.

Some basic Uzbek that could come in handy:

| Cyrillic | Uzbek | English |
|----------|-------|---------|
| Càëìì | Sa<u>lom</u> | Hello (literally, peace) |
| Xàéð | Xayr | Goodbye |
| Èëòèìîñ | iltimos | please (request) |
| ðàyìàò | rahmat | thank you |
| Aðçèìàéäè | Arzimaydi | You're welcome. |
| Kå÷èðàñèç | Kechir<u>as</u>iz | Excuse me. |
| yà | ha | yes |
| Éœš | yo'q | no, not, there is/are not |
| Áîð | bor | there is/are |
| Áó íîìà? | Bu ni<u>ma</u>? | What is this? |

Source: www.oxuscom.com/250words.htm

## THE PRESENTATION

Recommendations regarding cultural sensitivities: Consider this to be part of a "listening" process. This means, be constantly aware of what people you interact with are saying and doing.

Working and living in the customer's community immerses you in the culture, and that gives you an opportunity to develop cultural awareness and sensitivities over time.

The key is to concentrate on communicating with whoever you are dealing with. This is difficult to do if dealing with a group. If dealing with an individual, the situation is less complicated, but there is no "one size fits all" technique. Each situation is different and each individual is different. The first priority is "listening" to determine what the individual is asking.

Listening to the words the individual is saying is important, but usually you find out more by observing body language, any "props" (documents, drawings, or photographs) that the individual may have, and any other clues that can be used in the situation. If possible, face-to-face contact is best, but as emails become more and more prevalent as a means of communicating, getting that face-to-face communication is more difficult.

Emailing requires a completely different set of "listening" skills.

**AFTER** "listening" to the individual and the description of the situation, try to ask questions that will help with any additional details that will allow you to learn more about the situation and what you can or cannot do to assist. Speaking slowly and being aware of how the individual is reacting is very important. If the person has limited English skills, the person is probably more intent on agreeing with everything you say and giving the impression that he does understand when he really does not or only partially understands. Before the conversation is over, always try to gain confirmation that the person understands what you intend to do to help him.

To summarize, the most important part of making a presentation, whether it's a formal presentation or on-the-job training, to an individual in Uzbekistan is communicating your message. Almost all of the communication occurs when you are "listening," not when talking. Anyone can make a presentation, but only a good listener can make a good presentation, because he or she is listening to what the students need.

Speak slowly and clearly. Make sure to allow enough time for the interpreter. Speak directly to the audience, not to the interpreter.

Engage participants in discussion. Vary your methods.

Make sure you start and end with the agenda and objectives. Check back to each item on the agenda when you go on to the next to see whether there are any questions before moving on to the next topic or section. Keep the program on track, but be flexible enough to allow for interaction and discussion. Start and end on time.

**Helpful websites and references include:**

- http://unece.org/gender
- www.advantour.com/uzbekistan/tashkent.htm
- www.climate-zone.com
- www.eastlinetour.com/uzbekistan/
- www.ilovelanguages.com
- www.kropla.com/electric2.htm
- www.oxuscom.com/250words.htm
- www.uzbekistan.org/uzbekistan/national_holidays
- www.wikitravel.org/en/Tashkent
- www.worldtravelguide.net

# Vietnam

**V**ietnam is a country rich with tradition. It is a largely agricultural region, but continues to get more attention from major corporations, which increases industry and exporting.

The information and examples for Vietnam come from Tristan B. de la Rosa, executive coach and leadership development, Banyan Way. Here is some of what to expect and helpful information for training, teaching, or presenting to international audiences from Vietnam.

## ??? THE REQUEST

The office and field supervisory and management talent pool in Vietnam is small relative to what the country needs to support its high-growth economy. The country pursued its policy of "doi moi" or "openness" in the early 1990s and foreign investments have since poured in, fueling economic growth second only to that of China. As a result, most companies have found that among their biggest challenges is identifying local supervisory and management talent to help run their businesses.

Major corporations like Coca-Cola, Procter & Gamble, Unilever, and Nestle are investing substantial amounts to develop in-house talent. For these corporations, it is often enough just for employees to be able to speak English and to show a fairly high degree of personal initiative and resourcefulness. With these basic qualifications, people are hired with the view that whatever else they need to be effective at work can be provided through in-house training.

Given this background, most training that is needed in Vietnam right now must address rudimentary office, management, and supervisory skills. With English as the adopted language of commerce, even by other Asian companies in Vietnam, English language instruction probably tops the bill among all business-related courses that are currently offered. After English, we would classify training requirements in Vietnam into three broad groups:

Basic office skills would include business verbal/writing skills, and handling customer complaints.

Basic Supervisory and Management Skills include goals and priorities, time management, conducting meetings, setting performance standards, giving feedback, building teamwork, and making effective presentations.

Other skills include technical, marketing, sales, advertising, and customer service.

## • • • GETTING THERE

A valid passport and a visa are required for travel to Vietnam. We recommend registering your trip with the U.S. State Department online at https://travelregistration.state.gov as a Short-Term Traveler. Allow ample time for processing. Visas may be obtained from the Embassy of Vietnam in Washington, D.C., or the Vietnamese Consulate General in San Francisco. Although the capital is Hanoi, it is primarily the political hub, and unless the audience will be government officials and bureaucrats, most likely your work will take you to Ho Chi Minh City (formerly Saigon).

Holidays in January (calendar new year) and February (lunar new year) are considered Tet holidays. Each is a week-long celebration causing businesses and government to come to a standstill. It is not advisable to schedule business or training for these months. Weather in Ho Chi Minh City is, in general, tropical. Their rainy season is May to September and the climate dries out between October and March. Pack conservative yet temperature appropriate business attire for your trip. The only other clothing tip to provide is not to wear shorts; they are only worn by children.

Vietnam is seven hours ahead of GMT, making it eleven hours ahead of Central Standard Time and ten hours ahead of Central Daylight Time. Such time differences and the length of the flight necessitate early arrival for your session to overcome jet lag. Reliable taxi service is available from the airport to the hotel; however, many of the major hotels provide complimentary or discounted airport transfers. Check with your hotel for their arrangement. The central business district is about forty-five minutes from the Ho Chi Minh airport. The Hanoi central business district is seventy-five minutes from the airport.

## PROGRAM DESIGN

Keep the program design as simple as possible.

- Begin with basic concepts. Explain the meaning of each concept and why it is important to a given program.

- Vietnamese is the official language and few people will be comfortable using much English. Use simple English words. You are going to most likely be working with an interpreter. Assuming the interpreter is very good, you will still lose about 30 percent of your meaning in the translation.

- Experiential methods like case studies or role plays will work well.

As much as possible, tap into the local knowledge and experience. I attended one program for which the trainer used the pit stop crew at Indianapolis 500 races as an example of efficient and effective teamwork. Nobody in the audience knew what he was talking about and he simply failed to get the point across. Instead, use soccer analogies. the Vietnamese are soccer-crazy. Every time Vietnam won last year's Southeast Asian Games, everyone ran wild in the streets waving the national flag, honking horns, and creating as much noise as they could. Obvious concepts to hit home with soccer are teamwork, coordination, and strategy.

Try to design the program to be as physically interactive and experiential as possible. Vietnamese, like many Asians, tend to be reticent and quiet in a classroom setting. However, they do not mind being involved in educational games that teach while they have fun. I remember teaching the fundamentals of capitalism to employees by introducing them to the board game, Monopoly. They don't typically expect to receive anything in the way of giveaways or prizes for participation, so incorporating a few surprises will spark participation and add fun to the educational experience.

## LOGISTICS

The major international courier companies operating in Vietnam are UPS, DHL, and TNT SkyPak. Getting your teaching aids and equipment into Vietnam should not be a problem.

Remember that Vietnam is a communist country and there are certain materials that are expressly prohibited from being brought in:

- Any material that can be construed as being against the government and the communist party of Vietnam

- Any material that seeks to undermine or overthrow duly-constituted authorities

- Pornographic material of any kind

- All other materials that might be deemed as offensive to Vietnamese culture and mores

Computers equipped with a modem are technically required to have an import license as a telecommunication device from the Ministry of Trade. This regulation also applies to mobile phones but is rarely, if ever, enforced. Check with your in-country contact about the current situation. If you do decide to bring your laptop, it should not contain any information that the Vietnamese authorities might see as pornographic or politically sensitive. Duty exemptions may be obtained for items shipped or brought into Vietnam for display or training purposes, but not for sale.

Local currency is the Dông (VND; symbol đ). Notes are in denominations of đ500,000, 200,000, 100,000, 50,000, 20,000, 10,000, 5,000, 2,000, 1,000, 500, 200, and 100. Coins are in denominations of đ5,000, 2,000, 1,000, and 500. Interestingly, it is technically illegal to set prices or accept U.S. dollars as payment, yet U.S. currency is widely accepted and even viewed as alternative currency to the Vietnam Dông. White collar employees interviewing for jobs quote their salaries in dollars, and owners of office building quote their lease rates in dollars. You can use dollars to buy souvenirs at the public market or buy groceries at the supermarket. Exchange rates are usually the current rate. Even after all this proof, if you are uneasy about this situation, credit cards are a reliable alternative to cash for hotels and restaurants in the cities. There has been some recent talk of credit card fraud, so do be cautious of when and how you use your credit cards. Traveler's checks are not as widely accepted, but should be purchased in U.S. dollars to avoid exchange rate charges. Automated Teller Machines are available in larger towns for local currency withdrawals.

## PROGRAM DELIVERY

As you begin meeting and greeting your session participants, be aware of a couple of the social norms in Vietnam. Connections and introductions are an important part of doing business here. Business cards are often exchanged at first meetings. The Vietnamese often use both hands to give and receive cards. This is very similar to Japanese customs, but it is not as formal. A slight bow may be incorporated into the exchange. This is a good opportunity to check the pronunciation of names and acknowledge title. Outside of formal meetings, a common, very polite hello and good-bye is "xin chao" (pronounced seen chao). Less formal is the simple greeting "chao" (pronounced chow) is used with the appropriate title, showing respect for age and status.

- Chao Anh: can be used for a male, older or those you want to show respect for
- Chao Chi: for female, older or those you want to show respect for
- Chao Em: to younger male or female

When you are uncertain of the person's age or status, err on the side of caution and use "chao anh" or "chao chi." When addressing someone directly and using his or her name, know that Vietnamese names begin with the family name, followed by the middle name, and finally the given name. Use given names with an appropriate title, for example, Mr. Nguyen Anh Khai is addressed as Mr. Khai. In the same way, a visitor named Mr. John Doe will be addressed as Mr. John.

In conducting your class, keep in mind that Vietnamese, like most Asians, regard politeness and courtesy among the highest virtues. Never cause anyone to lose "face" or embarrass him or her in public. Avoid direct confrontation or any situation that could result in open conflict. When a student gives a wrong answer to your question and you do not require a precise response, you should avoid a direct statement such as, "You're wrong." Instead, try to direct the student toward the right answer by asking a series of questions that will eventually get him or her there. Good examples of leading questions are: "Why do you say that?" or "What if you looked at it another way?" Give them the opportunity to save face and adjust their answers.

As with audiences in our own country, ground rules are important. This is especially true when it comes to cell phone usage. As with so many people today, Vietnamese like to show how busy and important they are by answering cell phones, even while in a conference or during training. You may want to ask the participants to suggest the ground rules before beginning the session and make sure that technology is addressed.

Working with translators and interpreters will be important aspects of training in Vietnam. Other chapters have extensively covered the factors to consider when using translators; there are not special concerns in Vietnam. Just remember to build this translation issue into your project plan and time schedule. Younger participants will be better able to sustain energy levels where interpreters are used. They will also be slightly more open to new ideas from both east and west and will have more energy to go through more rigorous training regimes with longer hours, more physical activity, etc.

Different training methodologies can all work well here. Case studies, role plays, and lectures will all work quite well. In fact, it would be good to vary the types used throughout one program in order to minimize boredom.

## TECHNICAL REQUIREMENTS

Equipment for PowerPoint, DVD, and other audio video presentations are universally available in the cities. Most of the hotels have function and meeting rooms that rent out equipment, or have them free with meals and use of the rooms. Any electronics you bring will require an adaptor. Electricity in Vietnam is 220 volts, accepting two-pin flat plugs. Video format is PAL.

The Internet isn't always as accessible as it is in the United States. Internet cafes can be found around the city and in the hotels, but access in your meeting room is unlikely. Vietnam has an extensive firewall system that limits access to outside sites and prohibits use of wide area networks (WANs). There are no local access numbers for international phone calls through U.S. long distance carriers. You will be required to place calls through the Vietnamese long distance carrier and most likely will be subjected to high surcharges added to service by the hotel. Cell phone usage is problematic as well. Speak with your in-country contact about the necessity of phone accessibility and discuss your options.

## ACCOMMODATIONS

Vietnam is among the safest countries in Asia for travel. Crimes against tourists are not tolerated and are punished harshly. As long as you are not engaging in something that might be construed as an act against the government or its duly constituted authorities, you should feel comfortable and safe moving around the country.

A number of major international hotels already operate in Vietnam, among them Sheraton, Hyatt, Sofitel, Omni, and Renaissance. These are all located in or close to the central business districts of either Ho Chi Minh City (the commercial capital) or Hanoi (the political capital). The local hotels, among them Caravelle, Majestic, Rex, and Bong Sen, are quite reputable and clean.

Stick to bottled water, which is widely available. For food, hotel fare is generally safe and hygienic and there are many fine restaurants offering the world's favorite cuisine (French, Italian, Japanese, Indian, Chinese, American burgers, and, of course, Vietnamese). The street food represents an adventure, although visitors are probably better off avoiding it.

## GETTING AROUND

The best and safest way to get around either Ho Chi Minh City or Hanoi is via taxi. These are clean, air-conditioned, and most have English-speaking (or at least English-understanding) drivers. Taxies have standardized meters so you know exactly how much you pay at the end of a fare. Insist that your taxi driver use the meter. If you are taking a motorcycle taxi or cyclo, negotiate the fare before you go. Caution is needed for pedestrians as well as drivers; watch where you are going and look for traffic. Roads have been described by visitors as chaotic.

If you are daring enough, you can rent a motorbike and go around as 95% of the locals do. Just be aware that there are certain unspoken laws of the road:

- A green light does not mean that you can automatically go ahead. You have to watch out for those coming from the other side trying to beat the red light. An orange light is a signal for the Vietnamese to hurry up rather than to slow down. And a red light is just another color to be beaten.

- In case of an accident, the one with the more expensive motor bike is always at fault. This holds true unless you are a foreigner, in which case even if your motorbike is a war remnant, you will always be at fault.

- Teenagers rule the road. You should always give way to them.

There are few buses, and their destinations are poorly identified. So unless you have the time to get lost and have an unplanned adventure, these would be a poor choice.

The human-powered bicycle carts locally called "cyclos" are fun if you want to do some sight-seeing. However, their routes have been limited in recent years to ease congestion so you probably won't get to where you want to really go using one of these contraptions.

 **THE PEOPLE**

Vietnamese are warm, welcoming, and friendly. For Americans who may be concerned about whether there are any lingering animosities because of the war, there is absolutely no reason to be. Sixty percent of the population were born *after* the war and therefore have no strong feelings about it. Those who lived during the war and fought for whichever side just want to get on with life and have little or no desire to look back. Quite on the contrary, they often have a great respect for American technology and popular culture.

There is still a strong traditional culture in Vietnam. There are areas of influence from China and other Asian countries as well as some Western influence. The Vietnamese shake hands with both men and women at the beginning and the end of a meeting. The handshake may be replaced with a slight bow of head. Vietnamese men may be uncomfortable socializing with foreign women. Women may be seated together at meals and other social meetings. It is not polite to touch someone's head. It is seen as an invasion of personal space because the head is viewed as the spiritual center of the person. Finally, in this culture it is not polite to point at someone, so use your whole hand to gesture to another.

The best way to win the hearts of the Vietnamese people is to learn as much as you can about them and their culture. Pick up a few Vietnamese phrases. Enjoy Vietnamese food—be daring and try the more exotic items in their menu list. Go and watch a water puppet show and other Vietnamese cultural presentations. Ask questions about their culture and don't pretend to know everything. The explanation of a custom can help build relationships. If given a compliment, the polite way to respond is by denying it. Modesty is considered a blessing in all Asian countries. Hold your tongue when it comes to political conversations and viewpoints. The government continues to monitor foreign businesspeople in public places. Translators have even been known to pass information on to the government.

Always extend utmost courtesy to the older people. Address them with greater politeness and civility than you would the younger ones. Women must be treated and referred to with utmost modesty. Avoid sexual innuendoes in your language and in your jokes.

Vietnam is still largely agricultural (rice, coffee, livestock). Industry has grown around products for export including garments, shoes, and textiles.

## !!! PREPARATION

Prepare for your presentation as you would any other audience in the world—with a lot of respect for the intelligence of the people and with the sincere desire to impart something of value to them.

Do not think that because the information and knowledge that you are going to provide is basic, that you can get away with sloppy preparation and presentation. Do not underestimate the intelligence and sensibilities of the Vietnamese audience. Nations have lost wars underestimating them.

Teachers are among the most respected in Vietnamese society and are therefore expected to act with the highest level of dignity and decorum.

Some Vietnamese words that will be helpful for you are

| hello | "chao" |
| thank you | "cam on" |
| excuse me | "xin loi" |

##  THE PRESENTATION

Unless you speak fluent Vietnamese, you will most likely have to use an interpreter. Be sure to use one who is familiar with business language. There are language instruction schools that specialize in business English so you may want to use an interpreter from one of these. If you hire freelance interpreters, be sure they are working with or used to working with an international, preferably American, company.

Speak slowly and deliberately. If you are using an interpreter, pause after each complete thought so that the interpreter can properly translate for you. A complete thought may be one complex sentence or two simple sentences that make up the same thought. Pause after no more than two sentences for your interpreter to be able to recall your message.

More than ever, visual aids are necessary to reinforce your message. Remember that teaching through an interpreter degrades your original message by at least 30 percent. You should try to design your visual aids so that they cover the gap.

Translate your visual aids into Vietnamese (you can have the English words in much smaller font).

Work out the training schedule to take into consideration the translation time. The Vietnamese language tends to use more words for the same idea as English, so a class that would normally last thirty minutes in an English-only setting will take up to ninety-minutes in a Vietnamese-English setting.

As mentioned earlier, the Vietnamese tend to be quiet and do not actively participate in class. Asking the teacher questions is perhaps seen as disrespectful, as this suggests that the teacher was not able to teach clearly or that the teacher's ideas are being challenged. Do not be discouraged by this. Instead, tell your students to ask questions, saying that this is not only acceptable but highly encouraged as a way of learning from each other. If need be, have prepared pre-determined questions and have these planted among volunteers who will then ask questions at the appropriate times.

Vietnam can bring you an opportunity to experience Asian culture first-hand with fewer formalities than most. First-time travelers to the region are particularly fortunate to have the chance to replace any old, preconceived notions about the country. You may have some kind of emotional reaction to Vietnam, but do yourself a favor and forego the old lessons from history class, travel with an open heart and mind about the people, the culture, and the country, and be pleasantly surprised.

**Try this helpful website and personal resource:**

- https://travelregistration.state.gov
- Tristan B. de la Rosa, Banyan Way, Executive Coaching and Development: www.thebanyanway.com

**PART FOUR**

# Australia

# Australia

Australia is a land of interesting creatures like the kangaroo, koala, wombat, dingo, emu, and kookaburra; and plants such as the eucalyptus and acacias. As soon as you hear of the Aborigines (indigenous people), didgeridoo (musical instrument), and boomerang (wooden throwing stick), you know we are talking about the wonderful country of Australia.

"I LOVED Australia!" Betsy Foss (Morgan Stanley) tells us. She said: "I caught myself thinking that I could live here without any hesitation."

Here are some insights and suggestions for successfully training, teaching, and presenting to Australians.

## ??? THE REQUEST

The request, in the example we will use for discussion, is computer training for a Fortune 500 company. Arrangements had been made for conducting the session at the company's location in Sydney (the largest city). Typical requests from Australia cover all topics. The Australians freely ask for training and provide training to other countries.

## • • • GETTING THERE

Getting there takes a really long time (about twenty-five hours from New York), so be prepared for entertaining yourself to pass the time. It takes 14½ hours on a direct flight from San Francisco. Make sure your passport, travel documents, and accommodations are all in order and arranged far ahead of time, so you won't have to scramble at the last minute. A U.S. passport or passport of any other nationality **must** have at least six months remaining validity from the day of entry into the country for which a visa has been applied for. If validity is less than six months Express Travel Services (ETS) will renew your passport (fees apply) at www.myvisapassport.com/Visa-Australia-Business.html.

Australian business visa requirements include:

- Valid passport for six months

- One visa application form, completed and signed

- Two passport-type photographs

- Non-U.S. citizens must present a copy of their "green card" or a valid visa back to the United States

- A letter of invitation from the host company in Australia

- An official letter (on company letterhead) from the company stating the purpose and duration of the trip, and that the company will take care of all the financial expenses of the applicant during his or her intended stay in Australia

- Copy of airline tickets or confirmed itinerary

Add two days for travel to your schedule, plus a day to get rested and acclimated to the new time zone and location. The time zone in Sydney is GMT +10

Holidays that may affect your travel and program scheduling include:

- January: New Year's Day (1st)

- January: Australia Day (last Friday or Monday)

- March/April: Good Friday, Easter Monday

- April: Anzac Day (25th), which marks the anniversary of the first major military action fought by Australian and New Zealand forces during the First World War. ANZAC stands for Australian and New Zealand Army Corps.

- June: Queen's Birthday (second Monday)

- August: Bank Holiday (first Monday)

- October: Labour Day (first Monday)

- December: Christmas Day (25th), Boxing Day (26th)

Located in Mascot NSW (New South Wales, Australia), Sydney Airport is approximately 8 km/5 miles from the central city. Sydney Airport is easily accessible by all modes of transport, including car, train, taxi, or bus. There are rail stations located at both the international and domestic terminals. The international rail station is located at the northern end of the terminal and is accessible from the arrival level.

Airport Link is a fast and convenient way to reach the centre of Sydney. Trains run approximately every ten minutes, and the journey into the city takes only thirteen minutes. The international and domestic rail stations link directly to the City Circle, which means that most city destinations are within a short walk of stations.

The State Transit Website (www.131500.com.au) has useful information regarding public transport options.

Each terminal has its own sheltered taxi area with supervisors available in peak hours to ensure a smooth flow of taxis for travelers. The approximate fare you can expect to pay to or from Sydney Airport to Sydney City is around $25. Passengers pay for any bridge or road tolls on top of the fare (these fares are in Australian dollars and are based on non-peak traffic conditions).

A $2.50 airport toll is payable by all passengers taking a taxi from any of Sydney Airport's taxi ranks.

Contacts have been provided below if you would prefer to pre-book your taxi.

- Taxis Combined Services: phone: 133 300 or
- Web: www.taxiscombined.com.au

## PROGRAM DESIGN

The software training program that Betsy Foss was presenting had been previously designed and tested. Designs in English work well with this English-speaking audience. You can design a program with mini lecture, small group discussion, case studies, or role plays for this audience. Keep it interactive. You can include practice exercises and games if appropriate for your topic.

## LOGISTICS

Try to make arrangements through company contacts. Although everything is in English, you should take care to make sure that requirements and agreements are clear. You should also send materials far ahead (three weeks) of time. Bring a hard copy with you, in case you have to make last-minute copies.

The Australian currency includes coins in denominations of 5, 10, 20, 50 cents, $1, and $2. Bank notes/Australian dollars come in denominations of $5, $10, $20, $50, and $100.

## PROGRAM DELIVERY

The surprises are in the language. Yes, it is English, but not American English . . . and that is actually the hard part. Don't assume that because you speak the same language that all words have the same meaning. This actually makes it more difficult, as you "assume" that everything has the same meaning and that the audience is taking the material in the meaning you are thinking. Betsy suggests that you say at the beginning of the program, on the first day, "If I say anything that offends and/or is confusing, stop me right then and there so we can be clear on what I thought I was saying."

Mini-lecture, small group discussion, and interactive projects work well here.

## TECHNICAL REQUIREMENTS

Bring a laptop that has an internal power supply that can detect and switch to different local currents. Let them know ahead of time what you are bringing and they can also have the same laptop model available. You can use the power cord from the other laptop. Same for the data-show/overhead projector that plugged into the laptop. You will want a universal monitor plug so there will be no issue.

For the training session, it is possible to set up a room with several PCs so that everyone has his or her own and they are all networked into the corporate network as well. This works extremely well, as participants can follow along and do training assignments as they are being shown to them. Make it structured but informal so they can ask questions at any time. This way you will be able to flip back and forth between presentation/ instructions and hands-on practice.

Electricity in Australia is 220 to 240 volts AC. If you bring electrical appliances that happen to use 110 volts instead, directly plugging them into an Australian plug will burn them out. Transformers are required, and these are probably best bought abroad.

Whether you need a transformer or not, make sure that your appliances are configured for the three pin Australian plug. If you cannot get one of these at home, you may be wise to wait until you get to Australia.

If you have a laptop computer, you will probably find that the transformer that comes with it automatically adjusts to 110 or 240 volts. Check though. If it is able to cope with both currents, you will still need an adapter for the Australian three-pin system.

Bring your program on a DVD or Flash drive. Any videos that you need for your program should have already been converted to PAL format before you leave home. Check ahead of time with your host to see if the Internet is available, if that is needed for your program, in the location where you will be presenting.

You can rent a cell phone with a SIM card if you need one from www.cellhire.com/content/cell-phone-aus.htm.

## ACCOMMODATIONS

Make arrangements to stay in a hotel that is near where you will be presenting the program. All of the major hotels are available in Sydney, such as the Hilton, Radisson, Marriott, Four Seasons, and Sheraton.

Don't walk alone at night. Have your hotel call for a taxi. Get a card from your hotel with their name and address for your return.

## GETTING AROUND

You can ask the hotel to arrange transportation for you, if you are not renting a car. If renting, make sure you have good directions and maps to make it easier for you.

Transport around the city is convenient by car, train, taxi, or bus. The State Transit website at www.131500.com.au is helpful in planning.

## THE PEOPLE

The Australians, in our experience, are very interested in the instructor having a good time—their hospitality is unmatched. In our example, the Australians asked during a conference call, prior to arrival, whether there was anything we would like to do while we were there. Since the instructors were going to be there for a couple weeks and three weekends, we went online and studied Australia in that general area, picking three things to do: going to Phillips Island to see the pygmy penguins, touring the local vineyards, and seeing an Australian football game if one was going to be playing in Melbourne, where we were going to be located. During the next conference call, when we mentioned that any one of those would be fine, we did not expect the hospitality that was offered. We were able to do all three, and different people took us to each. One of the gentlemen and his mother loved the penguins and offered to be our escorts, and we saw a Koala preserve on the way as well. Another man and his wife loved the particular football team that was going to be playing one of the weekends, and another person offered to take us through wine country and while doing so we visited an old resurrected historical gold mine town nearby.

The people were great, friendly, helpful, and, in retrospect, a lot like people in Canada.

The earliest known inhabitants of Australia were the Indigenous Australians. The Dutch called the coastlines New Holland. The British called the Southeast New South

Wales and established a penal colony there. Thus, most Australians are European descendents, with only about 2 percent being of the Indigenous population, mainland Aborigines and Torres Strait Islanders.

The Commonwealth of Australia is a constitutional monarchy with a parliamentary system of government. Australia consists of six states, two major mainland territories, and other minor territories. The states are New South Wales, Queensland, South Australia, Tasmania, Victoria, and Western Australia. The two major mainland territories are the Northern Territory and the Australian Capital Territory.

This enormous country covers 2,988,888 square miles. Australia has a liberal democratic political system and remains a Commonwealth Realm. The capital city is Canberra. The population is twenty-one million, concentrated in the mainland state capitals of Sydney, Melbourne, Brisbane, Perth, and Adelaide.

There is no state religion. Most Australians consider themselves Christian.

Popular sports include cricket, hockey, netball, rugby league, rugby union, cycling, rowing, and swimming. Other popular sports include Australian rules football, horse racing, football (soccer) and motor racing.

## !!! PREPARATION

Candy is called lollies. The students are very pleased when lollies are available during the training session. These can be purchased at the local store. Having some available for each day makes the day more fun.

- "G'day" is "hullo," pronounced "Gidday," which is a shortened form of "Good Day," and used mostly in informal situations. More formally we would say "Hullo," "Good Morning," or "Good Afternoon."

- Goodbye is Goodbye. Although some people say "Hooroo," pronounced " 'ooroo."

- Bloke is an Aussie male who generally is a hard worker and does the right thing, for example: "Bill's a good bloke."

- Mate is friend, mainly for males. Everyone in Australia is a mate, so we would often say "G'day, mate" or "Thanks, mate."

- Onya means "well done," a shortened form of "good on you," a fine "Aussieism."

For some reason Australians shorten words wherever possible, especially peoples' names. They are generally shortened to one syllable and then have a suffix added to the end. Here are a few examples:

- A cup of tea or coffee becomes a "cuppa."

- Angela becomes Angie.

- Australian becomes Aussie.

- Barbecue becomes barbie

- Elizabeth becomes Lizzie

- Football becomes footy, pronounced with a soft "t" somewhere between T and D.

- Burgess becomes burgo

- Johnathon becomes Johnno

- Smoko means a break from work for a smoke, which now means a tea break, even if you don't smoke.

By the way, liquor stores are called bottle shops.

## THE PRESENTATION

It might be good for a presenter to acknowledge that he or she might say something that he or she did not realize might be offensive and apologize beforehand. Warn the participants (particularly if they have never been out of Australia themselves) that sometimes words have different meaning in different countries and this difference is not always known. Put the students at ease to clue you in whenever possible. Obviously, talking to someone who has either lived or worked there before or a native Australian who is in the United States can help. They might not think of everything taboo either, but even a couple items can give someone enough of a forewarning to possibly not make as many mistakes. Sometimes we don't think of another country where they speak the same language as needing the same courtesy of finding out about them before going over. For example, one does NOT say "fanny" in Australia. It has extremely derogatory sexual association. Pity the poor visitor who goes there and has that as a first name. Do not bring someone any Fanny Farmer candy.

Another example is that they "barrack" for their favorite team. They do NOT "root" for their favorite team—another word that has sexual connotation wherein a female is doing sexual favors for team members in their locker room. This embarrassed not only the poor gentleman who had offered to take one of us to an Australian football game, but we had asked him who he "rooted for" in front of his wife and children. When a very strange reaction was received, we then asked, "What did I say?" and he said to ask one of the female employees at work, whom we asked the next Monday. Needless to say, apologies were made and relayed to his wife as well. He was very gracious about it and said he realized that it was probably a mistake. The Australians truly are very kind and gracious people. Words of advice: Be aware that if you say something and get a strange reaction, you may have stumbled on a cultural difference. Depending on how well you know the people, you can ask forthright what indiscretion you performed and it may give them a chuckle or you may want to ask a specific individual at a later time. It might even be a good idea to talk to the person whom you are working closely with when you arrive to clue you in on anything you are doing that is "inappropriate."

G'day!

**Helpful websites and references include:**

- www.airportlink.com.au

- www.aussieslang.com/features/australian-slang-basics.asp

- www.australia.gov.au

- www.convertunits.com/info/kilometeres

- www.myvisapassport.com/Visa-Australia-Business.html

- www.131500.com.au (State Transit website)

- www.sydneyairport.com

- www.sydneyontheweb.com

- www.taxiscombined.com.au

**PART FIVE**

# Europe

# Denmark

Cool crisp waters create the backdrop behind the famous Little Mermaid statue in Copenhagen harbor in Denmark. This Scandinavian country is as famous for its Viking history as it is for its progressiveness. The Kingdom of Denmark, a constitutional monarchy, is the southernmost of the Scandinavian countries and is a member of the European Union. The mainland is located north of Germany, southwest of Sweden, and south of Norway. Denmark also includes two off-shore territories, Greenland and the Faroe Islands. The national capital and "one of the best places to live" is Copenhagen. This section will provide information regarding what to expect and tips for success when training, teaching, or presenting in Denmark.

## ??? THE REQUEST

The example we will use for Denmark is a request for a leadership and organization development (OD) program presented in Copenhagen, the capital.

When asked to conduct leadership training for an international company in Denmark, it is easy to be both excited and a little nervous.

## • • • GETTING THERE

A valid passport is required to enter the country.

Copenhagen is also known as København. The native name of Denmark is Danmark.

The Copenhagen airport is large and modern. Copenhagen Airport (København's Lufthavn), Kastrup is the major airport for both Copenhagen, Denmark, and Malmö, Sweden. Copenhagen Airport has all the world's major airlines represented in all terminals. Copenhagen Airport is located in Amager, south of the city center and only a few minutes from the Öresund Bridge, which connects Denmark with Sweden. Accessibility to and from the Copenhagen Airport is by taxi or bus right in front of the entrance and the railway station beneath Terminal 3, where the Copenhagen Metro connects you to all major Danish cities, and the Öresund Railway that takes you directly to and from Sweden.

Danish holidays that may affect your travel and program scheduling include:

- January: New Year's Day (1st)
- March/April: Maundy (Holy) Thursday, Good Friday, Easter Monday
- May: Worker's Day (1st), Common Prayer Day, Ascension Day, Whit Monday
- June: Constitution Day (5th)
- December: Christmas (24, 25. 26), New Year's Eve (31st)

Because of Denmark's northern location, the length of the day with sunlight varies greatly. There are short days during the winter when the sun rises around 9:30 A.M. and sunset is at 4:30 P.M., as well as long summer days with sunrise at 3:30 A.M. and sunset at 10 P.M. The shortest and longest days of the year have traditionally been celebrated. The celebration for the shortest day corresponds roughly with Christmas (Danish: *jul*) and modern celebrations concentrate on Christmas Eve, 24 December. The celebration for the longest day is Midsummer Day, which is known in Denmark as *sankthansaften (St. John's evening).*

The weather in Copenhagen is mild through all the four seasons. Summers bring temperatures averaging around 68 degrees F (20 degrees C), while in mid-winter temperatures hover just above or below 0 degrees C. Rainfall is moderate too, but spread throughout the year, so showers are possible in any season. Grey skies are the norm rather than the exception in Copenhagen.

The climate of Denmark is in the temperate zone. There is a lot of wind, which is stronger during the winter and weaker during the summer. Denmark has an average of 170 rainy days. The greatest rainfall comes in November.

Denmark is in the Central European Time Zone (CEST), one hour ahead of Greenwich Mean Time (GMT+1). Daylight saving time +1 hour.

We arrived a few days early to get a sense of the city of Copenhagen and get over jet lag. We took a cab to the hotel.

## PROGRAM DESIGN

The needs assessment in our program had already been conducted, and the standard program was designed to accommodate international audiences. This included lecture, speakers, learning teams for discussion, games, and role plays. We found that the program was most successful if we designed opportunities for the Danish participants to bring in and use their own examples of situations they were dealing with.

Make sure that any research data that is part of the program design is based on international research, not what is done only in one country. Participants don't seem to like data that is always from the same country and is not representative of theirs. (This is true wherever you present internationally.)

The city of Copenhagen has developed from a fishing village to a busy center of commerce. Most people speak some English in addition to Danish so our program design was in English.

## LOGISTICS

The location was an office setting in a conference room with standard equipment, all available as requested. Materials were shipped ahead of time. Unfortunately, in this case, no one checked to make sure they had been delivered to the correct room, so much time was lost searching for materials.

The currency of Denmark is the krone (kr), the plural form is "kroner." One krone is divided into 100 øre. Coins are in denominations of 25, 50 øre, 1, 2, 5, 10, 20 kroner. Bank notes come in denominations of 50, 100, 200, 500, 1,000 kroner. Almost all banks (including the Danske Bank at the airport) exchange money. Most hotels cash traveler's checks and exchange major foreign currencies, but they charge a substantial fee and give a lower rate. Although Denmark is part of the European Union, they have opted out of using the euro.

## PROGRAM DELIVERY

The room for our training was set up in pods with six at a table. There were name tags, but it would have been even more helpful to have additional tent cards for their names as well. There were nineteen participants from Germany, Spain, the United Kingdom, and the Netherlands, with varying degrees of capability in the English language. The materials had all been bound in booklets for each of the four days of the program. They were in English. The experience of the participants varied from six months to twenty-four years of service with the company. The German participant found it harder to understand the English spoken by the British and American participants and instructor than the English spoken by the other participants in the program. The reason for this was that those who speak English as a second language spoke in shorter, slower, simpler sentences and were therefore easier to understand.

The company's philosophy is that English is the language of business, so leadership training should be conducted in English. Another company goal is to ensure diversity by having a cross section of divisions and countries represented in each program.

The content of our program included change management, listening, and Situational Leadership. The program was designed to be interactive, which works well in Denmark.

## TECHNICAL REQUIREMENTS

To use your electric-powered equipment, bring a converter and an adapter. The electrical current in Scandinavia is 220 volts, 50 cycles alternating current (AC); wall outlets take Continental-type plugs, with two round prongs.

In our case, technical requirements were covered with the host and agreed on prior to the program presentation. The office location provided access to a variety of equipment and facilities.

We find it helpful to have a remote control to advance the slides on our computer. We bring our own computer and DVDs and have the technical expert on-site make sure that we are connecting everything correctly.

It is also important to have a technical expert available in case equipment does not work and needs to be fixed or replaced. Ask your host ahead of time, so that he or she will be available to help and how to contact them.

High-speed Internet is readily available, but check to make sure it is in the location that you need.

## ACCOMMODATIONS

Hotels in Copenhagen are very nice, and typical chains are represented, such as Hilton, Marriott, and Radisson. Three hotels were recommended to the participants prior to our program, so they were encouraged to select one and make their own reservations. This resulted in people staying in three different locations and being separated from each other, which did not help collaboration and relationship building.

Remember that it is light until around 10:30 P.M. and again at 2:30 A.M. in the summer, but dark most of the hours in the winter. This can be a little strange to most people and takes some getting used to. Bring a sleep mask in case you have trouble sleeping when it is light.

It is fine to drink the water. Food was excellent in any of the restaurants we tried.

Safety is not a major concern for this city, but for any emergencies you can dial 112 to report a fire or to call the police or an ambulance. State your phone number and address. Emergency calls from public telephones are free (no coins needed).

Telephone: International country code to call Denmark = +45.

For local phone calls, phones accept 1-, 5-, 10-, and 20-kroner coins. Pick up the receiver, dial the number, always include the area code, and wait until the party answers; then deposit the coins. You have roughly one minute per krone, so you can make another call on the same payment if your time has not run out. When it does, you will hear a beep and your call will be disconnected unless you deposit another coin. Dial the eight-digit number for calls anywhere within the country. For calls to the Faroe Islands (tel. 298) and Greenland (tel. 299), dial 00, then the three-digit code, then the five-digit number.

For international calls dial 00, then the country code (1 for the United States and Canada, 44 for Great Britain), the area code, and the number. It's very expensive to telephone or fax from hotels, although the regional phone companies offer a discount after 7:30 P.M. It's more economical to make calls from either the Copenhagen main rail station or the airports.

For an international operator, dial 113; for a directory-assisted international call, dial 115. To reach an AT&T operator, dial 80-01-0010; for MCI, 80-01-0022; for Sprint, 80-01-0877.

 **GETTING AROUND**

It is easy to get around Copenhagen using the Metro, buses, or taxi. There are lots of bicycles.

It seems quite safe to walk around the city. Some streets are blocked off for walking. People are willing to help with directions, and many people walk.

A traditional suburban train network in the greater Copenhagen area called S-Trains, or S-Tog (in Danish) are electric trains connecting the city center with the suburbs of Copenhagen. The numerous trains leave at ten- or twenty-minute intervals.

The railway connects Denmark with Sweden and Germany. Denmark has good highways. Always be on the alert for bicycles when driving and walking.

## THE PEOPLE

The Danish people are hearty, kind, blond, proud people who will willingly help you if you ask them. The primary language is Danish. Most people speak English. They are very friendly people.

Copenhagen has welcomed many immigrants. The foreigners and immigrants typically come from Western European countries such as neighboring Sweden and Norway, but also Great Britain, Eastern Europe (mostly Poland, Latvia, and Lithuania), former Yugoslavia, the Middle East (Turkey, Iraq, the West Bank/Gaza), Somalia, Pakistan, and Vietnam.

Simplicity and minimalism are the characteristics that best describe the simultaneously self-aware and receptive Danish culture. This can be seen everywhere in the architecture and furnishings.

Denmark is divided into five regions (Danish: *regioner*, singular: *region*) and a total of ninety-eight municipalities. Copenhagen is located in Region Hovedstaden.

The primary church in Denmark is Evangelical Lutheran, but many Danes do not consider themselves very religious.

Favorite sports include Danish football, ice hockey, handball, rugby, and cricket.

The Kingdom of Denmark is a constitutional monarchy. The Danish Constitution states that the monarch is not answerable for his or her actions, and his or her person is sacrosanct. The monarch appoints and dismisses the prime minister and other ministers. Executive authority is exercised on behalf of the monarch by the prime minister and other cabinet ministers who head departments. The cabinet, including the prime minister and other ministers, collectively make up the government.

Denmark's economy includes efficient agriculture, up-to-date small-scale and corporate industry, extensive government welfare measures, very high living standards, a stable currency, and high dependence on foreign trade. Denmark is a net exporter of food and energy.

The Danish economy is highly unionized; 75 percent of the labor force has membership in a trade union. Relationships between unions and employers are generally cooperative.

## PREPARATION

Find out the common mode of dress for the organization and culture ahead of time, if possible. Dress formally, including suit jackets, below-the-knee skirts for women, and ties for men, and you should be fine to present in any situation.

Find out the safety information for the facility so you can provide it at the beginning of the program to the participants. This includes what to do in case of emergency, escape routes from the building, and where they should all meet to make sure that everyone is there. If you don't do this, they ask for this information to be shared before starting.

Create one-page summary sheets of critical points for participants. This helps for the learners to know what they should have learned for each topic and/or each day of the program. This is especially helpful when participants are trying to learn in a language that is not their first language.

We found that scheduling a dinner on the second or third night of the program helped people to get to know one another and developed group camaraderie. We originally used an end-of-the-program celebration dinner and found that a group dinner earlier in the program was a great addition.

It is important to arrive early in order to set up the classroom and locate all of the materials. Finding the location of the presentation and the amount of time it takes to reach the location in traffic during the morning rush hour also requires additional planning.

Provide tent cards and markers, as well as name tags for the participants. Ask participants to write their names on both sides of the tent cards, to make it easier for everyone to learn others' names.

Basic Danish phrases and words that might come in handy include:

| | |
|---|---|
| Hello | "Hei" |
| Yes | "Ja" |
| No | "Nej" |
| How are you? | "Hvordan har du det?" |
| Fine. Thanks, and you? | "Fint, tak. Hvad med dig?" |
| Very good | "Meget Godt" |
| Good morning | "Godmorgen" |
| Good evening | "Godaften" |
| See you tomorrow | "Vi ses i morgen" |
| Open/Closed | "Åben/Lukket" |
| Do you speak English? | "Taler du engelsk?" |
| I don't speak Danish | "Jeg kan ikke dan" |

| I don't understand | "Det forstår jeg ikke" |
| Please | "Tak" |
| Sorry | "Undskyld!" |
| Thank you very much | "Tak skal du have!" |
| Good-bye | "Farvel" |

## THE PRESENTATION

The first morning of our program includes an overview of company values, businesses, and general information. Participants were given the results of their Myers-Briggs Type Inventory (MBTI) feedback. They were seated according to their MBTI types and mixed by type at each table. This did not work well because the introverts were dominated by the extroverts in their discussion. The next time, we made a revision to ensure that the discussion was more balanced in each group. We now start with an overview of different types and explain that introverts may be less likely to speak up and extroverts may have to provide silence and encouragement to hear from introverts. The feedback from the participants indicated that they would like one-on-one feedback on their reports, not just be given data and asked to discuss it at their tables, then present back to the large group. At one point a participant actually turned her back on her team and no one even noticed. When this was brought up to the large group by the instructor, the participant said that she had already been through this exercise and did not want to bias the others in her group—but no one in her group even noticed that she had turned her back and stopped participating!

The program activities work well when small group discussions are encouraged at each table, ideas are recorded on an easel/flip chart and presented back to the large group (for topics other than the MBTI results).

Work actually starts at 9 A.M. in this office. The participants were asked to be there by 8:30 A.M. These differences in starting times resulted in several of the participants arriving late, in addition to the fact that they each took separate transportation from the three hotels and many were delayed in traffic.

The distribution of participants at three different hotels also meant there was little interaction at dinner. A few people met for dinner, but there was no group activity or interaction with the entire group.

In the beginning of the program (the first morning), people arrived and did not socialize or talk. They immediately plugged in their computers and went to work. Everyone had his or her own computer, cell phone, and personal digital assistant (PDA). They were asked to close computers and turn off their phones and digital assistants for the duration of the program. At lunch people socialized only about fifteen minutes, then proceeded to eat lunch and work on their computers. Dinner was held around 7:30 or 8 P.M. and was leisurely for those who attended.

During the program, we served healthy food such as fruits, vegetables, cookies, sandwiches, and beverages. The portions were appropriately small and health-conscious.

As always in an international situation, speak slowly and simply in order for people with varying skills in English to comprehend. Also check for understanding by asking questions. Reinforce important learning by stating information in different ways and using different mediums, such as audiovisuals, workbooks to write in, and summary pages of important points.

The typical audiovisuals, presentation, and activities format works well with this audience.

When asked if anyone would like to volunteer to use their own examples for role plays, 50 percent of the participants had scenarios that they were eager to share. They were willing to have feedback and appreciated the comments of others.

It is often exhausting for the instructor to try to understand the accents of the various participants.

We have found participants in the program to be open and hungry for knowledge.

**Helpful websites and references include:**

- http://copenhagen.com/airport/
- www.single-serving.com/Danish/TB/basics.php
- www.timeanddate.com/worldclock/city

# England

**B**ig Ben tolls. The bell in the enormous clock that overlooks the awe-inspiring crypts of Westminster Abbey tells Londoners that the guards, who must protect the royal palace, will change. The Changing of the Guards at Buckingham Palace is a spectacle to be experienced. The guards are stiffly dressed in brilliant red and wearing very tall black fur hats balanced perfectly on their heads. Reverence for the Monarchy stands concurrent with respect for the elected Prime Minister. A short way down the River Thames, the Tower Bridge and the Tower of London receive visitors from all over the world to see the prison cells of famous prisoners and stunning crown jewels. London provides a glimpse of the fascinating country of England, but there is much more than even this to experience in England.

This chapter will provide information regarding what to expect and tips for success when training, teaching, and presenting in England.

## ??? THE REQUEST

Your company or client has determined the need for training in England. You breathe a sigh of relief because this "foreign" country, although you have never been there, doesn't seem so foreign. You probably have met or are even friends with someone from England; you speak the same language, share similar pop cultures, and have many of the same interests. It is true, yet don't be fooled into thinking there isn't some preparation necessary for your trip "across the pond."

Your destination could be London or a smaller city elsewhere in the country. There are countless possibilities for where your training may occur. The great thing about sharing a language with your host country is that all their resources are readily available to you, from Internet to written materials; you can reference them all with little difficulty, and plan the best trip and event possible. This is not to say that your in-country contact will not be invaluable; he or she will, but much of the research can be done by you personally to prepare yourself for success.

For the example we'll use in this chapter, we were asked to conduct a program that conveys corporate changes that need to be adopted across the world. This was a very challenging assignment, when people had to be persuaded to change, especially when they had not been consulted about the changes. In our case, processes need to be totally redesigned to obtain productivity improvements. This involves a great deal of work by people who already have enough to do in their daily assignments.

## • • • GETTING THERE

Passports are necessary, but no visa is required to travel to England. Flights to London are anywhere from thirteen hours from the West Coast to nine hours from New York. With numerous flight options, England is very easy to reach. London alone has five international airports. As with any travel of this length, it makes sense to arrive a day early so that you are well rested and able to inspect the location and room setup where the program will be delivered. This allows time to meet the local management and administrative staff as well as prepare transportation to the location. Suggestion: Plan the trip so you can stay through the weekend to do some sightseeing. Take into consideration the time difference and when you are traveling. We've made the mistake of leaving on Monday morning, arriving Monday evening (12 P.M. London time, 6 P.M. Chicago time) and teaching the following morning. Unable to sleep at my internal clock time of 6 P.M., I fell asleep around 5 A.M. local time for about an hour. It was then that the alarm went off to ready the training room for the day's activities. Some of us fall asleep better than others in new surroundings. What kind of traveler are you?

If London is not your final destination, you can reach most other large cities with a domestic flight from there, or you may choose rail travel. England has one of the largest railway networks in the world. Work with your travel agent on the best itinerary for you.

Holidays that may affect your travel and program plans include:

- January: New Year's Day (1st)
- March/April: Good Friday, Easter Monday
- May: Bank holidays (first Monday, last Monday)
- August: Bank holiday (last Monday)
- December: Christmas (25th), Boxing Day (26th)

 ## PROGRAM DESIGN

Conduct your typical needs assessment for your session. Get to know your audience and their backgrounds through your in-country contact. Assess their level of knowledge of the subject. Tailor your course to meet their needs. The program should be designed in English. Make sure you are using proper dictionary English and avoid slang or jargon. Include handouts and visuals as well as case studies and worksheets. Exercises should incorporate group and individual assignments. As you work, be mindful of the differences in our languages. Though we all speak English, you will still have some translation issues to deal with to ensure understanding. Time should be built into your schedule to address these differences and occasional misunderstandings that wouldn't normally occur with audiences at home. This is particularly important if you are using materials straight from your typical classrooms. Don't assume that you can take these materials off the shelf with no customization. Start the process by localizing, swapping terms, examples, illustrations, and references for British ones. Every audience appreciates an effort made to get into their shoes. Additionally, we have found that audiences in England are much more likely to be made up of participants from countries other than England. Many companies use London as a hub city to bring in other European employees. Clearly identify your audience and build your course around the language needs of these individuals. Schedule more frequent breaks because active listening across languages is tiresome and challenging.

Similarly, if your content is aimed at communicating corporate changes or procedural differences, involve as many people as you can who are directly affected by the changes. You will learn, from their perspective, how it will feel to hear these ideas and you will learn the best way to approach the most difficult topics of your session. This is particularly true if your audience will be made up of individuals from several countries. Their involvement and advanced buy-in will lend itself to a more successful program on-site.

Finally, here's a word about humor. It seems more and more British humor, music, and pop culture are blending. Many of their comedy and reality shows are broadcast worldwide. Through the magic of television, many of us have been exposed to authentic British TV in our homes. If you are at all familiar with these programs, you have some insight into British humor and can store it in your toolbox of tricks for England. It has been said that jokes in England are smaller and smarter.

## LOGISTICS

Upon arriving, use the ATM at the airport to get the best exchange rate on currency you can start using immediately. English money is the Great British Pound (*GBP* = **£**). It is made up of 100 pence. The singular of pence is a penny. 50 pence is written 50p. Coins are in 1p, 2p, 5p, 10p, 20p, 50p, £1, and £2 amounts. Notes are in 5-, 10-, 20-, and 50-pound denominations. The slang term for a pound is a quid.

Plans should be made for the occasional bank holidays when businesses are closed and very little work can be accomplished. There is one scheduled each season, not all of the UK is affected by every one.

Easels are an excellent tool to capture ideas throughout the program, keep people on task, and to reinforce important concepts in writing, therefore avoiding some of the language pitfalls you may encounter.

Shipping is quite reliable; however, it is always advisable to bring a hard copy and electronic copy of all materials in your carry-on luggage just in case the boxes do not arrive at the correct location on time. Remember to format your documents to A4 paper, which is slightly large than a standard 8½ × 11. Most software offers accommodation for this in their "page setup" area.

## PROGRAM DELIVERY

Depending on the size of your group, consider using a large round or oval table for smaller groups in situations in which your topic includes building or gaining support and addressing questions and concerns. This allows for free discussion and an informal feel to the program delivery. Spoken British English is surprisingly difficult to clearly understand. There are several terms that can be misunderstood and require clarification throughout the program, even when we are all speaking English. In our training experience, the French, German, and Italian participants who had joined us all spoke English. It takes some time to get used to their accents and so it is important to be very patient with each other. Competitive learning games work well in this culture. Role plays, case studies, and practice exercises are effective if they are well designed to reinforce critical learning points.

We had a significant learning during one particular session. What we did not expect was the strong negative reaction to being "pressured" by the main office to participate in a program that had been developed without the input of each country. The next time we learned our lesson and involved these people in the beginning of the program design. The output was significantly improved by their participation in the early stages of training development. Tea time is the perfect time to work through some of these issues. Schedule a morning and an afternoon tea break with biscuits. This is a more casual social event when some of the questions from the day can be discussed in a less formal way. Of course, you will have those who will leave the room during this time. Be clear how long the break time will be since, as with all audiences, you will have those participants who will push these timeframes.

## TECHNICAL REQUIREMENTS

Electrical outlets will be 240 volts. Bring a converter, European plugs, and extension cords, in case they are needed for a laptop. It is likely that you can bring your presentation on a storage device and request that a laptop and projector be set up in the presentation room ahead of time. You may also request an overhead projector and microphones, if necessary. Video equipment will most likely require PAL format. Some equipment will switch between PAL and NTSC, but most will not. You will have to have your videotape converted to PAL before coming to the country and then send it in advance to your in-country contact so he or she can test it.

You will need to check ahead to see whether your location offers high-speed Internet, if you need it for your program presentation.

## ACCOMMODATIONS

Accommodations are very nice and simple. You should feel very at home in most hotels. In some hotels, the tub has an attached spray device that can be used to shower soap off of you, but it is not attached high enough to stand under it. So you need to use one hand to hold the spray device. Some do have a bidet in the bathroom, not a familiar fixture to us, but you don't have to use it.

The British breakfast with tomato and beans is a bit of a surprise, but you quickly get used to it. Pub food in any town is quite delicious and the comfortable atmosphere is relaxing and friendly. We always love to try the local favorites and be sure to sample bangers and mash (sausage and mashed potatoes), fish and chips (fried fish and French fries), or shepherd's pie at a pub before you go home. When in London, you can taste some of the best foods in the ethnic restaurants such as Indian, Swiss, French, and Italian.

The Hilton, Radisson, and Marriott hotels offer the accommodations that you are used to—but it is always fun to try a different hotel as well. Just check online to see whether they offer whatever you require.

In general, London is considered a safe city, but you will need to be aware of opportunities for pickpockets (on public transportation and in crowded places), not give money to beggars (this only encourages them to continue), and always walk on well-lit, busy streets.

## GETTING AROUND

When you arrive in London, you may choose to ride the "tube" (the underground subway), which has lines that crisscross the city of London, but its reliability has over the years not remained up to standard. Chances are you are on a bit tighter schedule and you need a more efficient mode of transportation. Regardless of the city you are in, taxis are a good choice. You may not want to brave driving in a new city on the opposite side of the street. Taxis are readily available and "black cabs" are more special, since drivers are required to pass a challenging test proving their knowledge ("The Knowledge" is the name of the exam) of the city and its history, making them tour guides. Expect that you may need to carry your luggage down several streets to a hotel.

IMPORTANT SAFETY NOTE: When walking, it is very dangerous if you do not learn to look both left and right twice before crossing, because traffic is coming from the opposite direction from what we are used to. You constantly have to remind yourself to look opposite of your usual habit.

The tour buses are two stories so you can really see everything and can purchase a day ticket that allows you to get on and off the bus wherever you want to. This is excellent for sightseeing. There are no other particular safety issues in England, just that basic travel precautions are necessary. The police can be called by dialing "999" at any phone.

If you rent a car, be sure to get an automatic. It is hard enough to drive on the opposite side of the road, but when you also have to shift with your opposite hand, it gets really confusing.

## THE PEOPLE

Everyone is very friendly and cordial. There is more familiarity between the sexes than you may be used to seeing in the office. It is very nice to have dinner arranged for all of the participants to get to know each other better. Soccer ("football"), lawn tennis, cricket, rugby, and golf are all good topics of conversation. The weather can also be an easy discussion starter.

Bring an umbrella. The weather is very changeable and unpredictable. Winters are cold and wet with occasional snow, and summers are generally warm with frequent showers. July and August are the warmest months, while January and February are the coldest; however, temperatures do not usually drop lower than 32 degrees F (0 degrees C). The most pleasant times to travel in England are spring (May and June) and autumn (September and October).

It is interesting for us to discover that the British consider it inappropriate for foreigners to wear shorts, but not a problem for British actresses to be naked in films.

Manners are very important. Eating is done with fork in the left hand and knife in the right. Stand in line (queue) awaiting a service. Men take off your hats when indoors. Say "excuse me" and someone will let you pass. Say "please" and "thank you" as appropriate. Cover your mouth when yawning. Say "sorry" if you bump into someone. Do not talk loudly, hug, or slap someone's back. Avoid staring at anyone. Smile. Shake hands when meeting someone.

History is very significant in this country. British people tend to know so much about their history and can describe events in great and interesting detail. Significant periods are prehistory, Roman Period, Arthurian Period, Anglo-Saxon Period, the Middle Ages, Reformation and Restoration, Age of Empire, 20th Century, and current. A fascinating experience is to ask about the history or one's family or the Royal Family and you will be able to gain a great deal of information in a short time.

The United Kingdom (UK) is a parliamentary democracy and a constitutional monarchy comprising four constituent countries—England, Northern Ireland, Scotland, and Wales—with the Queen/King as head of state. The UK uses a parliamentary government based on strong democratic traditions. The position of prime minister, the UK's head of government, belongs to the current leader of the political party that can obtain the confidence of a plurality in the House of Commons. The prime minister and his or her cabinet are formally appointed by the monarch to form Her/His Majesty's Government. However, the prime minister chooses the cabinet, and by convention, the queen/king respects the prime minister's choices.

Although the Christian religion is most common and there is a link between church and state, England also has followers of Islam and Indian religions such as Hinduism, Sikhism, Buddhism, and Jainism.

Financial services, tourism, auto manufacturing, and the chemical and pharmaceutical industries (GlaxoSmithKline and AstraZeneca) are all significant for England.

London is the capital of England and of the United Kingdom. It is one of the world's leading business, financial, and cultural centers.

A number of major sports originated in the United Kingdom, including football (soccer), rugby, cricket, tennis, and golf.

## !!! PREPARATION

Dress professionally. In addition to reviewing and practicing the presentation, it is very important to prepare yourself physically and emotionally to be at your very best. This means getting enough sleep before leaving home and arriving with extra time to get rested and set up. This all pays off in more confidence and better interactions. It is so much easier to deal with change and misunderstandings when you are rested.

A4 (long) paper is the most common format, so keep this in mind if you are preparing handouts (instead of 8½ × 11" paper). Easels and large pads of paper can be provided. They may not be very sturdy for writing on, but will allow you to tape prewritten pages to them for display. Bring your own markers, just in case none are readily available.

In our experience at hotel conference or meeting rooms, you will be doing the bulk of your own setup. Be prepared to be responsible for everything from locating and carrying your shipped materials (or arranging for a hotel bellman to do so) to setting up AV (audiovisual) equipment and arranging tables. Find out early from the hotel/conference service whether they have any services they can provide to help. You will typically not find a bellman available at 6 A.M. when you want to ready your classroom.

The "lift" is an elevator. "Bonnet" is the hood of a car. "Lorry" is a truck. "Loo" is the bathroom (also referred to as the "WC" [water closet] or just plain toilet). Just ask if you do not understand words that are being used when someone is speaking to you.

## THE PRESENTATION

Classroom tips that can help to ensure smooth delivery of your presentation

- Keep it simple: let the complexity be in the discussion and clarification of ideas and concepts.

- Keep it short: allow enough time for translations and examples to be shared.

- Facilitate the learning points in smaller groups and guide discussions, and you will be more effective than during lecture.

- Don't use slang. It is not appreciated. Be careful to speak proper English. That is what is expected and accepted.

- If you are teaching multiple sessions or for several days with the same group, consider handing out and requiring evaluations to solicit feedback about how the session is going.

- Ask specific questions about the things you observed during the day. Adjust your sessions accordingly.

Cheers!

**Sources of further information include:**
- http://en.wikipedia.org/wiki/United_Kingdom
- www.culturebriefings.com
- www.meetengland.com

# France

The French really know how to savor their food and wine, and they have many ways of enjoying life. Paris, the "city of lights" is a feast for the eyes. Positioned on the River Seine, Paris provides spectacular views from the Eiffel Tower, incomparable art in the Louvre, and spiritual awe in the Notre Dame Cathedral. The gardens are adorned with statues and fountains. People read and discuss as they pause and walk throughout the city.

The French countryside provides beautiful, peaceful, pastoral scenes. You can stay in elegant chateaus, 18th century palatial estates where they serve you hot, fresh croissants and jam, small town inns, or even a farmhouse where they trained knights in the past.

Here is what to expect and tips for success when asked to train, teach, or present in France.

## ??? THE REQUEST

If you have been asked to present a program in France, the program is typically requested by an organization or company. The topic and audience for this program will be defined by the requestor. Ask for clarification and confirmation of the specific outcomes that are expected.

Jeremy Blain (Partner: Cegos) tells us that French companies and individuals usually dislike to be trained through non-native corporate programs. This is mainly a matter of autonomy. The participants are generally hungry to learn and challenging for tutors and instructors. The tutors need to be prepared and immersed in "real-world issues." Jeremy says that students like new technology learning with high audiovisual capability. They like to be engaged and interactive.

The most common location for the program would be Paris.

You can best communicate, before the program, with the secretary to request appropriate room setup. Speak very, very slowly and ask the person if he or she understands (if you are speaking in English). Do not assume that anyone will be able to follow you.

## • • • GETTING THERE

Check to ensure that your passport has at least six months before its renewal date and fulfill any visa requirements at www.traveldocs.com/fr/er.htm. At this time, no visa is required for U.S. citizens to stay for under three months.

If possible, arrange to have transportation from the Charles de Gaulle (CDG) Airport in Paris through your hotel, because it is very confusing to take the train if you do not speak French. You can take a bus from the airport to your hotel, but you will need to ask for help if you do not speak French. Some people may not be helpful, but usually you can find a kind person who is willing to help and will speak English with you. You will need to exchange your money for the Euro to be able to pay for any transportation.

Holidays that may affect your travel and your program:

- January: New Year's Day/Jour de l'an (1st)
- May: Labor Day/Fête du premier mai (1st)
- May: WWII Victory Day/Fête de la Victoire 1945; Fête du huitième mai (8th)
- July: Bastille Day/Fête nationale (14th)
- August: Assumption of the Blessed Virgin Mary/Assomption (15th)
- November: All Saints Day/La Toussaint (1st)
- November: Armistice Day/Jour d'armistice (11th)
- December: Christmas Day/Noël (25th)
- December: 2nd Day of Christmas—in Alsace and Lorraine only (26th)

French local time is GMT +1 (GMT +2 between the last Sunday in March and last Sunday in October).

## PROGRAM DESIGN

Program design must be done with the French customer's input. It will not easily be accepted if it is designed without continuous collaboration with the French. It should be designed in French and obviously reflect the French culture and language. Ask your French colleague or your host to review the design ahead of time, to ensure that it will be effective in their environment.

Any videotaped material should be designed to be reproduced in SECAM format and subtitled in French. Design interactive activities such as discussions, games, and case studies.

##  LOGISTICS

Check with your hosts to determine whether they will photocopy materials for the program or whether they would prefer that you ship the materials directly to them ahead of time.

Whiteboards and flip charts, overhead projector, and computer (beamer) will most likely be available for your program if requested. Arrange for an interpreter if you do not speak fluent French. You may have to have French-speaking participants on one side of the room and those who understand English on the other side, so that the interpreter can aid discussion, as needed.

The currency is the euro (EUR). Coins frequently used are: 1, 2, 5, 10, 20, 50 cent, €1, and €2. Banknotes frequently used: €5, €10, €20, and €50.

Most restaurants and hotels automatically add a 15 percent service charge, so a tip is not necessary, although another 2 to 3 percent is customary if the service has been good. If service is not included, then 15 percent is customary. Taxi drivers expect 10 to 15 percent of the fare. Hotel staff generally receives €1.50 a day and tips of €1 are given to washroom and cloakroom attendants and museum tour guides. Tour bus drivers and guides are also tipped.

The international telephone access code for France is +33. The outgoing code depends on what network is used to dial out on (for example, 00 for France Telecom), which is followed by the relevant country code (for example, 0044 for the United Kingdom). Other codes are used if using different networks. The area code for Paris is (0)1. Most public telephones accept phone cards, which are available in newsagents. Most hotels add a surcharge to calls, which can be very expensive. The cheapest way to call abroad is often with a phone card from a public telephone or at a post office. The local mobile phone operators use GSM networks and have roaming agreements with most international mobile phone companies. Internet cafes are available in towns throughout France.

Northern France, including Paris, has a climate similar to southern England, with warm summers, cold winters, and rainfall throughout the year. The western coast, from the Loire Valley to the Pyrenees, is milder, and summer days are generally very hot. During the second half of July and August, most French take their five-week vacation to the coasts and mountains, and empty cities tend to shut down accordingly.

## PROGRAM DELIVERY

Even if the participants can speak and understand English, they will most likely prefer to have the program delivered in French.

The French are especially proud of their language, and culture. You show respect for them if you learn as much as possible about them and try to speak the language.

## TECHNICAL REQUIREMENTS

Electrical current is 220 volts; 50Hz. European two-pin plugs are standard.

Be sure to bring 220-voltage converters, plugs, and backup systems to use if needed. Bring your program on an electronic storage device, send it to your host ahead of time, and hand carry hard copies of translated and English versions of handouts. Bring video-tapes reproduced in SECAM format and subtitled in French. DVDs should work fine if you bring your own computer. Internet capability is common, but check with the location for your presentation to make sure that high-speed Internet is available, if you need it.

## ACCOMMODATIONS

Accommodations at hotels, bed and breakfasts, and inns are plentiful in Paris. Karen Brown's books on accommodations are excellent (www.karenbrown.com). Taxi, trains, and metro (underground) are efficient. Most people walk to their destination, if possible.

Make reservations at an accommodation that advertises their ability to speak English, or you will have much difficulty making arrangements for your stay and transport. Unless you stay in a Western (Canadian or U.S.) hotel, you will not be likely to have a stand-up shower stall. You will most likely have a tub with a hand-held sprayer. Washcloths are not typically provided (they are considered a personal item). Plugs and converters will be required or you will burn up any electrical items that are not able to be switched to 220 volts.

We have found that French food and wine are excellent. The water is fine to drink.

Although Paris is relatively safe for a large city, watch for pickpockets; also watch your bags and luggage. Do not walk the street alone at night. Take a taxi to your destination.

Ask about the price before you climb into the taxi. Watch the meter and ask questions if you are concerned about the fare. Pedestrians should be very careful walking because the driving is frantic and fast. It is not recommended to drive in Paris.

The following numbers can all be dialed toll-free from any phone in France (including pay phones):

- Medical emergencies: Dial "15"

- Fire brigade: Dial "18"

- Police: Dial "17"

## GETTING AROUND

Obtain French maps in the airport, train station, or hotel. Practice your French questions so that you can be understood. Point to the location on the map and ask for help. Friendly English-speaking people should be helpful. Do not expect everyone to want to help.

Within the city of Paris, you can walk; take the Metro, or take a bus to your locations.

## THE PEOPLE

We have found that the French people love all things French. They have a reputation of not liking very much from other countries. They are very proud of their country and critical of other governments. It is very important that you compliment anything you like, avoid giving any criticism, be open to surprises, and be respectful, thankful, and polite—even if people seem abrupt or distant.

Here's a quick timeline of French history:

- 58–51 BC: Caesar's Gallic Wars

- 2nd century AD: Romans bring Christianity to Gaul

- 732: Charles Martel defeats Muslims stopping Arab invasion

- 755: Franks protect the church against Lombards and create the Papal States

- 800: Pope Leo III crowns Charlemagne Holy Roman Emperor

- 814–840: Louis the Pious succeeds Charlemagne as emperor

- 1095: Pope Urban II preaches for the First Crusade

- 1066: William of Normandy invades England; Battle of Hastings

- 1189–1192: Third Crusade; crusaders fail to recover Holy Land

- 1202: Fourth Crusade launched; Constantinople captured

- 1337–1443: Hundred Years' War

- 1453: English out of France except for Calais

- 1494–1559: France and Austria fight over Italian territories

- 1515: François I crowned King

- 1519: Leonardo da Vinci dies in the arms of François I

- 1547–1559: Reign of Henry II

- 1562–1598: The Wars of Religion

- 1572: Massacre of Protestants on St. Bartholomew's Eve in Paris

- 1589–1593: Henri IV becomes 1st Bourbon King and converts to Catholicism, ending Wars of Religion

- 1608: Founding of Quebec

- 1617: Louis XIII crowned at the age of 17

- 1624: Cardinal Richelieu becomes principal minister

- 1643–1715: Louis XIV becomes king

- 1682: Royal court moves to Versailles

- 1715: Louis XIV dies and Louis XV accedes

- 1762: Rousseau's Social Contract

- 1769: Napoleon Bonaparte born in Ajaccio, Corsica

- 1774: Louis XVI becomes king

- 1778–1783: The kingdom supports the American Revolution

- 1789: French Revolution, storming of La Bastille

- 1792: Louis XVI tried for treason and convicted; monarchy abolished

- 1793: Louis XVI and Queen Marie Antoinette guillotined in Paris

- 1794: Robespierre overthrown and end of Reign of Terror

- 1870–1871: Franco-Prussian War

- 1871: Third Republic

- 1889: Eiffel Tower built

- 1895: Lumière brothers build a portable movie camera

- 1914–1918: World War I

- 1919: Versailles Treaty

- 1929–1939: The Depression

- 1939: France declares war on Germany

- 1940: Paris falls, Vichy's government formed

- 1944–1945: D-Day and Allied victory and Fourth Republic led by de Gaulle

- 1946–1954: War in Indochina

- 1954–1958: War of Algeria

- 1958: De Gaulle initiates 5th Republic

- 1968: General strikes and students' riots in Paris

The French Republic is a democracy that is a unitary semi-presidential republic. The executive branch itself has two leaders: the President of the Republic, who is elected directly by vote for a five-year term and is the head of state, and the government, led by the president-appointed prime minister.

France is bordered by Belgium, Luxembourg, Germany, Switzerland, Italy, Monaco, Andorra, and Spain. France is divided into twenty-six administrative regions. Paris is the capital.

Tourism, aerospace (Airbus) and agriculture are primary industries in France. Wheat, poultry, dairy, beef, and pork, as well as an internationally recognized food and wine industry, are primary French agricultural exports.

France is a secular country. Religions include Catholicism, agnostics or atheists, Muslim, Protestant, and Jewish.

Favorite sports include football (soccer), both codes of rugby football, and, in certain regions, basketball, handball, cycling, and tennis.

**Some Protocol Tips**

- The handshake is a common form of greeting.

- Friends may greet each other by lightly kissing on the cheeks, once on the left cheek and once on the right cheek.

- First names are reserved for family and close friends. Wait until invited before using someone's first name.

- You are expected to say "bonjour" or "bonsoir" (good morning and good evening) with the title Monsieur or Madame when entering a shop and "au revoir" (good-bye) when leaving.

## !!! PREPARATION

Make sure you can arrive with time to rest and recuperate from your trip before conducting your session. If you are rested, it is easier to calmly respond to the challenges of being in another country. If possible, leave time to go sightseeing and enjoy some of the French culture after you have completed your program. If you do become ill at any time, the pharmacist can prescribe solutions for your ailments, without ever having to see a doctor. Your hotel will know which pharmacy is open all night if you need it.

Dress and fashion are very important. Attend to every detail of your appearance. It will be noticed!

Some basic French that may be helpful is listed below:

| English | Pronounced | French |
|---|---|---|
| Hello | sah-**loo** | "Salut" |
| Glad to meet you | on-shohn-**tay** | "Enchanté" |
| Good-bye | oh ruh-**vwar** | "Au revoir" |
| How are you? | kom-mohn tah-lay **voo** | "Comment allez-vous?" |
| Fine thanks and you? | bee-ehn mer-**see** ay voo? | "Merci et vous?" |
| Excuse me/sorry | ex-koo-**zay** mwah | "Excusez-moi" |
| Do you speak English? | par-**lay voo** zon-**glay** | "Parlez-vous anglais?" |
| Good morning/good day | bon-**zhoor** | "Bon jour" |
| Good evening | bon-**swar** | "Bon soir" |
| My name is | juh mah-**pell** | "Je m'appelle" |
| I'm sorry | day-zoh-**lay**/pahr-**dohn** | "Desolé/Pardon" |
| I don't understand | jhuhn kom-**prohn** pah | "Je ne comprends pas" |
| Please | seel voo **play** | "S'il vous plait" |
| Thank you | mare-**see** | "Merci" |
| No | nohn | "Non" |
| Ok | dah-**core** | "d'accord" |

## THE PRESENTATION

Jeanne Heinzer (Heinzer Consulting) tells us that the most likely locations for program delivery would be at the office of the organization (cheaper than a hotel) or at a hotel.

She reminds us to ask people to provide their experience and ideas throughout the program.

The French will adapt your program for their needs and implementation. If you offer guidelines and suggestions in formats that allow the participants to revise them, they will be much more receptive than if you act as if this is the one way to do things. Anything that has been developed or already revised in France is more acceptable than programs that have been developed elsewhere. If you can train a French person to deliver the program, it will be appreciated and understood better than if you deliver it with a translator.

Jeremy Blain (Cegos) gives us some tips for success:

- Participants should play an active role in their own learning.

- Participants should be regularly surprised, amazed, and asked to contribute.

- It is best to have participants use their own situations or ones that are similar to their own, throughout the training.

- Allow participants to try things out and experiment with new behaviors and skills.

- Start the training with why this is important.

- Have participants explain what they have learned and construct their own summaries.

- Provide ways for participants to be prepared to enter the training and develop action plans at the end of the program.

- Provide information and ongoing support after the training.

**Some helpful websites and resources include:**

- http://goparis.about.com/od/planningyourtrip/a/Paris_Safety.htm

- www.kwintessential.co.uk/resources/global-etiquette/france-country-profile.html

- www.traveldocs.com/fr/er.htm

# Germany

**W**e walked out onto the balcony and looked across the Rhine River at the ancient castle that was bathed in light. This is Germany! It is off season, so our room rate is low and the balcony room was available, so we are happy. We had just finished a delicious German supper with fresh Rhine wine. The cool evening allowed us to leave the balcony doors open to watch the Castle as we fell asleep.

Here is what to expect and some tips for success when training, teaching, and presenting in Germany.

## ??? THE REQUEST

You have been asked to present a program in Germany.

One of the most likely venues in Germany will be Munich (München).

Ask your host what the outcomes of the program should be. Send drafted objectives and a detailed outline for their review. Make agreements regarding length of the program, dates, times, and location.

## • • • GETTING THERE

Check to ensure that your passport has at least six months before the renewal date. Daily flights are available to Munich. Hotel photos and customer satisfaction ratings are available through Expedia. Ask your hotel, when making the reservation, whether they will provide a car for transport from the airport. If so, ask how much it will cost. If not, you can take a shuttle or taxi to your hotel. You will need to exchange your money for the euro to be able to pay for any transportation.

If you take the train to reach central Munich, follow the S-Bahn signs to the commuter rail station in München Airport Center. There, you can buy tickets from vending machines or a ticket counter. Trains depart six times an hour from 6 A.M. until 10 P.M., with less frequent service during the night. Major downtown stops include the Hauptbahnhof (main railroad station) and the Marienplatz. The journey takes about forty minutes, depending on the train and where you plan to get off. If you have bulky luggage, stow it by the flip-up jump seats near the doors.

### Some Tips for Using S-Bahn

- Two lines—S1 and S8—run from the airport to downtown Munich. Their routes are slightly different, but both will get you to the city center.

- When traveling **to the airport** on the S1 line, be sure to use a car labeled "Flughafen." (These cars are at the back of the train, which splits at Neufahrn.)

- The inexpensive **Munich Welcome Card** includes a roundtrip S-Bahn ticket to the city center, free public transportation in Munich, and discounts on museums and tourist attractions. The card is issued by the Munich Tourist Office, and you can buy it at the Service Center in München Airport Center near the S-Bahn entrance.

- You can pick up a tiny pocket-size schedule for the S1 and S8 lines from brochure racks in the airport. You'll also find schedules, ticket prices, and other S-Bahn information at the multilingual site: www.mvv-muenchen.de/en/.

- If you have luggage, grab one of the free baggage carts in the airport. You can use it all the way from the baggage-claim area to the S-Bahn platform.

Lufthansa buses connect the airport with Munich's main railroad station every twenty minutes during the day. However, they cost more and are less convenient than the train.

A cab ride into central Munich takes about thirty-five minutes (or longer in rush hour) and can easily cost 60 euros, depending on your destination.

**To rent a car,** follow the "Mietwagen" signs to the car-rental area. MUC has the best rental facilities: You just complete your paperwork at the rental counter, and then you step through the adjacent doorway to get your car. There's no need to take a shuttle bus or wait for a car to be delivered.

Germany's standard time zone is UTC/GMT +1 hour: Daylight saving time: +1 hour, six hours ahead of New York.

Holidays that may affect your travel or program schedule include:

- January: New Year's Day (1st), Epiphany (6th)
- March/April: Good Friday, Easter Monday
- May: Labour Day (1st)
- Spring: Ascension Day, Whitmonday, Corpus Christi
- August: Peace Festival (8th), Assumption Day (15th)
- October: German Unity Day (6th), Reformation Day (31st)
- November: All Saints Day (1st), Repentance Day (Wednesday before the 23rd)
- December: Christmas Day (25th), St. Stephen's Day (26th)

## PROGRAM DESIGN

Strength, precision, and quality are hallmarks of the German culture. When designing a presentation and preparing to deliver a program to members of the German community, it is especially important to make sure that you have all the facts succinctly and correctly displayed. It is critical that everything be accurate and double-checked because any incorrect component will greatly detract from the attention of your audience.

Technical subjects are easily respected and learned. When teaching the softer subjects, it may be a bit more challenging to obtain active participation. Crisp, clear directions can be delivered and will probably be rather well accepted in English, if necessary. Special care must be taken when designing and delivering a program to make sure that all aspects of the program will run perfectly. There is not much allowance for error, and mistakes will take away from your credibility and attention.

Design a clear structure and agenda for the program. Ask whether all of the participants understand English, and design the program so it can be translated into German for those who do not.

Design the program to be primarily lecture, because this is what the Germans are used to and will expect.

## LOGISTICS

Check with your hosts to determine whether they will photocopy materials for the program or to see whether they would prefer that you ship the materials directly to them ahead of time.

Request flip charts, projector, and computer to be provided and tested before the program. Arrange for an interpreter if you do not speak fluent German or request that a German-speaking participant in the room agree to help interpret for others.

Have water and coffee available as refreshments.

The currency is the euro (EUR). Coins frequently used are: 1, 2, 5, 10, 20, 50 cent, €1, €2. Banknotes frequently used: €5, €10, €20, €50.

The weather in Germany is temperate throughout the country with warm summers and cold winters. Prolonged periods of frost or snow are rare. Extreme temperature lows and highs are rare. Winter temperatures vary from west to east, with around freezing temperatures in the west and well below freezing in the east of Germany. Summer temperatures are typically between 20 degrees C and 30 degrees C, with more rainfall during the summer months. Rain falls throughout the year. The average January daytime temperature is 3 degrees C (38°F) and in July is 22 degrees C (72 degrees F). Extremes commonly reach–10 degrees C (5 degrees F) in winter and 35 degrees C (95 degrees F) in the summer months.

Munich can be very cold in the wintertime and does not get extremely warm in the summertime. So bring warm layers of clothing that can be shed as needed to be comfortable.

Clothes can be worn that are light- to medium-weight in summer, medium- to heavy-weights in winter. Frequent changes of weather make forecasting difficult. To be on the safe side, be sure to bring a sweater and wet-weather clothing with you.

## PROGRAM DELIVERY

The most likely locations for program delivery would be at the office of the organization or at a hotel. Even if the participants can speak and understand English, they may require help understanding some concepts, so speak slowly.

Jeanne Heinzer (Heinzer Consulting) reminds us that that this is a very formal environment. People are on a last-name basis, and if somebody has a title such as doctor (on his or her business card) use it (example: Dr. Meyer). The German people expect structure and an expert. Begin the program with the agenda for the training and stick to it. Start on time and finish on time. Use primarily lecture style. Have regular breaks, start and stop on time.

## TECHNICAL REQUIREMENTS

Be sure to bring 220/240 voltage converters, plugs and backup systems to use if needed. Bring your program on an electronic storage device, send it to your host ahead of time, and hand carry hard copies of translated and English versions of handouts. Bring video-tapes reproduced in PAL format and subtitled in German, if possible.

Check ahead of time to see whether Internet capability is available in the location for your presentation, if you need it.

## ACCOMMODATIONS

Accommodations at hotels and bed-and-breakfasts are plentiful in Munich. Karen Brown's books on accommodations are excellent (www.karenbrown.com).

Typical hotels such as Hilton, Marriott, and Sheraton have some of the amenities that you may need. Check online ahead of time for required services to see whether they are available in the hotel you choose.

Make reservations at an accommodation that advertises their ability to speak English, to make your stay easier. Unless you stay in a Western hotel (U.S. or Canadian), you will not likely be provided with washcloths (considered a personal item). Plugs and convert-ers will be required so that you will not burn up any electrical items that are unable to be switched to 220/240 volts.

Be prepared for good, hearty German food served with pride and the local beverage of world-renowned beer or wine.

## GETTING AROUND

Obtain German maps in the airport, train station, or hotel. Practice your German ques-tions so you can be understood. Point to the location on the map and ask for help. You will easily find friendly English-speaking people who are very helpful.

The MVV Munich public transit network's site (www.mvv-muenchen.de/en/) pro-vides excellent information regarding transportation. The information includes bus and rail schedule and prices.

## THE PEOPLE

Hierarchical-thinking and formal in a business environment (quite easygoing outside of work), Germans are primarily focused on the tasks to be accomplished. Building on a relationship is second. Do not spend too much time on chit chat, and get to the point quickly.

The participants may think that they are the experts. They may think that you are there to tell them what to do, and they do not like this. Stereotypes they hold of North Americans:

U.S. citizens think they have all the answers, all are obese, and they always wear sneakers (avoid them); they have no culture and no clue of what's going on around them. You will need to show them that this is not the case.

Everything seems large, and the Germans know how to have fun in a big way, as you can see by the size of their beer steins.

Germany is bordered to the north by the North Sea, Denmark, and the Baltic Sea; to the east by Poland and the Czech Republic, to the south by Austria and Switzerland, and to the west by France, Luxembourg, Belgium, and the Netherlands.

Germany is a parliamentary federal republic of sixteen states (*Bundesländer*), including Munich and Berlin. The capital city and seat of government is Berlin. The Chancellor is the head of government and exercises executive power, similar to the role of a prime minister. Federal legislative power is vested in the parliament consisting of the *Bundestag* (Federal Diet) and *Bundesrat* (Federal Council), which together form a unique type of legislative body. The *Bundestag* is elected through direct elections; the members of the *Bundesrat* represent the governments of the sixteen federal states and are members of the state cabinets, which appoint them and can remove them at any time.

Christianity is the largest religious denomination in Germany. The second-largest religion is Islam, followed by Buddhism and Judaism, Hinduism, or no religion.

Most of Germany's exports are in engineering, that is, automobiles, machinery, metals, and chemical goods. Germany is first in the world for generating electricity from wind power and it is also the main exporter of wind turbines.

World-famous composers such as Beethoven, Bach, Brahms, and Wagner are all from Germany.

Favorite sports include football (soccer), handball, volleyball, basketball, ice hockey, tennis, and motor sports.


## ▌▌▌ PREPARATION

Schedule a meeting with your interpreter ahead of time to explain the program and what you will be presenting. Review any technical terms or acronyms and invite questions so that the interpreter can be fully prepared to help you present the program.

Make sure you can arrive early with plenty of extra time to ensure you will not be late to conduct your session. Dress formally (better overdressed than too casual). Attend to every detail of your appearance.

Call the hotel or secretary to check to see whether everything is ready. Ask about any equipment that you will need.

Here are some common words and phrases that may be helpful:

| English | Deutsch | Pronunciation |
|---|---|---|
| yes/no | "ja/nein" | yah/nine |
| please/thanks | "bitte/danke" | BIT-tuh/DAHN-kuh |
| You're welcome. | "Bitte" | BIT-tuh |
| Excuse me | "Entschuldigen Sie!" | ent-SHOOL-de-gen zee |
| Where's the restroom/toilet? | "Wo ist die Toilette?" | vo ist dee toy-LET-uh |
| Hello | "Guten Tag!" | GOO-ten tahk |
| My name is . . . | "Ich heisse . . ." | ich HYE-suh |
| Good morning | "Guten Morgen!" | GOO-ten morgen |
| Good night | "Gute Nacht!" | GOO-tuh nahdt |
| Good-bye | "Auf Wiedersehen!" | owf VEE-der-zane |

## THE PRESENTATION

Any gruff exterior behaviors are good covers for the true warmth of the German people. When presenting, display your professionalism and self-confidence and meet your participants on common ground. The room may not be buzzing with conversation before the program starts, but you will get an attentive audience for your presentation.

Typically, the preferred learning style is from lecture. We have had reports of interactive techniques "bombing" and not resulting in effective responses from the participants.

Prepare and try out examples and activities that your audience will relate well to. Practice your presentation to ensure perfect delivery and prepare well for backup and contingency plans, so that all runs smoothly and precisely on time.

There is a great deal of history that forms the foundation of this proud culture, so it is very important to be sensitive to historical details and relationships. If your participants are from other countries, you must be very sensitive to possible sensitivity and animosities, especially in your seating setup. Let people choose who they want to sit with and where they want to sit, unless you have a very reliable German contact who can ensure that this is done correctly. Avoid jokes, cartoons, and humor, because they can easily backfire. Display confidence in your expertise with a good dose of respect for their culture and capability. Avoid competitive games, but include individual practice of techniques with unbiased feedback that has already been built into the activity, so it does not appear to be biased in any way. Make sure that everyone can always clearly tell where you are in the program, where you are going, what you will be doing, and by when. Surprises are not well received.

Arrive early, stay late, and double-check everything.

A good example of being aware of different audiences is a management training course that Michael Rockelmann (president, Driving Results) designed and delivered in an international medical device manufacturer. This was to be the foundation course in a management curriculum for the entire company and all employees who managed others, from supervisors to vice presidents, were to attend the foundation course and then enter their respective training programs for their roles.

The introductory course was a one-day overview that focused on introducing the basic management model and the company's approach to leading others. The course was designed to include experiential learning activities, with a large amount of interaction, and it relied heavily on social learning. The seven hours of training time included one hour of time during which the instructor presented ideas. The remaining six hours were all activities and discussions led by the participants. The course was designed to pull out the prior experiences, good and bad, that participants had being led or leading others. The purpose was to find the best practices already used by each participant within the company and build on those.

The course was delivered to 75 percent of the participants in North America and received high remarks on all Kirkpatrick level 1 and 2 measures (over 4.0 on a 5.0 scale). In addition, participants wrote wonderful comments on the course design, and there was a waiting list to attend the next event.

When preparing the course for delivery in Germany, the local training team was concerned about the format of the training. They felt the lack of instructor-led portions and the large number of activities relying on information from the participants would not be accepted by the local audience. After much debate and severe pushback from the North American training organization, a few modifications were made and some activities were replaced with lecture, but the overall course remained interactive and social.

The result: The pilot course bombed (and that is putting it nicely). Participants rated the course at a 1 or 2 on a 5-point scale, and their comments reflected their dissatisfaction with attending a training program during which they had to work more than receive useful information. Some participants even stated that the course was a waste of time and that there was a lack of information provided.

So we went back to the drawing board and took the wonderful information provided during training in North America and included this in the German version as content delivered by the instructor. We altered the format, took out a majority of the activities, and the course now resembled a typical training course: 70 percent of the time the instructor was speaking, 20 percent the class was discussing what the instructor said, and 10 percent was focused on team and individual activities.

The new design was concerning and a disappointment to the North American training organization, but the result could not be argued with. The newly designed German course received all of the high ratings and good comments that the original course did in North America. It was clear that the course that was successful in North America did not work in Germany, and that the German course would not have been as effective in North America.

So why did a course with the same objectives and content end up having two drastically different delivery methods but receive the same results? The answer is in knowing your audience and the difference in learning preferences.

One caution before we discuss this in more detail. These results are based on level 1 reaction and level 2 learning measures, and we did not have the data on whether the groups actually applied the skills to the job after attending the course. But both groups had an equal comprehension of the foundation when entering their respective management programs, and there was an increase in employee satisfaction with the manager's ability to manage. These measures do indicate that both training programs were effective in reaching their objectives.

So why are there major differences in learning preferences? Do people in North America learn better from interaction and activities, while Germans learn better from lecture? Are we fundamentally different in the way we learn?

The answer to this (Michael Rockelmann tells us) is no: All people learn in similar ways, through introduction of material then application and finally feedback. This does not change between people or cultures. The real difference is in the way people prefer to be introduced to the material. Research shows that people retain more when they are actively involved in the introduction and learning of the material. In North America training has been in an evolution toward more interaction for thirty years, and it is being more widely accepted, but there is still resistance from some learners. This is not the case in all cultures, especially in more formal cultures such as Germany.

So the key is to understand your audience, especially if it is an international audience. Make sure this is part of your needs assessment. Know what will be accepted and what won't be accepted and design accordingly. But remember that it is okay to push the envelope; don't design a full lecture because the audience expects it. We know that learning and retention will be strengthened by having the participants actively engaged, so build it in where possible, Rockelmann tells us.

Jennifer Britton, CEO of Potentials Realized, conducted annual staff retreat programs for a multi-national team and a two-week training program for new global program staff. Here are our questions and her tips for training in Germany:

**How do you prepare for conducting a program in this country?**

The first time I was called to Germany, it was on a last-minute "help us out" call, which did not give a lot of time for preparation, other than being open to using my intuition and training and coaching skills. I was lucky to be paired with a local counterpart who brought me up-to-speed on major issues once I arrived. Observation played a key role.

**What advice can you give to someone who has never done this before?**

- Do be on time. Germany is a country where things, including buses and trains. are on time. (When they say 7:13, they really mean 7:13.)

- Do be open to the wonderful culture of Germany and Europe. With the changes in the last few years in the European Union, it is very common to hear several languages spoken throughout the major German cities. Technology is very pervasive, and Germans are very well educated.

- Don't be late.

**What works best with this audience?**

Participatory approaches, theoretical underpinnings, practical approaches.

**What surprised you?**

The level of technology and efficiency in business surprised us. How cosmopolitan Bonn, Germany, is for example. It is easy to get around.

**What language did you conduct the training in?**

English

**What technical preparations had to be made (voltage, plugs, equipment, audiovisuals)?**

There were no major adaptations that needed to be done to the presentations, which were on PowerPoint. We were able to use the company's equipment and did not have to worry about voltage issues and plugs.

**What techniques work best with this audience (case studies, role plays, discussion . . . )?**

Mini-lecture, group work, case studies, scenarios, participatory approaches all work well.

**What customs are important to consider?**

Holidays are important, as are outdoor activities. Germans are very active people.

**What are the people like?**

People are friendly.

**What would you like to add about your experience in this country that would help others?**

Depending on where you deliver the training, most German cities and large urban centers are very similar to North American urban centers. People are friendly yet busy. It is easy to travel around, if you familiarize yourself and ask questions.

**Helpful websites and references include:**

- www.enjoy-europe.com/hte/chap11/electric.htm
- www.german-way.com/electric.html
- www.karenbrown.com
- www.greenwichmeantime.com/time-zone/europe/european-union/germany/currency-converter.htm
- www.greenwichmeantime.com/time-zone/europe/european-union/germany/munich/index.htm
- www.mvv-muenchen.de/en/
- www.worldtravelguide.net/country/99/public_holidays/Europe/Germany.html
- www.wordtravels.com/Travelguide/Countries/Germany/Climate/

# Hungary

H ungary is a landlocked country in Central Europe, bordered by Austria, Slovakia, Ukraine, Romania, Serbia, Croatia, and Slovenia. Hungary is a member of the European Union. Its capital is Budapest. The music of the brilliant Hungarian piano composer Franz Liszt ("Hungarian Rhapsodies") is loved all over the world. The Rubik's cube, holography, and the ballpoint pen were all invented by Hungarian scientists. Hungarian castles and mansions number over two thousand. This is a fascinating country!

Here is information regarding what to expect when training, teaching, or presenting in Hungary and tips for success.

## ??? THE REQUEST

The most probable city in Hungary for teaching would be Budapest, as many programs are requested for presentation at the university there. You should make agreements with your host regarding the dates, location, and syllabus of the program. They will tell you who the audience is and what the administration expects as outcomes of the program.

Dr. Sharon Badenhop (USA East Associates Inc.) teaches how to do business or teach in foreign countries. She always has her business cards translated and printed (on the reverse side) in the language of the country she will be visiting. If you do the same, send the draft of the card for approval to your contact in the country where you will be teaching before having them printed. Do NOT have the printer translate for you.

It is very important to do the necessary homework before teaching in another country. If Sharon does not have an associate to contact in-country, she goes to the library and takes out all of the books she can find on the country, reads them, and prepares.

A few key phrases for translation that she will need when speaking there are essential (e.g., thank you, please, etc.). Then she has the phrases reviewed by her host in the country to make sure no errors or cultural problems exist. Sharon remembers one time when a seemingly simple translation actually turned out to be vulgar, so she had them correct it before she started using it. She asked someone who is from a school that teaches English as a second language to do translations for her.

If possible, ask how fluent the participants are in English, but don't always believe the response. They may tell you ahead of time that people will understand, but then you might find that the participants look at you as if they do not understand much English. It is best to hire an interpreter if you do not speak Hungarian.


### • • • GETTING THERE

You will need a valid passport with six months left before its expiration to travel to Hungary. No special visa is required for entry to Hungary if your trip is less than ninety days long.

There are non-stop flights available to Budapest from New York. They are about nine hours in length. If you cannot fly direct, plan on an additional three hours of travel time, depending on the layover between flights. Standard local time is GMT +1, Eastern Standard Time +6 hours.

When you are making reservations with your hotel, ask them whether they can send a car to pick you up at the airport. If they can pick you up, ask what the cost will be. If they cannot, plan to take a taxi to your hotel. It is customary to tip your taxi driver up to 10 percent, based on your level of satisfaction with the ride.

Hungary's climate is temperate; with cold, cloudy, humid winters and warm summers.

With the Alps to the west and the flat, open great plain to the east, Budapest has warm summers and cold winters, with plenty of rain all year round. Winters are fairly short. The coldest weather arrives in mid-December, usually cloudy and damp with a few bright sunny days and frequent, but light, snow. In summer, from April to September, Budapest has a high proportion of sunny, warm days with relatively high humidity. The sun shines for about ten hours a day.

The average temperature in Budapest (listed in Fahrenheit) by month is:

| | |
|---|---|
| January: 29 degrees F | February: 39 degrees F |
| March: 50 degrees F | April: 62 degrees F |
| May: 72 degrees F | June: 78 degrees F |

July: 80 degrees F     August: 80 degrees F

September: 74 degrees F     October: 61 degrees F

November: 46 degrees F     December: 39 degrees F

Check national holiday calendars before scheduling training sessions and avoid the Christmas and New Year's holidays (mid-December to mid-January), as well as Friday afternoons during the summer. Most people take their family holidays during these times of year.

Holidays that may affect your travel and program schedule include:

January: New Year's Day (1st)

March: Revolution Day/National Holiday (15th) to celebrate independence from Hapsburg rule

March/April: Easter Monday

May: Labor Day (1st), Whit-Monday (day after Pentecost)

August: National Day/St. Stephen's Day (20th)

October: Remembrance Day (23rd)

November: All Saints Day (1st)

December: Christmas Day (25th), Boxing Day (26th)

## PROGRAM DESIGN

The official language of Hungary is Hungarian. Unless you are certain your audience will understand English or you speak Hungarian, you will want to incorporate the use of a translator into your program. This is a design consideration from the standpoint of time and complexity. When using a translator, as mentioned in other chapters, your time of development increases by at least one-third. The amount you will be able to cover in a session decreases based on the additional time and attention that will need to be paid to ensuring your audience has understood your content.

You can design the program so that it will be presented via PowerPoint. If the program is designed in English, leave enough white space on each page for it to be translated. Allow enough time to send the presentation to your host for reproduction and translation, if required. Short case studies and role plays could be designed into the program, as appropriate. These breaks from lecture relieve the stress caused by the additional concentration needed to have an interpreter in the classroom. Presenters grow weary of precisely articulating their points, translators grow weary of perfect interpretation, and participants grow weary of active listening. Exercises allow everyone to take a mental break from the additional work. They also allow participants to apply what they have heard. Expect to walk around the room and join into a conversation with the help of the interpreter.

## LOGISTICS

If the mailing of materials is an important component of presenting a successful program, send them very early to make sure that everything is there in your location when you arrive, ready to be used in your program. Email the presentation and handout materials ahead of time. Bring the program on an electronic storage device and/or hard copy in your carry-on luggage to be sure that you will have it when you arrive.

In preparing the presentation, Dr. Sharon Badenhop suggests that you make friends with the executive assistant. This can be most helpful. A series of emails with small requests will be more likely to assure that the agreements are understood, such as: "Do you have a computer with a projector?" The next email might read: "Are you the person I send the PowerPoint to? Will you set up the computer, load, and pre-run it to make sure that it works?" Then it is easy to send the presentation via email and bring it on a 2 gigabyte USB port, instead of carrying a computer on the plane.

Hungarian currency is the forint (HUF = Ft) divided into 100 fillér. Coins come in the value of 1, 2, 5, 10, 20, 50, and 100. Notes are in the value of 200, 500, 1,000, 2,000, 5,000, 10,000, and 20,000 Ft. Hungary is a member of the European Union, but has not completed its adoption of the euro currency.

Banks are open Monday through Thursday from 8 A.M. to 3 P.M., Friday from 8 A.M. to 1 P.M. All banks are closed on Saturdays. There is usually a commission of 1 percent for cashing traveler's checks at banks. Money can also be exchanged at exchange offices, hotel reception desks, and travel offices. Currency exchange machines and ATMs operate after hours in Budapest and other cities. It is recommended that all money exchange receipts be kept. Foreign currency should be exchanged for Forints only in authorized exchange offices. You can use your bank or credit card to get cash at post offices throughout Hungary. More than 3,200 post offices nation-wide provide this service.

Major credit cards (AmEx, Visa, and MasterCard) can be used in shops and businesses with the logo displayed at the entrance. ATMs operate twenty-four hours a day. Major credit cards and banking cards are accepted. Most stores will not accept traveler's checks.

## TECHNICAL REQUIREMENTS

Electricity in Hungary is 220 volts with European two-pronged plugs. An adaptor and/or voltage converter is necessary for electronic equipment. If you request a computer and projector ahead of time from your in-country contact, it will help to reduce your need to bring converters, plugs, and cords. It may be a good idea to purchase these items ahead of time and bring them with you, just in case there is an issue with your loaner equipment. Luxury hotels have Internet service available in your room; other hotels may have it available in their business office.

Hungary uses the PAL (phase alternation line) format for videos, so it is important to make sure that any video you will be using has been converted before you leave home.

For telephone, you can purchase a prepaid Hungary SIM card and rent a world cell phone, if you want convenient phone usage.

## ACCOMMODATIONS

Try to stay in the same hotel where you will be making your presentation or near the location where you will be teaching. If this is not possible, you can ask your host to make a recommendation or reservation for you. You will find familiar hotel chain names such as Marriott and Ramada, as well as smaller, local boutique hotels, all with amenities you normally expect. Wherever you stay, make sure to enjoy the delicious goulash and stews of Hungary.

Safety and security should not be a major problem in this country. As in any large city, in Budapest you should take the appropriate precautions, such as keeping your money out of sight, watching your belongings when traveling, and walking on well-lit streets where there are other people walking.

- Hungary's telephone country code is 36
- Budapest's area code is 1 (+7-digit number)
- International pre-dial 00 + country code + local number
- Domestic long distance pre-dial 06 + area code + local number
- Cell-phone numbers are 9-digit, after dialing 06, the first two numbers depend on the telephone company: 20, 30, or 70.
- Ambulance:104
- Police: 107
- Fire department: 105
- Directory assistance: 198
- International directory: 199
- Public phones require 10, 20, 50, or 100 Forint coins or a pre-purchased phone card (sold at newsstands, supermarkets, hotels, and post offices).

- Fax machines are available for tourists in main post offices and in many city hotels' business centers.
- International collect calls can be made from a private line or public payphone. A coin or phone card has to be inserted to initiate the call. International operators: AT&T: 00 8000 1111; MCI: 00 8000 1411: Sprint: 00 800 0 1877

Restaurant prices in Hungary generally do not include a service charge, and it is therefore customary to give a tip, generally equivalent to 10 or 15 percent of the bill.

The biggest health issue in Budapest is dirty air; there is still a fair amount of pollution from cars. Additionally, smoking continues to be prevalent.

Tap water in Budapest is generally safe to drink.

Public restrooms can be a bit grungy, often with no soap or only bar soap, a shared cloth towel for hand drying, and no toilet paper. It is recommended that travelers carry hand sanitizer and extra tissues to overcome this problem.

## GETTING AROUND

If you are giving your program at a university or office building, take a taxi that has been called from your hotel. Before entering the taxi, ask what the fare will be to your destination. Your hotel can give you guidelines on what is reasonable. If you plan to sightsee and explore the city, Budapest has an excellent and affordable public transportation system that operates from 4:30 A.M. to 11:00 P.M. Tickets are available at tobacco shops, subway stations, hotels, or street vendors and are purchased in advance. Tickets are checked frequently on all lines. You may choose from buses, trams, trolley buses, and subways. All are reliable and economical.

Violent crime is relatively rare in Budapest, although petty theft is rampant, especially aimed at tourists. Pickpocketing and bicycle thefts are common. Travelers should use caution and common sense when on crowded trams or in tourist-heavy areas.

## THE PEOPLE

The culture in Hungary tends to be conservative, having had a strong communist past. They are very happy about their relatively newfound independence, but still very proud of their history. There is little eye contact or emotion shown on the streets, especially from the older people. The people are very serious and do not smile easily.

There is a lot of bumping when you are in a crowd. Do not expect anyone to say "Excuse me." The dress is conservative. Suits and mid-calf-length skirts are appropriate for women. Women are treated as equals. This still carries over from their communist past. It is not easy to engage the people in conversation. They are curious about other cultures, however. They will not speak against their political parties and do not understand how anyone would speak against the leaders of their own country. It is easier to not discuss politics. Hungarians prefer to be called "central Europeans" rather than "eastern Europeans."

Family is very important to Hungarians. Generations of extended family often live together. The grandparents play an important role in helping raise the grandchildren. The family provides both emotional and financial support to its members.

Hungarians expect friends to share private and intimate details of their personal lives. If you ever feel you are being asked personal questions, this is part of the getting-to-know-you process.

Both men and women greet by shaking hands, although a man should usually wait for the woman to extend her hand. The older generation may still bow to a woman. Close friends kiss one another lightly on both cheeks, starting with the left cheek. In the business context, it is safe to address people by their titles and surnames.

We found a very interesting website that allows you to take your home culture and compare it to your host culture. Hungary is among the countries listed, as are many others. Take some time to look at the different dimensions highlighted by the website (www.kwintessential.co.uk/) and you can begin to formulate conversations and communication. As with many cultures, relationship-building is a key to business success.

The official language of Hungarian is spoken by 98 percent of the population. Minority languages include German, Croatian, Romani, Slovak, Romanian, Serbian, and Slovene.

Primary Hungarian religions are Roman Catholic and protestant.

Ruled or invaded at times by Huns (Attila), Denmark, Spain, Mongols, Ottomans, Hapsburgs, Communists, Romania, Germany, and the Soviet Union, Hungarians are used to loss and struggle.

The government is a parliamentary democracy. The president and prime minister are elected by Parliament.

Hungary is divided into nineteen counties. The country is divided in two by the Danube River. In addition to the nineteen counties, the capital city (*főváros*), Budapest, is independent of any county government.

The Hungarian people include Magyarok and several ethnic minorities: Roma ("Gypsies"), Germans, Slovaks, Croats, Romanians, Ukrainians, and Serbs.

Hungarians enjoy their football (soccer), water sports, and fencing.

## !!! PREPARATION

Dress and act professionally at all times and you will gain the respect of your students.

Check a world weather site on the Internet or Yahoo for several days before you go, to see what the weather will be like. Typically, winters are cold, but not bitter, and summers warm, but not hot. Budapest is at about the same latitude as Duluth, Minnesota.

Meet with your interpreter ahead of time to make sure he or she understands what you are planning to accomplish in the program. Help the interpreter to learn any technical terms or concepts that might be difficult to translate. In addition to reviewing and practicing your presentation, it is important to prepare yourself physically and emotionally to be at your very best. This means getting enough sleep before you leave your homeland, drinking plenty of water, and arriving with enough time to get rested and set up.

Here are some helpful words and phrases in Hungarian, with the pronunciation in italic:

| English | Hungarian | Pronunciation |
|---|---|---|
| Yes | IGEN | *ee*gen |
| No | nem | *nem* |
| Please | KÉREM | *kay*rem |
| Thank you | KÖSZÖNÖM | *køsønøm* |
| Good Morning | JÓ REGGELT KIVANOK | *yaw reggelt* |
| Good Afternoon | JÓ NAPOT KÍVÁNOK | *yaw noppawt* |
| Good Night | JÓ ÉJSZAKÁT KIVANOK | *yaw aysokkaht* |
| Hello/Later | SZERVUSZ | *servus tere* |
| Goodbye | VISZONTLÁTÁSRA | *vee*sawntlahtahshro |
| What is your name? | HOGY HÍVJÁK? | *hawd heevyaak* |
| My name is . . . | VAGYOK | *vodawk* |
| How are you? | HOGY VAN | *hawd von* |
| I'm fine, thanks, and you? | KÖSZÖNÖM JÓL, ÉS ÖN? | *køsønøm yawl, aysh* |
| I understand. | ÉRTEM. | *ayrtem* |
| I don't understand. | NEM ÉRTEM. | *nem ayrtem* |
| Do you speak English? | BESZÉL ANGOLUL? | *besayl ongawlul* |
| I don't speak much Hungarian. | NEM TUDOK (JÓL) MAGYARUL. | *nem toodawk (yawl) modorul* |

## THE PRESENTATION

The participants are used to presentations with interactive lecture. Speak slowly for the interpreter to have enough time to translate. Reconfirm their understanding by asking a student to tell you what you just said. A small role play can be used if you make it short, with time constraints and an explicit goal. Discussion can be difficult when using an interpreter.

Give breaks every hour or hour and a half, depending upon how long your session(s) is/are. Tell them that the break will last for five minutes, but expect that it may be fifteen. If you have a lot of material to cover, you can tell them that you are on North American time, and explain that this means if you give them a ten-minute break you expect them to be back in ten minutes. Hungarians are prompt and will be there at the right time to start the program. It is appropriate to start at 9 A.M. and teach until 5 P.M. But it is a long day for people to be concentrating on a translation. One hour for lunch is usually adequate.

Sources that can be used include:

- www.cusd.claremont.edu
- www.expatica.com/
- www.germanvideo.com/service_pages/video_format_chart.html
- www.gotohungary.com/information/
- www.kwintessential.co.uk/
- www.wordtravels.com/Cities/Hungary/Budapest/Climate
- www.wikipedia.org/

# Italy

**A** more (love), ancient ruins (the Coliseum), art (Renaissance), religion (the Vatican), wine, and pasta create the right atmosphere to think about Italy. Beautiful photographs of intriguing cities like Rome, Venice, Florence, Milan, and Pisa, small towns of the Italian Riviera, and the rolling countryside of Tuscany invite people to visit and immerse themselves in the Italian culture. This is a land where life is to be savored and enjoyed. Family is everything. Long walks and conversation are daily traditions. Gelato (Italian ice cream) and pizza are irresistible and unforgettable flavors that draw you into the tiny shops everywhere. Bellissimo (wonderful)!

Here is what to expect and tips for success when training, teaching, and presenting to an Italian audience:

## ??? THE REQUEST

A likely request might come to present a program in an easy-to-reach city like Rome or from a company in Milan (business center). If you are asked to conduct a program in Italy, ask your host what is expected, such as the purpose of the program and objectives. Send drafted objectives and a detailed outline for their review. Make agreements with them regarding length of the program, dates, times, and location.

Work with the hotel and/or office secretary to confirm administrative details.

# • • • GETTING THERE

You will need a valid passport to enter the country. Current travel information can be obtained from the Italian embassy or consulates before entering Italy.

Examples of likely locations for a program in Italy would be Milan or Rome. You will probably be flying into the city. The flight will take between nine and twelve hours, depending on which coast your flight originates from. All of Italy is on GMT +1. Add this to your travel time and determine how far in advance of your session you should arrive in your host city.

Ask your hotel when you make your reservation whether they will send a car to pick you up at the airport and, if so, how much it will cost. If they are not sending a car, take a taxi to travel to your hotel. But keep your eyes closed! The trip will be very hectic. Do not rent a car unless you want a very stressful entry. A taxi may cost you about 40 euros. A 10 percent tip is customary.

To take the train:

Rome's airport, sometimes known as Leonardo da Vinci Airport, is still referred to by its old name, Fiumicino, after the city it is near. Terminal B is a mix of domestic and international, and Terminal C is where you'll find major international flights. The airport code is FCO. It's twenty-six km from Rome (sixteen miles). The train to Rome's Central Station (Roma Termini) runs frequently between 6:37 A.M. and 10:52 P.M. and takes thirty-one minutes.

To get to Central Rome (Termini Station), after you've picked up your luggage, follow the signs to Stazione FS/Railway Station. You'll have to go up *two* floors to find it. Buy a ticket "Per Termini" at the FS ticket counter or from one of the machines in the station. A ticket costs *about* 11 euros. *Note*: You must validate your ticket by inserting it in the validation machine before you enter the train.

Upon returning to the airport from Termini, you'll find the train on Track 24. You can buy a ticket at the Alitalia office at Track 22 or from other places and machines in the station.

If arriving in Milan, dress well and pay attention to your appearance. Style is very important there.

The climate varies in Italy from north to the south, so check the local weather on the Internet before packing. Beachwear is limited to the beach; even on hot days, shorts are not worn. The climate is temperate, with occasional rainfall, but can get hot in the summer. In winter, conditions in Milan, Turin, and Venice are dominated by cold, damp, and fog. Tuscany's winter temperatures approach freezing, while temperatures in the south of the country are more favorable, averaging 50 to 60 degrees F (10 to 20 degrees C).

Holidays that may affect your travel and program scheduling include:

- January: New Year's Day (1st), Epiphany (6th)
- March/April: Easter Monday
- April: Anniversary of Liberation (25th) at end of World War II
- May: Labour Day (1st)
- June: Republic Day (2nd) for birth of the Italian Republic, 1946
- August: Assumption Day (15th)
- November: All Saints Day (1st)
- December: Immaculate Conception (8th), Christmas Day (25th), St. Stephen's Day (26th)

## PROGRAM DESIGN

The participants may speak a little English, but don't expect a lot. Design the program so that it can be translated into Italian. Build in interaction, fun, and time for breaks. Add translation time and time for working with your interpreter prior to the session. The rule of thumb is that an additional 33 percent of time is needed to address translation needs.

The Italians will participate in role plays, discussions, games, and case studies, so you can design these into your program as long as you allow a lot of time for the activity and the discussion after it. Design alternate ways to make a point, just in case they don't understand what you are saying.

## LOGISTICS

Request the necessary equipment to be set up and tested in the room before your arrival. If they cannot provide the equipment, bring your computer, projector, converter, plugs, and extension cord. Send your program to your hosts ahead of time as a backup precaution. Check with your hosts to determine whether they will photocopy materials for the program or to see whether they would prefer that you ship the materials directly to them ahead of time. Arrange for interpreters if you do not speak fluent Italian.

Italy is part of the European Union and does use the euro (EUR = €), which is divided into 100 cents. Coins come in denominations of 1, 2, 5, €10, 20, and 50 cents. Notes are in 5, 10, 20, 50, 100, 200, and 500 denominations. Banknotes are the same across EU (European Union) countries. Coins have the same fronts and country-specific back sides. ATMs are readily available and credit cards are accepted in most locations in

Italy. Travelers checks are becoming less accepted and are therefore not the best method of payment in Italy.

Food is important to attendees, so make sure you have some for the breaks. Have water available at all times.

## PROGRAM DELIVERY

The most likely location for program delivery would be at a hotel.

Speak slowly enough for your interpreter to keep up. Use simple words and concepts and be willing to explain in a variety of ways if people do not understand.

## TECHNICAL REQUIREMENTS

Be sure to bring 220/240 voltage converters, plugs, and backup systems to use if needed. Bring your program on an electronic storage device, send it to your host ahead of time, and hand carry hard copies of translated and English versions of handouts. Bring videotapes reproduced in PAL format and subtitled in Italian.

Major hotels have installed Internet service, but you may not have access in your sleeping room. Kiosks are available at airports and other public places for connections as you travel around the cities.

## ACCOMMODATIONS

Attempt to stay close to or in the location of your training to make it easy and quick for you to arrive.

Accommodations at hotels and at bed-and-breakfasts are plentiful. Karen Brown's books on accommodations are excellent (www.karenbrown.com). The local hotels are lovely and provide more interest than the larger hotel chains.

Make reservations at an accommodation that advertises their ability to speak English, so your stay will be comfortable. Unless you stay in a Western (U.S. or Canadian) hotel, you will not likely be provided with washcloths (considered a personal item). Plugs and converters are required or you will burn up any electrical items that are not able to be switched to 220/240 volts.

Always be very careful for pickpockets. They are plentiful. With the unemployment rate extremely high in the south of Rome, many opportunists come to the city to make their living. On buses and trains, distraction is used and your money is quickly taken. Sometimes a mother with a young baby will distract you and take your valuables before you even know what has happened. That is why you should keep only small amounts of money in your pocket and most of your money (with your passport) in an under-your-shirt pouch around your stomach.

## GETTING AROUND

Obtain maps in the airport, train station, or hotel. Practice your questions in Italian so you can be understood. Point to the location on the map and ask for help. The Italian people are very helpful and friendly.

Rome is such a busy city. It is so full of sights to see that it is filled with tourists. Flights into the country are plentiful. Transportation to your hotel can be an experience. Close your eyes and don't watch how they dart in and out, because it can be very stressful just to be a passenger in a taxi.

Milan is a busy, high-style city where fashion and trends are set. Milan is the business center for Italy and is the location for some major international companies (such as General Electric, Hewlett-Packard, Expedia, and Oracle). Traveling throughout the country of Italy is not difficult by train or car and is highly recommended, especially if you have additional recreational time to add to the end of your trip.

In major cities, it is not that hard to find people who understand and speak a little English. They are very happy if you try to speak Italian for basic phrases and questions and will be more easily able to help you. Your tour book, Italian phrase book, and maps will be most helpful to find your way around. The buses within Rome are a bit confusing and take a while because they make local stops. Italy, in general, has had issues with strikes affecting public transportation. Stay on top of the local news if you wish to rely on public transportation for your work or just for sightseeing. A taxi is more expensive, but may be a more sure way to reach your location.

## THE PEOPLE

Italians know what is important: family, food, wine, and art. You will see these wherever you go in Italy. The old ruins are right alongside of the newest buildings. Progress is evident, but there is always a reverence for the past.

Food and wine are, of course, very important to everyone. Meals are to be enjoyed leisurely and not interrupted by work. Most places even close down for staff afternoon lunches and reopen later in the afternoon through early evening. The family is central to everything. With over 90 percent of the population Roman Catholic, religion plays a large part in traditions, beliefs, and customs. Restaurants are most often family owned and operated. Emotions are easily displayed. Grand gestures and voices are used to welcome visitors. Everyone is made to feel like part of the family.

Learning is important, so teachers and presenters will be admired and attended to, as long as the program does not interfere with daily life.

Use examples of those things that are important to the participants and you will have their attention. That means you will need to do your homework by reading and watching current events (such as who is currently winning at football/soccer) and listening to their daily concerns, to show how your presentation will help them to obtain what is most important to them.

In addition to football, rugby, cycling, auto racing, basketball, and skiing are sports they enjoy. The first four of these can be used in examples that many Italians will relate well to.

Italian industries include tourism, machinery, iron and steel, chemicals, food processing, textiles, motor vehicles, clothing, footwear, and ceramics.

The history of Italy is interesting. The Roman Empire dominated the early world by spreading its land holdings as far north as England and Scotland and as far south as Egypt and Morocco. But Italy has been a divided nation for most of its history. Sections of the country have been owned at various times by countries such as Germany, France, Spain, and Austria-Hungary, and ruled by such famous persons as Napoleon and Mussolini. Italy's city states were often at war with each other and it was not considered a country until "recent" history. 1870 marked the complete unification of peninsular Italy into one nation under a constitutional monarchy. In 1946, Italians voted to abolish the monarchy and become a republic. Italy is a Republic with an elected President and Prime Minister, who often come under much public scrutiny. Most Italians love to talk about politics and their government and will easily give their opinions.

The Italian people are warm and friendly, but they are also hot-headed and passionate. So do not be surprised if mama breaks a dish and storms out of the restaurant with papa following behind to console her and bring her back in to cook the meal they will be serving to you (this was our experience). Men still love to watch women and touch if possible, as a compliment. Just be on your guard and do not react, but go about your business and it will stop.

## ‼️ PREPARATION

If presenting in Milan, make sure you have the latest fashion to wear. Dress very professionally and conduct yourself appropriately at all times. Other locations are less formal and more casual.

Call the hotel or secretary to check to see whether everything is ready. Ask about any equipment that you will need. Arrange to meet with your interpreter, if you are using one, well before the training to discuss the agenda and objectives and to answer any questions he or she might have.

Be prepared to really enjoy your visit to Italy. The people, culture, food, wine, and environment all make you feel like you are in a very special place. You are!

Here are a few helpful Italian phrases:

| English | Italian | Pronunciation |
| --- | --- | --- |
| Good Morning. | "Buongiorno" | bwon jorno |
| Good Evening. | "Buonasera" | bwona sayra |
| Do you speak English? | "Parla inglese?" | parla eengglaysay |
| I do not speak Italian. | "Non parlo italiano" | non parlo eetaleeaano |
| Thank you. | "Grazie" | grahtsyeh NOT grat-zee |
| Please | "Per favore" | pehr favoray |
| Please write it down. | "Lo scriva, per piacere." | lo skreeva pehr peeachayray. |
| Where is . . . | "Dov'è?" | doveh |
| Where is the bathroom? | "Dov'è la toeletta?" | |
| How much is that? | "Quanto costa?" | kwanto kosta |
| I'd like . . . | "Vorrei" | vorrehee (used when ordering in a restaurant, i.e., vorrei un caffè per favore, I would like a coffee please.) |
| Excuse me. | "Mi scusi" (for attention); "Permesso" (to pass) | |

## THE PRESENTATION

Speak slowly and clearly. Make sure to allow enough time for the interpreter. Speak directly to the audience, not to the interpreter.

Engage participants in discussion. Vary your methods. Keep it interactive and fun.

Make sure you start and end with the agenda and objectives. A relaxed enjoyable presentation will be effective as long as you end on time or a little early. Don't expect everyone to be on time to start the program, but you can start and let them catch up on their own without stopping the presentation. Allow an hour and a half for lunch. Wine will most likely be consumed at lunch, so plan the hard work for the morning of the program instead of the afternoon.

The Italians do not like to change, so if you are presenting a major change, you can expect that they will not respond positively. They are not very comfortable with role play, but will participate if it is requested. If you are using a case study, give it to the trainees the day before, so they can review it ahead of time. Their English may not be very good, but they will try to speak and understand you, if needed. They can understand written English better than spoken English. There is respect for money and age. Private school is seen as an advantage.

You can read their body language to tell whether you are being understood. If you look at people and see glassy eyes, you will know that you need to try a different approach to providing a good learning experience. Be willing to vary your techniques. Watch the audience's responses and you will be able to tell what is working and what needs to be modified for understanding.

Arrivederci (Good-bye/See you later)!

**Helpful websites and references include:**

- www.enchantedlearning.com/languages/italian/subjects/commonphrases.shtml
- www.goeurope.about.com
- www.infoplease.com
- www.wordreference.com

# Romania

**R**omania is a country in Southeastern Europe. It shares its border with Hungary and Serbia to the west, Ukraine and Moldova to the northeast, and Bulgaria to the south. Romania has a stretch of seacoast along the Black Sea. The Danube River forms some of the natural border between Romania, Serbia, and Bulgaria and flows into the Black Sea. Romania is probably most famous for Transylvania and Dracula's Castle (Bran Castle), rumored to have been owned by Vlad Tepes (Dracula).

This chapter provides more detailed information regarding what to expect and tips for success for you when training, teaching, and presenting to a Romanian audience.

## ??? THE REQUEST

If you have been asked to present a program in Romania, the most likely locations for a program to be presented would probably be Bucharest (the capital and center of Romania's business world) or Timisoara (considered the avant-garde for new ideas and openness). The revolution in 1989 to overthrow the Communist regime started at Timisoara.

## • • • GETTING THERE

Flights are easily available to large cities such as Bucharest. Other possible cities for a presenting a program, might be Timisoara, Brasov, Cluj, or Iasi. A valid passport is required to enter the country. The passport must be valid for three months beyond the expected stay of the traveler.

From the Otopeni (Henri Coanda Bucharest International) Airport near Bucharest, to get to the city you can take an official airport taxi (FLY TAXI) from outside of the airport (set the price at the beginning, pay no more then $15). A ride to the center of Bucharest should cost between RON 25 and 30 (EUR 6 to 8). You also can use the bus or the city shuttle, which are much cheaper. Suggestion: Go to the ground floor in the airport and buy a special bus ticket (for two uses) for the 783 line, which is less than 2 euros and will take around forty minutes.

Time is GMT +3 (summer), GMT +2 (winter)

National holidays that may affect your travel and program schedule include:

- January: New Year's Day (1st), day after New Year's (2nd)
- March/April: Easter Monday
- May: Labour Day (1st)
- December: National Holiday (1st), Christmas (25th), Boxing Day (26th)

## PROGRAM DESIGN

The example we are using for a program in Romania is program on coaching.

The program is designed in English and uses mini-lecture, notebooks, easels, class discussion, and activities throughout the program.

Translation can be made into the Romanian/Moldovan language for handouts that will help participants who have difficulty with English.

## LOGISTICS

Materials need to be mailed far ahead of time (four to six weeks) to ensure that they will arrive on time for the program. Bring your own computer with converter, plugs, extension cords, and a projector to make sure you will have what you need. Also bring your program saved on an electronic storage device that can be used on a computer that may already be available and working for you. Have a backup plan, such as hard copies of your program.

The currency of Romania is the new leu (RON). New notes come into denominations of 1, 5, 10, 50, 100, and 500. One new leu consists of 100 bani.

Romania's climate is temperate, with four distinct seasons. Spring and autumn are cool and pleasant. May and June, and September and October are the best months to visit. Summers are hot from July to August, and winters are harsh and very cold between

December and March, with snow falling throughout most of the country. Spring and summer are the wettest seasons, but rain can be expected throughout the year. In Bucharest, the temperature ranges from –29 degrees C in January to 29 degrees C in July, with average temperatures of –3 degrees C in January and 23 degrees C in July.

In general, Bucharest is safe for traveling. In comparison with many other major cities in Europe, violent crime and serious risks are low. However, street crime can be a problem in Bucharest, and travelers should be aware of the dangers associated with potential petty theft.

Pickpocketing is one of the most common dangers for tourists in Bucharest. Purse snatching is less common than pickpocketing, but it does also occur. These crimes are most likely to happen in crowded areas such as city centers and on public transportation. The most common perpetrators of this crime are children, generally orphans who live in the streets of Bucharest.

## PROGRAM DELIVERY

Gabriela Casineanu (a professional coach) shares her experience regarding Romania:

She says that the program would most likely be held in a hotel, although that depends on who your target audience is. Hotels would be a better location, because they are more closely related to the image of the people you want to reach. We asked Gabriela to answer the following questions for us:

**How would a program have to be modified for delivery in Romania?**

Gabriela responds that she likes the coaching program model of small group session, discussion, and activities so much that she would not change anything.

**If we wanted to present a course in your home country, how should it be prepared it so that it would be successful?**

The program, as it is designed, attracts people who are drawn to new/creative ways of living their lives. Participants are willing to discuss, role play, and actively participate in simple games.

## TECHNICAL REQUIREMENTS

Work with your host to explain technical requirements and capabilities.

Electrical current is 220 V; 50 cycles. Outlets take plugs with two round prongs. A plug and power adapter is necessary for most appliances requiring 110 V. Power adapters can be purchased many places, such as Wal-Mart, Radio Shack, or in most airports. Often they come with plug adapters for anywhere in the world.

You can often tell whether you need a power adapter by looking at the transformer or on the appliance itself to see what voltage it is rated for. If it says 220 or 240 volts, you are probably all right. Sometimes it will say 110 to 240 volts. Many laptops are now rated for up to 220, but you should look on the power supply or in your owner's manual before plugging in. It takes just seconds to ruin a good piece of equipment if it cannot handle the higher voltage.

The country is well covered with GSM 900/1800 mobile phone networks. Email and Internet are freely available in the cities and larger towns.

Romania's video format is SECAM, so you must make sure that your video has been converted before you leave home.

##  ACCOMMODATIONS

If you are presenting at a hotel, it is most convenient to stay there. There are recognized hotels available, such as Marriott, Hilton, and Ramada. Check for availability of rooms on the dates needed, as well as photos and customer satisfaction ratings on Expedia.

The direct dialing country code for Romania is +40, and the outgoing code is 00, followed by the relevant country code (e.g., 0044 for the UK). There are numerous area codes applying to cities, towns, and villages, for example, (0)21 for Bucharest. The country is well covered with GSM 900/1800 mobile phone networks.

**Food to enjoy: try the** desserts (tasty pies called ***poale -n brâu*** or huge traditional Christmas and Easter cakes called ***cozonac***), but also the meat rolls in sauerkraut leaves, accompanied by polenta, or in vine leaves (both kinds are called ***sarmalute***). Meat or vegetable soup seasoned with ***bors*** (a sour liquid made from bran and water), the pilaf of Turkish origin, and also baked eggplant salad, the small broiled sausages called ***mititei***, and the Oriental moussaka are the tastiest dishes of the southern region of Muntenia. Actually, the people of both Moldavia and Muntenia are the country's great epicures, whereas the natives of Banat and Transylvania are more of the gourmet kind, often using fruit to enhance the flavor of meat. The famous Romanian plum brandy (***tuica***) is an appetizer; the red and white wines the peasants make themselves add to the Romanian cuisine.

It is best to drink bottled water to make sure you do not experience stomach upset.

##  GETTING AROUND

Bucharest's Metro is a quite efficient means of transportation. One can easily get around by using a Metro map, which can be supplied from any Metro station. Prices are quite cheap. One ten-trip ticket can cost you only 60,000 Leu. In a city that lately has become paralyzed by traffic, Bucharest's Metro is by far the most reliable form of public transport. Built in 1979, the Metro is clean, cheap, safe, and covers the city pretty well. Tickets can be bought at the booths inside the stations; a ticket for two rides costs about $0.65, while a ticket for ten rides costs about $2.15. There is also a one-month pass for about $6.50. Avoid traveling during the rush hours from 7 to 9 A.M. and 5 to 7 P.M.

Even though the public transport network is cheap, extensive, and reliable, taking a bus, trolleybus, or tram can be a headache because they are very crowded (especially during the rush hours). A ticket valid for one journey costs 0.25 E and must be purchased before climbing aboard, then punched in one of the strange-looking devices located all over the vehicle (watch how others do it first).

Buses (petrol) and trolleybuses (electric) are the second-most-common means of transportation in Bucharest. Covering more areas than the subway, with more stops, the bus system is used by many. Bucharest is not yet divided into zones. With one transport ticket you can make a single ride (no getting off) from end to end of a bus line. Prices: for one ride ticket: 1.1 RON or approximately 0.3 EUR. A one-day ticket is 7 RON, approximately 1.9 EUR. A seven-day ticket is 15 RON, or about 4.1 EUR, and a fifteen-day ticket is 22 RON, about 6 EUR. Two-trip magnetic cards are available, as are ten-trip, and one-month Tickets are sold in the station, but there can be stations not selling tickets, so it's best to be prepared. Buses can be pretty crowded, mostly in rush hours. Beware of pickpockets in crowded buses. It's better to take a cab than to lose your money to pickpockets.

If you are taking a taxi, have your hotel recommend and obtain a taxi for you to go to any of your destinations.

##  THE PEOPLE

Lots of people speak English in Romania—from businessmen to teenagers, teachers, and engineers. It is their way to stay connected to the world.

If you go to large cities such as Bucharest, Timisoara, Brasov, Cluj, or Iasi, Gabriela Casineanu tells us you'll not see much difference between Canada and Romania. You will see less cultural diversity. Romanians are also interested in what people from other countries could teach them. They are very open and communicative.

A small alarm bell: There are Romanians who think that strangers are rich and they (Romanians) would like to take advantage of this. In the business world, most of them are looking for their profit (not only in Romania). Gabriela believes that there are more honest people in universities.

The Romanian people are mostly ethnic Romanian, with small minorities of German, Hungarian, and Roma (Gypsy) populations. Traditional Romanian music with violin and woodwind instruments is popular.

Here's a brief chronology:

| | |
|---|---|
| 1541 | Moldavia and Walachia are part of the Ottoman Empire. |
| 23 Dec 1861 | United Rumanian Principalities is formed. |
| 12 July 1866 | Rumania |
| 9 May 1877 | Independence from Ottoman Empire declared. |
| 13 Jul 1878 | Independence recognized internationally. |
| 26 Mar 1881 | Kingdom of Rumania |
| 6 Dec 1916 to 29 Nov 1918 | Occupied by Austria-Hungary and Germany. |
| 9 Apr 1918 | Bessarabia (see Moldova) annexed from Russia. |
| 1 Dec 1918 | Transylvania incorporated into Rumania. |
| 29 Dec 1918 | Bessarabia and Bukovina and incorporated into Romania. |
| 27 Jun 1940 | Bukovina and Bessarabia annexed by Soviet Union. Southern Dobruja annexed by Bulgaria. |
| 30 Aug 1940 | Under German pressure a major part of Transylvania is retroceded to Hungary. |
| 25 Jul 1941 to Aug 1944 | Rumania annexes Bessarabia, Bukovina, and Transnistria from the Soviet Union. |
| 15 Sep 1947 | Retroceded part of Transylvania is de jure, returned to Rumania (de facto since 11 Mar 1945). |
| 31 Aug 1944 to 10 Feb 1947 | Occupied by Soviet Union. |
| 30 Dec 1947 | Rumanian People's Republic. |
| 21 Aug 1965 | Socialist Republic of Rumania |
| Feb 1966 | Spelling officially changed to Romania. |
| 29 Dec 1989 | Romania. |

Key industries include textiles, footwear, light machinery, auto assembly, mining, timber, construction materials, metallurgy, chemicals, food processing, and petroleum refining.

Agricultural products include wheat, corn, barley, sugar beets, sunflower seed, potatoes, grapes, eggs, and sheep.

Romania began the transition from Communism in 1989 with a largely outdated industrial foundation and lack of productivity. After an extremely difficult three-year recession, the country began to recover at the turn of the century (2000), due to a strong demand in European Union export markets. Despite a major slowdown over the following two years, strong domestic activity in construction, agriculture, and consumption allowed for growth. In 2001, the government signed an International Monetary Fund (IMF) standby agreement that was approved in 2003 (the first time Romania successfully concluded an IMF agreement since the 1989 revolution). This move was accompanied by slow but steady gains in privatization, deficit reduction, and the curbing of inflation. In July 2004, the IMF's executive board approved a twenty-four-month standby agreement; this agreement is merely precautionary, according to most Romanian authorities. Romania still experiences widespread poverty and corruption in the business environment.

Romania is a democratic republic, with an elected president and appointed prime minister.

Romania is a secular state. Most people are Romanian Orthodox.

Favorite Romanian sports are soccer, handball, tennis, gymnastics, rugby, basketball, volleyball, and oina (similar to baseball).

## PREPARATION

Do not expect the advances and comforts that you may be used to, such as high-speed Internet in every room. Bring low-tech alternatives to teach critical points. Be prepared to use a variety of ways to communicate.

Some helpful basic Romanian phrases include:

| English | Romanian | Pronounced |
|---------|----------|------------|
| Good Morning! | "Bună dimineaţa" | BOO-nuh dee-mee-NYAH-tsah |
| Good Evening | "Bună seara" | BOO-nuh SYAH-rah |
| Good day! (when in doubt use this) | "Bună Ziua" | BOO-nuh ZEE-wah |

| | | |
|---|---|---|
| I'm sorry | "Imi pare rau" | um PAH-reh row |
| Thank you | "Bine" | been-e |
| You're welcome | "Cu plăcere" | coo pluh-cheh-reh |
| Where is the bathroom? | "Unde este toaleta?" | OOHN-deh YES-the twah-LET-ah |
| Yes | "Da" | dah |
| No | "Nu" | noo |

## THE PRESENTATION

When making your presentation, watch the responses of your participants. You will see whether they understand by the looks on their faces or the sound of their voices when asking questions.

They will be willing to try new things. Ask them to explain what they have learned so far. Keep your presentation simplified to start and move on to more complexity when they clearly understand the basic concepts in your program.

You can use pictures of the Romanian flag, castles, palace, and cathedral to show respect for this fascinating country.

**Helpful websites and references include:**

- www.countrystudies.com
- www.gocurrency.com
- www.itcnet.ro
- www.romanianlessons.com
- www.tripadvisor.com
- www.wordtravels.com
- www.worldstatesmen.org

# chapter TWENTY-SEVEN

# Switzerland

**M**ajestic snow-covered mountains, reflected in crystal, clear blue lakes; chalets that look like gingerbread houses; and hearty outdoor people are all vivid images of Switzerland. You can hear German, French, or Italian spoken as the dominant language, depending on your location in Switzerland—German in the north, east, and center of the country; French to the west; and Italian in the south.

When you travel in this country, you will experience a unique mixture of pastoral old countryside with progressive modern cities.

Here is what to expect and tips for success when training, teaching, or presenting to the Swiss people.

## ??? THE REQUEST

When presenting a program in Switzerland, some of the most likely locations would be Geneva (French-speaking section of Switzerland) or Zurich (German-speaking section). Several of our corporate managers are brought in or stationed in Switzerland for extended periods of time to work and train other employees.

Many of the programs in our Switzerland experiences have been leadership, management, or human resource development programs. When asked to present to a Swiss audience, it is important to ask your host and confirm the purpose and objectives of the program. Send drafted objectives and a detailed outline for their review. Make written agreements regarding length of the program, dates, times, and location.

Work with the hotel and/or office secretary to confirm administrative details.

### • • • GETTING THERE

Of course you will need a valid passport to enter the country.

Depending on the location you will be working with, the names of Switzerland will vary from Schweiz (German), Suisse (French), to Svizzera (Italian). So do not be confused when making hotel or travel reservations, if you see any of these names.

The time in Switzerland is standard time zone: UTC/GMT +1 hour

Daylight saving time: +1 hour

You will probably be flying into Geneva or Zurich. Ask your hotel when you make your reservation whether they will be sending a car to pick you up at the airport and, if so, how much it will cost. If not, take the train, bus, or taxi or rent a car to travel to your hotel.

The Geneva airport is located just 5 km from the city center. See www.gva.ch/en/ for detailed information.

#### Transport from the Geneva Airport

- *Rail Link*: The train departs every ten minutes from the airport to Gare Cornavin. SFr. 5.20 for adults. It is about a six-minute trip.

- *Bus*: The number 10 bus departs approximately every ten minutes to Gare Cornavin. SFr. 2.20 for adults. It is a twelve-to-eighteen-minute trip. Tickets are good for one hour, including transfers.

- *Taxis*: Taxis are available at the taxi stand. There is a maximum of four passengers. The average cost is approximately SFr. 25–35 per trip, and the duration is fifteen to thirty minutes.

#### Transport from the Zurich Airport

- The Zurich Airport has its own railway station, which is located under Terminal B. About six trains run hourly to and from Zurich's main station.

- The trip takes only ten minutes, while cars can take up to forty-five minutes during rush hours.

- The Zurich Airport site has information about all scheduled flights to and from Zurich.

The following holidays are legal holidays all over Switzerland. They may affect your travel and program scheduling:

- January: New Year's Day (*Neujahr/jour de l'an/capodanno*) (1st)

- March/April: Good Friday (*Karfreitag/Vendredi Saint/Venerdi Santo*) (first Sunday after the first full moon after the Spring Equinox, usually late March)

- Spring: Easter Sunday/Monday (*Ostern/Pâques/Pasqua*) (second and third day after Good Friday)

- Spring: Ascension Day (*Auffahrt/Ascencion/Assensione*) (forty days after Easter Sunday)

- Spring: Whit Sunday and Monday (*Pfingsten/Pentecôte/Pentecoste*) (tenth and eleventh days after Ascension Day)

- August: National Day (*Bundesfeier/fête nationale/festa nazionale*) (1st) Celebrates the Oath of 1291, which is considered the start of the Swiss Confederation

- September: Federal Fast (*Bundesfast/Jeûne federal*) (second Monday of September, except in Geneva where the Genevan Fast is celebrated on the first Thursday of September. These two dates are occasions of feasts rather than fasts)

- December: Christmas Day and St. Stephen's Day (*Weihnachten/Noël/Natale*) (25th and 26th). Note that St. Stephen's Day is not always a holiday, as it often depends on a company's good will.

## PROGRAM DESIGN

The primary groups in Switzerland are the French and Italian-speaking people, and the German-speaking Swiss. Ask ahead of time if English is acceptable and, if so, the handouts can be in English. The German-speaking participants may be more comfortable with English than the French-speaking students, so it is good to have the program translated into both French and German versions (if possible, also Italian). Design your slides so that they have extra room on each slide for the translations. For example, your slides may be in English, but you can have handouts of the slides available for the French, German, and Italian translations, in case they are preferred by your participants. Make sure the slides include simple words and concepts that can be easily understood or looked up in a dictionary.

Design a clear structure and agenda for the training and make sure each section of the program is easily referenced back to the agenda. This ensures that participants can check and see where you are in the program at any time. Some lecture is okay, but try to design much of the program to be interactive.

Practice the design to know the precise timing. This audience needs to have everything go on time, as planned. You will need to decide what has to be dropped to keep to the agenda as promised. So prepare your contingency plans to keep the program on track and on time.

## LOGISTICS

Request the necessary equipment to be set up and tested in the room before your arrival. If they cannot provide the equipment, bring your computer, projector, converter, plugs, and extension cord. Send your program to your hosts ahead of time as a backup precaution. Check with your hosts to determine whether they will photocopy materials for the program or whether they would prefer that you ship the materials directly to them ahead of time. Arrange for interpreters if you do not speak fluent French, German, or Italian, as needed.

Have fruit and lots of water available as refreshments. The Swiss are very health-conscious.

The official currency is the Swiss franc (CHF) divided into 100 Rappen (German) or centimes (French). Although they are not part of the EU (European Union), many prices are indicated in euros and some merchants may accept euros. Visa, MasterCard, and American Express are widely accepted. ATMs are widespread; many are equipped with the Cirrus or Maestro systems. Banks offer the best exchange rates for traveler's checks and foreign currency, but it is also possible to exchange money at major hotels, main train stations, and airports. Banks are open Monday to Friday only.

## PROGRAM DELIVERY

The most likely locations for program delivery would be at the office or at a hotel. Even if the participants can speak and understand English, they may require help understanding some concepts, so speak slowly.

Jeanne Heinzer (Heinzer Consulting) explains that this is a formal environment, but you do not have to use "mister" when addressing male participants. Stick to the program agenda. Start the program on time and finish on time. The Swiss like discussion. A good mixture of techniques will be welcomed. A bit of humor is expected, but review it ahead of time with your host to make sure that it will work for this audience. You should speak slowly; the Swiss's English can be poorer than you think. Ask them how comfortable they feel in English. Have regular breaks and, again, start and stop on time.

## TECHNICAL REQUIREMENTS

Be sure to bring 220/240 voltage converters, plugs, and backup systems to use if needed. Bring your program on an electronic storage device, send it to your host ahead of time, and hand carry hard copies of translated and English versions of handouts. Bring videotapes reproduced in PAL and SECAM formats and subtitled in German and French, if possible.

Electricity in Switzerland is 230 volts, alternating at 50 cycles per second. There are three main types of voltage converters. Resistor-network converters will usually be advertised as supporting something like 50 to 1,600 watts. They are lightweight and support high-wattage electrical appliances like hair dryers and irons. However, they can only be used for short periods of time and are not ideal for digital devices.

Transformers will have a much lower maximum watt rating, usually 50 or 100. Transformers can often be used continuously and provide better electricity for low-wattage appliances like battery chargers and laptop computers. They are heavy.

Some companies sell combination converters that include both a resistor and a transformer in the same package. This kind of converter will usually come with a switch that toggles between the two modes. This is good if you need both types of converter.

Outlets in Switzerland generally accept one type of plug with two round pins.

Check ahead of time to see whether Internet capability is available where you will be presenting, if you need it.

## ACCOMMODATIONS

Accommodations at hotels and bed-and-breakfasts are plentiful in Switzerland. Karen Brown's books on accommodations are excellent (www.karenbrown.com).

Make reservations at an accommodation that advertises their ability to speak English. Unless you stay in a Western hotel (U.S. or Canadian), you will not likely be provided with washcloths (considered a personal item). You will not see most of the typical chain hotels in Geneva or Zurich, so check with your travel agent or online for location, cost, photos, and customer satisfaction ratings, as well as Internet availability in your room. Plugs and converters will be required, or you will burn up any electrical items that are not able to be switched to 220/240 volts.

Geneva is considered by many travelers to be safe, expensive, friendly, clean, and international. Zurich is considered walkable, safe, polite, clean, not as expensive as Geneva, and quaint.

- International country code: +41 (Switzerland)
- Telephone for Zurich: area codes: (0) 44 / (0) 43
- Telephone code for Geneva: city/area code: (0) 22

- The outgoing code is 00, followed by the relevant country code.

- Mobile phone GSM 1800 and 900 networks operate throughout the country.

- Visitors who wish to use a prepaid SIM card from Swisscom Mobile (NATEL easy) will be required to register with the service provider and produce identification.

- Internet cafes are available in the main towns and resorts; some public phone booths also have Internet and email access.

## GETTING AROUND

Zurich has two self-service transport systems: the Zurich Transportation Authority (VBZ), and the Greater Zurich Transport System (ZVV). The modern tram, bus, and S-Bahn network offers daily service from about 5:30 A.M. until midnight, with services every six minutes during rush hours. An English leaflet containing a detailed outline of the route network and information on the use of the ticket machines is available at all Ticketerias, located at the train stations and major tram/bus stops. A single ticket is all you need. Fares and tickets in the greater Zurich area are based on a system of fare zones. You buy a ticket for one or several zones. The period of validity varies with the number of zones you buy. Tickets must be purchased before boarding and can be obtained at any tram or bus stop from an automatic ticket machine. They must always be validated before boarding. Inspectors do make random checks, and traveling with an invalidated ticket brings a fine of 60 Swiss francs.

Taxis in Zurich should be ordered by telephone or obtained at taxi ranks. Hailing a taxi in the street usually doesn't work. The fares are always metered and include a tip. There are additional charges for luggage, extra passengers, and waiting time. Call a taxi at 044 222 2222, 044 444 4444 or 044 777 7777. There is also a specialized taxi service for the disabled (01 272 4242).

Obtain maps in the airport, train station, or hotel. Practice your French and German questions so that you can be understood. Point to the location on the map and ask for help. Friendly English-speaking people will be helpful.

**In Geneva** the bus and tram services are run by the TPG (***Transports Publics Genevois***). Buses and trams run from 06:00 to 24:00, depending on the service. Each bus and tram stop has timetables and maps covering the entire Geneva network. Bus and tram tickets are sold at the vending machines at stops. Monthly bus passes and Noctambus passes can be bought at the Gare Cornavin or from the TPG office. Tickets can also be bought directly from the driver. Pre-paid discount cards (the Cart@Bonus) can be bought from newsagents. Taxis are expensive.

# THE PEOPLE

Swiss citizens are subject to three legal jurisdictions: the commune (communities or municipalities), canton, and federal levels. The federal constitution defines a system of direct democracy. The Swiss Confederation consists of twenty-six cantons. Geneva and Zurich are considered cantons.

The Swiss are formal, but very nice. They expect a lot of information (direct democracy). They are a relationship-oriented culture. Spend some time to establish trust. Tell them about yourself and who you are as a person. This is a much less hierarchical, consensus oriented society, where everybody has a word to say. Make sure you involve them. They take their time. They may speak slowly. "Slowly but steadily" is one of their mottos.

Switzerland is a small country situated in the heart of Central Europe and shares a lot of its *history* and its *culture* (four national languages spoken in different regions) with its neighbors Germany, France, Italy and Austria.

### Some Basic Swiss History

- Archeology shows that Stone Age hunters had been living in Switzerland before the last Ice Age (approximately 350,000 B.C.).

- Switzerland's official Latin name, "Confoederatio Helvetica" goes back to a Celtic tribe called the Helvetians.

- The majority of Switzerland's "native" population settled during the Germanic Migration of Nations that set an end to the Roman Empire in Western Europe at about 400 A.D.

- The Old Swiss Confederacy was founded in the first days of August, 1291 (hence Switzerland's national holiday is celebrated on August 1).

- Switzerland was officially accepted as an independent nation by its neighbors in the 1648 European peace treaty.

- The Swiss Revolution and the Helvetic Republic have set an end to the rule of a small number of privileged cities, valleys, and families over the majority of the country.

- Today's borders and Switzerland's neutrality were defined at the Vienna Congress of 1815 ending the wars of Napoleon.

- Switzerland's modern federal constitution dates back to 1848 (with total revisions in 1874 and 1999). The New Federal Constitution combines elements of the

U.S. constitution (federal/state with central and cantonal [state] governments and parliaments) and of French revolutionary tradition.

- Switzerland remained neutral during WWI and WWII

- Recent history is characterized by political stability, economic progress, increased social security, and a new openness and tolerance.

Banking, tourism, pharmaceuticals, and chemicals are important industries in Switzerland. The manufacture of precision instruments for engineering is important, as is watch-making, and the biological sciences industries. Several of the world's largest companies are headquartered in Switzerland. Among these are Nestle, UBS AG, Credit Suisse, Novartis, ABB, and Swatch. Switzerland is ranked one of the most powerful economies in the world.

Switzerland has no official state religion. Christianity is the predominant religion, divided between the Catholic church and various protestant denominations. Immigration has brought Islam (predominantly Albanians) and Eastern Orthodoxy.

The Swiss are big fans of football (soccer), wrestling, and Hornussen, which is like a cross between baseball and golf.

Customs will depend on which area of Switzerland you are in, that is, German areas respect and are closer to German customs and traditions, the French areas honor French traditions, and the Italian sections of the country exhibit Italian customs.

## !!! PREPARATION

Make sure you can arrive early with plenty of extra time to ensure you will not be late to conduct your session. Smart, casual dress is perfect. The Swiss expect professionalism, promptness, and precision.

Call the hotel or secretary to check to see whether everything is ready. Ask about any equipment that you will need.

Many of the Swiss people speak German, Swiss, Italian, and English.

Swiss German is not standardized, and pronunciations vary greatly depending on where you are. Here are a few of the changes in pronunciation:

- The "ch" sound you find in "chlöibi" is somewhat similar to the noise you make when you clear your throat. It is similar to the Scottish sound "ch" as in "loch."

- Words that end in "ä" such as "ladä" (store), the ä here is pronounced similar to the ending in British English "father" (dropping the r)

- An "äi" is similar to the sound you utter when you say "buy," "lie," or "my." This depends on where you are, however. In Bern, it sounds more like the diphthong in "way."
- If you find a double vowel, that usually indicates the length of the vowel, that is, it is a long vowel, for example: Maa (man).

Some basic vocabulary that you might find helpful is listed below.

| English | Swiss German |
|---|---|
| Hello | "Grüezi hoi! saluti!" (auch: saletti) |
| Hello everyone | "Grüezi mittenand" |
| Hi everyone | "Halo mittenand" |
| Fine, thank you | "Guet, merci" |
| I lost my wallet! | "Ich (i) (y) ha mis Portmonnaie verlore!" (I, y are like English "e") |
| I feel sick/not well/upset | "Y fühle mich schlacht" |
| Where is the police station? | "Wo isch dr Polizei Poschte?" |
| I have to/must report something | "I mües öppis määlde" |
| Hospital | "Spital" |
| Is there a hospital nearby? | "Het's es Spital in dr Nöchi?" |
| I/we am/are lost!! | "I bi velore/mir sind verlore" |
| Can you please tell me where . . . is? | "Bitte säge si mir wo . . . isch?" |
| train station | "Bahnhof" |
| post office (prononced "pay-tay-tay") | "PTT" |
| church | "Chile" |
| Monday | "Mäntig" "Mentig" |
| Tuesday | "Tsischtig" |
| Wednesday | "Mittwuch" |
| Thursday | "Donnschtig" |
| Friday | "Fritig" |
| Saturday | "Samschtig" |
| Sunday | "Sunntig" |

Swiss French is similar to Belgian French. Some basic phrases with their pronunciation include:

| | | |
|---|---|---|
| Hello/Good day | "Bonjour" | *bohn-zhoor* |
| Good evening | "Bonsoir" | *bohn-swahr* |
| Good night | "Bonne nuit" | *bun nwee* |
| Hi/Bye | "Salut" | *sah-lew* |
| Good-bye | "Au revoir" | *ohr-vwah* |
| Please | "S'il vous plait" | *seel voo pleh* |
| Thank you (very much) | "Merci (beaucoup)" | *mair-see boh-koo* |
| You're welcome | "De rien/Je vous en prie" | *duh ree-ahn/zhuh voo zawn pree* |
| Welcome | "Bienvenu(e)" | *bee-ahn-vuh-new* |
| See you later | "A tout à l'heure/A plus tard" | *ah too tah luhr/ah plew tahr* |
| See you soon | "A bientôt" | *ah bee-ahn-toh* |
| See you tomorrow | "A demain" | *ah duh-mahn* |
| Sorry! | "Désolé (e)!" | *day-zoh-lay* |
| Excuse me! | "Pardonnez-moi!" | *pahr-dohn-nay-mwah* |

 **THE PRESENTATION**

Speak slowly and clearly. Make sure to allow enough time for the interpreter. Speak directly to the audience, not to the interpreter. If it is too speedy, the quality can suffer and that is what they may think.

Engage participants in discussion. Vary your methods. Keep it interactive and fun.

Make sure you start and end with the agenda and objectives. Check back to each item on the agenda when you go on to the next item to see whether there are any questions before moving on to the next topic or section. Keep the program on track, but be flexible enough to allow for interaction and discussion. Start and end on time.

Salut!

**Helpful websites and references include:**

- www.geneva.angloinfo.com/information/11/busses.asp
- www.history-switzerland.geschichte-schweiz.ch/
- www.geneva.info/airport/
- www.gva.ch/en/
- www.ielanguages.com/french1.html
- www.karenbrown.com
- www.switzerland.isyours.com
- www.treehouse.ofb.net/go/en/voltage
- www.timeanddate.com
- www.travelnotes.org/Europe/switzerland.htm
- www.wikitravel.org/en/Swiss-German_phrasebook
- www.wordtravels.com
- www.zurich-relocation.ch/content/transportation/public_transportation.html

# The Netherlands/Holland

Costumes, wooden shoes, and windmills are still part of Dutch life, but you can quickly see that The Netherlands has moved out of the past into a progressive future. The Dutch people are welcoming and fun to be with, but look out for all the bicycles that pause for no one. Famous Dutch painters such as Rembrandt and Van Gogh created masterpieces that we continue to admire in the amazing museums of Amsterdam, such as the Rijksmuseum and Van Gogh Museum. Here is an example for a training program delivered in Holland. This provides more detailed information regarding what to expect and tips for success when training, teaching, and presenting to the Dutch people.

## ??? THE REQUEST

As an example, say we have been asked by Xerox management to present a program in Holland on continuous supplier involvement for engineering design teams. Each team member is an expert in his or own field, such as engineering, manufacturing, parts supplier, finance, or procurement. Xerox wants to present the program in early spring at their design and manufacturing site. The program sponsor is the chief engineer for the product.

We need to determine how best to communicate with the audience before the program, invite participants and make arrangements with the local managers and administrative staff.

The Netherlands is often called Holland. This is formally incorrect, as North and South Holland in the western Netherlands are only two of the country's twelve provinces.

Travel arrangements in our example were booked through the corporate travel agency for the dates selected by the local manager. He and his administrative staff determined the dates that most of the participants could be available and asked them to hold the dates on their calendars for this important event. The flight arrangements were made to fly into Germany because the presentation location was just over the border. We had our passports in plenty of time, and there are no visa requirements to enter either country.

Landing in Germany was a little unnerving with all of the military around. The luggage did not make the flight, so we had to travel into Holland (the scheduled location of our session) and wait for a call from the airport. The next day the luggage arrived (luckily, the presentation was in a carry-on bag) and we were required to travel back into Germany so the luggage could be personally brought through Customs. So now we were in business! The next day we traveled to our training delivery site. Signs read "der smakkderhide." What was that? We made up stories of possible translation, such as "small furry animals that were smacked by your car if you went too fast." We eventually found out that it indicated the manufacturing plant area. We continued on to find our site. It was a snooker club! Billiards is the closest that we could translate into something familiar. We were asked: "What time would you like us to bring tea?"

Holland is the low-lying northwest region of the Netherlands and comprises the provinces of North Holland and South Holland. Although the whole country is commonly known as Holland, the official name is actually The Netherlands.

For most presenters, a likely location for a program would be in Amsterdam. This is a city that is easy to reach by air. From Schiphol Airport there is a direct train to Amsterdam Central Station, for € 3.60, in fifteen minutes. You can buy the ticket from the machine, because at the counter you may pay an extra charge (€ .5); beware: the machines may not accept credit or debit cards. If you buy the ticket at the ticket office you will also be given advice as to the next train and at what platform. The train station at Schiphol is located underground, under the main airport hall. Watch out for pickpockets and baggage thieves. A common trick is a knock on your window to distract you so that an accomplice can steal your luggage or laptop. Another trick is to have an accomplice jam the doors and then steal your luggage. The thief jumps out, and the door immediately closes, making it impossible to catch the person.

Taxis from Schiphol are expensive: legal taxis have blue number plates, others should be avoided. Some hotels in Amsterdam and around the airport have a shuttle bus service.

Time zone: Central European time zone. Standard time zone: UTC/GMT +1 hour: Daylight saving time: +1 hour: Current time zone offset: UTC/GMT +2 hours: Time zone abbreviation: CEST or Central European Summer Time

This implies that the **time** difference with EST is +6 hours and with PST +9 hours. Daylight saving period: clocks are turned forward one hour at the end of March and back one hour at the end of October.

Holidays that may affect your travel and program scheduling include:

- January: New Year's Day (1st)
- March-April: Good Friday, Easter Monday
- April: Queen's Birthday (30th)
- May: Liberation Day (5th)
- May-June: Ascension Day, Whit Monday
- December: Christmas Day (25th), Boxing Day (26th)

## PROGRAM DESIGN

The needs assessment and design in our example were done by a multi-national team of technical experts to ensure that we were meeting the needs of the participants and the management. The design was based on benchmarking data that revealed that costs could be reduced by early product design decisions and teamwork from a variety of experts on the design. Because each technical expert is familiar with his or her own requirements, the experts are often unable to understand the competing requirements of other team members from other countries. The program was designed in English (the most common language), with the capability of being translated into the other appropriate languages. The course objectives included the ability to share information, work together, and make decisions that would result in a high-quality, low-cost product that could be manufactured and delivered to customers. Case studies, role plays, and videos were designed to help participants learn from best practices and avoid common mistakes through applying solid company practices and procedures.

Expect to hear a lot of questions, so prepare a detailed list of information regarding what the participants can expect to get out of the training, based on your needs assessment conducted beforehand.

**LOGISTICS**

Electronic and hard copy materials should be sent ahead of time for reproduction in Holland. Equipment must be requested and was in working order when we arrived. The copies were reproduced on A4 paper instead of the 8½ × 11" paper size that they had been designed for, so they looked very funny in the notebooks that we shipped for handouts. Now we know to format the electronic version for A4 paper to avoid this situation in the future. The room had large pillars, which obstructed the participants' view of the speaker from several seats in the room. Our setup was intended for small groups at tables, so we rearranged the tables that had been set up for us. We asked for a small table in front for the speaker materials and one in back for additional handout materials to be distributed at specific times in the program. We asked what time they usually had breaks and adjusted our presentation schedule to accommodate their expectations.

Always ask beforehand whether the program can be conducted in English and the manual can be provided in English. Most Dutch with a good educational level will feel comfortable with a presenter who speaks to them in English.

Work with the hotel or office secretary to check about equipment, plugs, and cords needed, and ask whether they will be provided and tested before the program starts.

The climate in Holland is temperate and very similar to that of the United Kingdom, with summer temperatures ranging from 20 to 25 degrees C in July and August and winter temperatures in December and January ranging from 0 to 10 degrees C.

The Netherlands receives a fairly steady flow of rainfall throughout the year, with April and May on average being the driest months.

The Dutch currency is the euro. Coins: 1, 2, 5, 10, 20, 50 cents, €1, €2. Bank Notes: €5, €10, €20, €50 €100, €200, €500.

If you are looking for an ATM, you won't find one, because they are called Geldautomaats or Chipknips. They are similar to ATMs and they prompt you to an English button.

There are many places to change money. Post offices usually give the best rates. The GWK (Travelex foreign exchange company) at Central Station is also good. Compare rates carefully at the exchange offices in town. Hotels are usually an expensive place to change money. Banks can be slow. There's an American Express on the Damrak, and a Thomas Cook on the Dam. Credit cards are not as widely accepted in The Netherlands as in many other lands, but it's growing steadily better. Always inquire first if you intend to pay by credit card. An ATM card will most likely work in The Netherlands, so you don't need to take traveler's checks. Check with your bank before leaving though.

Let them know where you will be traveling, so they expect withdrawals and charges from your location.

## PROGRAM DELIVERY

Our program participants had traveled to Holland from a variety of European countries. Their languages included British English, Dutch, French, Italian, and German. We were told that all could speak English, but quickly realized that was an overstatement for some. A few had brought translators with them. They represented many different fields of expertise. Most were from the same company, but some were external suppliers of parts to Xerox and therefore worked for much smaller companies. Some seemed very nervous and others very confident, so we knew we had to level the playing field and make them all feel equal and comfortable enough to participate. We gave them a simple activity to have each identify how he or she provided service to Xerox customers.

The Dutch like to have a good mixture of techniques, such as discussion and role play, with not too much lecture. They like interactivity and are willing to ask questions.

The people are open and fun-loving, and willing to try out different practice exercises. The difficulty comes when participants try to read and speak in a language that is not their first. It would help them if you sent copies of the materials ahead of time so they can take their time to read and understand it. It can also be a challenge for the participants to get along with each other. Countries have often had centuries of hostilities between them and are now being asked to strike up an instant cooperation. Everyone is very cordial, and each participant was on his or her best behavior.

## TECHNICAL REQUIREMENTS

We were able to design the program with relatively simple technical requirements. The main thing that we had to prepare for was different video equipment standards. It is important to inquire about this long before the program so you can be prepared with the PAL video format that was necessary. Some equipment is capable of switching from NTSC format to PAL, but you should bring both types of tapes just in case. An additional fallback plan is a script of the video that can be duplicated and read if the equipment does not work.

The voltage requirement is 220/240, 50 cycle, so make sure you have a converter and international plugs (two-prong), as well as an extension cord, if you are bringing your own computer and/or projector.

Check to make sure that the location of your program has high-speed Internet capability, if you will need it.

## ACCOMMODATIONS

The hotel in our example (hotel de Bovenste Molen), was incredibly beautiful (hard to find because it was really in the countryside), settled on a lovely quiet lake with swans floating and no one but the guests on the entire lake. We noticed that the candy bars in the vending machines were Snickers and purchased one. But to our surprise there were no nuts in it as expected. The recipe is changed for other countries. It's the simplest surprises that catch you off guard!

The food was another big surprise. There was lots of buttermilk, ham, and cheese for breakfast. Some restaurants proudly displayed their freshly killed poultry in the front window. Others allowed you to select your own live turtle that they would then make into soup for you. Herring stands and beer are popular among the Dutch people.

In Holland on another trip, we checked into a pensione (bed and breakfast), unpacked and asked the owner where he suggested we go for dinner. Many, many hours later, after being lost in a town that was much larger than we thought, we still had not found a place to eat and did not know the name and address of our lodging. All of our things were there, and we did not know how to find it!

Lesson learned: always take a business card or have the owner write down the name and address of your lodging in the language of the country so you can show it to someone to get help.

An important thing to remember about all public toilets in Amsterdam, apart from being called "toiletten" or "WC" and not "rest room," is to pay the person who sits at the entrance. There will be a little saucer or cup on a table where you can put the entrance money, which is usually only a bit of change.

Amsterdam has Marriott, Radisson, Sheraton, and Hilton hotels, which provide the typical amenities that you may be expecting.

You should be careful with your belongings because there are people who will steal them in Amsterdam.

## GETTING AROUND

If you rent a car, it can give you freedom but also can get you lost. Make sure that you have a map in the language of the country and detailed directions from the car rental agency to make your trip easier. If you are located in a major city such as Amsterdam, you can rely on taxis and public transportation instead of a car.

Watch out for the bicycles when you are walking or driving. They are everywhere!

You can rent a bicycle too. It is an excellent way to get around.

The tram (fifteen lines) is the main form of public transport in the central area, and there are also dozens of bus routes for regional buses and suburban buses. Most tram stops have a detailed, but not very legible, map of the system.

Tickets can be bought on the bus or tram, but it is always cheaper to buy them before boarding. The standard ticket for bus, tram, and metro is the *strippenkaart*. They are available from machines in the metro and railway stations, from the GVB (Gemeentevervoerbedrijf or Municipal Transport Corporation) office opposite Central Station, and from supermarkets, newsagents, and tobacconists. This ticket consists of a number of strips, which must be stamped in a validator prior to entering the metro, or by the driver or conductor when boarding a tram or bus. A strippenkaart is also valid for use on NS trains *within* Amsterdam; validate them on the platform. They are *not* valid for train trips to Schiphol airport. You can use them on buses to Schiphol, but generally it's faster to get there by train. Multiple people can share one strippenkaart.

Travel for one hour through a single zone costs two strips; two zones cost three strips; and so forth. Typically, tourists will only be traveling through the central zone of Amsterdam, unless they plan on visiting outer areas. Alternatively, you can get a 24-, 48-, or 72-hour all-zones bus/rail/tram pass for a reasonable price (€ 10 for 48 hours). Don't forget to stamp it before your first trip. If you stay longer in Amsterdam, you can buy discounted weekly or monthly tickets from most post offices or other ticket sale points.

A new national ticketing system is being introduced, based on a contactless card (swipe card). The system is operational on the Amsterdam metro, at first in parallel with the old system. Trams and buses are being converted to the new system.

Most trams these days have conductors, old trams at the rear and new trams more toward the center. The former can be boarded either via the front or rear doors, and passengers leave through the center doors. The newer trams can be boarded either via the front or the last set of doors, and passengers leave through doors at the rear and between the entrance doors. There are still two or three lines without conductors; all doors can be used for entrance, and all except the front doors for exit. Enter buses only via the front door.

## THE PEOPLE

Dutch hospitality is excellent. Everyone was welcoming and helpful to us.

The Dutch are informal and will quickly get on a first-name basis with you. They like speed and are speedy people, according to Jeanne Heinzer (Heinzer Consulting).

They are easygoing, but want a lot for their money. They are a consensus-oriented culture.

The Netherlands is bordered on the north by the North Sea and on the south by Belgium and Germany. Amsterdam is the capital city, known for its impressive architecture and canals that crisscross the city.

The Netherlands was part of the Holy Roman Empire and has historically been dominated by surrounding countries such as Germany, France, and Great Britain, plus conquests by Austria/Germany and Spain. The Dutch language has been influenced by the German, French, and English languages. Many Dutch people can speak these languages in addition to Dutch. Inhabitants of larger cities may be immigrants, so you may hear additional languages spoken as well.

The Netherlands has a prosperous and open economy. Industrial activity is predominantly in food processing (for example, Unilever and Heineken International), chemicals (DSM), petroleum refining (Royal Dutch Shell), and electrical machinery (Philips).

Amsterdam is the financial and business capital of The Netherlands and one of the most important cities in Europe in which to do business. Many large Dutch corporations and banks have their headquarters in Amsterdam, including ABN Amro, Akzo Nobel, Heineken International, ING Group, Ahold, Delta Lloyd Group, and Philips. KPMG International's global headquarters is located in nearby Amstelveen, as is the European headquarters of Cisco Systems.

There is much freedom, and the city of Amsterdam has become known for its casual policies on prostitution and drug use. Such freedom also breeds crime, so you should be aware of your possessions and surroundings at all times.

## !!! PREPARATION

In addition to reviewing and practicing the presentation, it is important that you prepare yourself physically and emotionally to be at your very best. This means getting enough sleep before your leave, drinking lots of water, and arriving with extra time to rest, find your way about, and set up.

Dress informally (better underdressed than overdressed). Expect an informal atmosphere. The Dutch like humor, fun, and enjoyment. Structure is important but not critical.

Be prepared for the Dutch to be direct.

Here are some basic Dutch phrases:

| Dutch | English |
|---|---|
| "ja" | yes |
| "nee" *or* "neen" | no ("nee" is used primarily by itself, and "neen" when as part of a sentence) |
| "alsjeblieft" | please (*familiar*) |
| "alstublieft" | please (*polite*) |
| "dank je" | thank you (*familiar*) |
| "dank u" | thank you (*polite*) |
| "hartelijk dank" | thank you very much |
| "graag gedaan" | you're welcome (literally: done with pleasure) |
| "hallo" | hi, hello |
| "goededag" | hello (literally: good day; can be used any time from morning until around 5 P.M.) |
| "goedemorgen" | good morning (used until around noon) |
| "goedemiddag" | good afternoon (used from noon until 6 P.M.) |
| "goedenamiddag" | good afternoon (less common, used from noon until around 4 P.M.) |
| "goedeavond" | good evening (used after 6 P.M.) |
| "Welkom!" | Welcome! |
| "Tot ziens!" | See you later! |
| "doei" | bye (informal, typically Dutch) |
| "daag" | bye (infomal, typically Flemish) |
| "goedenacht" | goodnight |
| "Een prettige dag!" | Have a good day! |
| "excuseer me" *or* "excuseer mij" | excuse me (to get attention or to get past someone); sorry |
| "sorry" | sorry |
| "geen probleem" | no problem, don't worry about it |

| "Spreek je Engels?" | Do you speak English? ( *familiar* ) |
| "Spreekt u Engels?" | Do you speak English? ( *polite* ) |
| "Spreek je Nederlands?" | Do you speak Dutch? (*familiar*) |
| "Spreekt u Nederlands?" | Do you speak Dutch? ( *polite* ) |
| "Ik spreek geen Nederlands." | I don't speak Dutch. |
| "Ik spreek niet goed Nederlands." | I don't speak much Dutch. |
| "Ik spreek een beetje Nederlands." | I speak a little Dutch. |
| "Ik spreek een heel klein beetje Nederlands." | I only speak very little Dutch. |
| "Alsjeblieft, spreek langzamer." | Please speak more slowly. ( *familiar* ) |
| "Alstublieft, spreek langzamer." | Please speak more slowly. ( *polite* ) |
| "Kan u dat alstjeblieft herhalen?" | Could you please repeat that? ( *familiar* ) |
| "Kan u dat alstublieft herhalen?" | Could you please repeat that? ( *polite* ) |
| "Ik versta het niet." | I don't understand. |
| "Ik weet het niet." | I don't know. |
| "Waar zijn de toiletten, alsjeblieft?" | Where's the toilet, please? ( *familiar* ) |
| "Waar zijn de toiletten, alstublieft?" | Where's the toilet, please? ( *polite* ) |

## THE PRESENTATION

The participants in our example, were pre-grouped by our hosts, but some adjustments needed to be made because some participants needed a translator with them in their groupings. The co-presenter made some initial jokes that fell flat and used some acronyms that no one understood. He said, "I'm going to pass out some handouts" and people feverously thumbed through their English dictionaries to figure out what he was saying and then they watched closely to see whether he really was going to "pass out."

Watch the faces of the students to see whether there is a lot of confusion. Enunciate and explain things clearly. Be willing to extend the amount of time for translations to occur and for misinterpretations to be clarified. If people are very patient with each other, a light and enjoyable atmosphere will continue.

Visual aids and handouts are very helpful for those who have difficulty with English. It is easier for them to read the language than to understand the spoken word.

It is important to stick to the agenda that you have shown at the beginning of the program, but of course, be flexible when it is needed to enhance the learning.

Start and end on time.

Check how well your participants understand your presentation and adapt your speed and wording, as needed, to make sure they are learning effectively.

Some learning/tips from our experience include:

- Bring or request extra extension cords and plug conversion kits.

- Bring a sense of humor.

- Always take a card from your hotel so you can find your way back with help.

- Schedule and practice your presentation with extra time allowed for interpretation.

Dag (Good-bye)

**Helpful websites and references include:**

- http://en.wikipedia.org/wiki/Amsterdam

- www.gvb.nl/english/aboutgvb/history.html

- www.holland.com

- www.smartphrase.com/Dutch/du_general_words_phr.shtml

- www.speakdutch.co.uk/phrases/basic_phrases

- www.us.holland.com

- www.virtualtourist.com

- www.wikitravel.org/en/Amsterdam

**PART SIX**

# The Americas

# Argentina

---

*"Don't cry for me, Argentina"*
Evita, *Andrew Lloyd Weber and Tim Rice*

---

It seems there is little reason to cry for Argentina any longer. The second-largest country in South America is coming out of a major financial crisis and making a dramatic recovery. The birthplace of tango, this vibrant country boasts a diverse landscape and a bustling world-class city, Buenos Aires. With an economy based in agriculture, tourism/services, and manufacturing, Argentina is also known for its superb wine. Spanish and Italian immigrants have flavored the local culture, making Buenos Aires become known as the most European city in South America.

## ??? THE REQUEST

It is estimated that about 80 percent of Argentina's population lives in urban areas with about one-third of the total population residing in the greater Buenos Aires area. With those kinds of statistics, the probability that you will be working in a city, specifically Buenos Aires, is pretty high. Also noteworthy is that Argentina has a phenomenal literacy rate, estimated upwards of 97 percent, because of free schooling in these urban areas. Industries that are thriving, and which may require your services, include agriculture, oil refining, automobile manufacturing, and services/tourism. Our experiences with requests include sales and leadership training in Argentina.

## • • • GETTING THERE

Travelers must have a valid passport to go to Argentina. At time of publication, no special visa is required for stays shorter than ninety days. As recommended for other countries, verify that your passport's validity is dated six months beyond your return date. It is always a good idea to verify visa requirements before traveling. The Department of State, via the Department's Bureau of Consular Affairs Internet website at www.travel.state.gov, provides up-to-date information about visas, travel warnings, political disturbances, and a number of other important travel topics. It is also recommended that you register your trip via the State Department's travel registration website before traveling.

The flight to Ministro Pistarini International Airport (EZE) is about nine hours from Miami, so your first day will be spent traveling, even if your final destination is Buenos Aires. The airport is in Ezeiza, a suburb of Buenos Aires, which is approximately a forty-minute drive to the city center if traffic is good. If your final destination is elsewhere, you will still fly into this international hub. Some of these domestic flights may leave from Airport Jorge Newbery (AEP) near downtown Buenos Aires. It is recommended that you secure a pre-paid taxi (Remise) from one of the business kiosks near the baggage claim in the airport, as opposed to hailing a taxi curbside. It may even cost you a few pesos more, but it is safer and more reliable, particularly if your Spanish is not very good. A minimum cab fare is $1.20, and tipping is not expected if you are not traveling with baggage.

Argentina is three hours behind GMT. This is two hours ahead of U.S. EST or one hour ahead of U.S. EDT. The time is expressed in a twenty-four-hour system, so 4:00 P.M. is 16:00 hours. Check the weather before packing your suitcase. Since Argentina is in the Southern hemisphere, their seasons are opposite ours. The summer months are December through March, with January and February the warmest. Business people dress conservatively and more traditionally, with both men and women wearing suits. Verify with your in-country contact the appropriate attire for your sessions. Consider the location and subject when selecting how to set the dress code for the session.

Holidays that will affect your training, travel and enjoyment of being in Argentina:

- January: New Year's (1st)
- March/April: Maudy (Holy) Thursday, Good Friday
- March: Memorial Day (24th)

- April: Malvinas Day (2nd)

- May: Labor Day (1st), Revolución de Mayo (25st)

- June: National Flag Day (20th)

- July: National Independence Day (9th)

- August: Anniversary of the death of General José de San Martín (17th)

- October: Columbus Day (12th)

- December: Immaculate Conception Day (8th), Christmas Eve (24th), Christmas Day (25th), New Year's Eve (31st)

## PROGRAM DESIGN

You will need an in-country contact to help you determine any translation issues or needs. It may very well be that your audience is fluent and comfortable in English. If they are not, you may be fluent in Spanish. If you are, it is still possible to have communication issues, so work with your in-country contact to make sure that the program design is localized for Argentina. Even if you do speak Spanish, consider hiring an interpreter for your audience if they are not fluent in English. If you do use an interpreter, extra time must be built into your project plan. An additional one-third the amount of time for the overall plan should be added to accommodate this additional work.

If you are translating your materials, have them proofread by a trusted person in-country. If your proofreader can suggest ways to localize the materials to include examples and references relative to their country, your program would benefit from it. As you probably already know, these small customizations can really make a difference to your audience.

Patagonia (beautiful mountains, glaciers, and natural wonders cover one-third of Argentina), Gauchos (famous horsemen and wanderers of the countryside), dramatic dance of the tango and the National Football Team (soccer) are all loved and recognized with pride by Argentineans. These can be used as examples for familiar visuals, discussion, and unity as you design the program to reflect the country's culture.

## LOGISTICS

Once in Argentina, customs laws require the registration of "personal working elements," which include laptops, cell phones, and other electronic devices. This process is required at entry and exit. It is possible to bring samples of such devices for training purposes (or sales/marketing presentations), as long as they don't have a commercial value. If they do have commercial value, a ninety-day bond may be required, but is refunded at the time of departure from the country. If you are shipping materials for your session, be sure to research the current customs forms and waivers that may be required for your packages. Be sure to keep your baggage claim tickets, because airport security is likely to check them before you may leave with your luggage. When you return home, you will be charged a departure tax to leave the country.

January is the least desirable time to try to schedule anything in Argentina. Not only is the weather at its summer peak, but many businesses slow or shut down completely for vacation. The best months to travel are April through November, avoiding the coldest months of July and August.

Besides the already mentioned registration of personal working elements (laptops, cell phones, and other electronics), there are no other common logistical considerations. As with any other training, if you are sending your course materials ahead, give them plenty of time to arrive safely at your destination. Verify their arrival with your in-country contact and have a back-up plan should something unforeseen occur.

Currency is the Argentine peso (ARS $) which is divided into 100 centavos. ATM machines are readily available and will often allow you to withdraw in US dollars or ARS. Check your local bank to verify that your ATM card can be used in Argentina and what the withdraw fees are, if any. Travelers checks are not always accepted in stores and restaurants, but credit cards, specifically Visa, are widely accepted. Sales tax is high, at time of publication 21 percent, but generally the tax is reflected in the price on the item. Ask if you have questions.

## PROGRAM DELIVERY

There are many possible approaches you can take to deliver or present your program. The choice depends on a number of factors. The most important factor to consider is the type of outcome required, for example, if the learner must be able to perform a task then skill building and practice should be part of the program. If learners need to be able to explain something to someone else, then lecture can be the primary delivery mechanism. The second most important factor to consider is: How can the learners best learn what they need to?

The work day in Argentina may be different from what your day is like at home. The day begins somewhere between 8 A.M. and 9 A.M., but more often 9 A.M., and runs through to anywhere between 5 P.M. and 7 P.M. A one-hour lunch break is typical. Breakfast meetings are not common, but business dinners are. They typically don't start until 9 P.M. or 10 P.M. Many people take a short nap before these evening events. With the late start, you will have more people arrive at your session on time if you begin your day a little later, between 9 A.M. and 10 A.M. One last schedule reminder: Be sure to check the national holidays so you don't schedule a conflict. We will talk more about dining later.

## TECHNICAL REQUIREMENTS

You will need your electrical converters when traveling to Argentina. Their electric currents have a voltage of 220V and a frequency of 50 Hz. There are two types of sockets used, the European two-prong and the Australian slanted plugs on most wall electrical outlets.

Your cell phone may need to be set for a special roaming service by your service provider. You may also choose to rent a local cell phone; they are available at most large hotels for a fee. In-country land lines are reliable for both local and long-distance/international calls, but placing calls from your hotel room is costly. Larger hotels also typically have Internet access. You will find Internet cafés in Buenos Aires, but do not count on Internet service in your classroom for teaching purposes unless you have made the arrangements yourself specifically.

For your reference, emergency phone numbers are 101 for police, 100 for fire, and 107 for ambulance.

The country code for Argentina is 54. Every region has its own area code with Buenos Aires mainly using the 11 area code, and sometimes the 15 area code for cell phones.

## ACCOMMODATIONS

Business travelers can feel very at home in Argentina. Many familiar hotel chains have comparable accommodations and service. Prices vary based on category. Solicit recommendations from your in-country contact to select a hotel that suits your needs and is close to your training site. Don't leave your high-priced personal belongings in your room; as with any large city, theft is a real possibility. Secure your laptop and other valuables in the hotel safe or keep them with you at all times. Some hotels will give you a discount for paying with cash, so ask at check-in.

The sales tax, known as IVA, is 21 percent. When reserving a hotel, that tax is sometimes not mentioned, so double-check the final price before you book.

Buenos Aires is considered a safe city and local police keep it that way by actively patrolling all tourist areas. Violent crime is rare, and smaller towns in Argentina are even safer than Buenos Aires.

Nevertheless, it is important to remember there a number of thieves who spend their time in tourist areas on the lookout for easy prey. Always protect your valuables and keep your passport and tickets in a safe at your hotel.

The water is supposed to be fine to drink, but we prefer to use bottled water to decrease any risk of health affects from water that is different from what we usually drink.

## GETTING AROUND

Driving in Argentina, specifically Buenos Aires, is generally dangerous. It is not recommended to rent a car, which is expensive, and drive to the city, which is dangerous. Driving is dangerous and so is walking across the busy streets. Pedestrians don't necessarily have the right of way, and traffic doesn't always follow the rules of the road. Keep your wits about you when walking to and from destinations. Take public transportation.

The subway (subterráneo or subte) and the buses (colectivos) are safe and widely used. The subway is inexpensive, more reliable, and less crowded than traveling by bus, but even better are the radio taxis or Remis (private car with a driver). As opposed to a taxi you can hail on the street, a Remis is an arranged ride. On the street, the taxi is yellow or black and the Remis is bright green. They basically charge the same rate, but for safety reasons the government recommends these radio taxis to travelers instead of hailing a taxi on the street. Tipping is not necessary unless you have baggage; however, rounding up to an even peso amount is polite. Taxis can be called from your hotel or restaurant. If you are uncomfortable obtaining a taxi on the street, go to the nearest hotel and get one there.

Tipping in restaurants or bars is usually around 10 percent, but cannot be added to your bill, so pay cash. Any other service provider expects a peso for his or her time. Paying cash for smaller bills is suggested to minimize the risk of credit card fraud, a popular crime.

## THE PEOPLE

The people of Argentina, as with any country today, vary greatly. Many are of Spanish or Italian descent. Inhabitants of Buenos Aires are called *Porteños* (those who live by the port); inhabitants of Salta are called *Salteños*. Another group worth noting is the famed Gauchos, who, like the American cowboy, have established a position in South American folklore. These wanderers of the Pampas work the cattle, live off the land, and are fodder for stories told to children.

The stereotypical idea of the "Latin Lover" and his passion are real here. Public displays of affection happen openly and cat-calling is common. For the most part, the unwanted attention directed toward women is harmless and a man's way of appreciating women. No need for sneers; just smile and keep walking. Another object of attention for passion is football (our soccer). Loyalties are high and rivalries are heated. This is one topic that is a great conversation starter. The two local teams are Boca Juniors and River Plate.

Tea is a social drink in Argentina. They call it "mate," and it is drunk through a straw. There is no specific time for this ritual, so be flattered if you are invited to join a group drinking mate. Consider serving it during your class since it is also a common drink at work.

As you venture out to the restaurants, here are a few quirky items we noticed:

- Tap water is not usually available, you must buy bottled

- There is no such thing as brunch; restaurants don't usually open until 7:30 or 8 P.M. and they don't get busy until after 9 P.M.

- There is no pepper on the table.

- Meals are very meat-heavy, with few salads to be found.

- Smoking is permitted in most public places and many people do smoke.

Argentina's university system has achieved world-wide levels of excellence. The country's public university system is free of charge.

There are twenty-three provinces divided into six major regions: Pampas, Gran Chaco, Mesopotamia, Patagonia, Cuyo, and NOA or Northwest. Buenos Aires is in the Pampas region, which extends west and south of the city center. Requests may also come from cities such as Cordoba, Santa Fe (Rosario), and San Luis, which are also in Pampas and from Mendoza in the Cuyo region.

- Main exports: Soya beans and oil, cereals, mineral fuels, beef, and leather.

- Main imports: Machinery and equipments, motor vehicles, chemicals, metal manufactured goods and plastics.

- Main trade partners: Brazil, United States, Chile, and China.

## ‖‖ PREPARATION

The dialect of Spanish spoken in the *Río de la Plata* area (Argentina, Uruguay, and Paraguay) differs from the standard Latin American variety in two distinct ways:

First, "ll" and "y," normally pronounced like the English "y," are both pronounced "zh." So, "*yo tambien*" sounds like "*zho tambien*." The exception is when y is at the end of a word; *estoy* is pronounced as it would be anywhere.

A bit trickier is the use of *vos* in place of the more common *tú*, which requires a different verb form in the present tense, except for some irregular verbs. For regular verbs, an accent is added to the second syllable: *tú comes* becomes *vos comés*. For stem-changing verbs, the original stem is used in place of the changed one: *tú tienes* becomes *vos tenés*. With "ir" verbs an "ís" ending is used: *tú vienes* becomes *vos venís*. And some forms seem just plain random: *tú eres* becomes *vos sos*.

Fortunately, you'll be understood just fine in Argentina if you use standard Latin American (or even European) Spanish. But keep the differences in mind and you'll have an easier time understanding the locals.

Here are some useful words and phrases:

| | |
|---|---|
| "Hola" | Hi. |
| "¿Cómo te va?" | How's it going? |
| "Encantado" | Pleased to meet you (male). |
| "Encantada" | Pleased to meet you (female). |
| "Presentar" | To introduce |
| "Presentarse" | To introduce oneself |
| "Mucho gusto" | It's nice to meet you. |
| "Gracias" (f) | Thank you. |
| "Con permiso" | Excuse me. |
| "¿Qué tal?" | How are you? |
| "¿Qué cuentas?" | What's new? |
| "¿Qué pasa?" | What's up? |
| "Hasta pronto" | See you soon. |
| "Muchas gracias" (f) | Thank you very much. |
| "Nos vemos" | See you later. |
| "Hasta mañana" | See you tomorrow. |
| "Adiós" (m) | Good-bye. |
| "Hasta luego" | So long. |

The U.S. Embassy is located at 4300 Colombia Avenue in the Palermo district of Buenos Aires. Mission offices can be reached by phone at (54) (11) 5777-4533/34 or by fax at (54) (11) 5777-4240. Mailing addresses: U.S. Embassy Buenos Aires, APO AA 34034; or 4300 Colombia, 1425 Buenos Aires, Argentina.

**Other Contact Information**

American Chamber of Commerce in Argentina

Viamonte 1133, 8th floor

Buenos Aires, Argentina

Tel (54) (11) 4371-4500; Fax (54) (11) 4371-8400

U.S. Department of Commerce

Office of Latin America and the Caribbean

International Trade Administration

14th and Constitution Avenue, NW

Washington, DC 20230

Tel (202) 482-2436; (800) USA-TRADE; Fax (202) 482-4726

Automated fax service for trade-related information: (202) 482-4464

## THE PRESENTATION

If you have worked in any of the Latin American countries before, you will be familiar with some of the challenges you may face in Argentina. If this part of the world is new ground for you, the biggest question you should have is about language. The official language is Spanish, with many other languages frequently spoken. Argentinean Spanish is spoken with some distinct differences. There are different regional vocabulary and specific pronunciation differences.

In general, business customs are a little more formal. Be on time for your meetings, but don't be surprised if the Argentineans are late. Distribute your business cards, and if you have the time before you leave, print some in Spanish. Establishing a relationship is important to Argentineans. Firm handshakes are an important first step. Shake everyone's hand upon arrival and at departure; don't stop with the first person you encounter and don't exclude the women. Kissing on the right cheek is customary for Argentinean men when meeting a woman, even for the first time. Men who are not from Argentina should not engage in this custom, but women should not be surprised if they are greeted that way. The next piece of groundwork can be laid by exchanging information about family, personal interests, hobbies, and sports. Do not refer to yourself or others as "American" or "from America" in Argentina. You are referring to the whole of North America with these uses. Instead, say more specifically that you're from the United States (for example) or from a specific town, such as New York.

**Some helpful resources include:**

- www.allaboutar.com/travel_facts.htm

- www.argentina.gov.ar

- www.argentinacafe.com/Background/argentina-language.htm

- www.cp-pc.ca/english/argentina/

- www.crazycolour.com/os/argentina_02.shtml

- www.gayot.com

- www.kropla.com/electric.htm (Everything you ever wanted to know about using your electrical appliances in a foreign country.)

- www.ontheroadtravel.com

- www.travel.state.gov

- www.worldtravelguide.net

# Brazil

*C*arnival parades with amazing costumes, as well as many religious celebrations and festivals seem to represent the Brazilian culture. The toucan, an exotic bird to most of us, gives us a brilliant sample of the tropical environment that shapes the Brazilian way of life. Here is what to expect and some tips for success when training, teaching, or presenting to Brazilians.

## !!! THE REQUEST

When presenting a program in Brazil, it is likely that you have been requested by a company or organization. The session may be at the company headquarters in Sao Paolo or Rio de Janeiro.

The majority of participants will speak Portuguese and not much English.

Work with the requestor and sponsor of the program to confirm details of learning objectives, program outcomes, and requirements, dates, times, location, number of participants, and background of the participants (job titles, level of experience with this topic).

If it is possible to send information to the participants ahead of time, you can request their questions regarding your topic (which you can answer in the program), provide any pre-reading material (don't assume that this will be read), and information about the program (so they will enter the session with a knowledge of why they have been selected to attend).

### • • • GETTING THERE

You will need a valid passport and visa. For business travel, Brazil requires a letter from the employer or sponsoring company, on their letterhead stationery, and signed by a senior manager (an equivalent to vice president or above), briefly introducing the person (specifying employment status/position held in the company by applicant), and clearly stating the precise nature of the business to be conducted by the applicant in Brazil. The employer or sponsoring company shall also specifically attest to each of the following statements: that the visa applicant will maintain his residency in the United States, that the visa applicant's trip to Brazil is of a short-term nature, that the goal of the visa applicant's trip to Brazil is strictly for business meetings not involving any technical assistance, not to exceed the legally authorized stay per visit, and that the visa applicant has no intention to immigrate to Brazil. Make sure you apply and obtain these with ample time for any problems to be resolved. Visa information and applications are available at www.brazilvisahq.com. Also bring at least one additional photo identification with you that you can use when asked to show an ID when entering buildings (instead of using your passport for this).

Arrange to have your vaccinations updated, such as boosters for tetanus and polio plus vaccination for yellow fever, at least ten days before you travel (so it can take effect). Bring your international vaccination certificate with you in case you are asked for it. You should check with your doctor and the Center for Disease Control and Prevention to determine the most up-to-date requirements at www.cdc.gov.

Air is the best way to get to Brazil and move around the country. Ask your host or sponsor if someone will be able to pick you up at the airport and bring you to your hotel. If they are unable to do that, then take a taxi or the bus to your destination.

Sao Paolo and Rio are three hours behind Greenwich Mean Time, one hour ahead of New York, three hours ahead of Chicago, and four hours behind London. The country of Brazil has three time zones.

Here are some of the holidays that may affect your program, travel, and celebrations:

- January: New Year's Day (1st)
- March/April: Carnival (Tuesday before Ash Wednesday), Ash Wednesday, Good Friday
- April: Tiradentes (21st)
- May: Labor Day/May Day (1st)
- May/June: Corpus Christi (62 days after Good Friday)
- July: Constitution Revolution Sao Paolo State (9th)

- September: Independence Day (7th)
- October: Our Lady of Aparecida (12th)
- November: All Souls Day (2nd)
- November: Proclamation of the Republic Day (15th)
- December: Christmas Day (25th)

## PROGRAM DESIGN

Design your program so that it can be translated easily into Portuguese. Leave a lot of extra space on each page for the translated version. English may work but it will be more easily understood if you have the translation already made. Email your handout materials ahead of time, so they can be duplicated for your presentation. Have handouts of everything that you can use to work from during your presentation. That way if someone's ability to read English is better than his or her ability to speak it, the person can follow and have something to take away. He or she also won't feel left out of the "conversation."

An online locator for translators and interpreters is provided at www.language123.com. This includes their credentials as well as samples, quotes, and photos. You can request references for their work by contacting them individually. Ask your host for a recommended interpreter. They may be able to tell you who has a good reputation for their type of work.

If you are presenting a computer application, make sure that you are prepared to show the actual application, not screen captures. It can be confusing if you are not showing the actual application as it is meant to work.

Andrea Mascarenhas (HR Manager for Latin America Region–South, Kodak) suggests that if someone is positioned as the expert, the audience will definitely want a lecture with the key insights of the expert, with time for questions. If the objective is skill development, then you can design the program with case studies and role plays, including a debriefing with the insights of the trainer.

Football (soccer) is the well-loved, exciting, and emotional sport that charges the energy and passion of all who participate and may make a common ground for beginning conversation or for examples.

## LOGISTICS

It is good to work with a local contact who will be responsible for room requirements and setup. This person may be the person who will also be responsible for receiving your handout materials and making sure that copies have been made or that what you have sent has been received and available in the room where you will present. Email is usually an effective way to make the arrangements, because the receiver can obtain help with the translation and clarification if needed.

The Brazilian currency is the real (R$). Coins come in denominations of 1, 5, 10, 25, 50 centavos, R$1. Bank notes come in denominations of R$1, R$2, R$5, R$10, R$20, R$50, and R$100. Get small bills so you don't have to wait for people to give you change. It can be a very long wait. Keep the receipt when you exchange money in case you want to convert it when you leave.

## PROGRAM DELIVERY

Even if the participants can speak and understand English, they will most likely prefer to have the program delivered in Portuguese. Have an interpreter available and find out ahead of time whether some of the participants would be able to help with ongoing translations during class discussions. We found it helpful for the morning session to be at our location for our presentation at 7:30 A.M. This provides time for setup and surprises to be handled.

Most Brazilians may have a preconceived idea about North Americans that includes arrogance and being cold. Never use the "OK" sign (middle finger to the thumb), it is considered a vulgar insult. Give a "thumbs up" instead.

Another contemporary custom you must avoid is the immediate use of first names. It is very important to let them take the initiative on using first names. Brazilians are more formal and protocol-oriented. This may be very difficult, but something you should try to keep in mind. Treat them formally until they give you some kind of a signal to use their first names.

Give breaks more frequently than normal. A person can only concentrate so long before either giving up or getting a headache, if the program is not delivered in their native language. Betsy Foss (Morgan Stanley) tells us that the first day is particularly hard because, even if the audience knows English, if they haven't been listening to it or speaking it regularly or lately, it takes a while for it to become more natural.

Andrea Mascarenhas (Kodak) reminds us that Brazilians tend to be informal, so a lot is accomplished by being friendly and open without being arrogant. The key thing is not to portray Brazil as an exotic location. To those who live and work there, it is daily life and there is nothing exotic.

In addition to football (soccer), sports such as basketball, volleyball, auto racing, and martial arts can be used as examples to gain people's interest.

## TECHNICAL REQUIREMENTS

The electrical current can vary between 100 to 240 volts, 50 to 60 Hz. There can be variations even within the same city. Be prepared for power surges. Current stabilizers are helpful but heavy. Request that they provide one for you. You should bring an adapter for your laptop and battery charger that can handle full voltage ranges. Always check before you plug anything in to make sure that you will not have a problem. Be sure to bring voltage converters, plugs (three prongs: two round and one flat) and back up systems to use if needed. Bring your program on an electronic storage device, send it to your host ahead of time, hand carry hard copies of translated and English versions of handouts. Bring videotapes (PAL-M is used exclusively in Brazil, and is a hybrid of NTSC and PAL), or DVDs that are already subtitled in Portuguese. If you bring your computer, you can request a data show projector to be available and set up in your presentation room. Check ahead of time to see whether Internet capability is available, if needed.

## ACCOMMODATIONS

Hotels and pousadas (like a bed-and-breakfast) are good accommodations. Safety and security are important. Use common sense when traveling. Travel with others. Don't look like a tourist. Be cautious but confident.

Dinner is generally between 8 P.M. and 10 P.M.

Always be safe by drinking bottled or filtered water. This will avoid stomach upset that could be caused by drinking water that may have ill effects.

Negotiate the price for your hotel and ask about the taxes that will be added to your bill. Sometimes breakfast is included. Staying in downtown Rio is not advised, because it is not considered a good neighborhood. Do not stay in motels. They are rented by the hour and are not generally used for business travel.

Hyatt, Hilton, Radisson, Marriott, and Sheraton Hotels provide standard amenities.

## GETTING AROUND

Obtain maps of Brazil and your city at the newsstand. Practice your Portuguese questions so you can be understood. Take a card from your hotel and have your destination written down so that you can show it to people when asking for directions. Subway, bus, and taxi are good means of transportation in Sao Paolo and Rio. At night it is better to take a taxi than to take the bus. Driving is not recommended.

## THE PEOPLE

The Brazilian people are very warm and welcoming, expressive, and open. They will go out of their way to be of service to you and take care of you. Hospitality is an important hallmark of this culture. A man will insist on walking a woman to her door and making sure she is safe. This is a very male-oriented society. Most women who work in businesses are secretaries.

Most events start and continue late. People usually go out to dinner at 9 or 10 P.M. You can go to dinner at 8, as most restaurants do not accept reservations, but most Brazilians considered that early.

Brazilians are proud of their culture and consider themselves as unique and different from other Latin Americans. They speak Portuguese, not Spanish, although many speak English. It is not appropriate to speak Spanish with them or imply that they are similar to other South Americans.

Brazil is the sixth most populous country in the world. Most people live along the coast and in major cities. The rest of the country is sparsely populated.

Brazil's regions are the Northeast, Amazon, Centerwest, and South. Nine major cities provide homes to two-thirds of Brazilians: Sao Paulo, Rio de Janeiro, Belo Horizonte, Porto Alegre, Salvador, Recife, Fortaleza, Brasilia, and Belem. Greater Sao Paulo has over seventeen million inhabitants, Greater Rio, more than ten million.

It is difficult to describe what a typical Brazilian looks like. Most Brazilians have a combination of European, African, Amerindian, Asian, and Middle Eastern ancestors. The intermingling of immigrants and the original indigenous population of the region results in a unique mix of races. Many original explorers married local women. In addition, many children were born of plantation chiefs and the slaves, who had been brought over from Africa to work on sugar and coffee plantations.

Many Italian, Spanish and Portuguese immigrants came to Brazil in addition to Japanese. Today, the largest Japanese population outside Japan is in Sao Paulo.

Many nationality groups came to Brazil to escape political or religious persecution, such as from Portuguese Africa. You can see a variety of influences in different regions of the country. People still speak German in the south, where many Germans and Poles settled.

In Brazil success depends both on what you know and who you know. Personal relationships and a respect for Brazilian traditions affect business as much as technological or financial capability.

Do not be surprised or upset if you have to wait for a meeting or to be picked up. Time is more relaxed in Brazil. Brazilians have a different approach to time. It is not a matter of being lazy or not caring about business.

You will be judged a great deal on your appearance. You should be very sensitive to attire. Wear discrete, conservative clothing. A grey or blue suit is appropriate. Casual dress can be considered an insult. In Brazil, it is unusual to wear a red tie. Brazilian dress is very sophisticated.

When it is offered, always accept the cafezinho, the demitasse of coffee. Not to accept will offend your host. Brazil is very proud of their superior coffee and people can get emotional about it.

It is normal to have people interrupted with phone calls or documents to be signed. Do not expect Brazilians to say "thank you" or "please" as often as people in other countries. Smile and be relaxed. Brazilians get personal very quickly, especially if they like you. They will ask a lot of questions. They want to get to know you. You should show personal interest in them before getting down to business. Brazilians do prefer long-term relationships.

Although Brazilians may say "stay a bit longer" or "drink another coffee," most of the time, they do not really mean it. They are just being polite.

People from the United States are frequently perceived as impatient, abrupt, and wanting immediate results. It is best to not be aggressive or pushy. Give them time to digest new information, concepts, and ideas. Brazilians are typically uncomfortable with blunt communication.

Brazilians show very energetic body language when communicating. People may stand a lot closer than in many cultures and may make physical moves such as pats or jabs. Greetings include kisses (between women or women and men), handshakes, hugs, and backslapping. Gestures are used often. Thumbs up means OK, hello, or thanks. Finger shaking to emphasize "no" is vigorous but not a threat. Avoid the common sign of the finger and thumb joining to form a circle, generally taken to mean OK, has a quite different meaning in Brazil. It is considered vulgar and obscene. It is just like giving someone "the finger." Instead, remember to use the thumbs-up sign. It is safe, and commonly used.

Some of our contributors share their experiences and observations with us:

- Handshakes are often prolonged compared to other standards and it may be accompanied by an abraço (hug).

- Brazilian women also shake hands upon meeting someone, but most commonly they greet with a kiss, usually twice on alternative cheeks. Often women kiss the air while brushing cheeks. One begins the contact with movement to the left.

- Even if a woman meets using a handshake, she is likely to take leave with a kiss.

- Greeting with kisses has come to be used between men and women as well. If a man gives a woman a kiss as a greeting, he generally only kisses one cheek.

- Greeting and leave-taking must be done comfortably and unflinchingly so as not to confirm a stereotype of being cold and distant.

- If you back away, you will hurt someone's feelings.

- Where some would likely refer to a business associate as "Mr. Smith," the Brazilian refers to business colleagues by their first names, for example, "Senhor Angelo" or "Senhora Clarice." Priests, physicians, and professors as well as other professionals usually go by their first names. Exceptions depend on the degree of formality of the individual. It is still a custom to use files and lists alphabetized by first name, rather than last, although telephone directories now list by last name.

- Brazilians stand very close while speaking and do not apologize for bumping or brushing against another person. They find the habit of constant apologizing in crowded situations very odd.

- In many places, such as a public market, no lines are formed. The person who pushes to the front of the booth is next.

- Women touch more than men, often walking down the street with arms around one another, arms linked, or holding hands.

- A woman may tug at the jewelry, shirt collar, or buttons of another while talking.

- A Brazilian who feels that your attention is wandering may grab your chin to redirect your gaze.

- Most touching occurs between peers and usually members of the same sex.

- In places where some people usually stare straight ahead (for example, in an elevator), Brazilians will look around at each other.

- While speaking, Brazilians maintain steady eye contact to a degree that others would consider it a stare. The exception is when speaking to someone of a different age or status. The younger or less powerful person generally looks away.

Although in many nations drinking alcohol is part of the culture, in Brazil it is not. Drinking and smoking, going to a pub or even to a disco may be associated with immorality or family problems.

## !!! PREPARATION

You will be encouraged to dress casually to be comfortable. It is still important to dress professionally and show confidence. Avoid any behavior that implies arrogance.

Find out whether there is someone who can review your materials ahead of time for anything that is inadvertently offensive or confusing. You can bring overhead transparencies in case the laptop does not work. Carry your presentation, transparencies, a hard copy of the handouts, and your laptop with you instead of checking anything with your luggage, just in case.

Try to get an agreement that someone in the class will alert you to any gestures or parts of your presentation that may be offensive, so you can apologize for it and not do it again.

Here are some helpful basic words and phrases in Portuguese:

| | |
|---|---|
| Hello | "Olá" |
| Hi | "oi" (informal) |
| Please | "Se faz favor"/"Por favor" |
| Sorry | "desculpe" |
| Thank you | "obrigado" |
| Good bye | "Adeus" |
| Goodbye | "até logo, tchau" (informal) |
| Good day | "Bom dia" |
| Good evening | "Boa tarde" |
| Good night | "Boa noite" |
| See you soon | "Até logo"/"Até a vista" |
| Yes | "Sim" |
| No | "Não" |
| I don't know | "Não sei" |
| Where? | "Onde?" |
| When? | "Quê?" |
| Why? | "Quem?" |
| What? | "Qual?"/"Quais?" (pl.) |
| Who? | "Como?" |
| How? | "Quanto?" |
| How much/many? | "Quanto"/"Quantos?" |
| Is/are there? | "Há?" |

| Thank you (very much) | "(Muito) obrigado/obrigada" |
| Excuse me | "Com licença"/"Desculpe" |
| I'm sorry, but . . . | "Peço desculpa, mas . . ." |
| That's a shame | "Que pena" |
| May I . . . ? | "Posso . . . ?" |

## THE PRESENTATION

The most likely locations for program delivery would be at the office of the organization or at a hotel. The presentation will most likely be in a conference room. Avoid using slang or acronyms that are not clearly defined when you present. Speak very slowly and enunciate your words so they can be understood and translated. Use simple sentence structure. Don't assume that you have been understood. Be very careful of body language and gestures. Be aware of any funny looks or uncomfortable silences from your audience, so that you alert yourself to a possible "faux pas." Humor doesn't always work. There are too many differences in interpretation, wording, and understanding.

Frank Petrzala (EDS) provides the following tips for success:

- Treat all individuals with respect.

- Smile.

- Be open and friendly.

- Listen when they speak, making eye contact. Actively acknowledge what they are saying.

- If the material allows, make it interactive. Ask questions to engage the participants. (Do not use a "gotcha" question to put someone on the spot.)

- If there is a language barrier, speaking louder does not mean that the information is communicated any better (they aren't necessarily deaf). Slow it down.

- In meeting women, they are lightly (or air) kissed on the cheek. (My first day, I shook hands. I was asked, "Why are Americans so cold?" I told them that we are conditioned to not enter a person's personal space. They replied, "We know when someone is being too friendly.")

- Be interested in their culture and willing to try new foods, etc.

- Do not wear white knee-high socks with shorts (fashion faux pas that they will laugh at!)

Ultimately, Frank says, people are people. Think about your response before replying. Treat people with respect and you will receive that in return.

**Helpful websites and references include:**

- www.brazilvisahq.com
- www.cdc.com
- www.language123.com

# Canada

*O Canada!*
*Our home and native land!*
*True patriot love in all thy sons command.*
*With glowing hearts we see thee rise.*
*The True North strong and free!*
*From far and wide*
*O Canada, we stand on guard for thee.*
*God keep our land glorious and free!\*
*O Canada, we stand on guard for thee.*
*O Canada, we stand on guard for thee.*

Canadian National Anthem

Canada is a vast land of serene natural treasures, dotted with a few large glistening cities. Most Canadians are proud, hearty nature lovers and are used to the cold weather that they experience for much of the year.

We have found the Canadian participants in all of our programs to be welcoming, fun, and willing to provide interesting conversation about their observations or current events. Here are some examples and tips for success when training, teaching, or presenting to Canadians.

## ??? THE REQUEST

The program that we will use as an example is a program that is held in both Toronto and Montreal, very typical venues for conducting programs in Canada. The request is to provide a course for coaching skills to approximately twenty-four participants who come from all over Canada. The program is scheduled three days of every month for five months and held in a downtown hotel. This is convenient for those who live farther away, because they can stay at the same hotel where the program is conducted.

## • • • GETTING THERE

Toronto and Montreal are easily accessed by plane or car. You need a valid passport to enter or to cross back and forth if driving through the border. The Canadian border is not difficult to cross by car, but returning may be more challenging, with the interchange often including many pertinent questions regarding your stay and your destination. Highways are very good, but get extremely congested when entering the city, so allow a lot of extra time if driving, because the time can vary in hours. You can rent a car and quite easily find your way with a map and directions, or take a taxi from the airport. Trains are also available for transportation throughout the country.

Canada uses six primary time zones. From east to west they are Newfoundland Time Zone, Atlantic Time Zone, Eastern Time, Central Time Zone, Mountain Time Zone, and the Pacific Time Zone. Toronto is in Ontario (Eastern Time Zone) and therefore GMT/UTC – 5 hours standard time and GMT/UTC – 4 hours daylight savings time. The time zone for Toronto is the same as New York. Montreal is in Quebec Province (Eastern Time Zone) and has the same time as Toronto: GMT/UTC – 5 standard time and GMT/UTC – 4 daylight savings time.

It is also good to know when holidays are going to be observed, so you can expect that they may delay or interrupt getting your materials prepared, your training program itself, as well as influence the excitement and attention level of your participants:

- January: New Year's Day (1st)
- January: Chinese New Year
- February: Valentine's Day (14th)
- March/April: Good Friday, Easter Monday
- May: Mother's Day, Victoria Day (Monday on or before the 24th)
- June: Father's Day

- July: Canada Day (1st)

- August: Civic Holiday (1st Monday)

- September: Labor Day (1st Monday), Grandparents' Day, Yom Kippur

- October: Thanksgiving (second Monday), Halloween (31st)

- November: Remembrance Day (11th)

- December: Christmas (25th), Boxing Day (26th)

## PROGRAM DESIGN

The program can be designed and delivered in English, unless it is being held in Montreal; then French is required. It is best to design in both English and French versions or translations so that you can have them both available for participants who prefer one over the other. The program design, of course, depends on the type of learning that is intended. The audience is typically quite flexible and appreciates interactive presentations as well as activities that reinforce the learning. For our example, the program design includes an instructor presentation using an easel and facilitation of activities where participants practice and obtain feedback on their skill development.

Pictures of Canadian nature (Canada goose), sports (hockey), Canadian Mounties (Royal Canadian Mounted Police), and the Canadian Flag (red maple leaf) all show respect for the Canadian way of life and interest in the participants.

When designing a program, keep in mind that Canadian society is a multicultural one. Approximately two-fifths of the Canadian population has an origin other than British, French, or First Nations. Canada has welcomed immigrants from China and South Asia as well as from countries all over the world such as Pakistan, Iran, the United States, Romania, United Kingdom, South Korea, Colombia, and others. This means that your program design should be created knowing that participants may have backgrounds that reflect their home countries in addition to their new home of Canada.

## LOGISTICS

Send your materials such as workbooks and handouts, with ample time to be delivered to your presentation location. Make agreements with your host or hotel regarding who they should be addressed and delivered to, as well as any setup requirements that are necessary. Contact the hotel to request the appropriate equipment and setup for your program, if being delivered in a hotel. Send your presentation ahead of time to your host, and bring your program materials with you, such as the program saved on an electronic storage device, as well as one hard copy of both English and French translations of handouts.

Canadian currency is the Canadian dollar ($ or C$). The most common coins include: 1¢, 5¢, 10¢, 25¢, $1 (often called "loonies"), $2 (often called "toonies"). The most common bank notes are $5, $10, $20, and $50. The best rate of exchange is usually found in banks. ATMs (often called an ABM) are typically the most convenient way to obtain Canadian currency.

Visa and MasterCard are commonly accepted credit cards.

## PROGRAM DELIVERY

Role plays, case studies, and PowerPoint presentations all work fine in the training sessions. Allow ample time for lunch, because it is difficult to get served at a restaurant and back to the room in an hour, so an hour and a half will provide enough time. The program can start as early as 8 A.M. and last until 5 or 6 P.M. If homework is given, you can count on it being completed as expected. Many people will drive from one to two hours away or take the train, so it is best not to end the program too late.

Introductions should be made at the beginning of the program that include the instructors, interpreter (if there is one needed for French), support staff, and any managers or sponsors in the room. Then participants should be asked to introduce themselves individually.

Canadian participants are typically comfortable with discussion, interaction, and asking questions of the instructor. We found them willing to participate in activities and role plays with interest and enthusiasm.

## TECHNICAL REQUIREMENTS

Canadian electrical current is 120/240. The typical plug is a three-prong plug like that used in the United States. Be sure to bring extension cords, plugs and back-up systems to use if needed. Bring your program on an electronic storage device, send it to your host ahead of time, and hand carry hard copies of translated French and English versions of handouts. Bring videotapes (NTSC format) or DVDs that are already subtitled in French if your presentation is in Montreal. If you bring your computer, you can request a projector to be available and set up in your presentation room.

Internet access is widely available in Toronto and Montreal.

## ACCOMMODATIONS

Hotels provide very good accommodations. Security is not a large problem, but if you are in the city, you should use common sense. The water is safe to drink and food is excellent and should not cause any intestinal problems.

Standard hotel chains are available, such as Sheraton, Weston, Marriott, and Radisson Hotels.

Toronto has a great variety of accommodations that can be accessed on www.toronto.com as well as information regarding travel, events, and traffic.

Webcams showing Montreal sights, accommodations, events, and information are included on the www.montreal.com website.

## GETTING AROUND

Everything is centrally located in Toronto. It is easy to get around by walking, car, taxi, or streetcar.

Practice your French questions so you can use French in Montreal. Point to the location on a map and ask for help. Friendly English-speaking people will be very helpful. You can get around Montreal by walking, car, taxi, or the Metro.

## THE PEOPLE

Canada is a vast land made up of ten provinces and three territories. Canadian provinces from west to east include:

- British Columbia
- Alberta
- Saskatchewan
- Manitoba
- Ontario
- Québec
- New Brunswick
- Prince Edward Island
- Nova Scotia
- Newfoundland and Labrador

Canadian territories from west to east include:

- Yukon

- Northwest Territories

- Nunavut

English, French, Scottish, and Irish immigrants were first to come to Canada's Ontario province, where Toronto is located. Immigration continued throughout the 20th century, with large numbers of people of Italian, German, Chinese, Dutch, Portuguese, Indian, Polish, and Caribbean origin arriving in the Ontario province. Now people from every country in the world live in Ontario. English is the official language. Ontario's Francophone population is the largest language minority. The automobile industry, mining, forestry, and tourism are dominant in the economy. Toronto is Canada's largest city and the capital of Ontario.

Montreal is Canada's second-largest city and the heart of French culture in North America. It is located in the Québec province. Amerindians of the Algonquin and Iroquois nations lived in the woodlands and river valleys of Québec. The northern part of the province was, and still is, inhabited by Inuit. The Canada River (the Saint Lawrence) was a rich homeland to agricultural people who lived in towns along its banks for thousands of years prior to the arrival of the French explorer Jacques Cartier in 1534.

The early French era included a thriving fur trade, a struggle for survival, and relatively friendly relations with the Aboriginal people north of the St. Lawrence. There was also an ongoing rivalry between the French and the Iroquoian people to the south. France was involved in worldwide rivalry with Britain over Québec. The French influence now is stronger than any other in Québec and French is the dominant spoken language.

Québec exports less than half of its total production, mainly from the forest industry (printing, lumber, and paper), mining (aluminum and iron ore) and transportation equipment manufacturing. Québec also exports electricity, engineering expertise, electronic products, and telecommunications equipment.

The people of Canada are very proud of their country, very kind and helpful, as well as hearty, outdoor lovers of nature and the environment. They are curious about the politics of other countries and concerned about national and international issues. Their health care is a frequent topic of discussion, but hockey dominates everything. Sports discussions are ongoing and detailed. Women know just as much about sports as men. Family is very important, but different depending on where you were raised (rural, city, coast, or mountains). Most stay in their provinces, even if they have moved to the city.

Hospitality is wonderful. Several participants invited us to stay in their homes instead of the hotel. We were invited to dinner at their homes and often surprised with cookies, candy, and honey. People freely offer and give rides to make sure that you do not get lost when going to a destination. They go out of their way and take extra time to bring us back safely to the hotel. Each person has been very gracious, but each person is different. You can tell that there is an interesting story behind each person's current life. Canadians think it is strange that some foreigners drink soda in the morning.

Some come from cities, either English-speaking or French-speaking. Some come from hearty rural areas where winter is difficult but lived with gusto. Some come from coastal shipping and fishing areas. And still others come from the Native Peoples locations, primarily in the West, with a pride and depth that continues to make us curious and interested.

Many of the participants in the course become lifelong friends. This was really unexpected and makes you want to return to Canada at any opportunity.

Marylou Atkins-Hayes (Kodak) explained some of the holiday traditions such as "crackers," which are small surprise packages that contain tiny gifts, jokes, and fun. Two people hold either end and pull to open the decorated package and see the surprises it contains. Each pair enjoys the joke being read as well as the surprise of the person receiving each item in the small package. It is an entertaining ritual from their British roots.

Canadian industry includes transportation equipment, chemicals, processed and unprocessed minerals, and food products.

Canadian agriculture includes wheat, barley, oilseed, tobacco; dairy products; forest products; and fish.

Canada's exports include motor vehicles and parts, industrial machinery, aircraft, telecommunications equipment, chemicals, timber, and crude petroleum.

Canada's type of government is a federal parliamentary democracy within a constitutional monarchy. The capital is Ottawa, Ontario. The Queen of England is the Head of State. The Governor-General is the representative of the Queen. The Head of Government is the Prime Minister of Canada.

## ‖‖‖ PREPARATION
•••

Dress professionally and show confidence. Avoid any behavior that implies arrogance.

Find out whether there is someone who can review your materials ahead of time for anything that is inadvertently offensive or confusing. You can bring overhead transparencies in case the laptop does not work. Carry your presentation, transparencies, a hard copy of the handouts, and your laptop with you instead of checking anything with your luggage, just in case your luggage is delayed by an airline.

Try to get an agreement that someone in the class will alert you to any gestures or parts of your presentation that may be confusing or offensive (so you can clarify or apologize, as needed).

Here are some helpful French phrases for your interactions with Canadians who are most comfortable with French:

| English | Pronounced | French |
|---|---|---|
| Hello | sah-**loo** | "Salut" |
| Glad to meet you | on-shohn-**tay** | "Enchanté" |
| Good-bye | oh ruh-**vwar** | "Au revoir" |
| How are you? | kom-mohn tah-lay **voo** | "Comment allez-vous?" |
| Fine thanks and you? | bee-ehn mer-**see** ay voo? | "Merci et vous?" |
| Excuse me/sorry | ex-koo-**zay** mwah | "Excusez-moi" |
| Do you speak English? | par-**lay voo** zon-**glay** | "Parlez-vous anglais?" |
| Good morning/good day | bon-**zhoor** | "Bon jour" |
| Good evening | bon-**swar** | "Bon soir" |
| My name is | juh mah-**pell** | "Je m'appelle" |
| I'm sorry | day-zoh-**lay**/pahr-**dohn** | "Desolé/Pardon" |
| I don't understand | jhuhn kom-**prohn** pah | "Je ne comprends pas" |
| Please | seel voo **play** | "S'il vous plait" |
| Thank you | mare-**see** | "Merci" |
| No | nohn | "Non" |
| Ok | dah-**core** | "d'accord" |

## THE PRESENTATION

The presentation location is most likely a conference room. Avoid using slang or acronyms that are not clearly defined when you present. Speak very slowly and enunciate your words so they can be understood and interpreted, if French translation is necessary. Use simple sentence structure. Don't assume that you have been understood. Be very careful of your own body language and gestures, because they will be interpreted more than your words by your audience. Be aware of any funny looks or uncomfortable silences from your audience. Humor doesn't always work. There are too many differences in interpretation, wording, and understanding.

The program presentation in our example includes low-tech audiovisuals. Easels work well to write, demonstrate, and record information. Activities include many pairs, trios, and group practice and action planning. Learning and the interactions of the individuals are the primary focus of instruction. Thus, everything proceeds quite smoothly. Participants are willing to experiment and learn.

Standard audiovisuals work well for Canadians. They seem quite comfortable with presentations made in PowerPoint slides projected from the computer or films on DVD.

When instruction is in English, it is a challenge for those whose primary language is French. They may willingly ask for clarification and discuss their ideas, but you can tell they are working much harder than the rest of us (because they are thinking and speaking in two different languages and translation is difficult when English is spoken quickly to present new learning concepts). It is helpful if you carefully watch to see whether there is a questioning look on someone's face. If so, then it is good to speak more slowly and ask whether the person has any questions. We also need to listen very carefully to clearly understand words that are spoken with an accent. It can be exhausting but very important to pay close attention to each word. Some people lose interest and are unable to focus intently on a speaker who is speaking in a strong accent. This is very insulting and hurtful to the speaker (they confide their reaction). Patience and flexibility are very important on these occasions. Saying: "I am sorry, I do not understand" and intently listening to their explanation is very helpful. Also asking questions helps you to stay focused on the learner. Show respect for his or her hard work in taking a course in a language other than his or her most comfortable one. They appreciate it. Try to learn some words and sentences in their language to make them feel more at home and accepted. In addition to just being courteous, it helps us to understand how difficult it is to speak another language.

Marylou Atkins-Hayes (independent businesswoman) tells us how instructors often come to present in another country, with their own examples prepared, but participants can't relate to their examples. She suggests that you research the country and local festivals, events, and weather and insert local information into your learning examples and stories so that everyone can relate. When teaching or meeting with Francophones (French-speaking Canadians), it is important to make sure that you do not have any working lunches (their response would be: "We don't do that"). Short lunches are not a good idea either. You should readjust your schedule to ensure that there is sufficient time for a good lunch and dinner.

Estela Sasson (professional coach) has told us that, when teaching and presenting to French Canadians, you have to speak French. She says, "This shows that you are on the same wavelength. It is very cultural and emotional. You have to show some familiarity and that you are in the same world. How you relate is so important. You have to be non-judgmental and establish a cultural link of trust as humans." She tells us that French Canadians are often irritated with people who speak English when they are in French-speaking sections of Canada such as Montreal.

Remember that hockey is the unifying and dividing force in Canada and is always sure to get people talking and excited. Comments about the beauty of the land are always appreciated as a constant source of agreement and pride.

**Helpful websites and references include:**

- www.frommers.com
- www.ielanguages.com
- www.infoplease.com
- www.nationalgeographic.com
- www.timetemperature.com

# Central America and the Caribbean

The region has been home to many indigenous peoples and advanced civilizations, including the Aztecs, Toltecs, Caribs, Tupi, Maya, and Inca. The Europeans came and settled with the native people, bringing the influence of the romance languages, especially Spanish. Each country has its own personality, but overall the pace is calming and welcoming.

Here is some information and a few tips for success when training, teaching, and presenting to audiences from this region. We will first cover some areas of Central America and then provide helpful tips and information for the Caribbean.

## ??? THE REQUEST

Sandra Edwards, regional vice president of AMA, shares some examples, in this chapter, based on her experiences as vice president of International Business Development at Achieve Global, presenting several times to groups from Central and South America. The topics included knowledge transfer, global account development, leadership, and building a high performance sales organization.

## • • • GETTING THERE

Central America includes Belize, Costa Rica, El Salvador, Guatemala, Honduras, Nicaragua, and Panama. Frequent flights are available to the capital of each country. A valid passport is required. It is important to check and complete the visa and entry requirements far ahead of time for each country (www.cibt.com). For example, at this time a visa is required for El Salvador and a tourist card for Panama, but visas are not required for Belize, Costa Rica, Guatemala, Honduras, or Nicaragua for U.S. citizens staying fewer than thirty days. Here are a few localized facts:

- Belize borders the Caribbean Sea, between Guatemala and Mexico. Capital: Belmopan. Time zone: GMT/UTC – 6 hours

- Costa Rica is in Central America, bordering both the Caribbean Sea and the North Pacific Ocean, between Nicaragua and Panama. Capital: San Jose. Time zone: GMT/UTC – 6 hours

- El Salvador is in Central America, bordering the Pacific Ocean, between Guatemala and Honduras. Capital: San Salvador. Time zone: GMT/UTC – 6 hours

- Guatemala is in Central America, bordering the Pacific Ocean, between El Salvador and Mexico and bordering the Gulf of Honduras (Caribbean Sea) between Honduras and Belize. Capital: Guatemala City. Time zone: GMT/UTC – 6 hours

- Honduras is in Central America, bordering the Caribbean Sea, between Guatemala and Nicaragua and on the Gulf of Fonseca (Pacific Ocean), between El Salvador and Nicaragua. Capital: Tegucigalpa (Tegus) got its tongue-twisting name from the ancient Nahuatl language, and translated means "silver mountain." Time zone: GMT/UTC – 6 hours

- Nicaragua is in Central America, bordering both the Caribbean Sea and the Pacific Ocean, between Costa Rica and Honduras. Capital: Managua. Time zone: GMT/UTC – 6 hours (daylight savings time in summer)

- Panama is in Central America, bordering both the Caribbean Sea and the Pacific Ocean, between Colombia and Costa Rica. Capital: Panama City. Time zone: GMT/UTC – 5 hours

 **PROGRAM DESIGN**

The materials should be translated into Latin American Spanish and culturally adapted. This can be done by having materials translated here and then sending them to be revised by your contact, so that changes can be made with cultural nuances and language adjustments, as needed.

The people in all of these countries speak Spanish as their primary language, except Belize which has English as their primary language and Spanish as secondary (Belize is formerly known as British Honduras).

Because the favorite sport is football (soccer) you can design examples with this as a common focus because most people can relate.

## LOGISTICS

Work with your hotel or conference center to request any equipment, hook-ups, and setup that is needed to ensure a successful presentation. They should be able to accommodate your needs. Reconfirm in writing to ensure clarification and understanding.

Large celebrations, festivals, and food mark the holidays, as well as most people taking the day off, so you will not be able to conduct classes on these dates and can use upcoming holidays as examples and conversation in your course or presentation. Belize celebrates the most holidays, as listed below. Other countries celebrate fewer, but will include some of these:

- New Year: January 1
- Baron Bliss Day: March 9
- Good Friday: March/April: Friday before Easter
- Holy Saturday: March/April: Saturday before Easter
- Easter Monday: March/April: Monday after Easter
- Labor Day: May 1
- Commonwealth Day: May 25
- National Day (St. George's Caye Day): September 10
- Independence Day: September 21
- Columbus Day: October 12
- Christmas: December 25 and 26

### Currency

*Belize:* The currency of Belize is called the Dollar (BZD). Dollar banknotes are issued in the following denominations: 2, 5, 10, 20, 50, and 100 Dollars. Smaller values are issued as coins, with 1 Dollar = 100 Cents. U.S. dollars are widely accepted. British Pounds and Mexican Pesos can also be used.

*Costa Rica:* The currency of Costa Rica is called the Colon (pl. Colones). Colon (CRC) banknotes are issued in the following denominations: 500, 1,000, 2,000, 5,000, and 10,000 Colones. All major currencies are accepted.

*El Salvador:* U.S. dollars are now used in El Salvador. Colones can still be used, but are not reissued by banks.

*Guatemala:* The currency of Guatemala is called the Quetzal (pl. Quetzales). Quetzal banknotes are issued in the following denominations: 1, 5, 10, 20, 50, and 100 Quetzales. All major currencies are accepted.

*Honduras:* The Honduran currency (HNL) is called the Lempira (pl. Lempiras). Lempira banknotes are issued in the following denominations: 1, 2, 5, 10, 20, 50, 100, and 500 Lempiras. Changing dollars into lempiras in Tegus is easy. There are many banks throughout the city, especially within the Boulevard Morazan and downtown areas. Banco Atlantida offers cash withdrawals from your Visa cards, and Credomatic located at Bulevar Morazan offers cash withdrawals for Visa and MasterCard.

*Nicaragua:* Nicaragua has its own currency: the Córdoba. The U.S. dollar is also accepted. The currency of Nicaragua is the Nicaraguan Gold Cordoba (NIO). A hundred centavos make one NIO, and coins can be obtained in 5, 10, 25, and 50 centavos as well as NIO1 and NIO5 denominations. Notes come in groupings of 10, 20, 50, 100, and 500 NIO. You can usually exchange your money at the airport, at banks or at any of the official foreign exchange bureaus found in most of the country's major cities.

*Panama:* Panama's official currency, the Balboa, is available only in coins, not in paper bills. The value, shape, and size of the Balboa coins are equal to that of the U.S. dollar. Most products and services are priced in Balboas; however, one can read the price as though it were written in U.S. dollars. Visa, MasterCard, and American Express credit cards are commonly used throughout Panama, including at car rental companies, hotels, and stores.

## PROGRAM DELIVERY

Critical to consider are the following points:

- When speaking in English, practice speaking VERY slowly as you will need to speak quite slowly when training.

- Ensure lots of time for discussion and dialogue.

- Allow for at least 90 minutes for lunch and half an hour for breaks.

- Practice exercises should be in teams and avoid competition.

- Case studies and discussions work very well.

- Video, if appropriate and not too Americanized, can be helpful.

- Positive reinforcement and recognition of participants' experience and expertise are important.

- The facilitator (instructor) is given great respect and really needs to be expert in the content as well as in facilitation. The instructor should have "lived" the topic and be able to illustrate with relevant, culturally accepted examples. Thus, it's vital to gather specific examples and case studies from the countries to ensure a high-quality experience for the course participants. You can also share cases and examples from other parts of the world to provide a global forum.

- The Latin participants take training very seriously and value the intellectual as well as the practical aspects. Games and toys diminish the seriousness and perceived value of the training experience.

- High energy, enthusiasm for the subject, and passion for the results to be achieved all play well in Latin America.

- Be prepared to socialize with participants (dinner, lunches) during the session and after hours if the training is more than a day. It is perceived as insulting if the trainer simply returns to his or her hotel room and does not wish to sample the culture outside of the classroom. As in many locations in the world, the Latin Americans want to share their culture, stories, foods, and arts with the visitor.

## TECHNICAL REQUIREMENTS

Voltage is typically 110V or 220V (El Salvador 110V: 100V to 160V; Panama 110V: 100V to 160V). Be sure to bring extension cords, plugs, and back-up systems to use as needed. Bring your program on an electronic storage device, send it to your host ahead of time, hand carry hard copies of translated and English versions of handouts. Bring videotapes (NTSC format) or DVDs that are already subtitled in Spanish. If you bring your computer, you can request a projector to be available and set up in your presentation room.

Do not expect Internet availability. Check to see whether it is available ahead of time if you need it for your program.

## ACCOMMODATIONS

Hotels provide very good accommodations. Marriott, Radisson, and Westin hotels are likely to provide what you would normally expect. You can check photos and customer ratings, as well as make reservations online through Expedia (www.expedia.com) or Travelocity (www.travelocity.com), as well as through your travel agent. Security is always important to consider when leaving your hotel. Drink bottled water only, to assure that you will not have stomach problems from water that your body is not used to having.

Make sure that you watch your possessions, do not show large amounts of money. (Carry a little money in your pocket, but most in an under-your-clothes pouch with your passport or place it in a secure hotel safe.)

## GETTING AROUND

Travel within each city can be arranged by your hotel. Ask them for the best advice for traveling within the city.

Here is an example, but you will want to get the most up-to-date local travel and safety advice from your hotel:

Honduras: Getting around Tegucigalpa can be a confusing experience. Taxis are plentiful in Tegucigalpa, they are not expensive, and will usually run under 40 lempiras for a trip. It is, however, a good idea to negotiate the rate before climbing into the vehicle.

The central market is extremely interesting; however, we must warn you, as in any other large market, you must keep an eye out for pickpockets. It is not recommended at all to venture into the market area after dark.

## THE PEOPLE

The people are fabulous to work with, Sandi Edwards (Achieve Global/AMA) tells us. They really value and appreciate intellectual discussion, new ways and ideas to discuss, evaluate, and try. They are eager to learn. The social aspect adds to the vibrant experience for all. Gift giving is not unusual, so don't be surprised if you are the lucky recipient of cultural wares.

Each of these countries has its own special history, traditions, and crafts. Common is the love of dance, food, color, and friendship. Nature and native peoples are strong and obvious influences. Mountains, beaches, volcanoes, and lush foliage are prevalent. The weather influences what people wear. For example, it is hot and dry in Panama from November to March and the rainy season is from May to November in Costa Rica, so check the weather for a week before your departure to know what to bring.

Because each country and city has its own history and current affairs, it is best to go online and review information specific to the location where you will be working.

## PREPARATION

Keep these tips in mind:

- Prepare and read up on the country so that you are able to at least say hello and good evening in Spanish.

- Be outgoing, sample the new ways, and enjoy the differences; don't make comparisons to your home country.

- Be prepared to go with the flow and allow more time than you think is needed, for almost every activity in the program. Don't rush people to meet the timeline, just ensure they see relevance, value, and application to their real world.

- Courtesy and gentleness are important if facilitating; dynamism and passion are important when presenting.

- Excellent presentation skills are highly valued and expected.

Here are some useful words and phrases:

| English | Pronunciation | Spanish |
|---|---|---|
| Hi | O-la | "Hola" |
| To introduce | Present-are | "Presentar" |
| To introduce oneself | Present-are-say | "Presentarse" |
| How's it going? | Comb-o tay vah | "¿Cómo te va?" |
| Pleased to meet you (male) | N-cahn-ta-doh | "Encantado" |
| Pleased to meet you (female) | N-cahn-ta-da | "Encantada" |
| It's nice to meet you | Moo-cho goo-sto | "Mucho gusto" |
| How are you? | Kay tall | "¿Qué tal?" |
| What's up? | Kay pah-sa | "¿Qué pasa?" |
| Excuse me | Pear-dohn-ah-may | "Perdóneme" |
| I'm sorry | Low sea-n-toe | "Lo siento" |
| Thank you | Grah-syas | "Gracias" |

## THE PRESENTATION

Sandi Edwards (Achieve Global/AMA) conducts programs in English. Here are some suggestions from her:

- Do enjoy the people and welcome the leisurely pace and love of learning.

- Don't make comparisons to your own country.

- Don't be negative about any government and avoid political discussions.

- Listen more than you speak.

- Encourage everyone to participate so that dominant players don't take over the session.

- Do ensure that you add plenty of time for the program. A rule of thumb might be: Add at least four hours to every day of your typical training,

What surprises Sandi is how slowly she has to speak to ensure understanding, even when everyone speaks English.

Here are some tips and helpful information from other trainers about some specific Caribbean locations.

## Caribbean: Antigua, Barbados

Working for the United Nations, Jennifer Britton conducted a number of governmental and UN training programs over a three-year period. Jennifer lived in these countries.

### Dos and Don'ts

- Do be professional, punctual, and well dressed.

- Do not wear beach attire to undertake training programs. Business dress is more appropriate (jacket and skirt/pants for women, shirt and tie for men).

- "Bajans" (people of Barbados) are very well educated and technically savvy; leverage the knowledge of the group.

- Don't inundate with PowerPoint; use as many participatory techniques as possible.

What works best with this audience?

There is a certain level of formality with training programs, which may include an opening address and closing address, and sometimes receptions. You should work as much as possible with a local counterpart to share skills and techniques and to build capacity within the host organization.

- Language: English

- Equipment: Most of the Caribbean islands have 110 volts and similar plugs to North America. You may want to invest in a surge protector for any electrical equipment.

- Techniques: All are applicable

- Customs: Sundays are still considered a "day of rest" and all stores are closed. Most Bajans will spend the day at home or at church. Saturday stores are open for a half day.

- People: Very well educated

Delivering training programs in the English-speaking Caribbean is a real pleasure and opportunities are generally not that frequent. Wherever possible, look to build local capacity by bringing a local counterpart on board to further develop their skills.

## Caribbean: Haiti

Jennifer conducted four-day supervisory skills training programs for one of the UN agencies.

Language: English and French. Materials need to be translated. One of the participants works as a translator to clarify those phrases that are not clear when speaking in a second language, French.

Haiti is a country that is coming out of a period of political unrest. Economically it is the poorest country in the Western Hemisphere. Trainers should communicate closely with the host organization regarding security, travel, and what materials to bring. Pack materials, copies, markers, and so forth. 110 V and North American plugs are typically available. Given that poverty is high, dress in a business-like fashion, but do not travel with a lot of valuables.

Given the security situation, it is not recommended to travel around other parts of Haiti. Keep to the hotel and to where the training is being delivered. It is very important that trainers who have a good command of French do training in most locations, particularly at the local level.

A main rule of thumb when working in any country or delivering any training in another country is to learn as much as you can about the country before you go. Connect with a local counterpart prior to travel and ask questions regarding dress, organizational culture, their past experience with training programs, what worked, what didn't, what they really want, as well as any technical questions. The number one rule in cross-cultural work: Don't Assume!

Observation plays a key role in cross-cultural success. Observe how others behave. Learn as much of the local language or dialogue as you can prior to the program and show interest in and respect for local customs. If at all possible, connect with expatriates from that country prior to delivering a training program there. If appropriate, work with local counterparts who can "translate" your information into the local dialect, even if the native language is English. The variety of cultures and traditions in this region of the world provides many opportunities to experience a great deal within a relatively small area. There is a common sensation, though, of being transported to another time and place when you enter and stay in each country.

Enjoy!

**Helpful websites and references include:**

- www.centralhome.com/ballroomcountry/video_formats.htm
- www.guardianfx.com/maps/southamerica.html
- www.honduras.com/hondurastips/english/tegucigalpa.htm
- www.infoplease.com
- www.nicaragua.com/currency/
- www.traveldocs.com/bz/vr.htm
- www.visahq.com/visas.php
- www.worldheadquarters.com/panama/currency/index.html

# Colombia

S truggle has been a continuous part of Colombia's history. Independence from Spain, struggle over territory, internal political strife, drug cartels, and guerilla insurgencies have plagued the country. Even now, kidnapping, robberies, and drug smuggling require the traveler to be on guard. This is a challenging environment that is not used to seeing a lot of foreigners but beginning to see more tourists. The people of Colombia are hospitable and open. Here is what to expect and tips for success for training, teaching, and presenting to audiences in Colombia.

## ??? THE REQUEST

The request (our example) includes an agreement between the school director and her board to initiate this activity as part of their improvement plan for the year.

Doug Cumming, Superintendent of Education, Ontario, Canada, suggests asking lots of questions by email to gain a composite picture before beginning to prepare. Also ask the same of a third-party person who knows the organization very well. Doug spends more than two hundred hours in the planning process, including research, dialoguing with former colleagues, and developing many visual materials.

### Agreements

The workshop leader needs to have a written contract, clearly written and agreed to by both parties before you leave home (this is critical, Doug reminds us). Ensure clarity and common understanding about details, such as who meets you at the airport; where you are to be lodged; how you are to be paid (cash? check? currency?), and when (ideally, while you are still there).

Confirm that the members of the audience are committed to attending and participating fully in the workshop. One good technique to help achieve this is to send ahead some assignment or task that becomes part of the overall presentation, such as identifying questions they would like to have answered in the program. This can help to determine content emphasis of a course, gather data and information regarding strategies, and plan for evaluation for the workshop. This is a critical aspect of the "buy in" for the participants. It signals the practicality of what they are going to learn.

### Pre-Work

Collect as much information as possible regarding the staff, community profile, the business or company. Your third-party contact is the obvious source of such information. If this person can't answer all your questions, ask him or her to recommend the best contacts for you.

## • • • GETTING THERE

A valid passport is required to enter Colombia. Check for the most current visa requirements at www.traveldocs.com/co/embassy.htm or with your embassy or consulate representative. (Business travel may require a visa, even when tourist travel does not.)

Colombia is in the northwest region of South America. It is bordered by Venezuela, Brazil, Ecuador, Peru, Panama, the Pacific Ocean, and the Caribbean Sea. Study the environment and geography prior to arriving there so you are familiar with the area.

Colombia's time zone is GMT/UTC – 5 hours.

Expedia and Travelocity offer flight and accommodation information and photos. Once you arrive by air, make sure you have a trusted driver to pick you up and take you to any destinations. This can be arranged by asking your host ahead of time to recommend a trusted driver.

Although Bogota would be the most likely location for a program, other possibilities might be Cartagena, San Andres, and Providencia, Caribbean locations.

Remember: January is summertime in Colombia. Climate is about 15 to 16 degrees C (approximately 60 degrees F) all year round in Bogota, but it can get cool at night. January through March and July through September are the dry seasons. Cartagena has a tropical location, so the climate changes little, with an average high of 32 degrees C

(88.6 degrees F) and an average low of 25 degrees C (77 degrees F) throughout the year. Cartagena also averages around 90 percent humidity, with a rainy season typically in October. Cartagena receives about 1,000 mm (40 inches) of rain per year. The best times to visit San Andres are January through February and September, with March and April a close second. San Andres and Providencia climate is average 30 degrees C (80 degrees F) all year round and gets quite a lot of rain from June through November.

Famous festivals include the Cali Fair, the Barranquilla Carnival, the Bogota summer festival, the Iberoamerican Theater Festival, and the Flower Festival. Many people visit Colombia during Christmas time, and the celebrations surrounding the Independence of Colombia.

The festivals and holidays will influence the timing, traffic, and atmosphere of your program:

- January: New Year's Day (Año Nuevo and La Circunsición) (1st), Epiphany (6th)
- March: San José (19th)
- March/April: Carnaval, Semana Santa
- May: Labor Day (Dia de los Trabajadores) (1st)
- May or June: Corpus Christi
- June: Sagrado Corazon de Jesús, San Pedro y San Pablo (29th)
- July: Independence Day {Dia de la Independencia} (20th)
- August: Simón Bolívar wins the Batalla de Boyacá (7th), La Asunción de Nuestra Señora (15th), and Feria del Orinoco (last week)
- October: Columbus Day (Dia de la Raza) (12th)
- November: Día de Todos Santos (1st), Independencia de Cartagena (11th),
- December: Inmaculada Concepción (8th), Christmas Day (Navidad) (25th)

## PROGRAM DESIGN

These are the topics that were requested to be presented, from our example with Doug Cumming:

- Curriculum Development and Management
- Effective Classroom Theory and Practice

The staff (forty members) includes mainly Colombians with four or five foreign teachers; as well as a few invited board members. These latter people attend the workshop occasionally.

The objectives of the program were that participants would be able to:

- Demonstrate an understanding of seven generic characteristics of a good curriculum
- Re-create a unit or course of study following the format presented
- Demonstrate an understanding of the integration of effective classroom management strategies with overall school improvement
- Learn and apply key tenets of learning style theory to classroom activities.

For translations, Doug relies on a combination of a third-party fully bilingual person accompanying him to the workshop site and his own ability to speak Castilian Spanish. All overheads are in English but with translation capability. All participants complete a written evaluation of the four-day workshop; results collated and returned in full copy to the director. Good models for curriculum from Canada and classroom management were used, but always with the perspective of applying and adapting ideas to Colombian curriculum. One weakness has been the lack of effective follow-up after the workshop.

Football (soccer), cycling, boxing, and bullfighting are popular sports in Colombia, so you can design examples, audiovisuals, or case studies with reference to these, as well as some basketball and baseball.

## LOGISTICS

Take as few multiple copies of materials as possible; rather, have copying done on site. It makes for lighter luggage. Just be clear to communicate expectations and make agreements about making copies, the need for equipment, and room setup before arriving.

The Colombian peso is used throughout the country. U.S. dollars are also widely accepted. You can use major bank machine cards such as Visa and MasterCard to receive Colombian pesos at several ATM locations.

The Colombian Peso (COP; symbol Col$) = 100 centavos. Notes are in denominations of Col$50,000, 20,000, 10,000, 5,000, 2,000, and 1,000. Coins are in denominations of Col$1,000, 500, 200, 100, 50, 20, 10, and 5.

Currency should be exchanged at hotels, banks, and bureaux de change only, although most places charge a commission. Travelers are advised against changing money on the street. The U.S. dollar is the easiest currency to exchange.

## PROGRAM DELIVERY

There is a nice easy Mediterranean-style atmosphere around protocols that can be aided by those who live in this country. Work with your local contact and engage some of the participants ahead of time, if possible, to have them help you understand what is most effective for the students' learning.

Lecture, discussion, and case studies are appropriate for this audience.

## TECHNICAL REQUIREMENTS

*Setup:* Send specific requests about equipment and room organization. Make agreements regarding the copying of materials. Also make an agreement regarding how many hours per day the group is expected to work.

*Tools:* all the equipment and paperwork that the participants would need must be requested in advance.

*Electricity:* in Colombia is 110 Volts, alternating at 60 cycles per second. If you travel to Colombia with a device that does not accept 110 Volts at 60 Hertz, you will need a voltage converter. Outlets in Colombia generally accept a two pronged flat blade plug, so you will need an adapter.

## ACCOMMODATIONS

Hotel ratings and photos can easily be found on Expedia and Travelocity.

Security is an aspect of a country like Colombia that a foreigner should know about before arriving. Kidnapping and violence are possibilities. Ask your host for a hotel recommendation.

Doug stayed in an 1800-vintage former Spanish mission house, now a private home, with its incredible dimensions and history.

For food, in Bogotá and the Andean region, ajiaco is the traditional dish. It is also a type of soup made of chicken, potatoes, and flavored with a locally grown herb called "guasca."

The best way to avoid stomach problems is to drink bottled water.

## GETTING AROUND

Have a car and trusted driver take you where you need to go. Make this part of your planning agreements with your host. The roads may be bumpy.

Safety and security are still concerns in Colombia. Check the most recent information and warnings at www.travel.state.gov and avoid taking public transportation as much as possible. Have your hotel make arrangements for transportation if your host does not.

The central and northern parts of the city of Bogota are more widely traveled by visitors to the city. Getting around in the city is simplified by the naming convention of the streets. Most of the older streets are named *carreras* running north and south or *calles* running east and west and are numbered. The newer streets may be *avenidas circulars* or *transversales*. Bus transportation is excellent. Large busses, called *bus*, smaller buses called *busetas* and buseta, smaller buses and the *microbus or colectivo* van size, travel the city streets, while the *Transmilenio* modern articulated buses operates now on selected main streets, but is expected to cover the entire city within the next decade.

## THE PEOPLE

About three-fifths of the people are mestizo, a mix of Indian and European blood. One-fifth are "white" European, and one-fifth are mulatto (this word may be considered offensive to some, so it is best not to use it), a mix of African and European blood or zambo, a mix of African and Indian. The language is Castilian Spanish.

The class system is strong with few opportunities to move into a higher class. The people continue to live in difficult conditions.

The predominant religion is Roman Catholic.

Violence is common and safety of a foreigner must be assured by having a reliable guide. You should check news and keep aware of the conditions on a constant basis. Also check for updated travel advisories at http://travel.state.gov. Kidnapping remains a possibility, as is street crime, violence, and scams such as phony policemen. Make sure you are escorted and driven to your destination safely.

Indigenous people/Amerindians and early Spanish explorers shape much of Colombia's culture. Wars, violence, and drug cartels mark much of the history of this country.

Mountains, coastline, volcanoes, cities, and the tropics provide a variety of geography and climate variations. Temperatures decrease as altitude increases. Rainfall increases as you go south through the country.

Colombia is a republic with an elected president. The constitution guarantees religious freedom, but most Colombians are Roman Catholic.

Colombia's main exports include manufactured goods, petroleum, coal, and coffee.

Music and dancing are very popular in Colombia.

An ancient game called *Tejo*, inherited from the muisco, is also played. The object of *tejo* is to throw a small metal disk at a gunpowder detonator in a small circular area. The winner is calculated by the number of explosions compared to number of throws.

## ‖‖‖ PREPARATION

Work with your interpreter ahead of time to help him or her understand what you are teaching. Review any terms or concepts that may be more difficult or complex. Encourage the person to ask questions so you can clarify anything that needs further explanation.

Arrive early to ensure that everything needed is available and working. Check the room setup and confirm that all materials are there.

Here are a few helpful basic phrases in Castilian Spanish:

| | |
|---|---|
| Good day | "Buenos Dias" |
| How are you? | "Como esta?" |
| Thank you | "Gracias" |
| Excuse me | "Perdoneme" |
| Please | "Por favor" |
| Yes | "Si" |
| No | "No" |
| Where is . . . | "Donde esta . . . ?" |

## THE PRESENTATION

The most important thing is to always remember that you represent another culture and country. You are not there to tell them what is wrong with their present practices or that you have the answers they need. Rather, you are there to learn from and with them, to offer suggestions for consideration, ideas they might adapt for their work. This approach, a.k.a. the "soft sell," typically yields better results.

### Cultural Sensitivities

One should never underestimate the cultural sensitivities aspect of working with a group in another country. Having worked in Colombia for an extensive period of time, Doug could walk into such a group reasonably confident of the proper expectations and protocols that one needs to observe as an outsider. One detail that could be problematic is that the director led Doug to believe the teachers all understood English; this turned out to not be the case and it could have posed a huge communications issue except for the fact that he is fluent in Spanish. Conclusion: If you are in a country where the participant group does not speak English widely, know this in advance, so you can make appropriate adjustments.

## Management Sensitivities

Being sensitive to management includes, first, a sensitive handling of questions from the participants that might be construed as critical of administration and second, sensitive handling of board members and key guests who are likely there to informally evaluate the financial worth of the workshop—in other words, are they getting their "money's worth"? You can answer participant questions by providing clear advantages for learning this information, as well as specifics of the return on investment that can be gained by attending your program.

## Follow-Up Suggestions

The lack of follow-up for Doug's workshop disappointed him. Shared email addresses, all participants encouraged to send questions/successes, and an offer for continued consulting at no charge to resolve any problems as they tried to incorporate some of his information into their curriculum yielded little. Apart from a nice thank-you note, there was very little continuing contact, even though they appreciated the work, as was reflected in the evaluations.

Conclusion: If appropriate, try to build a follow-up component into the original agreement, if you see it as helpful in enhancing the long-range benefits of the workshop. You can do this by providing an ongoing newsletter with hints and updates as well as typical questions and answers to reinforce the learning from the program.

**Helpful websites and references include:**

- http://travel.state.gov
- http://treehouse.ofb.net/go/en/voltage/Colombia
- www.traveldocs.com/co/embassy.htm
- www.worldtravelguide.net/country/59/money/South-America/Colombia.html

# Guyana

**G**uyana is a fascinating country of diversity, very friendly and very open to learning. Guyana is part of South America, but as it was formerly British Guyana, English is the main language. Guyana is more formally aligned to CARICOM* (Caribbean Community) and the Caribbean than the rest of South America, in part due to former challenges in traversing the terrain. Guyana is bordered by the Atlantic Ocean, Suriname, Brazil, and Venezuela. Guyana is a developing nation on the north coast of South America.

## ??? THE REQUEST

Jennifer Britton, CEO of Potentials Realized, lived and worked in Guyana for a six-year period. She says that a main rule of thumb for running programs in Guyana, like other developing nations, is: "Be as self-contained as possible and have a number of contingency plans." Materials may not arrive, technology may not work, so be prepared so that you can enjoy the training with the participants.

## • • • GETTING THERE

A valid passport is needed to enter Guyana. Visas are not typically needed. Flights are available to Timehri/Georgetown (GEO), the capital and largest city.

*The CARICOM member states are Antigua and Barbuda, The Bahamas, Barbados, Belize, Dominica, Grenada, Guyana, Haiti, Jamaica, Montserrat, Saint Lucia, St. Kitts and Nevis, St. Vincent and the Grenadines, Suriname, Trinidad, and Tobago. CARICOM associate members include Anguilla, Bermuda, the British Virgin Islands, the Cayman Islands, and Turks and the Caicos Islands.

Taxi fares are listed at the airport and are fixed. They do vary slightly according to which taxi service you use. You should agree to a fare beforehand. Taxis from Cheddi Jagan International Airport to Georgetown should cost less than $20 or about $4,000 GUY. Use the official airport taxi service. Look for uniforms and ID badges.

The departure tax is equal to GYD$4,000.00/US$20. Hotel room tax is 10 percent in hotels with sixteen or more rooms.

Driving is on the left-hand side of the road. Public transportation is available to most parts of the country. Car rentals are also available.

The Guyana (GUY) dollar is the only currency accepted in this country. Visitors may exchange their currencies at banks, cambios, and most hotels. The rate of the dollar fluctuates. Major credit cards and traveler's checks are generally accepted.

Guyana is one hour ahead of EST and GMT/UTC – 4 hours.

Holidays that may affect your travel and program scheduling include:

- January: New Year's Day (1st)
- February: Mashramani (23rd) Republic Day
- Spring: Phangwah–Holi–Hindu Spring Festival of Colours
- Spring: Eid-ul-Fitr
- Spring: Youm Un Nabi
- Spring: Good Friday, Easter Monday
- May: Labour Day (1st), Indian Arrival Day (5th), Independence Day (26th)
- July: CARICOM Day (first Monday)
- August: Emancipation Day (1st)
- Fall: Diwali–Indian Festival of Lights
- December: Christmas (25th), Boxing Day (26 or 27th)

 **PROGRAM DESIGN**

Primary languages are English and Creole. Different parts of the country (particularly if you are delivering community-based training) speak different Creolease dialects. So while English is the main language, English-speaking trainers may need to adapt their language. Confirm which Guyana location you are training in, as there is Guyana, former Dutch Guyana (Suriname), and also French Guyana (Guiana).

## LOGISTICS

If at all possible, try to "walk" with all of your materials. Flip charts, Blue Tack, and markers can be difficult to source in parts of Guyana. Likewise, photocopying arrangements should be discussed prior to the training sessions. It may be advantageous to bring your own copies, or send the material for copying prior to the event.

The local climate is tropical and generally hot and humid, although moderated by northeast trade winds along the coast. There are two rainy seasons, the first from May to mid-August, and the second from mid-November to mid-January.

The currency is the Guyanese dollar (GYD). Coins come in $1, $5, and $10. Banknotes are in $20, $100, $500, and $1,000 denominations.

Banks offer exchange facilities. Bureau de change offer free conversion of currencies. Electricity is 110V 220V (50-60 Cycles).

## PROGRAM DELIVERY

The techniques that work best with this audience are small group discussion and lectures. Case studies and role plays may be appropriate with some groups.

### Dos and Don'ts

- Do have a welcome address at the start of the training program from a governmental or company representative.

- If it is a multi-day program, you may want to include an afternoon reception.

- Provide lunch during the training program.

- As much as possible, have back-up plans in case something does not arrive, power shortages occur, or materials are not available.

- Try to be as self-sufficient as possible.

- Don't dress inappropriately. Guyanese of all walks of life take personal presentation and dress very seriously.

- Presentations are usually very structured, with a strong emphasis on etiquette. For men, a shirt and tie (or shirt jacket) would be appropriate wear, for women a blazer and pants or skirt.

## TECHNICAL REQUIREMENTS

Throughout the country you will find a mix of 110, 120, and 240 voltage. Check with the location where you are undertaking your training. Surge protection for electrical equipment is important. If you are delivering training at the community level or in the hinterland, electrical supply may be limited or unavailable. Check it out or use flip charts.

Do not expect Internet accessibility. You can check to see whether it is available, but have alternative hard copy examples as handouts.

## ACCOMMODATIONS

Tourist facilities are not developed, except for hotels in the capital city of Georgetown and a limited number of eco-resorts. The vast majority of the Guyanese live along the coast and the interior of the country is largely unpopulated and undeveloped. Travel in the interior of Guyana can be difficult; many interior regions can only be reached by plane or boat.

Hotels in Georgetown can easily be booked through Expedia and Travelocity, which show photos and customer ratings.

Phone access number is 159 (www.att.com/traveler)

Creole, Chinese, Indian, and international restaurants are available. Dress code is casual.

## GETTING AROUND

Taxis can be used in Georgetown. Buses can be used for transport throughout the country. Avoid walking alone.

Pick-pocketing, purse snatching, assault, and theft occur in all areas of Georgetown, so watch your personal belongings at all times.

## THE PEOPLE

The people are very friendly and personable. They are also very open to learning and are very well-versed when it comes to world issues.

Jennifer Britton (Potentials Realized) lived and worked in Guyana for a six-year period and had the privilege of working throughout the length and breadth of the country. There are significant distinctions between the capital, coastland communities (where approximately 85 percent of Guyanese live), and locations in the hinterland. Given the diversity of the country and the range of training environments (governmental or community-based training), programs will look different and be structured differently. Wherever possible, connect with local counterparts to get more information on the location and what's worked well in past training initiatives. Try to bring as much as you can with you, in terms of personal supplies, as shopping can be limited to local markets.

Primary religions are Christianity and Hinduism.

Guyanese cuisine has many similarities to that of the rest of the Caribbean. The food is diverse and includes dishes such as chicken curry, roti, and cookup rice (a style of rice with different kinds of vegetables accompanied by chicken, beef, or fish). The food reflects the ethnic makeup of the country and its colonial history and includes dishes from the Africans and creoles, East Indians, Amerindians, Chinese, and Europeans (mostly British and Portuguese).

The major sports in Guyana are cricket (Guyana is part of the West Indies as defined for international cricket purposes), softball cricket (beach cricket), and football.

The main economic activities in Guyana are agriculture (producing rice and Demerara sugar), bauxite mining, gold mining, timber, shrimp fishing and mineral mining. The sugar industry, which accounts for 28 percent of all export earnings, is largely run by Guysuco, which employs more people than any other industry. Many industries have a large foreign investment. The mineral industry, for example, is heavily invested in by the American company Reynolds Metals and the Canadian Alcan. The Korean/Malaysian Barama Company has a large stake in the logging industry.

*Guyana* is an Amerindian word meaning "Land of many waters." The country can be characterized by its vast rain forests dissected by numerous rivers, creeks, and waterfalls.

Population of around 749,970 persons live in Guyana.

Guyana has 83,000 square miles and is located on the northeast shoulder of the South American continent. There are distinct areas—the coastal belt, the forested and mountainous area, hilly, sand, and clay and the savannah zone. Guyana is notable for its mighty rivers, the three most important being the Demerara, Berbice, and the Essequibo.

Guyana is a representative democratic republic, where the president of Guyana is the head of government. Executive authority is exercised by the president, who appoints and supervises the prime minister and other ministers. The president is not directly elected; each party presenting a slate of candidates for the assembly must designate in advance a leader who will become president if that party receives the largest number of votes.

### ‖‖‖ PREPARATION

The training can be conducted in English. The materials do not need to be translated.

Average temperature ranges from between 75 to 87 degrees F, so bring professional but comfortable clothing.

## THE PRESENTATION

The techniques that work best with this audience are mini-lecture, small group work, and group presentations.

The most wonderful surprise is how friendly Guyanese are.

**Helpful websites and references include:**

- http://travel.excite.co.uk/travel/guides/south_america/guyana/Currency
- http://travel.state.gov/travel/cis_pa_tw/cis/cis_1133.html
- www.caribbeantravel.com/destinations_guyana.asp
- www.caricom.org/jsp/community/member_states.jsp?menu=community

# chapter THIRTY-FIVE

# Mexico

**M**usic, colorful costumes, food, and crafts immediately come to mind when one thinks of Mexico. The vitality, energy, and love of life are so evident when speaking with Mexicans. One gets the feeling that everyone is welcome and all are family. It seems that there is always some type of celebration just beginning, whether it is a holiday, baptism, wedding, anniversary, or just a get-together of people. Here is what to expect and tips for success when training, teaching, and presenting to the people in Mexico.

## ??? THE REQUEST

For a session or presentation that has been requested for Mexico, the best location will be a hotel in Mexico City, Guadalajara, or Monterrey. These are the three major cities that would be the most likely location of a training program or presentation.

Working with the requester of the program, you should confirm the dates, times, locations, and objectives for the program.

## • • • GETTING THERE

You will need a valid passport to enter Mexico. Check www.cibt.com for any changes to visa requirements. Check the travel website www.travel.state.gov for current document requirements, health, safety, and travel tips. You can arrive by plane or car. Check with your local travel agent as well as online at Expedia (www.expedia.com) and Travelocity (www.travelocity.com) sites for the best travel options within your time frame and budget.

Mexico City, Guadalajara, and Monterrey are on Central Standard Time (same time as Chicago, +1 for New York and +6 for London).

Mexico charges an airport tax on all departures. Passengers leaving the country on international flights pay in dollars or the peso equivalent. It has become a common practice to include this departure tax in your ticket price, but double-check to make sure so you're not caught by surprise at the airport.

Mexico charges a "tourism tax." Your ticket price may not include it, so be sure to have enough money to pay it at the airport upon departure.

It is very important to be aware of celebrations and holidays that might affect the timing and atmosphere of your program. Some official holidays may result in difficulty traveling, as well as being unable to begin training:

- January 1: Año Nuevo (New Year's Day) is an official Mexican holiday.
- January 6: Día de los Santos Reyes is the day when Mexicans exchange Christmas presents. This day culminates the Christmastime festivities.
- January 17: Feast Day of de San Antonio de Abad or Blessing of the Animals.
- February 2: Día de la Candelaria or Candlemas, best seen in: San Juan de los Lagos, Jalapa; Talpa de Allende, Jalisco; and Santa Maria del Tuxla, Oaxaca.
- February (movable holiday): Carnaval is a five-day celebration before the Catholic Lent. Port towns such as Ensenada, La Paz, Mazatlán, and Veracruz are excellent places to watch Carnaval festivities.
- February 5: Día de la Constitución an official holiday that commemorates Mexico's Constitution.
- February 24: Flag Day.
- March 19: St. Joseph's Day, Día de San José
- March 21: the birthday of Benito Juárez
- April: Semana Santa, Holy Week from Palm to Easter Sunday
- May 1: Primero de Mayo
- May 3: Holy Cross Day Día de la Santa Cruz,
- May 5: Cinco de Mayo
- May 10: Mother's Day
- June 1: Navy Day
- June 24: Saint John the Baptist Day

- June 29: Fiesta of Saint Peter and Saint Paul

- September 1: Annual State of the Union

- September 16: Mexican Independence Day

- October 12: Día de la Raza

- November 1 and 2: Día de los Muertos

- November 20: Revolution Day

- December 12: Día de Nuestra Señora de Guadalupe or the day of the Virgin of Guadalupe

- December 16 through January 6: Las Posadas

- December 25: Navidad

## PROGRAM DESIGN

It is important that trainers, teachers, and presenters be aware of the culture. The program slides and materials should be in Mexican Spanish because many participants may not speak English well enough to understand the content. Role plays, case studies, and PowerPoint presentations all work fine in the training sessions.

Make sure to design the program to allow for translation time so you will not have a program that seems rushed. The pace in Mexico is not always as fast as in other places, so allow for ways to not speed through the program content. This may mean designing handouts and job aids that need no explanation, just in case you do not have the time to review all of them.

Soccer is a commonly loved sport, so examples or case studies can be created around the love of the sport in Mexico.

Family and holidays are also unifying characteristics of the Mexican culture, so these can be used a positive examples of common activities or visuals when designing a program.

Bullfighting and baseball are additional interests for some.

## LOGISTICS

In addition to mailing the materials for your program, it is good to bring them with you (one hard copy each of both English and Spanish translation handouts and presentations), as well as electronic copies of the presentation. Make arrangements with your host for any equipment that is needed.

The currency is the Mexican peso. Try to exchange a small amount of money ahead of your arrival to pay for transportation to your hotel. *Casas de cambio* (exchange houses) are generally more convenient than banks because they have more locations and longer hours; the rate of exchange may be the same as at a bank or slightly lower. Before leaving a bank or exchange-house window, count your change in front of the teller before the next client steps up. Keep small bills because small bills and coins are not easy to get and large bills are hard to cash. $1 bills are convenient for tipping.

## PROGRAM DELIVERY

Estela Sasson (Mexican Consulate) makes a few recommendations for the success of your program: Don't use clichés such as "siesta time" or negative references to the Mexican people. Many Mexicans feel inferior because they have been conquered and/or abused by other countries' militaries, such as the Spaniards and Americans. There is a long history here that must be respected and we need to be very sensitive to the pain these people have felt at the hands of others. They appreciate understanding of their culture and history as well as respect for their people. Acknowledge all good things. Acknowledge the difficulties they have.

Role plays, case studies, and PowerPoint presentations all work fine in the training sessions. If there is any physical contact during activities, you should separate the men from the women and not intermix them. Mexican men are typically known to be macho and jealous when it comes to women.

Any educational program should involve lots of food, eating, and socializing. Short presentations work well if held over lunch at a restaurant.

## TECHNICAL REQUIREMENTS

Mexico uses 120V two-prong plugs. Be sure to bring voltage converters, plugs, and backup systems to use if needed. Bring your program on an electronic storage device, send it to your host ahead of time, hand carry hard copies of translated Mexican Spanish and English versions of handouts. Bring videotapes (NTSC format) or DVDs that are already subtitled in Mexican Spanish. If you bring your computer, you can request a projector to be available and set up in your presentation room.

Check with your location for availability of internet access if you will need it for your presentation.

## ACCOMMODATIONS

Expedia provides travelers' reviews that are helpful in choosing your accommodations in Mexico City and Monterrey at www.expedia.com. Travelocity provides customer reviews and hotel photos for Guadalajara at www.travelocity.com. Security is important. Use common sense when traveling. If possible, travel with others. Don't look like a tourist (no sneakers). Be cautious but confident. Always be safe by drinking bottled or filtered water.

## GETTING AROUND

A taxi is likely to be your best form of transportation. Have your hotel call a secure taxi company to arrange your travel. Have your hotel write the destination on a piece of paper in Spanish so you can show it to your driver. Make sure to take a hotel card that has the name and address of the hotel, so you can show it to your taxi driver for your return. Keep the name and number of the secure taxi company to call for your return. It can be dangerous to hail a taxi and it leaves you open to robbery and kidnapping.

Watch your valuables and do not show large amounts of money. These only provide temptations and opportunities in a very poor country.

## THE PEOPLE

The Mexican people are typically very friendly, open, smiling, trusting, accepting, passive, and eager to be of service.

The population is stratified into upper class, middle class, and lower class. The richest people have bodyguards. Understand that the Mexican people do not feel safe and protected by their government officials or representatives who are supposed to protect them.

The Mexican people are used to being paid less and not valued. Labor is cheap and not protected by unions or laws. There is a huge youth population who are very eager to work. Often employers will have three people employed to do one job. Corruption and bribery have caused mistrust. There are no social institutions to help the poor. There are plenty of universities and small industries.

Mexico has many people, tasty food, huge markets, weather that is fantastic, and friendly people. You will see begging in the streets because there is so much poverty. Crime is a part of life because there are few jobs and they do not pay much. Some Mexicans do not like Americans because they took Mexican territory. Others may feel that all their ills are because of the Americans. The government does not stop this kind of thinking because it benefits them. The Mexican people do benefit from the tourists who come to their country and many wish they could live in America because of the work available there.

Mexico is a republic with two legislative houses; its chief of state and head of government is the elected president.

Mexico has no official religion, but most of the people in Mexico say that they are Roman Catholic. It is the nation with the second-largest Catholic population, after Brazil and before the United States.

Industries include the automobile industry, petrochemicals, cement and construction, textiles, food and beverages, mining, consumer durables, and tourism.

At least three great civilizations—the Mayas, the Olmecs, and later the Toltecs—preceded the wealthy Aztec empire, conquered in 1519 to 1521 by the Spanish under Hernando Cortés. Spain ruled Mexico as part of the viceroyalty of New Spain for the next 300 years until September 16, 1810, when the Mexicans first revolted. They won independence in 1821. From 1821 to 1877, there were two emperors, several dictators, and enough presidents and provisional executives to make a new government on the average of every nine months.

The years after the fall of the dictator Porfirio Diaz (1877 to 1880 and 1884 to 1911) were marked by bloody political-military strife and trouble with the United States, culminating in the punitive U.S. expedition into northern Mexico (1916 and 1917) in unsuccessful pursuit of the revolutionary Pancho Villa. Since a brief civil war in 1920, Mexico has enjoyed a period of gradual agricultural, political, and social reforms.

Following World War II, the government emphasized economic growth.

## ‼️ PREPARATION

You will be encouraged to dress casually to be comfortable. It is still important to dress professionally and show confidence. Avoid any behavior that implies arrogance.

Find out whether there is someone who can review your materials ahead of time, for anything that is inadvertently offensive or overly confusing. Bring overhead transparencies in case the laptop does not work. Carry your presentation, transparencies, a hard copy of the handouts, and your laptop with you instead of checking anything with your luggage, just in case.

Try to get an agreement that someone in the class will alert you to any gestures or parts of your presentation that may be confusing or offensive.

Here are some useful words and phrases to learn:

| English | Pronunciation | Spanish |
|---------|---------------|---------|
| Hi | O-la | "Hola" |
| To introduce | Present-are | "Presentar" |
| To introduce oneself | Present-are-say | "Presentarse" |
| How's it going? | Comb-o tay vah | "¿Cómo te va?" |
| Pleased to meet you (male) | N-cahn-ta-doh | "Encantado" |
| Pleased to meet you (female) | N-cahn-ta-da | "Encantada" |
| It's nice to meet you | Moo-cho goo-sto | "Mucho gusto" |
| How are you? | Kay tall | "¿Qué tal?" |
| What's up? | Kay pah-sa | "¿Qué pasa?" |
| Excuse me | Cone pear-me-so | "Con permiso" |
| I'm sorry | Low sea-n-toe | "Lo siento" |
| Thank you | Grah-syas | "Gracias" |
| See you Soon | Ah-stah prawn-toe | "Hasta pronto" |
| See you later | No-s ve-mo-s | "Nos vemos" |
| See you tomorrow | Ah-stah mahn-yahn-ah | "Hasta mañana" |
| Good-bye | Ah-dee-oh-s | "Adiós" |

## THE PRESENTATION

Julie Ponce teaches English to Mexicans and tells us that you have to be lighthearted, able to joke around, and yet very respectful. The people are very sensitive that other cultures tend to "blow them off."

Presentations will most likely be in a conference room. The sessions could also be held at a company or organization office location, and a less likely location would be a university (unless it is a scientific, political, or engineering topic).

Avoid using slang or acronyms that are not clearly defined when you present. Speak very slowly and enunciate your words so they can be understood and translated. Use simple sentence structure. Don't assume that you have been understood. Be very careful of body language and gestures. Be aware of any funny looks or uncomfortable silences from your audience. Humor doesn't always work. There are too many differences in interpretation, wording, and understanding.

Show the participants that you are genuinely interested in their families, them, and their lives. Talk around the issue before you start being direct. Establishing the relationship and valuing them as people are very important.

When correcting students, you must say something good first and be very gentle and calm. There should be no raised voices or confrontation at all. They would sooner not give their opinions, evaluations, or complaints. They will not contribute at all if they interpret a comment as being a direct affront or feel that they have been shot down in a disrespectful manner. Usually, you will never know that you slighted them, but you will lose them.

It is very important that you do not come across as ignorant about their culture or act as though you are superior. Having respect is considered a basic human right.

In short: Be calmer, gentler, warm up to them, have a relaxed way of doing things, and be friendly. They will respond well to all of these behaviors.

**Helpful websites and references include:**

- www.cibt.com
- www.expedia.com
- www.infoplease.com
- www.travelocity.com
- www.travel.state.gov

# The United States

The Statue of Liberty in New York Harbor's plaque reads: "Give me your tired, your poor. . . . " This is the symbol and gift from the French that has greeted millions of immigrants to the United States. These immigrants have left their home countries in pursuit of freedom and a better life for themselves and their families. The streets are not "paved with gold," as some believed when they traveled to the United States, but this is the "land of opportunity" where even the poorest people can work hard and achieve success.

Here is what to expect and tips for success when training, teaching, and presenting throughout the United States of America (USA).

## ??? THE REQUEST

The request for a program to be conducted in the United States might come from any of a variety of organizations, universities, or government. There are so many possible locations that it would be difficult to list them here, so we will cover some of the more common locations and regions of this enormous country. We will cover regions of the country such as New England, the Midwest, the South, and the West Coast, as well as some of the major states and cities such as New York City, Boston, Chicago, Orlando, Florida, Los Angeles, Atlanta, and Dallas, where a program is most likely to be held.

## • • • GETTING THERE

A valid passport is required to enter the United States from other countries. Visa and entry requirements should be checked and completed at www.us.gov. U.S. locations are often accessed by plane, train, or car. A car can be easily rented at the airport with a good map and directions to your destination. Some large cities have good public transportation, but Americans love their cars and, that is the most common form of transport. Check to see whether your hotel has a shuttle from the airport when you make reservations. Ask how much it will cost for your transport to the hotel and be prepared to tip the driver 15 to 20 percent of your fare, in U.S. dollars. If the hotel does not have a shuttle, you can take a taxi, which will be waiting outside of the airport for people to take. Ask approximately how much it will cost to go to your hotel, so you can be prepared with the payment and tip. Most taxis have meters that you can watch to see how much it will cost. There is often a charge for luggage, so ask how much that will be, as well.

The United States uses nine standard time zones. From east to west they are Atlantic Standard Time (AST), Eastern Standard Time (EST), Central Standard Time (CST), Mountain Standard Time (MST), Pacific Standard Time (PST), Alaskan Standard Time (AST), Hawaii-Aleutian Standard Time (HST), Samoa Standard Time (UTC-11), and Chamorro Standard Time (UTC + 10).

- Eastern time zone locations include New York, Boston, Atlanta, and Orlando = GMT/UTC – 5 hours EST, or – 4 hours EDT.

- Central time zone locations include Chicago and Dallas = GMT/UTC – 6 hours CST, – 5 hours CDT.

- Mountain time zone locations include Phoenix and Denver = GMT/UTC – 7, – 6 MDT (except for Arizona).

- Pacific time zone locations include Los Angeles and San Francisco = GMT/UTC – 8 hours, – 7 PDT.

In areas of the United States that observe Daylight Saving Time (DST), local residents will move their clocks ahead one hour when Daylight Saving Time begins. As a result, their UTC or GMT offset would change from UTC – 5h or GMT – 5h to UTC – 4h or GMT – 4h. In places not observing Daylight Saving Time, the local UTC or GMT offset will remain the same year-round. Arizona, Puerto Rico, Hawaii, the U.S. Virgin Islands, and American Samoa do not observe Daylight Saving Time.

Holidays when government offices and many businesses are closed include:

- January 1: New Year's Day

- Third Monday in January: Martin Luther King's Day

- January 20: Inauguration Day, every forth year, after the presidential election

- Third Monday in February: President's Day

- Last Monday in May: Memorial Day

- July 4: Independence Day

- First Monday in September: Labor Day

- Second Monday in October: Columbus Day

- November 11: Veterans' Day

- Fourth Thursday in November: Thanksgiving

- December 25: Christmas

Check the weather report for a week before you leave for your destination to determine what to pack at www.weather.com/. The weather varies so much by location that it is always good to check ahead of time to be prepared.

## PROGRAM DESIGN

The program can be designed and delivered in English. Spanish is spoken, especially in the Southwest and some southern states as well. If you are teaching in an area that has a majority of Spanish-speaking participants, you can have a translation available, but it is not typically expected. Check this ahead of time with your hosts.

Most Americans like to be entertained. They are used to Hollywood movies, computer games, large-screen presentations, and active learning. The more you can get them to get up and move around, the better. Although much of the early education is lecture, it does not keep people's attention. Define and gain agreement on the specific program objectives with your host or requester. Once these have been confirmed, design the program around each objective, asking yourself: "What is the best way to achieve this objective?" If people have to learn a skill, you should demonstrate and then require them to perform the skill, with feedback provided. If the participants are to learn how to explain something, design the presentation with vivid memory joggers such as photos and graphics that will be remembered easily. Include a variety of activities in the program that require active participation. Design an evaluation that is appropriate to the hosts' requirements. Case studies, role plays, competitive games, and small group discussion all work well with most U.S. audiences. If computer training is required, make sure that you show the actual application, not just screen captures, to keep people's attention; and have at least one computer per every two students for them to practice the software application.

There are some regional differences that could be considered in your program design. Many people from New England are more likely to be introverted and those from the Mid-Atlantic region may not be very talkative, so you may want to build in opportunities to discuss in small groups and not require people to ask questions in a larger group. Instead you could have them write questions and submit them for a response. New Englanders are often more reserved than Californians, for example. You will likely find New Yorkers to be very direct communicators. In the South and Northwest, paces may be slower and more relaxed than the fast pace of the urban Northeast. People from Texas, Oklahoma, Arkansas, and Louisiana are known to like visiting their neighbors and friends and likely do it more than people from other parts of the country. Pacific Coast residents are often more isolated from friends and relatives because of the distance between them, so any examples you give should take these sensitivities and characteristics into consideration. (Anderson, Lustig, & Andersen, 1987). Here are some regional points of interest:

- Atlanta, Georgia, is the site of global corporations such as Coca-Cola and Delta Airlines, CNN, plus the Centers for Disease Control and CARE.
- Charlotte, South Carolina, is the center of a new southern industrial belt of manufacturing and banking.
- Miami, Florida, has a large immigrant population of Hispanic and Caribbean people from Cuba, Haiti, and Latin America, so there are many Spanish-speaking people there. Orlando is a common tourist destination (Disney World).
- Texas and the Southwest are heavily involved in oil production and have many ties to Mexico.
- Los Angeles and Southern California have an ethnically diverse immigrant community; provide ports for global trade, plus centers of the entertainment and tourist industries.
- San Francisco is considered the capital of the world's high-tech industry.
- Seattle, Washington, is the site of Starbucks and Microsoft companies.
- New York is the largest point of entry of immigrants from many countries and is ethnically diverse.
- Boston, Massachusetts, contains much of the original history of the country and is made up of many small neighborhoods.
- Chicago, Illinois, is the third-largest city in the United States.
- Washington, D.C., is the seat of government.

These are some of the characteristics that influence each of the major locations and their people. Examples from and awareness of these can show that the trainer, teacher, or presenter has done his or her homework. Searching for the current news of the city you will be in ahead of time will help you to make comments regarding what the local sports team is doing, what the weather is like, and some of the daily interests of the citizens of the city. This shows you are interested in the things that are affecting the participants and will be appreciated by them.

## LOGISTICS

You can easily send your presentation electronically to your hosts and ask them to pre-load their computer- and ensure that it works with a projector. Hard copy materials can easily be shipped to any location. Bring one hard copy with you in case you need to make additional copies at a local store such as Kinko's or Staples. Save your presentation on an electronic storage device that can be plugged into any computer. This will enable you to travel light and not have to bring a computer, projector, or extension cords. Call or email to double-check that everything has been received and will be set up, double-checked, and working for your arrival.

The currency is the US $1. Coins most commonly come in denominations of 1, 5, 10, and 25 cents. Dollars most commonly come in denominations of $1, $5, $10, $20, $50, and $100 bills.

## PROGRAM DELIVERY

Role plays, case studies, and PowerPoint presentations all typically work fine in training sessions. If you are showing a computer application, make sure that there is at least one computer for every two students to practice exercises as you present. It is critical that the software that you will be showing has been loaded onto all of the computers and has been tested before you begin the program. This assures that there will not be a lot of time lost that should be used for training. Allow an hour break for lunch. The program can start as early as 8 A.M. and last until 5 P.M. If homework is given, you can not always count on it being completed as expected. Many people may drive from one to two hours away or take a train, so it is best not to end the program too late.

## TECHNICAL REQUIREMENTS

It is best to work with the technicians at the location of your presentation. They can make sure that all technical aspects are covered and check to see whether microphones or specific projection devices are required. Videotape format is NTSC. Most computers will also support DVD in addition to CDs. If the program will be videotaped, your approval should be requested ahead of time. All of the United States uses 110/120 volt outlets. Plugs should be two- or three-pronged. Make sure you have brought an extension cord, just in case you need it to reach an outlet. Some locations will be equipped for wireless that can be used if you have a wireless card in your computer. Most locations will be able to provide a computer and projector, so you will only need to bring your program on a storage device. Check to ensure that the equipment is provided and working ahead of time. Send your program to your host ahead of time, as a backup precaution. If you are wearing a microphone, be sure to turn it off when visiting the rest room or having private conversation. This is easy to forget.

Internet accessibility is widespread.

## ACCOMMODATIONS

Hotels are very good accommodations and so are bed and breakfasts (B&Bs). These are readily available online using Expedia (www.expedia.com) or Travelocity (www.travelocity .com). Security is not a large problem, but if you are in the city, you should use common sense, such as keeping valuables out of sight and only walking where it is well lit and where there are a lot of other people are around. The water is safe to drink and food is excellent and should not cause any intestinal problems, as in some other countries. All of your typical presentation needs can be provided by the hotel, such as equipment and refreshments, if prearranged.

## GETTING AROUND

The car is used by the majority of people from the United States. Taxis are most often available in the cities. You can ask approximately how much it will cost and how long it should take to reach your destination. Most taxi drivers should be able to give you that information. Most taxis will have meters, so you can see how much it will cost. Have U.S. dollars available to pay taxi, bus, or train fares. A tip is expected for a taxi ride of 15 to 20 percent. In some large cities, trains, subways, buses, and streetcars are available, but this is not as common as one would think.

Most people from the United States are very friendly and talkative. You can ask anyone on the street for help. Some will be more helpful than others. Have a map that will help them to help you find your location.

Most major cities have at least one major form of transportation in addition to taxis, cars, and buses. New York City has the subway. Boston has the **T**. Chicago has the **L**.

Dallas has the DART bus, trolley, and rail system. Los Angeles and Orlando have no public transportation that go for any long distance, so you will need to rent a car to get around.

## THE PEOPLE

Most Americans like to talk and laugh unless they are in a hurry. If you see someone acting as if he or she is in a hurry, it is best to not stop the person to ask questions.

They love to eat and will be very happy to tell you about good places to eat or go out. They typically love to give their opinions freely. Many U.S. citizens are not very worried about criticizing their own government (especially in larger cities, more likely in the North than the South), but they are quite proud of their heritage and history. Do not expect them to know much about it though. They are not like the people of some countries who have memorized everything about their countries. Most Americans will have to look up information instead of trying to remember it all.

As with any culture, history shapes much of what people like and what they are sensitive to. When North America was discovered, Indigenous American tribes spoke thousands of different languages. Europeans came as immigrants and established some of the regional cultures that can be seen today. Puritans came from eastern England to Massachusetts. Quakers from England's north midlands and Wales settled in the Delaware Valley. Settlers came from Northern Ireland, Scotland, and Northern England to Appalachia. After that, immigrants have come from every country in the world and often establish communities in large cities or rural areas that continue to keep their language, food, and customs active in daily life. There is an amazing diversity of cultures that is evident, especially in large cities, but each person still responds to memories of growing up in his or her own particular culture, especially around holidays, when many may travel across the country to be with family.

The courage and motivation that immigrants had to have to leave their countries, families, and friends and travel across the ocean to an unknown land is still evident in the rugged individualism that is seen in American behaviors, politics, and media. There is a strong belief that individuals should be self-motivated to set their own goals and achieve them independently. These beliefs include that individuals have the power to determine their own destiny rather than favoring group decisions or having someone else decide for them. This is, of course, very different from Asian cultures.

The legal system promises equal treatment to all, but evidence does not always bear this out in action, especially for people of color and women. Great strides have been made and every day brings some bright advance for individuals who have been struggling to be recognized.

People often conform to what is "in" regarding fashion, technology, and tastes. There is a strong faith in the scientific method of solving problems. Events are seen to have causes rather than being random. Causes are studied. Objectivity, empirical evidence and facts are valued and expected. Science and technology are strong influences and persuaders.

People from the United States are known for their materialism and belief that possessions are important in life. People are encouraged to buy things through the heavy marketing in the media, and they see work as a means to buy more things. This system encourages high turnover, disposability, and "super-sizing" (getting food and drink in a larger size).

One's identity is defined by his or her occupation. Work is very serious and competitive, and is separated from play, which has spawned a large recreation industry. High value is placed on efficiency and practicality. Time is money. Expectations are that products and services should be provided quickly, accurately, and politely.

Change is good and there is a continuing faith in the future. New things are readily accepted, but changing practices and locations take time and persuasion. Consistent with the belief in the scientific method, there is a belief that humans are rational and they act on the basis of reason (Jandt, 2004).

These are some of the characteristics of this population that the trainer, teacher, or presenter can be aware of and use in examples that can enhance the learning process.

## !!! PREPARATION

Dress professionally and show confidence.

Many Americans respect expertise more than age or seniority.

Ask often whether anyone has comments or examples for what you are presenting. Americans like to be engaged in active dialogue about a topic and are not shy about giving their opinions.

Build in breaks at least every two hours. They will enjoy coffee, soda, and snacks any time during the day or evening.

Weather in the United States varies from snow and cold in New York and Chicago to hot and dry in Los Angeles and Dallas, and hot and humid in Atlanta. Check the weather a week before you go and follow it to make sure you are bringing clothes that will be comfortable for the weather.

Check how the local football (fall/winter), basketball (winter), baseball (spring/summer) team is doing so you can use this in conversation or as examples in class.

## THE PRESENTATION

The most common venues would be office conference or training rooms or hotel conference rooms. The presentation will most likely be in a conference room. Explain any acronyms or technical terms that you use during your presentation. Provide a glossary if there are a lot of unfamiliar terms or concepts to be covered.

Americans do not like lectures and typically lose interest quickly if they are not asked to be involved in some way. Easels with newsprint or whiteboards are often used to write, demonstrate, and record information. Good activities include pairs, trios, group practices, and competitive games. Participants are willing to experiment and learn. Ask for people's experience and opinions as often as possible. This can be done by providing a round table or small group set up, periodically including exercises that require the participants to discuss a topic, list key points on an easel page, and then share a comment from the group with the large group. Americans love competitive games, so you can include an activity that requires them to remember key points and compete as a team against the other tables of participants. If you have small (surprise) prizes such as candy, cookies, pens, magnets, or gift certificates, they will be more motivated to compete. They do not like role plays very much, but will do them if they are learning and practicing skills such as interviewing or conflict resolution.

The participants will like to be praised for good performance. It works well if they receive small rewards (books, mugs, mouse pads) for successfully participating in activities. Humor works well. Check it before you use it with someone who can give you an honest reaction to the joke. Keep people moving around as much as possible. This can even include counting off and regrouping for activities (each person takes a number from 1 to 4, then the 1s are matched with other 1s and so on). Good videos are typically well accepted, as long as they are obviously connected to the topic being discussed. "How to" videos and demonstrations are often welcomed by the participants. They like case studies that they can discuss and then get some feedback regarding their recommendations.

People from the United States are familiar with evaluation and feedback. Although they may not like them very much, they are used to tests, quizzes, and critiques. They do expect to be able to provide feedback regarding the program they have participated in and are usually ready to give their opinions about anything. Most participants are not worried or cautious about asking questions and carrying on discussions, practice, and performance of tasks. It is important to not embarrass anyone or force their participation if they decline.

Follow-up of a program or presentation is greatly appreciated. Even an email or newsletter reminds them of their participation in the program with some key points for them to practice and reinforce their learning. Most participants appreciate it if you provide additional resources that can be recommended for further study.

**Helpful websites and references include:**

- Anderson, P.A., Lustig, M.W., & Anderson, J.F. (1987). Dominant U.S. cultural patterns. *Communication Monographs, 54, 128–144.*

- www.timetemperature.com/tzus/gmt_.shtml

- www.time-for-time.com/zonesus.htm

- www.us.gov

- www.weather.com/

**PART SEVEN**

# Conclusion

# Human Resource Development Around the Globe*

Three-year-old Liu Xiao had never seen a foreigner up close. On February 5, a tall, blonde, blue-eyed stranger greeted her as she arrived home from preschool. With my limited Chinese vocabulary, I said, "Ni Hao, Wa ei ni" as we met. My "Hello, I love you" was welcomed by the only English Liu Xiao knew. With shrieks and laughter, she ran around the room shouting, "Happy Birthday to you!" Experiencing Chinese culture first-hand and developing "guanxi" (the Chinese word for "relationships") was an unexpected and wonderful benefit of my business trip to China, where I had gone to deliver a train-the-trainer course in human resource development.

Globalization is a hot topic of discussion among many HRD professionals. Whether it is concerns about outsourcing the HR function, off shoring jobs, takeovers from a global giant or an organization's expansion into developing corners of the world an HRD professional can no longer deny their need for global knowledge. How comfortable you are with globalization inevitability may depend on the organization you are with, how familiar you are with globally diverse business cultures, how well you can adapt to the

*Reprinted with permission of Donna Steffey, President of Vital Signs Training

global marketplace, and how well you are able to conduct training and development with international business partners.

Whether you work as part of a multinational organization or as an independent consultant, you will probably soon be dealing with global issues. In the emerging borderless economy, cultural barriers are presenting both new challenges and new opportunities for HRD professionals. The marketplace is becoming increasingly diverse, and business is undergoing a major transformation. As these changes occur, we need cultural as well as business information to prepare our corporate partners and ourselves for the journey ahead.

As HRD specialists, our calling is becoming broader than human resource development. We have an opportunity to create collaborative relationships to foster international understanding and respect in a multicultural world. While national governments have the primary responsibility for maintaining peace, they are limited in what they can actually do to ensure a peaceful world. Individuals and organizations can make tremendous contributions through their actions abroad. Two years ago I was part of an all volunteer training team that went to East Africa to deliver train-the-trainer courses to NGO directors so they could educate widows and teen orphans on how to run small business. I was also part of a training team in China on September 11, 2001. I saw first-hand how a practitioner could make a global difference. Many of our participants had never met an American before our training. When the buildings fell, we cried together. They saw our grief. They had grown to know our training team and could put a face on the buildings that had fallen thousands of miles away in a country that was formally "foreign" to them.

Our goal can be to increase our ability to think and act in culturally respectful ways. It is a starting point in our quest for knowledge about international HRD best practices and challenges. We can learn about regional and global trends affecting international business development and, therefore, human resource development. We can read about cultural differences and suggestions on how to prepare ourselves for business abroad—including how to avoid being "The Ugly American." We can discover more about diverse global regions, their national challenges, cultural differences, and HR practices. So grab your suitcase and your passport and let's start our learning journey.

## GLOBAL BUSINESS TRENDS

Globalization is defined by the World Bank Group as "the growing integration of economies and societies around the world." Over the past two decades, there has been a far-reaching move toward capitalism and consumerism around the globe. With the proliferation and convenience of modern technology and the systematic erosion of trade barriers, many companies have developed a global presence—in spite of fluxes in the U.S. and world economies.

Many U.S. corporations have turned to cheap labor in developing countries to keep prices and expenses in line. As a result, a tsunami of U.S. jobs has swept onto foreign shores. While the United States has tried to discourage companies from outsourcing to lower-cost locales such as China and India, the economics of "offshoring" may just be too powerful for business to resist. Human resource departments will have to be able to manage a more cross-cultural, diverse, and foreign workforce as this trend continues.

One challenge of globalization is waiting for the building of infrastructures, including electricity, roads, and phone lines in developing countries. Beyond this, it is likely that sporadic backlashes against globalization, language barriers, high illiteracy rates, environmental concerns, and clashing social norms will present even greater challenges.

According to researchers, other trends that will present challenges during globalization include:

- *Baby Boomers Retire:* The baby boomer retirements in the United States, Europe, Canada, China, and elsewhere where aging populations exist will have a great impact on the workforce over the next decade. Organizations need succession plans to handle the exodus of workers and their knowledge.

- *Young Populations:* By the year 2015 there will be three billion people worldwide, with 550 million from India alone, under the age of twenty-five. We need plans in place to develop that group of human resources (World Bank News & Broadcast, 2003).

- *Growth of Developing Countries:* Developing countries are projected to grow at twice the rate of developed countries. Many will need help to build the gap between rich and poor—usually meaning educated and uneducated (World Bank News & Broadcast, 2003).

- *Technology:* The spread of technology has boosted economic growth in developing countries. "Any business that does not require physical presence can be co-sourced," says Azim Premji, CEO of Wipro, one of India's largest companies. According to the International Monetary Fund chief economist, technology also helps widen the gap between rich and poor.

- *China's Growth:* China's economy is likely to continue to grow in ranking to the second-largest economy by the year 2020. It is expected to continue to grow at a rate of 7 to 9 percent per year. China needs a growth rate of at least 8 percent to provide jobs for the millions joining the workforce each year. Fear of worker unrest is a big concern. China also has retirement concerns. There are three hundred million baby boomers, yet only 5 percent have guaranteed medical benefits. (*T&D* magazine, 2006; India and China Inc. "High-Flying Dragons in China, by Alice Law)

- *Ethnic Conflicts:* The number and intensity of ethnic conflicts will increase and continue worldwide as terrorism continues.

- *Economics Versus Environmentalism:* As economic development expands globally, pollution, deforestation, and global warming will hasten, causing more political conflicts.

Given all these challenges, the role of human resource development must change. We will need to build and develop the capabilities of the organization to thrive amid these global issues, rather than simply reacting to more traditional issues such as performance management, class size, blended learning approaches, and even ROI—and we have to do it in a culturally responsive way. An HR system that is common practice in your country may be considered offensive in another. Differences in employment laws, compensation packages, job security, and learning styles are just a few examples of what an HR professional might face working globally versus locally.

Learning and teaching styles differ among cultures as well as individuals. For example, the entertaining instructional style of the U.S. facilitator does not find a receptive audience in many corners of the globe. A few years ago, I spent some time facilitating programs in the UK. The evaluations had a consistent message: "Too American." How could it be? I had changed all my business examples! It took me about a week to realize that it was my style and not my content that was "too American." By easing the British audience into my entertaining style rather than overwhelming them with it, they reacted more like frogs put into cool water instead of boiling water. They were able to bathe in the knowledge, as opposed to hopping out of the classroom, overwhelmed by my "Americanism."

The bottom line for multinational organizations—no matter where they're based—is the need for the development of globally literate leadership. New educational strategies are needed to cultivate global leaders. By helping leaders build core competencies for success in the global marketplace, we will become indispensable to businesses and surely give them the return on investment of training dollars that organizations are looking for.

## CULTURAL IMPACT ON HRD

"Culture is the collective programming of the mind which distinguishes the people of one category of people from another," says Geert Hofstede (Global Business Culture, 2002), a Dutch interculturalist. Each nation indoctrinates its members with a common array of behavioral norms that leads to sets of national behavioral characteristics. These characteristics permeate every aspect of life, including behavior in the workplace, and impact the way organizations do business.

When we look at individualism versus collectivism, for example, we know there is a difference between the East and the West (Sarkar-Barney, 2003). During every stage of education and "programming" in the West (Europe, the United States, Canada), people learn to accept personal responsibility and view themselves primarily as individuals. Conversely, at every stage of personal development in the East (Japan, China, Singapore), people learn to see themselves as small parts of a larger society and emphasize the importance of group agreement and a consensus approach.

Language often reflects cultural differences, even among nations that share a common language. When Donna Baylor of Transition Seminars taught in the UK, she referred to her purse as her "fanny pack." After a few days, someone finally informed her that she was using a dirty word. Cynthia Hernandez Kolski of Communication Education says that when she went to Mexico to teach stress management and communication skills, she had to be very careful with her communication. Even though she speaks Spanish, she realized that literal translations and conveying her intended meaning resulted in two very different messages.

Another important difference is how verbosely or concisely a particular culture speaks. In Italy, for example, the ability to speak well using a large volume of words is a sign of being intellectual. In other countries, however, being talkative is viewed differently, perhaps negatively; or it may even cause problems. Wei Xian Lin, my co-facilitator and translator while I was training in China, was interpreting a rather lengthy program for me. We were alarmed when we heard a loud thud. Not only had one of our participants fallen asleep, but he had actually fallen off his chair. He was out cold! In this case, my verbosity caused a potentially serious problem!

Culture influences approaches to everyday situations in the work environment in hundreds of ways. National characteristics play an important role in determining corporate strategies, incentive programs, personnel policies, and training strategies. It is dangerous to ignore these differences. Most organizations know they must invest the time and money to research government rules and regulations and regional market conditions, but in HRD, we sometimes make the mistake of thinking that "people are people" and will all learn effectively through the same learning materials as long as we change the examples. Or we may believe that we can use the same incentive programs overseas that work in the United States. In order to minimize the potential risks of working internationally, it is important to look first at the people and their culture to understand what drives and motivates them.

Before looking at specific regional characteristics, though, let's check ourselves and be sure that we are culturally and socially literate—seeing, thinking, and acting in culturally mindful ways.

## GET READY TO GO GLOBAL

Bags all packed, briefcase and passport in hand, we're ready to go. But are you aware of the "cultural" items in your suitcase that you are about to subconsciously communicate to your unsuspecting global partner? Chances are you aren't. Our culture is the paradigm through which we see the world, and unless we are conscious of it, we probably won't be able to really see and learn about the culture we are about to experience. For instance, what are some of our collective attitudes that sometimes cause locals to label us "Ugly Americans"?

1. Americans (people from the United States) believe in having control over their environment. Problems in one's life (such as poverty), they conclude, are due to laziness and an unwillingness to take responsibility and work harder. This can create an attitude of superiority.

2. U.S. Americans see change as good, leading to development and progress. Many older, more traditional cultures see change as disruptive to their ancient heritage. This American attitude can manifest itself as disrespect.

3. These Americans are more concerned about accomplishing things on time than about developing interpersonal relationships.

4. Equality is cherished in the United States. The concept of equality is strange to seven-eighths of the world, which view status and authority as desirable.

5. Competition is the "American Way." Americans believe it brings out the best in any individual.

6. Informal and casual attitudes permeate every aspect of American life. Bosses even encourage workers to use first names.

7. Many other countries have developed subtle, sometimes highly ritualistic ways of informing others of unpleasant information. Americans prefer the direct approach.

It is easy to become overwhelmed when you think of all the ways you must prepare yourself to go global. Tucker International, a full-service, international HRD company, advises us to gather as much information about current events in that country as possible (Tucker International, 2001). We also need an understanding of any tensions that exist between our host country and home country. Not only must cultural differences be understood socially, but also differences in business practices, laws, and governmental policies must be understood.

Culture shock is to be expected, and an adaptation period is normal. A few additional points follow.

## REGION-SPECIFIC DATA

This section serves as a brief overview of several globally diverse regions around the world. It is designed to increase your cultural awareness, but it is not extensive enough to prepare you to do business in other countries. Prior to any overseas assignment, it is recommend that you do thorough research on any organization you will be working with, just as you would in the United States. Then do additional research on the host country and its culture. Read books (including novels) to learn about their modern and ancient history and culture, view foreign films; talk to people who have lived in the country and ask them to compare the two cultures. Read the local newspaper online, and try to learn some of the language or expressions. People you meet will appreciate your effort.

Here are several regions at a glance, with more expansive data to follow.

### Made in China

China's entry into the World Trade Organization has brought its labor force unprecedented business and job opportunities. However, change didn't just start then. China's economy has grown 9 percent a year for twenty consecutive years and is targeted to be the second-largest economy by the year 2020. The Chinese government is preparing its workforce to be white-collar professionals. Yet Chinese enterprises did not pay much attention to human resource development until the country carried out "reform and opening up" policies around 1980. The first reform was the era of the agricultural economy, when land was the most valuable resource. Next was the industrial economy, in which capital or money was the most valuable resource. Under the information economy, the importance of human resources development has become obvious, especially since high-caliber employees are increasingly pulled away from local enterprises by foreign firms. Many Chinese CEOs now list talent related issues prominently as a concern.

While Chinese enterprises are experiencing increasingly severe competition for talent from foreign companies, training—which in the past was usually available only to senior managers and regarded as more of a perk than a targeted training effort—is now seen as valuable. Only in the past few years have attitudes toward training begun to change.

Previously, enterprises did not think they had the responsibility to train employees. They felt employees should be qualified enough to meet job requirements and felt it was the duty of employees to train themselves. Although training efforts in China have increased, they are still applied unsystematically. Most companies don't have detailed training/development plans due to explosive growth and scarcity of managerial talent. A large number of low-skilled workers must be retrained or let go from the increasingly competitive marketplace. The "iron-rice bowl" is no longer iron, and workers over age forty are finding it difficult to find or keep jobs.

China's aging workforce and economic growth spark the need for successful talent management. The need is to develop "global" managers; managers who have the ability to manage locally but act globally.

## India Rising

"India and China can together reshape the world order," said Prime Minister Singh to Chinese premier Wen Jiabao when he visited New Delhi in 2005. India and China have 2.4 billion people combined. India is the second-fastest-growing economy after China. The global market growth in India has only been strong in the last decade, even though India has always had brilliant, educated people. I once co-facilitated a leadership-training course for Infosys Technologies, one of India's largest software companies and an outstanding learning organization. A student asked his fellow participants to raise their hands if they had been the top students in their university classes. Every hand in the room went up. According to an article in *BusinessWeek* (2003), "If India can turn into a fast-growth economy; it will be the first developing nation that used its brainpower, not natural resources or raw muscle of factory labor, as the catalyst."

It wasn't until July 1991 that radical economic liberalization measures were launched in India. Between 1947 and 1991, there was a protected market with strict foreign exchange regulations and lengthy licensing procedures. Then the IT boom occurred in 2000. India now possesses some basic underpinnings of a strong, market-driven economy: democratic government, Western accounting principals, and the widespread use of English.

Still, this country—with its abundance of low-cost, high-IQ, English-speaking brainpower—has its challenges. Only 59 percent of India's billion-person population is literate, and only slightly more than that have electricity in their homes. Another challenge is bridging communication gaps, even though English is the primary language. A common practice is to respectfully say "yes" to any project request, even when "no" is the answer. Tensions between Hindus and Muslims are problematic, and the risk of war with nuclear-armed Pakistan is ever-present.

India is the world's youngest country. Fifty percent of India's population is under the age of twenty-five, while populations in the United States, China, and Europe are aging.

Training and development have grown rapidly in India. Spending on training has tripled in the past four years. The percentage of employees receiving training has jumped from less than half to nearly two-thirds. The biggest challenge is battling wage inflation and turnover of quality talent. Since much of India's business involves Western partners, they feel a strong need to incorporate Western concepts, models, and theories. Don Overbey of SunCatcher Productions recently consulted with a company in Mumbai, India. The Indians wanted to operate their new marketing division like the Americans do, so they contracted with Don to recommend a "world-class" Western structure. They adopted his company's recommendations, but Don was concerned about the cultural differences. The Indians, however, have become proficient at adapting American concepts to fit their culture. As a whole, the Indian economy today is following the pattern set by its Western counterparts with a slight difference. Narayana Murthy, the recently retired cofounder of Infosys, has a theory of "compassionate capitalism." He believes corporations must create wealth, but that they must also create "goodwill in the society." Many Indian CEOs share that philosophy: to create a market economy that is environmentally sustainable and reduces inequality (Kamdar, 2007).

## Japan's Workforce Becomes More Fluid

As Japan's workforce moves from the concept of "lifetime employment" to a more fluid model along international standards, changing jobs in Japan is no longer rare. This is good news for the foreign associate interested in hiring talented, experienced workers. There will still be some challenges, however, since the Japanese view Western business in a negative light. Japanese see a greater likelihood of dismissals from Western companies—compared to Japanese companies—due to an about-face from leaders in offshore international headquarters.

Japan's economy roared in the 1980s, but the country faced a slowdown since the 1990s. In 2002, Japan began showing signs of economic growth with recovery and long-term growth continuing into 2006 (Human Development Resources Bureau, 2007). This resurgence has led to a lower unemployment rate and increased worker productivity, but has left companies scrambling to hire enough personnel. Japan has great manufacturing capacity, advanced technology, heavy investment in education—with 75.9 percent of its workforce having attended universities—and a disciplined workforce (Ministry of Education, Culture, Sports, Science and Technology, 2007).

Japan's strong cultural influences affect its workforce. The emphasis placed on seniority in the workplace is a unique characteristic of the Japanese labor market. It is no surprise that younger workers are opposing that tradition in favor of performance promotions. Indeed, with the additional complication of Japan's declining labor population due to an aging society and low birth rates, the securing and development of young personnel is becoming an increasingly important issue for companies. This is leading to a more flexible workplace than in previous times, with a significant increase in the number of "non-regular workers" who enjoy more flexible schedules, selection of jobs or contracts, and a higher level of specialization.

According to the Ministry of Health, Labour, and Welfare, 53.9 percent of offices provide systematic on the job training for regular employees and 72.2 percent provide off-the-job training. In fact, 68.4 percent of companies in Japan acknowledge that skills development is the responsibility of the company, rather than the individual. In-house training comprises as much as 66.5 percent of the training used with private education/training, and public service education/training coming in second and third. However, traveling as an international consultant may bring its own peculiarities in Japan, where a relaxed learning style is the norm.

## Africa and the Middle East

Africa and the Middle East regions, except for the oil-rich countries, will have to create five to six million jobs each year if current unemployment is to be reduced. Recent downward trends in birth rates have not significantly impacted the labor force yet. According to the International Labor Office's Report on Global Employment Trends (2008), in Sub-Saharan Africa, 8.2 percent of the population is unemployed; but with 85.4 percent of those still earning less than $2 a day, underemployment is a serious problem. In North Africa, unemployment is running between 20 and 30 percent. The public sector and the informal economy continue to account for most jobs. At least 20 percent of the total population in this area are between ages fifteen and twenty-four, and unemployment has affected youth more than others. In the Middle East, unemployment is about 11.8 percent.

Female workers in the region concentrate in a small number of economic activities, are less mobile, and face barriers in many professions. The good news is that current market reforms are creating more jobs for women. For example, in the Middle East, women had an increase of 7 percent in employment for 2007 (ILO, 2008).

Too many training programs in the region produce poor results. Often funded from payroll contributions, they are costly, supply driven, and dominated by governments. They often serve as programs of last resort for educational dropouts. These training programs lack facilities and equipment and are not sufficiently geared to the needs of the market.

Fortunately, things are improving. Nancy Kramer, director of business and industry services at Harold Washington College in Chicago, knows this first-hand. Nancy decided to foster collaborative relationships and international understanding and increase her cultural mindfulness by becoming a Peace Corps volunteer in Zimbabwe. She made a difference in the way training was delivered when she taught "How to Start a Small Business." When she arrived in Masvingo, she found that local Zimbabwe entrepreneurs wanted to learn everything the American way. But as Nancy began to understand the culture, she realized that American ways were not the best ways in Zimbabwe. She taught the curriculum and invited the local business owners to be guest speakers so that they could expand on the reality and application of ideas in Zimbabwe. She utilized role playing in her classes as well. Once the students learned it, they loved it. Nancy said, "Everyone was a ham. They especially loved pretending to be the manager." Nancy says that this experience helped her to learn to laugh a lot, especially at herself!

## Europe Unites

In the last decade, the European Union has made overhauling the stereotypic image of corporate training one of their primary goals, including calling for a "substantial annual increase per capita investment in human resources" at the EU summit meeting in 2000. The European Union is facing many of the same difficulties as the United States with increased outsourcing and difficulty in retaining qualified personnel. The emphasis on training is becoming more evident.

According to Anne Bagamery, a writer for the *International Herald Tribune,* investments in training are viewed as symbolic of a company's commitment to the community, the economy, and the employees. In 2003, for example, the list of one hundred best companies to work for in Britain was highly determined by the training offered by these companies. Britain has been spending roughly $35 billion each year on worker training, with a governmentally appointed agency (the Adult Learning Inspectorate) involved in evaluating trouble programs and terminating government-funded businesses if training doesn't measure up.

This seems to be more effective than in France, where companies spend about $26 billion on training each year, but most training is focused on top executives and employees of big companies, rather than on entry-level training for the unemployed or workers in smaller businesses.

In Eastern Europe, on the other hand, the unemployment rates and general economic growth rates have been improving consistently over the last ten years, but this has only returned these countries to where they were before the fall of the Soviet Union. These countries continue to face a job population that moves between jobs quickly and most well-skilled nationals leave the countries entirely (ILO, 2007), making training in these countries a more delicate endeavor.

### Canada Can Do

A wide assortment of circumstances challenges the Canadian economy today, including geopolitical tensions and continued sluggishness of the U.S. economy. Despite these factors—and a softer labor market—signs of a healthy economy are appearing. Along with economic recovery will come a growing need for human resource development. The increased employment of knowledge workers and the growing number of Canadian employers who report having difficulty recruiting qualified employees raise questions about what Canada is doing to respond to an apparent employee shortage. According to the annual report of the Canadian Council on Learning, by 2015, 70 percent of the projected 1.7 million new jobs will require a post-secondary education. According to the report, Canadian firms also invest less in training than other industrial nations, with less than one-third of Canadians taking part in any formal work-related learning activities and 1.5 million Canadians reporting that their learning and training needs are going unmet. Hewitt, a global human resource outsourcing and consulting firm, surveyed Canadian companies nationwide and found that average salary increases for 2008 are projected to be 3.8 percent overall, which is expected to outpace the inflation rate (Hewitt, 2007).

The peak for traditional students of post-secondary education will be in 2013 and then will decline for two decades, according to current demographic projections. The aging population means that HR managers are now called upon to provide effective succession planning at a time when fewer and fewer young people live there. Another demographic prediction indicates that by 2011, the net growth of Canada's population will be entirely related to immigration. HR must be prepared to manage the integration of cultures and diversity in the workplace.

## WHERE DO WE GO NEXT?

Human resource development experts have a challenging job, given the realities of the U.S. and the global marketplace. Healthcare costs are soaring, workplaces are becoming increasingly diverse culturally, and profits are sagging. Baby Boomers everywhere are aging, and there aren't enough young skilled workers to plug into the labor force.

The American Society for Training and Development, with global networks around the world, reports that organizations with above-average training and development budgets outperform competitors and achieve a higher total shareholder return. Many of the top firms clearly understand this concept. Our skills are needed, and our industry future looks bright.

Our HRD challenge, then, is to build world-class organizations by designing training strategies that augment participants' knowledge about their businesses, cultivate current global leaders and develop new ones, and help companies identify and build the core competencies necessary to excel in the global marketplace. We can continue to use the HRD tools and techniques that have taken us this far, but our focus must be on our end goal and not just on the process to get there. And what is the end goal for HRD professionals? Is a goal of "helping to build world-class organizations" enough? Peter Block, respected author and humanist, said in a article (Block, 2003), "If an organization exists to be efficient and customer focused, is that compelling enough to retain and motivate employees? Organizations that have a compelling purpose matter most to employees." So our challenge may go even deeper. As HRD professionals we possess certain insights and intuitions about people due to our access and observation of employees and management. Perhaps our challenge is to push the boundaries and help shape management's thinking, perhaps even global thinking. We have the power to use our understanding of basic cross-cultural human behavior to influence organizations and countries to identify and achieve more than being an "efficient and customer focused" organization. With our influence organizations can be compelling positive "world-class" forces.

## References

ASTD. (2002). *The 2002 ASTD international comparison report.* Alexandria, VA:, American Society for Training and Development. astd.org.

Bagamery, A. (2004, May 12). The workplace: Training: The new power tool. *The International Herald Tribune.*

Bierema, L. (2002). The global pendulum. *Training & Development.*

Block, P. (2003, March 1). Changing our thinking about action. *Link and Learn Newsletter.* www .linkageinc.com.

*BusinessWeek.* (2003). The rise of India. www.businessweek.com/magazine/content/03_49/ b3861001_mz001.htm

Canadian Council on Learning. (2007). *Report on Learning in Canada 2007: Post-secondary education in Canada: Strategies for success.* Ottawa, Ontario: Author.

Central Intelligence Agency. (2008). *India.* www.cia.gov/library/publications/the-world-factbook/ geos/in.html

Economic Research Forum. (2001). *Labor market and human resource development.* Cairo, Egypt: ERF.

Galagan, P. (2003, December). The future of the profession formerly known as training. *Training & Development.*

Global Business Culture. (2002). *Does culture matter?* www.globalbusinessculture.com.

GlobalEDGE country comparison feature. wwwglobaledge.msu.edu.

Gross, A. (1998). Trends in human resources practices in Japan. *SHRM International Focus.* wwwlpacificbridge.com.

Hewitt. (2008). *Canada Salary Increase Survey.* www.compensationcenter.com.

Human Resources Development Bureau. (2007). *Report from the Research Association on Lifelong Career Development Support and Corporate Organization.* Ministry of Health, Labour and Welfare.

International Labor Organization (2008). *Global employment trends.* Geneva, Switzerland: International Labor Office.

Kamdar, M. (2007). *Planet India.* New York: Macmillan.

Ministry of Education, Culture, Sports, Science and Technology. (2007). *Japan's education at a glance, 2006, school education.* www.mext.go.jp/english/statist/07070310.htm

Paradise, A. (2007). *State of the industry report.* Alexandria, VA: American Society for Training and Development. www.astd.org.

Sarkar-Barney, S. (2003). *The role of national culture in enhancing training effectiveness: A framework.* www.elsevier.com.

Surgue, B. (2003). *State of the industry report.* Alexandria, VA: American Society for Training and Development. www.astd.org.

Tsukudo, T. (2002). *Brain drain or gain.* Kathmandu, Nepal: WorldLink, CIPD/PPL.

Tucker International. (2001). *Best practices make for perfect international assignments.* www.tuckerintl.com.

Willins, R., & Rioux, S. (2000, May). The growing pains of globalizing HR. *Training & Development.*

Workforce Management. (2003). *Enter the brave new world: Trends affecting international business development.* www.workforce.com.

WorldLink. (2002). *IPM South Africa regional report.* Kathmandu, Nepal: WorldLink, CIPD/PPL.

WorldLink. (2003). *EAPM regional report.* Kathmandu, Nepal: WorldLink/World Federation of Personnel Management Association.

# Dealing with the Unfamiliar and Coping with Change

**M**ost of us like to be comfortable. We like the familiar way things are in our own homes and workplaces. Traveling to strange exotic places and trying to communicate with people in different cultures and in different languages are activities that many people avoid. Some of us are excited by these opportunities, but this section is especially for those who have some fears or discomforts about global assignments. Here are some practical tips that can help.

Explore what makes you most uncomfortable, such as interrupting your daily routine, meeting people who are very different from you, changing time zones, or getting lost. The reasons will be different for each of us, but if you can make a list of the concerns that are most on your mind, then you can explore each one and put a plan in place to reduce your anxiety.

If safety and security are major concerns for you, watch the news to be fully aware of what is happening in the city and country where you are presenting. Arrange for transportation and accommodations through a reputable travel agency. Ask your hosts or sponsors for their recommendations to increase your security. Ask them to recommend a trusted guide and/or driver for your stay. Ask your hotel to arrange a car for you and tell you how much it should cost before going anywhere. Ask your driver how much it will cost before you get into a car. If you are not happy with the price or feel uncomfortable about the driver, say "Thank you, but I have changed my mind" and look for another alternative. Only walk on well-lit and well-traveled streets. Always have the name and address of your hotel with you whenever you go out, in case you need directions. Carry a small amount of cash with you, in small bills, in the currency of the country, in your pocket. This can be quickly and conveniently accessed when you need it, but this avoids showing large amounts of money to possible pickpockets. Avoid carrying backpacks, purses, or computer cases whenever possible, as that only invites problems. Only wear your underclothes money belt with some cash and your passport. Always be aware of what is going on around you, and move out of the area if you feel anxiety. People will typically be very helpful. Carry a small dictionary of the local language with you and point to the words when you need to ask a question. Learn a few basic words in the local language, such as "Good morning," "Excuse me," "Where is the bathroom?" and "Thank you."

If change in your routine is a cause of stress for you, planning a familiar routine in a new location can help you. Bring a picture or tiny item that reminds you of home, and keep it with you or place it on your nightstand to remind you of familiar things. Get up earlier than usual to give yourself time to acclimate to new surroundings.

Make sure to get enough sleep. It is easier to be patient, courteous, and flexible if you feel rested.

Watch and listen. You will learn a great deal about the culture. See how people interact. Do they talk a lot or very little? Are they loud or quiet? Do they smile much, or are they very serious? What do they wear? How do they relax? How do they eat? Try to be part of the environment and not make gestures that will attract a lot of attention. Smile and say "hello" in the language of the locals. Learn how to say "I am sorry, I do not understand" in the local language. People will be extra patient with you if you tell them that.

Purchase maps and guidebooks before you leave for a trip. Plan how to travel from the airport to your hotel and from your hotel to your presentation site. Once you arrive in your destination country, purchase a map in the language of the country because the signs will be in their language. Ask for written directions to your destination. Before leaving home, you should purchase a small compass to attach to your bag. It is very easy to become disoriented when you are on the other side of the world.

Be friendly and politely curious. Avoid discussing politics, religion, or other emotionally charged topics by sticking to the weather and people's favorite sports as easy topics to discuss and make friends.

Bring the things that remind you to relax, such as music and pictures.

Enjoy the experience!

# Mentoring Global Employees

**T**he common definition of a mentor is someone who has experience that can be beneficial to a person who does not yet have that experience. A mentor is not the person's supervisor. They are usually not in the same organization that the person to be mentored (mentee) is in. This provides perspective to the mentee. With no direct supervision over the person, the mentor can be honest but does not hold the mentee's future in his or her hands (that is, mentors do not appraise employee performance, decide pay or promotion for the mentee). A person who wants to explore the possibility of living and working in another country and culture may want a mentor to share experiences with him or her.

The mentoring relationship is a partnership based upon agreed goals, where the mentor guides the person and the mentee completes agreed action items to get them to their goals. The relationship is strengthened when both participants complete an agreement form that includes information such as what is to be achieved, how often they will meet, and how they will work together.

A mentor can be trained or self-developed. Many books are available to guide a mentor in how to be most effective. Skills and competencies of a mentor include good communication skills, technical and professional experience, networking capability, cultural awareness, and "political" savvy.

If asked to be a mentor, you can prepare an agreement that you will discuss with the mentee. This agreement should clearly state the amount of time to be spent, such as one hour per month for three months before reassessing to see whether you will continue for another three months. Find out what the mentee's goals are for the mentoring partnership. Be prepared to suggest some goals in case the person has not thought that through. Because the mentee is from another culture, do your homework ahead of time by reading and learning about his or her culture. This will help you to avoid any mistakes or embarrassment and better connect with his or her needs and motivations. If the person's first language is not English, you must speak especially clearly, using short words that could be looked up in a dictionary if necessary. You can also use an interpreter, but always speak to the mentee and not to the interpreter, to be respectful.

Mentoring relationships can be encouraged by an international organization and made available on a voluntary basis. This is not something that works as well when it is mandated. Generally, executives are encouraged to come to an information session, given tools for the mentoring process, and invited to be available as needed. If you are in charge of providing mentors, find out all that you can about each volunteer's background and skills. Hold information sessions to explain the process, introduce potential candidates to available mentors (perhaps via conference call or webcam), and help matches to occur. Time zones and languages will be important criteria for matching. It is a difficult challenge for a mentor to be twelve hours behind a mentee's time. This requires one person to start very early in the day and the other to stay late in the evening. It is easier for all parties if the time zones do not exceed five hours' difference. It is also most helpful if the mentor has had some previous experience with a person who speaks the language. Even though many people speak English very well as their second language, it is often difficult to understand a strong accent. International mentoring is usually done via phone and/or computer, and it is a challenge to understand every important word that is spoken over the phone if someone has a very heavy accent. This can lead to misunderstanding and frequent requests to repeat comments. This can strain the mentoring relationship.

International mentoring can be enhanced by using written documents. Short outlines or discussions should be typed and sent ahead of time so that both parties can review and discuss them. This helps to avoid misunderstanding and provides a common ground for discussion.

Another possibility is to use "mentoring quads," small groups of three mentees and one mentor. With this type of arrangement, the mentees can learn from and support each other as well as learning from the mentor. For example, a mentoring quad was begun when a new manager from Shanghai asked an experienced manager from New York to be her mentor. As soon as the mentee began to speak with other women in Shanghai, they asked to be included and wanted to be helped with their careers in the company. The new group was so excited about this process that they asked to meet every week and stayed at work until 9 P.M. so they could call the New York mentor at 8 A.M. in New York. The mentor began by asking each person to introduce herself and to all tell what they wanted to gain from the mentoring relationship. They talked about what they had in common, such as career advancement, as well as issues they were facing as women in the workforce. Using an agreement form for each person worked especially well. Everyone had the opportunity to review her own goals and have the others discuss the goals, as well as suggest ideas for achieving them.

Because global mentoring is generally done over the telephone or by email, it is very helpful for each person to send pictures to the others that they can use to introduce themselves and show what is most important to them. The mentor in our example showed family photos, but the mentees showed only photos of themselves. It took six months before one of them showed a picture of her husband and son. The discussions were very business-focused. The mentor asked questions about the city in China (weather and location) as well as the culture (foods they liked, favorite customs for holidays). The women asked business questions such as how to talk to their manager regarding work projects, how to get along with difficult co-workers, and how to network more effectively.

This relationship continued for eighteen months. They discussed how the relationship was going quarterly and decided whether they wanted to continue. They discussed what was working or not working. All were very complimentary, although the mentor assumed that this was because the Chinese culture does not encourage giving negative feedback.

When two of the three mentees were moving on to new jobs, they decided that they should close this mentoring quad. They all talked about what they had gained from each other and how much they had enjoyed this process. They said goodbye and moved on to the next steps.

A mentor must go into an international mentoring relationship with a willingness both to help and to learn. Mentors must be open, supportive, and curious. They should not pass judgment, but simply give guidance. It does take extra energy to listen carefully when people are speaking over the phone with heavy accents. Clarification should be requested whenever needed. Writing down the information to be discussed ahead of time often helps everyone to understand the words being spoken without struggling through the pronunciation. This process can be done through the computer so that both mentor and mentee(s) see the same information.

The virtual mentoring relationship in the example above was a huge success because the participants were patient and motivated to make it work, because everyone had been properly prepared, and because the mentor had done her homework.

# Technology Considerations When Presenting to International Audiences

## PREPARATION

Presenting outside the United States offers special technological challenges. Here are some tips we've collected that can help you.

Pat Maley (VisualsEtc@yahoo.com) recommends that, when presenting in a location outside the United States, you hire an international AV specialist company such as Crews Control (www.crewscontrol.com) or a local media company in the location where you will present. This ensures that all the correct equipment, voltages, cords, and connections will be used to enable flawless technological support for your presentation. Use a checklist of requirements for your program to cover every possible need and confirm each one with the specialist.

Bring extra supplies, and always have one or two backup plans for everything. Copy your entire presentation onto a storage device or CD/DVD. Carry this with you at all times and do not keep it with your computer. Make sure you copy your English version as well as all translated versions.

Send your presentation to a trusted manager or administrative assistant who will have it in case you need it. Save the presentation in earlier versions of the software you are using and label them with the version number, in case the computer you are using on-site uses an older version of the software. This will cover the possibility that the version you are showing looks like gibberish. (And don't use words like "gibberish" or other slang in your presentation, as they will not be understood.)

Ask a person from the organization or hotel to provide a computer, projector, and hookups in case your computer does not work there or you have insufficient/incompatible cords. Ask them to set the equipment up and test it to make sure that everything is working for you when you arrive.

Keep your computer with you at all times. They have a way of quickly disappearing.

If you are using video, make sure that you have brought all formats and translations because some machines will allow more than one format, and some will require a specific format and will not work otherwise. NTSC is the most common format for U.S.-produced videos. They have to be converted on a separate tape to PAL format for most British-based countries and SECAM for French-speaking countries.

Prepare and carry a hard copy of your presentation with you so that you can use this as a fallback plan.

Make a request for easels and easel paper for your presentation room that will allow you to collect input, ideas, and comments from participants as well as providing you with an alternative method of presentation if equipment fails.

Make a request for rectangular pieces of cardboard and markers for each participant. They can write their names on them and create "tent cards" if they are seated at tables. This will be helpful to see from a distance in addition to name tags that participants can be wearing.

Decide how you would like the room to be set up to ensure optimum visibility and learning and make a request that the furniture be placed in the room according to the sketch that you send.

## SESSION SETUP

Pat Maley suggests that you always ask for permission before you do anything on-site. This respects the culture as well as the technical specialists who can guarantee your success technically. Create a partnership with the technologists who are in the location of the presentation. Have a way to immediately contact them in case of emergency.

Check room setup to make sure there is sufficient seating capacity for the number of participants.

Check to see whether materials have been delivered. Set up materials for ease of distribution.

Check and double-check all equipment to ensure that it is working.

Sit in various seats to see whether the view is sufficient from several locations in the room.

Place materials, tent cards, and markers at each person's seat, if you have them seated at tables. Put handout materials on each person's seat if there are no tables, or ensure that they are available to be picked up by each person as people enter the room.

## THE PRESENTATION

Present directly to your participants, even if there is an interpreter. It is very disrespectful to speak to the interpreter, but often a temptation because that's the person who speaks your language.

Have someone continuously monitor every technical aspect of the presentation. This person must be someone who can quickly implement a backup plan without the participants being very aware of the transition.

It is important to remember not to give the OK sign with your thumb and index finger joined in a circle, because this can be a tremendous insult in South American and Middle Eastern cultures. A "thumbs up" may be a better choice, if you absolutely are required to gesture.

If your audience does not speak English, show your slides in their language and have an interpreter read the content to them. Watch to see people's reactions. If you see questions on their faces, ask the interpreter to ask whether they have questions regarding this information.

If they seem bored, ask whether they want to take a short break. Find out why they are bored from someone you trust and make appropriate adjustments to the program, such as going faster over information that they already know or inserting some activity into the program.

### Virtual Presentations

Often virtual presentations are made to a mixed audience via phone, computer, or electronic devices. In this case, many cultures may be attending the program from several locations.

### *Phone Conferencing*

To set up a phone conference call with an international audience, work with your phone company to ensure that enough phone lines are available for the call and obtain the specific call-in information that will ensure everyone's successful connection to the call. Be sure to schedule the call at times that are reasonable for all international participants. This may mean that you schedule two calls, one in the morning and another at night, so you will not be asking people to attend the conference at unreasonable hours. Ask for the costs for having the phone company host and moderate the call, and decide whether that is appropriate for your needs. For example, if you have a large number of people attending from different international locations, a moderator can mute the phone lines so that only the speaker can be heard and then, at an appropriate time, open the phone lines for questions. This prevents a lot of background noise that comes in from different callers' locations. If you have a small number of people attending, then you can ask people to put their own phone lines on mute until you indicate that it is time for questions.

Start the call approximately ten or fifteen minutes ahead of time, so that people can call in early. Greet those who are coming online, as well as those who are patiently waiting for the program to begin, by telling them the name of the program and how many minutes it will be before the program begins. At the start time, welcome all attendees and introduce the program. If it is appropriate, ask for brief introductions such as name and location of the callers. Describe the purpose of the call, the agenda, and any protocols, for example, when making a comment or asking a question each person should identify him- or herself before speaking. Start and end the call on time. Provide a person's name and phone number to call later, if additional questions occur. Speak slowly, using simple terms. Provide a technical help phone number to call if anyone has problems phoning in or hearing. Courtesy and patience are absolutely critical. Provide a written script or notes of the conference before and after the program. This will be most helpful for those who do not speak the language as well.

### Web Conferencing

Engage a web-casting service such as WebEx and obtain training to prepare and deliver your program via this technology.

PowerPoint is the most common format for this delivery method. Prepare, practice, and test your presentation to ensure that it flows well and can be delivered within the agreed time frame.

Contract with your phone company or broadcasting service to have the phone lines moderated and muted. They will provide a person who can open up the phone lines at appropriate times for questions. Make sure that you have clearly provided directions to everyone calling in about how to get online and what the technical help phone number is in case they have problems or are disconnected. Have an online location where participants can retrieve documents and the presentation, in case they cannot access the program while it is being broadcast. Contingency plans must be developed for all kinds of technical difficulties in order to reduce frustration of participants who are having difficulty. Taping of the program ensures that participants can access the program as soon as the live broadcast is complete, in case they did not make it at the time it was broadcast or they want to review the program again.

Make announcements before the program begins, welcoming participants to the program and telling them that the program will begin in ten minutes, nine minutes, eight minutes, and so forth. Music can be used while people are waiting for the program to begin.

Introduce presenters and show their photos. Review objectives of the program and the agenda. Explain how questions will be handled and where to go to find the program documents, and make participants feel welcome. Always start and end on time.

### Podcasting

Podcasting is the preparation and distribution of audio files using RSS (Really Simple Syndication) to the computers of subscribed users. These files may then be uploaded to digital audio players (DAPs) such as the iPod.

**Steps for Podcasting**

- Create an audio file.
- Save the file as an MP3 on your computer.
- Upload it to a website.
- Insert the URL into an RSS feed.
- Publish the RSS feed.

These programs can be used to teach, provide homework, reinforce learning, and listen to the program at a later date. This is a very portable and accessible medium.

### PDA Programming

Personal digital assistants (PDAs) are carried conveniently by many people to track their appointments and emails, so they are perfect devices to deliver just-in-time training. Programming that is designed for PDAs must be short, clear, and easy to follow so that the learner can access what he or she needs anywhere, at any time. For example, when the learner is waiting in the airport or for a meeting he or she can complete a sales training module on a PDA. If someone needs information regarding how to perform a task, he or she can look it up and then more effectively perform the task. This type of training can be developed by a company or provider that does this type of programming on an ongoing basis or by someone who knows how to design computer-based training in modules. The programs should be designed for global use by ensuring that simple terms are used and that formatting includes enough space for translation into the language needed.

### Computer Simulations and Games

Some organizations are finding that training developed in computer simulation or game formats are very well received by learners. Basic instruction for a new assignment can be delivered via interactive, fun, and visually exciting ways. When developing these programs, it is best to engage a trusted and successful vendor who has done this type of development for global audiences. Ask to see examples and ask for references. Talk to the organizations that have used these vendors and determine how successful they have been at translating the programs into acceptable and effective learning programs. There are many variables to consider, such as language translations, visuals, formats, and delivery mechanisms.

The complexity of presenting to global audiences cannot be underestimated. Failure or insults can have such tremendous ramifications for international relations, so presenting internationally via a simulation or game is not something to be attempted without assuring that the contents show respect for all of the cultures that might be using the programs. This type of design typically takes longer and is more complicated to fix if you find that something is disrespectful or inappropriate. Other types of programming are often easier and faster to revise, and you can also obtain more immediate feedback on the success of the learning approach.

## OVERALL CONSIDERATIONS

It is important to remember that the primary purposes of using technology are to enhance the learning of the participants in a program. It is easy for presenters to become so caught up in the details of making sure that everything works, that we forget about the people and their learning experience. If the presenter can have someone else responsible for worrying about the technological detail, he or she can then focus on the learners. If you do not have the luxury of technical support, then practice and contingency planning are critical to ensure you are able to create an environment in which the participants will not even notice that technology is a part of the program. They will be so engaged in the learning experience that they will focus on their own growth in knowledge and skill.

# Learning in a Second Language: L2

*Edited by C. Pinto, Transware Inc.*

The rapid processes of globalization, immigration, and the movement of capital and ideas are shaping the 21st century in ways that had not been expected. Similarly, the economic trends that drive these global forces are defining the actions of individuals, groups, regions, nations, and corporations in peculiarly coherent and contradictory manners. It is within this environment that individuals and organizations alike are challenged by how to engage, learn, and grow in a way that allows them to continue to participate successfully in this complex 21st century economy.

Without a doubt, one specific challenge to organizations is that the makeup of the workforce, at all levels, is no longer homogeneous in culture or language. This reduces the impact and benefits of being the provider or recipient of a mono-cultural, mono-lingual learning environment within the organization.

There is no glossing over the fact that the cultural work heritage of many people is a prevailing influence each day in all types of organizations. The expected cultural foundation people come into the workplace equipped with now has to take into account the roots and learning foundations of their "diverse" cultures. The premise being that global clients and global organizational learning needs are equivalent.

Keeping in mind that as the individual responsibilities of title and position increase within an organization so does the "stress" on the fundamental aspects of learning. What an administrative assistant has to know and learn in order to function and be efficient within the organization differs markedly from the expectations that an organization has for its chief financial officer. Add to this organizational learning spectrum the variables of distinct second languages or second culture challenges to learning and you have a clear picture of what most of the Fortune Global 2500 organizations and their privately held equivalents face on a day-to-day basis.

How is a company to achieve new efficiencies, introduce new products, confer with its distribution channels, create prospects, and satisfy clients if the underlying learning environment of its own organization is not creating the "level learning playing field" for the participants of the organization for the markets it serves?

The intrinsic complexity of global organizations is fundamentally rooted with their people, their shared objectives, and their understanding of how it is that they contribute to the attainment of those objectives—objectives that, without a constant state of reinforcement via learning, will become diffused in the organizational culture and thus create pooled confusion of the business objectives of the organization.

The individual participant in an organization moves among multiple functional environments on a daily basis. The work environment is but one of them. If that individual is moving within multi-lingual and multi-cultural environments then the organizational environmental messaging and reinforcement is further diluted, unless the learning environment can be adapted to be closer to what the individual relates to culturally and linguistically.

What are the challenges to an individual recipient within an English mono-cultural, mono-lingual learning environment?*

- Individuals may lack knowledge of grammar and syntax and therefore may read word by word, resulting in lower overall comprehension. They may encounter too much unfamiliar vocabulary to grasp the overall concept conveyed in the sentence. They are also challenged when reading idiomatic expressions and unfamiliar grammatical constructions.

- Readers may have difficulty with more complex and compound sentences. They may lose the meaning of references within the text, such as with frequent use of pronouns. Pronoun usage may be different or less frequent in the native language. Connectives may be overlooked or misunderstood, resulting in a loss of the relationships between concepts and ideas.

*Excerpt reprinted from Transware collection, David E. Stone, Ph.D. © 2005 Southern Polytechnic State University

- Readers may have difficulty adjusting their reading strategies to match the author's intent or purpose. They may not be familiar with a particular story "grammar" or the organizational patterns of informational text. They may not be familiar with specific genre and the literary devices used in text.

- From a purely linguistic standpoint these factors may also come into play:

  - Different conceptual frameworks may be activated that misguide their reading

  - Expectations of what is normal may differ and cause breakdowns in coherence

  - Cause and consequence chains can differ and/or be more emotional, evoking strong reactions in the reader

  - Symbols may differ

  - Pedagogy may differ

  - There may be differences in what to attend to and what to ignore

- Readers often use strategies that are applicable to the orthographic system and the grammatical and syntactic patterns of their L1 (first language). These may or may not transfer into the L2 text.

In the case of web-based or non-classroom based learning, the level of comprehension may be further eroded by the fact that there is no readily available support from co-workers as the training is being presented. Web-based training is also often enhanced by integrated video or audio sequences, which affords a further challenge to the second language learner in that the rates of comprehension decline in comparison to text comprehension.

If you want to find research to back up the evaluation of your current learning program, you can conduct a complete search on the topic of the source, impact and ultimately the value of training and learning for a second language trainee by conducting a literature search at www.infotrieve.com, (www4.infotrieve.com/search/databases/newsearch.asp) a document delivery search engine. From the website, for a fee, you can download the document that you select and read up on the topic as researched by a variety of researchers in various disciplines.

Some suggested topics to search on would be:

- Learning in a Second Language

- Listening Comprehension

- L2 Learners

This all points to the fact that inward-looking translation and acculturation of the learning environment is an absolute requirement for all learning ecosystems, including those that are meant for prospective clients and clients alike.

The underlying truth to operate as a multicultural, multilingual organization is the specter of liability and regulatory disapproval which can be generated when labor or product events conspire to make things go very badly for an organization.

Worst-case scenarios of product training materials that do not clearly demarcate the scope and span of use of a product or a production objective that is understood by one business unit in Germany to mean "good quality" and in another in Turkey to mean "quality is acceptable" could have odd consequences to the bottom line. Similarly diversity, language, and cultural requirements span state to constitutional edicts, so there is little reason to not take the diversity of your clients to be equivalent to the diversity of your employees.

One of the clearest and most entertaining lessons, albeit fictional, of what the learning challenges might be for an L2 person in a mono-cultural, mono-lingual environment are the learning adventures of Viktor Navorski ("The Terminal"), played by Tom Hanks. Viktor finds himself sealed in at JFK Airport while awaiting the resolution of diplomatic ties between his homeland of Krakoshna and the United States. Learning English by watching TV, comparing an English book to its equivalent Krakoshnian edition, and his interaction with a seemingly endless repertoire of language groups beyond English was the basis of his knowledge. The result was that, when offered the ability to exit the airport via a legal loophole, he does not understand the statement or consequences of the proposed exit process.

It may be that within an organization that only offers a mono-cultural and mono-lingual learning environment, the existence of a "Viktor range" of learners must be forming at many layers of the organization. Perhaps simple anonymous surveys of the organization can begin to detect the existence of a "Viktor Index" to measure the cognition and coherence of knowledge with regards to an organization's objective, which in turn could be used to structure learning programs that level the learning field.

Similarly, the translation and localization of training and learning programs within the organization can often not only be effective in creating greater knowledge and understanding of the business objective, but also create a more coherent organizational culture. As this multi-lingual learning concept is applied at first retroactively to existing programs and then projected into future programs, organizations can, via sustainable technologies, process and maintain global learning communities from which the organization can grow.

The client/market side of the equation is revenue-critical in that client and markets not only expect products and services in their respective languages, but often will penalize organizations that do not extend their knowledge into the local language and culture. The most obvious presentation of obliviousness in this regard is organizational websites with no extension to other languages, offering only a mono-lingual experience. Learning and training elements of products and services directed at markets should always have some option to be experienced in the language and culture of the recipient target clients.

In summary, one might consider that language and cultural inclusivity are the most effective ways to create long-term value for organizations and their communities. Learning and training programs that support language and cultural inclusivity in a localized manner will go a long way toward creating sustainable global organizations.

Mr. Pinto is the director of marketing for Transware. He has extensive experience in international communications and business development. A graduate of UC Berkeley, he has consulted and directly participated in the development of multiple multi-lingual sales and marketing programs in the Americas and Europe. Transware is leading provider of translation and localization services to the global training and learning industries. The company provides, via its global operations centers, multilingual, media, and cultural program management for the top companies in training and supports all language aspects of marketing and global communications programs for organizations.

# A Workshop, Webinar, or What?

Organizations face a number of challenges when rolling out company-wide initiatives across the globe. Cost, culture, language, and technology are a few of the major considerations everyone must face. Sending a message from the president to all employees around the world isn't difficult, but communicating it in a way that is consistently understood is where things become troublesome. Imagine the challenges facing multinational organizations in rolling out a two-day workshop about effective communication or one on conducting effective performance reviews. Or how should new employees get up-to-speed on the company and learn about the products? With all of the technology, delivery methods and cultural implications, how does one determine the best way to accomplish the organization's goals for learning and development?

In this appendix, we take a look at some of the different ways to accomplish these goals, as well as some of the advantages and disadvantages for each. We will look at the following options:

- Conduct a face-to-face workshop there (where the participants work)
- Conduct a face-to-face workshop here (at the headquarters)
- Train-the-trainer

- Master trainer simultaneous workshops
- Virtual training

## FACE-TO-FACE WORKSHOP THERE

In this option, facilitators (either internal employees or contractors) go on the road and take the workshop to their audiences around the globe.

### Advantages

- Content can be customized and adapted to meet the needs of different audiences and cultures.
- Facilitators can pick up on learning transfer success and react/adjust as needed on the fly.
- Traveling to the various locations helps the company to learn about customers and/or audience culture.
- Employees feel valued because they are receiving the same treatment as corporate does, but on their own turf.
- Getting to know leaders and people from corporate can help instill loyalty, foster shared understanding, and create the desired culture.
- Typically, there may be more learning, skills transfer, and team building in a workshop versus other methods.
- Contractors can be hired if internal resources are an issue or aren't available to do the work.

### Disadvantages

- Facilitators may encounter inconsistent facility or technology at the various locations, which makes it hard for consistent delivery of content.
- Employees attending training in their office facility may be distracted with emails, phone calls, and other job responsibilities.
- Travel takes facilitators and leaders out of their office, which could impact other work.
- Language barriers or culture differences may affect the delivery of content.
- Financial costs of travel abroad are high.
- Travel, preparation, and repeated facilitation takes its toll on facilitators.

## FACE-TO-FACE WORKSHOP HERE

This option brings employees to the corporate headquarters location to participate in the face-to-face workshop.

**Advantages**

- The employees feel valued by being brought to "corporate."
- Being at the corporate location is a great opportunity to learn or reinforce the culture of the company.
- Employee relationship building with corporate staff is likely to occur. This helps bridge the "geographic gap."
- Typically, there may be more learning, skills transfer, and team building in a workshop versus other methods (for skill-based or relationship-based learning content).

**Disadvantages**

- Financial costs of employee travel may be cost-prohibitive, depending on the size of the company and number of employees attending the workshop.
- Need to factor in the lead time, expense, and potential restrictions for obtaining passports/visas required for travel.
- Employee travel takes them out of their office, which could impact other work.
- Fatigue factor (such as jetlag) or culture shock could affect learners.
- Participants could experience language barriers, even when everyone speaks English.

## TRAIN-THE-TRAINER

This scenario has several options. One would be for "Master Trainers" (experts on the workshop and in training trainers) to travel to train additional facilitators on the content and in the techniques needed to actually facilitate the workshop.

Another variation includes facilitators (perhaps managers or subject-matter experts) who will be facilitating the workshop coming to the corporate headquarters and attending a train-the-trainer session to learn the content and facilitation techniques.

A third variation of this option would be to train independent facilitators and have them partner with in-country employees to roll out the workshop. The independent facilitator would most likely be an expert in the content, while the in country co-facilitator would be an expert in the company and the culture. Working together, this team could support each other to deliver a successful workshop.

**Advantages**

- More people will know the content and can help spread the word.

- Content can be localized and customized to better meet the needs of the learners.

- With more facilitators and people versed in the content, the odds of having champions and follow-up for the initiative/training is greater.

- May be the most cost-effective in terms of time and money (versus sending all employees to another country to take the training or having a few corporate facilitators trying to do all the workshops abroad).

- Roll-out could be completed in a shorter timeframe with more people trained to deliver the training.

**Disadvantages**

- Quality and consistency may be reduced when newly trained facilitators are delivering around the globe.

- Management support and follow-up may be reduced unless leaders voice and show support.

- The newly trained facilitators will likely not be dedicated resources, so mind share and skills may be an issue.

## MASTER TRAINER SIMULTANEOUS WORKSHOPS

Yet another variation of the train-the-trainer includes a master trainer/satellite option. In this case, a master trainer would be in one location and there could be several groups in attendance around the world. For example, the master trainer could be located in New York and there would be groups of employees in India ready to be trained (let's say in Pune, Bangalore, Chennai, Delhi, and Mumbai). Each satellite meeting room with a facilitator is connected to the master trainer via video conference or webcast. The master trainer opens the session, greets participants, and presents the first module of content. When an assignment is given, the local facilitators take over and lead the groups through the assignment. When the assignment is complete, the entire group reconvenes and the local facilitators offer some comments, insights, or questions from the group. The master trainer handles those and moves on to the next module. This approach continues for the duration of the training. This method works well when the organization needs a level of continuity in the training.

What about logistics? The New Yorker will likely start the session at 8:00 p.m. Eastern time, so the learners in India can participate during their work day. If this is an eight-hour workshop, consider breaking it up into four to five segments to give participants and facilitators time to take a break.

What about getting the facilitators in synch? The local facilitators need to be trained on the content, what to expect, and their roles during the session. As you guessed, this can be done with the master trainer presenting the material in advance to facilitator groups across one country or across different countries. Be sure to account for differing time zones when planning this facilitator preparation session.

### Advantages

- Can train many people/workshops at one time.
- Will have more consistency with master trainer environment than with many facilitators doing it their own way.
- Will likely have less travel and travel-related issues.

### Disadvantages

- May have time zone issues.
- Will need to train facilitators.
- Different groups will have different experiences, but hopefully the main points will all be covered.

## VIRTUAL TRAINING

This option could include presenting content via live or recorded webcasts, and/or e-learning.

### Advantages

- Cost-efficient in that e-learning typically saves money with large audiences, as compared to incurring travel costs for participants.
- Webcasts can be recorded and repeated by the same or different learner audiences.
- Electronic media events can reach greater audiences for each event.
- This delivery method is convenient for all involved (no travel required).
- Significant time advantage for participants due to not having to travel.

### Disadvantages

- Company's values and culture may not be passed along as easily as during face-to-face training delivery methods.

- Retention and learning transfer may be compromised (particularly for skills training), unless practice exercises are included.

- To accommodate differing time zones, the master trainer may need to work during unusual hours if facilitating a live webinar.

- The content may not be sensitized and localized for varied cultures, unless different versions are created.

- Technology challenges could be daunting.

- Not all learning styles/learners respond best to virtual training methods.

This is just a very quick review of some methods and some of their strengths and weaknesses. It is not intended to be complete, but only to help you think about considerations when designing learning events for global audiences. Each of these options has a particular strength and can be combined with other methods to provide a strong blended learning event. When it comes time to decide on a method, look to the objectives of the learning event to help choose the best option. Keep in mind that there are no wrong choices. The key is: Whatever choice you make, do it well!

## RESOURCES

### Websites

- http://globalproducts.kodal.com/travel.htm—Growing resource with good information on travel and tips
- http://travel.state.gov—Use to check for updated travel advisories
- www.cdc.gov—Center for Disease Control and Prevention to determine the most up-to-date requirements for vaccinations and health
- www.cia.gov—Provides country background and information
- www.crewscontrol.com—An international audiovisual specialist company you can hire to support all of your technology needs
- www.cyberlink.com—Good information on communications; links to other websites (regional and country)
- www.cyborlink.com, International Business Etiquette and Manners
- www.executiveplanet.com/business-etiquette/—Good information on negotiation; links to other websites for each country
- www.frommers.com—You can order *Frommer's Travel Guides* for any country
- www.globesmart.com—Provides country customs, protocol, and other information
- www.globetrekkertv.com—Globe Trekker
- www.hbsp.harvard.edu, Harvard Business Articles and Newsletters
- www.independenttraveler.com—Airport security questions and answers
- www.karenbrown.com—Karen Brown's books on accommodations are excellent

- www.lonelyplanet.com—Gives country details such as dialing codes, time zone, plugs, tips, transport suggestions, currency, and more

- www.travelchannel.com—Broadcast information on countries is provided here with additional information

- www.travel-guide.com—Very navigable site for handling all travel information needs by country

- www.towd.com—In addition to the site above, provides links to official country tourism sites

- www.timeanddate.com—World time zones and weather

- www.tsa.gov—Transportation Security Administration

### Organizations

- ASTD (The American Society for Training and Development): www.astd.org

- East West Center: www.eastwestcenter.org

- National Communication Association: www.natcom.org

- Peace Corps: www.peacecorps.gov

- Professional Society for Sales and Marketing Training: www.smt.org

- SIETAR (Society for Intercultural Education): www.SIETAR.org

### Publications

- *The Economist*

- *National Geographic*

- *Frommer's Guides*

- *Lonely Planet*

### Books

Adler, Nancy J. *International Dimensions of Organizational Behavior.* Cincinnati, OH, South-Western, 2002.

Cushner, Kenneth, & Brislin, Richard W. *Intercultural Interactions: A Practical Guide.* Thousand Oaks, CA: Sage, 1996.

Friedman, Thomas L. *The World Is Flat.* New York: Farrar, Straus and Giroux, 2006.

Jandt, Fred E. *An Introduction to Intercultural Communication.* Thousand Oaks, CA: Sage, 2004.

Jandt, Fred E. (Ed.). *Intercultural Communication: A Global Reader.* Thousand Oaks, CA: Sage, 2004.

Kirrane, Diane E. (Ed.). Training and Learning Styles. *Info-line*, Alexandria, VA: ASTD Press, 2005.

Kohls, Robert, & Bussow, Herbert L. *Training Know-How for Cross-Cultural and Diversity Trainers*. Duncanville, TX: Adult Learning Systems, 1995.

Landis, Dan, & Brislin, Richard W. (Eds.). *Handbook of Intercultural Training*. New York: Pergamon Press, 1983.

Nadler, Leonard, & Nadler, Zeace. *Designing Training Programs: The Critical Events Model*. Houston, TX: Gulf, 1994.

Morrison, Terri, & Conway, Wayne. *Kiss, Bow, or Shake Hands: The Guide to Doing Business in More Than 60 Countries*. Avon, MA: Adams Media, an F&W Publications Company, 2006.

Morrison, Terri & Conway, Wayne, *Kiss, Bow, or Shake Hands: How to Do Business in 12 Asian Countries*. Avon, MA: Adams Media, an F&W Publications, Inc., 2007

Myers, Isabel Briggs. *Introduction to Type: A Guide to Understanding Your Results on the Myers-Briggs Type Indicator*. Mountain View, CA: Consulting Psychologists Press, 1998.

Sussan, Stephanie. (Ed.). *Instructional Systems Development*. Alexandria, VA: ASTD Press, 2002.

Jon Anderson, Partner, Lake Point Partners, www.lakepointepartners.com

Thomas Archibald, Peace Corps Volunteer, Gabon, Africa

Marylou Atkins-Hayes, HR Manager, Eastman Kodak Company, Canada

Marcie Austen, Director Human Resources, Shure, Inc.

Sharon Badenhop, President, USA East Associates, Inc., Linking Business Innovators with Overseas Opportunities, sbadenh1@rochester.rr.com

Jojo Barraquias, Jr., UFC Philippines, Inc. and Southeast Asia Food, Inc. Customer Business Development Head, Domestic & International Sales, jbarraquias@yahoo.com

Janice Berntson, Manager of Leadership Development, Eastman Kodak Company

Cori Bjorklund, Writer and Designer

Jennifer Britton, Potentials Realized Founder, Group Coaching Essentials jennifer@potentialsrealized.com, UN Caribbean Representative

Jeremy Blain, Partner, Cegos, United Kingdom, www.cegos.co.uk

Aldrin Bogi, Student Mobilization Center, Youth with a Mission, South Asia

Chungme Lee Bogi, Director Bangalore, India, Youth with a Mission

Jiggu Bogi, Associate National Director, India, Youth with a Mission

Gabriela Casineau, Coach, Canada; Romania

Linda Cegelski, Manager, Learning and Development, General Electric Corporation

Deborah Coleman, CTI Coach and Trainer

Douglas Cummings, Superintendent of Schools, Canada

Tristan B. de la Rosa, Banyan Way, Executive Coaching and Development, www.thebanyanway.com

Brian Dietmeyer, President, Think! Inc., Negotiating, www.e-thinkinc.com

Denise Devlin, Education Specialist, Carestream Health

Drake Resource Group, Custom Learning Solutions, www.drakerg.com

Sandra Edwards, Regional Vice President, American Management Association; VP International Business Development, Achieve Global

Betsy Foss, Financial Consultant, Morgan Stanley

Butch Fremmer, Welocalize, www.welocalize.com

Nicholas Gauss, Writer and Student

Stephen Gawrys, Sergeant, Chicago Police Dept.

Caroline Hall Otis, CTI Coach and Trainer

Jeanne Heinzer, Heinzer Consulting, Intercultural Training and Personal Coaching, www.heinzerconsulting.com

Cathy Hwang, Educator and Student

John Hwang, Director, Student Mobilization Centre, South America, Youth with a Mission

Alicia Irwin, Graduate Program Assistant, Cornell University; Peace Corps Volunteer, Thailand

Julie Jacques, Training and OD Leader, Chicago area

Bina Joseph, Online Tutor, www.tutorvista.com

Kathy Leck, Executive Vice President, Corporate Education, Lake Forest Graduate School of Management, http://www.lakeforestmba.edu/

Nicholas Lee, Esq., Factor & Lake, LTD

Gretchen Linzing, Manager–Training and Communications, Recruitment Services, UnitedHealth Group, gretchenlj1976@yahoo.com

Patrick Maley, Owner, VisualsEtc@yahoo.com

Andrea Mascarenhas, Training Manager, Latin American Region, EKC

Andrea Nierenberg, President, The Nierenberg Group, Inc., www.selfmarketing.com

Fr. Symon Ntaiyia, Pastor: Kenya and Sodus, New York

Susan Onaitis, President, Global Learning Link, www.GlobalLearningLink.com

Jo Paulson, Consultant/Facilitator/Coach, India, HR Anexi Pvt Ltd, www.hranexi.com

Francis Petrzala, International Trainer, EDS

Kenneth Philips, Philips Associates, Performance Management Consultant, www.philipsassoc.com

Claudio A. Pinto, Marketing Director, Transware, rich-media globalization and localization, www.transware.com

Amy Pletcher, Independent Writer, Editor, and Consultant, www.amypletcher.com.

Julie V. Ponce, Writer, Trainer, Educator, Professional Musician and Singer

Michael Rockelmann, Driving Results, President, www.drivingresults.com

Marilyn Sadler-Bay, Organization Development Consultant

Ronnie Sarkar, Senior Vice President, Digital Solutions, R.R. Donnelley

Estela Sasson, Mexican Consulate; Montreal, Canada, Professional Coach estelathecoach@yahoo.ca

Mika Sato-Foley, Sakura Translations, mika@sakuratranslations.com

Elizabeth Seon, Designer, Chicago area

Ruth Soskin, Training Consultant and Technical Writer, Trainology, Inc., ruthsoskin@trainology.com

Donna Steffey, President, Vital Signs, www.vitalsignstraining.com

Dr. Cisca Sugiro, Research Scientist, Kodak

Susan Sul, President, MorningWare, Inc. www.morningware.com

Louann M. Swedberg, Writer and Instructional Designer, lmswedb@aol.com.

Carole Wald, Account Manager, Corporate Education, Lake Forest Graduate School of Management, http://www.lakeforestmba.edu/

Christopher Watkins, Corporate Design and Usability, Corporate Marketing Office, EKC

Ronald Webb, Boeing, Tashkent, Uzbekistan

Bill Wiggenhorn, Principle of Main-Captiva. LLC, Founder and Former President of Motorola University

# INDEX

## A

Accommodations: African, 86–87; Argentina, 319–320; Brazil, 329; Canada, 341; Central America/Caribbean, 351–352; Chinese, 121–122; Columbia, 361; Denmark, 224–225; Egyptian, 100; England, 235–236; France, 244–245; Germany, 255; Hong Kong, 130–131; Hungarian, 267–268; India, 139; Indonesian, 145–146; Italy, 276–277; Japanese, 157–158; Malaysian, 166; Mexico, 375; Netherlands/Holland, 306; Philippines, 172; Romanian, 284; South African, 109–110; South Korean, 178; Switzerland, 292–294; Thailand, 187; United States, 384; Uzbekistan, 195; Vietnam, 205

Accommodators learning style, 41

Activities: best practice tips for, 38; considerations when adding, 37; icebreakers for Chinese participants, 124; "Mad Minute," 141; recommended for U.S. presentations, 387; scenario for including, 37–38; using series of successes through, 67; team-building welcome, 66; See also Presentations

ADDIE model: Analyze phase of, 27–32; Design phase of, 32–39; Develop phase of, 39–43; Evaluate phase of, 46; Implement/Program Delivery phase of, 43–46

Adler, N., 69

Africa: accommodations available in, 86–87; consulate and embassy information for countries of, 90–93; global business growth of, 400–401; historic background information on, 77–78; logistic issues related to, 84–85; the people of, 87–88; regions of, 78–79; safety issues in, 86–87; traveling to, 79–80, 86–87; See also Egypt; South Africa

African presentations: kinds of requests/questions to ask for, 79; preparation for, 88; program delivery issues for, 85–86; program design considerations for, 80–84; suggestions for giving, 88–89

AIDS, 80

American Society for Training and Development (ASTD), 403

American Translators Association, 54, 57

The Americas: Argentina, 315–324; Brazil, 325–335; Canada, 337–346, 402; Central America and the Caribbean, 347–356; Colombia, 357–364; Guyana, 365–370; Mexico, 371–378; United States, 379–388, 396

Analyze phase (ADDIE model): communicating with potential participants, 31; doing your homework during, 31–32; gathering additional information during, 30; issues to consider during, 27–28; leverage communication vehicles during, 28–30; presenting your proposal during, 32; review the request and obtain information, 28

Andersen, J. F., 382

Anderson, J., 124

Anderson, P. A., 382

Apartheid (South Africa), 79, 83–84, 105

Archibald, T., 89

Argentina: accommodations in, 319–320; important organizations information, 322–323; logistics of, 317–318; people of, 320–321; traveling to and in, 316–317, 320; websites on, 324

Argentine presentations: preparation for, 321–323; program delivery of, 318–319; program design for, 317; request for, 315–316; technical requirements for, 319; tips for successful, 323–324

Asian countries: China, 115–126, 397–398; Hong Kong, 127–133; India, 135–142, 398–399; Indonesia, 143–149; Japan,

Central America/Caribbean: accommodations in, 351–352; logistics of, 349–350; people of, 352; traveling to and in, 347–348, 352; websites on, 356

Central America/Caribbean presentations: preparation for, 352–353; program delivery of, 350–351; program design for, 348–349; request for, 347; technical requirements of, 351; tips for successful, 353–355

Chandra, J., 141

China: accommodations in, 121–122; economic growth and challenges, 393–394; global business progress by, 397–398; holidays in, 117; logistics of, 119–120; people of, 122–123; traveling to and in, 116–117, 122; websites on, 126

Chinese presentation: preparation for, 123–124; program delivery for, 120–121; program design for, 117–119; request for, 115–116; technical requirements for, 121; tips on giving a successful, 124–126

Classroom interpreters. *See* Interpreters

Clothing: Brazilian social customs regarding, 331; Danish social customs regarding, 226; Egyptian social customs regarding, 102; English social customs regarding, 237; general tips on appropriate, 17; German social customs regarding, 256; Guyanese social customs regarding, 367; Hungarian social customs regarding, 268–269; Indonesian social customs regarding, 148; Italian social customs regarding, 278; Malaysian social customs regarding, 167; Muslim countries and recommended, 80, 148; Netherlands social customs regarding, 308; Philippines social customs regarding, 173; Thailand social customs regarding, 188

CNN foreign/world news and current events, 89

Coca-Cola, 199

Collaborative learning style, 40

Colombia: accommodations in, 361; logistics of, 360; people of, 362–363; traveling to and in, 358–359, 361–362; websites on, 364

Colombian presentations: preparation for, 363; program delivery of, 361; program design for, 359–360; request for, 357–358; technical requirements for, 361; tips for successful, 363–364

*Communicating with Japanese in Business* (JETRO), 154

Communication: email, 29; five dimensions of cross-cultural, 68–69, 151; with your hosts, 63; for intercultural presentation evaluation, 72–74; leveraging vehicles for, 28–30; with potential participants or SMEs, 31; practice exercise to identify confusing, 49–50; using simple and clear language for, 45; throughout the program tips for good, 69–70; time zone differences affecting, 19; *See also* Body language; Telephone communication

"Compassionate capitalism" theory, 399

Conaway, W., 24

Conference calls, 29

Convergers learning style, 40

Costa Rica, 348, 349

Credit cards: Africa and use of, 84; Argentina and use of, 318; Canada and use of, 340; Central America/Caribbean and use of, 350; China and use of, 119–120; Columbia and use of, 360; Egypt and use of, 98; Guyana and use of, 366; Hungary and use of, 266; Indonesia and fraud with, 144; Italy and use of, 275–276; Japan and limited use of, 155; Netherlands/Holland and use of, 304; South Africa and use of, 108; South Korea and use of, 177; Switzerland and use of, 292;

Thailand and use of, 186; Vietnam and use of, 203; *See also* Currency

Cross-cultural issues: communication throughout the program, 69–70; evaluation and intercultural communication, 72–74; five dimensions of communication, 68–69

Cultural differences: body language, 16; cultural sensitivity/respect for, 14, 64–65, 363–364; as email communication issue, 29; exploring and learning about, 18–22; five dimensions of, 68–69, 151; language reflecting, 50, 217–218, 395; region-specific data on business and, 397–402; sensitivity to, 14, 64–65, 363–364; website comparing U.S. and other, 269; *See also* International audience; Participants; Social norms

Cultural sensitivity, 14, 64–65, 363–364

Culture: definition of, 394; high power versus low power distance, 68; HRD impact of, 394–396; long-term versus short-term orientation, 68, 69; masculine versus feminine, 68, 69

Culture shock, 397

Cumming, D., 357, 359, 360, 361, 363–364

Currency: African, 84; Argentine, 318; Australian, 213; Brazilian, 328; Canadian, 340; Central America/Caribbean, 349–350; Chinese, 119–120; Columbia, 360; Egyptian, 98; English, 234; exchange rates, 12–13; French, 243; Germany, 254; Guyana, 366, 367; Hong Kong, 129–130; Hungarian, 266; Indonesian, 144; Italian, 275; Japanese, 155; Malaysian, 165; Mexican, 374; Netherlands/Holland, 304–305; Philippines, 171; Romanian, 282; South African, 108; South Korean, 177; Swiss, 292; Thailand, 186; United States, 383;

of history of, 245–247; tips on
protocol to use in, 247–248; traveling to and in, 242, 245; websites
on, 249
French presentations: preparation
for, 248; program delivery of, 244;
program design for, 242–243;
request for, 241–242; technical
requirements of, 244; tips for
successful, 249
Friedman, T. L., 1, 123, 142
*Frommer's: South Africa* (de Bruyn), 89

## G

Gawrys, S., 112
Gender issues: African presentations
and possible, 85–86; Hungary and,
268–269; Muslim countries and
recommended clothing, 80, 148;
South Korean, 179–180; Vietnam
social norms regarding women,
206, 207
German presentations: preparation
for, 256–257; program delivery for,
254; program design for, 253;
request for, 251; technical
requirements for, 254–255; tips for
successful, 257–261
Germany: accommodations in, 255;
logistics of, 253–254; Munich
Welcome Card of, 252; people of,
255–256; using S-Bahn in, 252;
traveling to and in, 251–253, 255;
websites on, 261
Gestrin, P., 89
Global business: Africa and the
Middle East's progress toward,
400–401; Canada and challenge
of, 402; China's progress toward,
397–398; developing globally literate leadership for, 394; European
Union's increasing, 401–402;
getting ready to move toward,
396–397; HRD and challenges of,
402–403; India's progress toward,
398–399; Japan's progress toward,
399–400; trends related to, 392–394
*Global Etiquette Guide to African and
the Middle East* (Foster), 89

Global Learning Link, 22
Global learning projects: best
practices for webcasts used in,
70–72; tips on managing, 19–21;
WebEx used for, 71, 72
Global webcasts, 70–72
Globalization: business trends related
to, 392–394; definition of, 392; as
important HRD issue, 391–392
Globally literate leadership, 394
Goals: establishing program, 66;
outlining day objectives and, 67
Graphics development tips, 41
Guatemala, 348, 350
*The Guide to Translation and
Localization*, 57, 59
Guyana: accommodations in, 368;
logistics of, 367; people of,
368–369; traveling to and in,
365–366, 368; websites on, 370
Guyanese presentations: preparation
for, 369; program delivery of, 367;
program design for, 366; request
for, 365; technical requirements for,
367–368; tips for successful, 370

## H

Haiti, 355
Harvard Business School Publishing
(HBSP), 89
Health issues: Africa and related,
80; Brazil and related, 326; China
and related, 116; jetlag, 13, 23, 26;
Philippines and related, 169
Heinzer, J., 249, 254, 292, 307
Hewitt, 402
High power cultures, 68
Hodell, C., 31, 46
Hofstede, G., 151, 394
Holidays: Argentina, 316–317;
Australia, 212; Brazilian, 326–327;
Canadian, 338–339; Central
America/Caribbean, 349; Chinese,
117; Columbia, 359; Danish, 222;
Egyptian, 97; English, 233; France,
242; Germany, 257; Guyana, 366;
Hong Kong, 128; Hungarian, 265;
India, 136; Indonesian, 143–144;
Italian, 275; Japanese, 153;

Malaysian, 164; Mexico, 372–373;
Muslim countries and observed,
97, 143; Netherlands/Holland, 303;
Philippines, 170; Romania, 282;
South African, 108; South Korean,
176; Switzerland, 290–291;
Thailand, 184–185; United States,
380–381; Uzbekistan, 192–193;
Vietnamese, 200
Holland. *See* Netherlands/Holland
presentations
Honduras, 348, 350
Hong Kong: accommodations in,
130–131; geographical divisions
of, 132; logistics of, 129–130;
people of, 131–132; traveling
to and around, 127–128, 131;
websites on, 133
Hong Kong presentations:
preparation for, 132; program
design for, 128–129; request for,
127; suggestions for successful, 133;
technical requirements for, 130
Host communication, 63
"How to Start a Small Business"
(Kramer course), 401
HRD (human resource
development): cultural impact on,
394–396; globalization as issue for,
391–392; globalization challenges
for, 402–403
Human Development Resources
Bureau, 399
Hungarian presentations: preparation
for, 270; program design for, 265;
request for, 263–264; special language issues of, 263–264; technical
requirements for, 266–267; tips for
successful, 271
Hungary: accommodations in,
267–268; logistics of, 266; people
in, 268–269; traveling to and in,
264–265, 268; websites on, 271
Hwang, C., 177
Hwang, J., 55

## I

Icebreakers, 124
Illness. *See* Health issues

ILO (International Labor Office), 400, 402

Implement/program delivery phase (ADDIE model): best practice tips for, 44–46; issues to consider during, 43–44; *See also* Program delivery

Independent learning style, 40

India: accommodations in, 139; global business progress by, 398–399; logistics of, 138; people of, 140; religions in, 140; special language issues of, 136–137, 141; traveling to and in, 135–136, 139–140; websites and resources on, 142

Indian presentations: preparation for, 141; program delivery of, 138; program design for, 136–137; request for, 135; technical requirements related to, 138–139; tips for successful, 141–142

Individualism, 68, 385

Indonesia: accommodations in, 145–146; holidays in, 143–144; languages of, 144, 147; logistics of, 144; people of, 146–147; traveling to and in, 143–144, 146; websites on, 149

Indonesian presentations: preparation for, 148; program delivery/technical requirements for, 145; program design for, 144; request for, 143; tips for successful, 148–149

Information quick references, 67

Infosys Technologies, 398

Initiating presentation: creating an environment, 66–67; creating bond through introductions, 65; establishing common program goals, 66; making everyone feel welcome, 66; starting with powerful beginning, 68–69; techniques for facilitating participation, 67

Inoculations, 13

*Intercultural Interactions: A Practical Guide* (Cushner and Brislin), 64

International audience: African presentations and, 81; cultural sensitivity toward your, 14, 64–65, 363–364; knowing your, 61–62; preparing to present to the, 10–26; typical problems when facing an, 9–10; *See also* Cultural differences; Participants

*International Dimensions of Organizational Behavior* (Adler), 69

*International Herald Tribune*, 401

International Labor Office (ILO), 400, 402

International Labor Office's Report on Global Employment Trends, 400

Internet access: Argentina, 319; Canada, 340; Central America/Caribbean, 351; Denmark, 224; Guyana, 368; Hong Kong, 130; India, 139; Italy, 276; Malaysia, 166; Mexico, 374; Philippines, 172; Romanian, 284; United States, 384; Uzbekistan, 194–195; Vietnam, 205; *See also* Laptops; Technical issues; Websites

Interpreters: for Argentine presentation, 317; for Brazilian presentations, 327; contacting your, 63; effective use of classroom, 53–55; for German presentations, 256; for Japanese presentations, 155–156, 160–161; for South Korean presentations, 177; for Vietnamese presentations, 200–201, 203, 206–207; *See also* Language; Translation

*Into Africa: Intercultural Insights* (Yale and Phyllis), 89

*An Introduction to Intercultural Communication: Identities in a Global Community* (Jandt), 73

*Introduction to Type* (Myers), 40

Introductions (participant), 65

Italian presentations: preparation for, 278–279; program delivery of, 276; program design for, 275–276; request for, 273; technical requirements of, 276; tips for successful, 279–280

Italy: accommodations in, 276–277; people of, 277–278; traveling to and in, 274–275, 277; websites on, 280

## J

Jacobs**, 40

Jacques, J., 156–157

Jandt, F. E., 73, 382, 386

Japan: accommodations in, 157–158; global business progress by, 399–400; logistics of, 155; people of, 158–159; traveling to and in, 152–153, 158; websites on, 162

Japan External Trade Organization (JETRO), 154, 162

Japanese presentations: preparation for, 159–160; program delivery of, 155–157; program design for, 153–154; requests for, 152; technical requirements related to, 157; tips for successful, 160–162

Jetlag, 13, 23, 26

## K

Kamdar**, 399

Kidnapping (Columbia), 361, 362

*Kiss, Bow, or Shake Hands: The Bestselling Guide to Doing Business in More than 60 Countries* (Morrison and Conaway), 24

Kohls, R., 70

Kolb, D., 40

Kolski, C. H., 395

Korean Chamber of Commerce, 175

Kramer, N., 401

## L

Lake Point Partners, 124

Landis, D., 65

Language: African presentation issues regarding, 82–83; cultural differences reflected by, 50, 217–218, 395; ESL (English as second language) participants, 71; Hungary and special issues of, 263–264; India and special issues of, 136–137, 141; Indonesia and special issues of, 144, 147; Japan and special issues of, 155–156,

160–161; learning cultural protocols using participant's, 54; practice exercise to identify confusing, 49–50; using simply and clear, 45; *See also* Body language; Interpreters; Translation

Language phrases: Argentine, 322; Australian, 216–217; Brazilian, 333–334; Cantonese (China), 132; Central America/Caribbean Spanish, 353; Danish, 227–228; Dutch (Netherlands/Holland), 309–310; French, 248; French Canadian, 344; German, 257; Hungarian, 270; Indonesian, 148; Italian, 279; Japanese, 159, 160; Korean, 180; Malaysian, 167–168; Mexican Spanish, 377; Philippines, 172; Romanian, 287–288; Swiss French, 298; Swiss German, 297; Thai, 189; Uzbek, 197; Vietnamese, 203–204, 207

Laptops: Australia and issues related to, 214; Romania and issues related to, 282; Vietnam requirements for importing, 202; voltage converters/plug adapters for, 99; *See also* Internet access

Learning: accommodating different styles of, 39–41; follow-up/reinforcement of, 47, 74, 364, 387–388

Learning styles: as Develop phase consideration, 39–41; types of, 40–41

Leck, K., 137

Lee, N., 180

Left hand use: in Egypt, 100; in India, 139; in Indonesia, 147

Linzing, G., 123

Lionbridge, 57

Liu Xiao, 391

Localization: meaning and implications of, 55–58; process of selecting program for, 58–59; resources for, 59; of training curriculum, 58

Lodging. *See* Accommodations

Logistics: Africa, 84–85; Argentina, 317–318; Australia, 213; Brazil, 327–328; Canada, 339–340; Central America/Caribbean, 349–350; China, 119–120; Columbia, 360; Egypt, 98; England, 234; France, 243–244; Germany, 253–254; Guyana, 367; Hong Kong, 129–130; Hungary, 266; India, 138; Indonesia, 144; Italy, 275–276; Japan, 155; Malaysia, 164–165; Mexico, 373–374; Netherlands/Holland, 304–305; Philippines, 170–171; Romanian, 282–283; South Africa, 107–108; South Korea, 176–177; Switzerland, 292; United States, 383; Uzbekistan, 193; Vietnam, 202–203

Long-term orientation, 68, 69

Low power cultures, 68

Lustig, M. W., 382

## M

"Mad Minute" activity, 141

Main-Captiva, 119

Malaria, 80

Malaysia: accommodations in, 166; logistics of, 164–165; people of, 167; traveling to and in, 163–164, 166–167; websites on, 168

Malaysian presentations: preparation for, 167–168; program delivery of, 165; program design for, 164; request for, 163; technical requirements of, 166; tips for successful, 168

Management sensitivities, 364

Mandela, N., 111

Mascarenhas, A., 327, 328

Masculine cultures, 68, 69

Materials. *See* Documents; Training materials

MBTI (Myers-Briggs Type Indicator), 40, 228

McClay, R., 70, 85, 142

Medications, 13

Meeting communication tips, 29–30

Melatonin, 13

Merrill Brink, 57

Mexican presentations: preparation for, 376–377; program delivery of, 374; program design for, 373; request for, 371; technical requirements for, 374; tips for successful, 377–378

Mexico: accommodations in, 375; logistics of, 373–374; people in, 375–376; traveling to and in, 371–373, 375; websites on, 378

Middle East globalization, 400–401; *See also* Muslim countries

Morningware, Inc., 180

*MultiLingual* magazine, 57, 59

Munich Welcome Card (Germany), 252

Murthy, N., 399

Muslim countries: clothing recommended for, 80, 148; customs to be aware of in, 83; holidays observed in, 97, 143; prayer breaks in, 148; *See also* Middle East globalization

Myers, I. B., 40

Myers-Briggs Type Indicator, 40, 228

## N

Nadler, L., 31

Nadler, Z., 31

Nestle, 199

Netherlands/Holland: accommodations in, 306; logistics of, 304–305; people of, 307–308; traveling to and in, 302–303, 306–307; websites on, 311

Netherlands/Holland presentations: preparation for, 308–310; program delivery of, 305; program design for, 303; request for, 301; technical requirements for, 305–306; tips for successful, 310–311

New product workshop: creating your deliverables for, 42–43; initial outline on components of, 34–35; podcasts included in, 35, 43

Nicaragua, 348, 350

## O

Objectives: establishing program, 66; outlining the presentation, 67

Octopus card (Hong Kong), 130, 131

"Offshoring" tend, 393

Onaitis, S., 22, 26

Outlines: developing a detailed, 35–36; new product podcasts included in, 35; new product workshop components included in, 34–35; pre-reading materials included in, 33–34

Overbey, D., 399

*Overcoming Jet Lag* (Ehret), 23

## P

Paige, M., 70

Panama, 348, 350

Participants: African presentation, 81–84; communicating with potential, 31; creating bond through introductions, 65; ESL (English as second language), 71; follow-up/reinforcement techniques for, 47, 74, 364, 387–388; making all feel welcome, 66; *See also* Cultural differences; Feedback; International audience; Presentations

Passport/visa issues: Africa and, 80; Argentina and, 316; Australia and, 211–212; Brazil and, 326; Canada and, 338; Central America/Caribbean and, 347–348; China and, 116–117; Columbia and, 358; Egypt and, 96; England and, 232; France and, 242; Germany and, 251; Guyana and, 365; Hungary and, 264; India and, 136; Italy and, 274; Japan and, 152; Malaysia and, 164; Mexico and, 371; Philippines and, 169; Romania and, 281; South Korea and, 175; Thailand and, 184; tips regarding, 12–13; United States and, 379; Uzbekistan and, 192; Vietnam and, 200; *See also* Traveling/transportation

Petrzala, F., 334

Philippines: accommodations in, 172; logistics on, 170–171; people of, 172–173; traveling to and in, 169–170, 172; websites on, 174

Philippines presentation: preparation for, 173; program delivery of, 171;

program design for, 170; request for, 169; technical requirements for, 171–172; tips for successful, 174

Pletcher, A., 89

Plug adapters, 99

Podcasts: creating workshop, 43; initial outline on use of, 35

Ponce, J., 377

Practicing presentation, 62

Prayer breaks, 148

Pre-reading materials: for creating deliverables, 42; initial outline inclusion of, 33–34

Pre-work, 358

Premji, A., 393

Preparation tips: basic questions to ask, 11; from Carole Wald on global learning projects, 19–21; food safety and security issues, 17; overall recommendations, 22–26; overcoming jetlag, 13; preparing and presenting training materials, 14–16; showing respect, 14; from Susan Onaitis, 22–26; traveling tips, 12–13; virtual presentation, 17–18

Preparing presentation: for African programs, 88; for Argentine programs, 321–323; for Australian programs, 216–217; being prepared for surprises, 63; for Brazilian programs, 332–334; for Canadian presentations, 343–344; for Central America/Caribbean, 352–353; for Chinese programs, 123–124; communicating with your hosts as, 63; contact your interpreter, 63; for Denmark programs, 226–228; for Egyptian programs, 102–103; for English programs, 238; for French programs, 248; general tips for, 11–26, 64–65; for German programs, 256–257; for Guyanese programs, 369; for Hong Kong programs, 132–133; for Hungarian programs, 270; for Indian programs, 141; for Indonesian programs, 148; for Italian programs, 278–279; for Japanese programs, 159–160;

knowing your audience as part of, 61–62; knowing yourself as part of, 62; for Malaysian programs, 167–168; for Mexican programs, 376–377; for Netherlands/ Holland programs, 308–310; for Philippines programs, 173; practicing presentation/checking materials, 62–63; for South African programs, 111; for Swiss programs, 296–298; for Thailand programs, 188–189; for United States programs, 386; for Uzbekistan programs, 196–197; for Vietnamese programs, 207–208

Presentation techniques: best practices for global webcasts, 70–72; evaluation and intercultural communication, 72–74; follow-up/reinforcement of learning, 47, 74, 364; initiating the presentation, 65–69; preparing to present, 61–65; for throughout the program, 69–70

Presentations: considerations for designing virtual, 47–48; designing program and, 27–50; follow-up/ reinforcement of, 47, 74, 364, 387–388; general tips for conducting, 44–45, 64–65; general tips on virtual, 17–18; global webcasts, 70–72; initiating the, 65–69; podcasts, 35, 43; pre-work on, 358; techniques for international audiences, 61–74; translation/ localization issues for, 51–59; written contracts for, 357–358; *See also* Activities; Participants; *specific countries*; Training materials

Procter & Gamble, 199

Program delivery: African presentations, 85–86; Australian presentations, 214; best practice tips for text, graphics, audiovisuals, 42; Brazilian presentations, 328; Canadian presentations, 340; Central America/Caribbean presentations, 350–351; Chinese presentations, 120–121;

Renie McClay has been in the learning and development field for over twenty years. She has managed sales training for three Fortune 500 Companies, including Kraft, Gerber and Pactiv.

Enjoying traveling the world, Renie has visited forty-nine U.S. states and over thirty countries (more by the time you read this!). She has facilitated face to face workshops to varied audiences around the world, including corporate, universities, and non-profit. In addition to face-to-face training, she has hosted many webcasts, broadcasts, and talk-shows for Asian, Australian, Latin American, European, and North American audiences.

She is a Certified Online and Synchronous Instructor. She takes existing curriculum and creates modules for presenting via webcast to groups in India, China, Australia, Europe, and North America. She also has experience managing the localizing and translating of sales aids and educational resources for Asia and Latin America.

Renie's passion is in people development. She reduces new hire learning curves by helping companies to improve their onboarding of new employees, including new hire orientations, mentoring, product training, and curriculum development. She increases effectiveness of new and veteran salespeople and sales management. Being strong at relationships, she helps people to become better communicators and to build better relationships with people they don't naturally connect with. She uses her Second City Improvisational training to help audiences use their creativity for better innovation.

Renie is the editor of *Sales Training Solutions*, published by Dearborn Tiado in 2006. She is a past president of the Professional Society for Sales and Marketing Training. She is on the board of the Chicago Chapter of the American Society for Training and Development, and is the editor for their magazine, *Training Today*. Renie can be reached at inspiredtolearn@gmail.com and visit her website at www.inspiredtolearn.net.

LuAnn Irwin, LAI Associates, has traveled to more than twenty-three countries and forty-nine states in the United States to teach and learn from people of other nations and cultures. She has worked as manager/director of training for Eastman Kodak Company, Xerox Corporation, and Hong Kong Shanghai Banking Company, all Fortune 500 companies. At Kodak, LuAnn managed training professionals, providing leadership development, sales training, and technical and interpersonal skills for international teams, delivered virtually through international webcasts and in person. LuAnn has been a mentor for Chinese managers and professionals in Shanghai and active in networks for Asian, African, Hispanic, and Native American employees.

As manager of technical training design for Xerox, LuAnn managed a team of designers and developers and led eight worldwide training development teams. The programs delivered included training, presentations, videos, case studies, role plays, and activities. As director of training for Hong Kong Shanghai Banking Company, LuAnn designed and delivered customer service and leadership training for all employees in the region. She was promoted to become an officer of the company, the youngest and only the thirteenth woman to be appointed.

She has also conducted training, teaching, and consulting projects for General Motors Delphi Division, Bausch & Lomb, the New York Governor's Office of Employee Relations, Blue Cross/Blue Shield, the New York State Department of Education, county and city government, Cornell University, Carnegie Mellon University, the University of Rochester, Rochester Institute of Technology, and many other companies, educational institutions, and non-profit agencies.

LuAnn has a master's degree in adult learning from the University of Rochester. She is past president of the American Society for Training and Development's local chapter and past president of Literacy Volunteers of Wayne County.

She has contributed to *Sales Training Solutions* ("Tech Talk: Delivering Technical Training to Sales Professionals") and been published in newsletter articles for the American Society for Training and Development, Literacy Volunteers, and Asia Pacific Exchange Network. She has presented at the Genesee Valley chapter of the American Society for Training and Development, Rochester Institute of Technology, Chamber of Commerce Small Business Association, and the Asia Pacific Exchange Network. LuAnn can be reached at luannirwin@hotmail.com or luannirwin@gmail.com.